PETER McKELLAR

Experience and Behaviour

*

PENGUIN BOOKS

Penguin Books Ltd, Harmondsworth, Middlesex, England
Penguin Books Inc., 7110 Ambassador Road, Baltimore, Maryland 21207, U.S.A.
Penguin Books Australia Ltd, Ringwood, Victoria, Australia

—

First published 1968
Reprinted 1971
Copyright © Peter McKellar, 1968

—

Made and printed in Great Britain by
Cox & Wyman Ltd
London, Fakenham and Reading
Set in Monotype Plantin

For

MARGUERITE

semper floreat

Contents

EXPERIENCE AND BEHAVIOUR

A New Zealander of a pioneering and medico-legal family, Peter McKellar graduated at Otago and London Universities. His concern with relations of Psychology to other disciplines, especially Medicine and Law, is apparent in this book. Also evident is a longstanding interest in the study of subjective experiences, and in other recently neglected areas of the subject. Professor McKellar is author of *A Text-Book of Human Psychology* (1952), and *Imagination and Thinking* (1957). His previous researches have been into visual perception, human aggression, remembering and testimony, experimental studies of mental abnormality, and individual differences in thinking. A Fellow of the British Psychological Society, Professor McKellar has held posts at the Universities of London, Aberdeen and St Andrews, and both in New Zealand and the United States. He enjoys a happy marriage to his Yorkshire wife to whom this book is dedicated. Peter McKellar is Professor and Head of the Department of Psychology at Otago University, New Zealand.

Acknowledgements

FOR permission to reproduce certain of the illustrations I am indebted to: the Editor of the *British Journal of Psychology* (Figures 6, 7, 8, 15); Professor G. Miller (Figure 14); Professor H. J. Eysenck and Dr S. B. G. Eysenck (Figure 15, from the *British Journal of Psychology*, 54:1, 1963); and the publishers McGraw-Hill (Figures 16 and 17, from *Psychology at Work*, by F. H. Allport, R. L. Schanck and M. Dickens, edited by P. S. Achilles, 1932). I have to thank Professor H. Kay and my former colleagues in the Department of Psychology at the University of Sheffield for many valuable suggestions and criticisms. For additional help in revision, specific suggestions, and permission to use unpublished data (acknowledged in the text) I am specially grateful to Messrs J. Clarkson, B. T. Dodd, D. Rossi, and M. Sime. Mr E. Eagle has very kindly helped in the preparation of the illustrations. Dr A. Usher, Department of Forensic Medicine, and Mr K. Patchett, Department of Law, colleagues in other Departments of the University, have contributed valuable help. Finally, for their patient help in preparing the manuscript, I should like to thank Miss J. Taylor and Mrs B. Ellwood of Sheffield.

Foreword

EVERY volume in the Pelican Psychology Series could be described as an 'Introduction to Psychology' since each has been written for the intelligent general reader who, with no systematic knowledge of the subject, wants to know what all this psychology is about. This is true of *Experience and Behaviour* which like most of the others was not designed as a text book. There can be as many introductions to psychology as there are fields of interest in this vast subject and as many as there are different approaches in each of the many fields.

In this book the general approach is that characteristic of the main stream of modern scientific psychology – the psychology of Galton in England, of Wundt in Germany and of William James in America. These writers conceived the subject as being the scientific study not only of modes of behaviour but also of various sorts of experiences – such expressions as hallucinations, hypnagogic images, day dreams, and the dreams of sleep. For writers in this main stream psychology is the scientific study of 'the personality as a whole' as displayed in outward behaviour and in 'inner experience'. This book is fresh, lively and well stocked with illustrative material. It amply meets the needs both of general readers and of students in universities and in the schools and colleges of post-secondary education. Its impressive list of references contain bibliographical material which could keep a serious student busy for many a long day.

C. A. MACE

CHAPTER ONE

Human Psychology

First Psychology lost its soul, then it lost its mind, then it
lost consciousness, but it still has behaviour of a kind.
                                        EDWIN G. BORING

HUMAN psychology deals with experience and behaviour. By
experience is meant the internal aspects of mental life that we
learn about through man's ability to reflect upon his thoughts,
perceptions, emotions and motives, and to communicate these
introspections. By *behaviour* is meant the externally observable
activities of the organism. Thus behaviour – unlike experience –
can be studied not only in man but also in animals, which lack
the human capacity for introspection and communication.

The activities of living organisms throughout the evolutionary
system are the subject matter of psychology. In dealing with
human psychology it is appropriate to place this branch of the
subject within the broader perspective of biological evolution.
As has been estimated by a distinguished European psychologist,
H. Hediger of Zürich, there are about a million different species
of living creatures. Hediger (1955) adds: 'This means a million
different kinds of behaviour, and a million different psychological
studies.' Thus, as Hediger points out, psychology, as a branch
of science, faces a huge task, which as yet it has hardly begun.
We know a little, but not much, about the behaviour of a few
species of animals. Moreover, Hediger, in speaking as he does
of 'living creatures', underestimates the extent of the task.
In addition to mammals, birds, reptiles, amphibians and
fishes are insects, which are the largest category of macro-
scopic living creatures; and there are about a million different
species of insects alone. Thus, in considering scientific psychology we begin with the realization that there are many
forms of life different from our own. This is obviously true
between species. One purpose of this book is to draw attention to

some of the psychological differences *within* the human species itself.

HISTORICAL ORIENTATION

Two and a half thousand years is a modest estimate of the age of psychology as an expression of human curiosity about experience and behaviour. Its history as a branch of science dates from the nineteenth century, when the subject, as taught in modern universities, began to emerge partly out of philosophy and partly out of physiology. An important date was 1879: in that year Wilhelm Wundt (1832–1920) established at Leipzig the first major laboratory for psychological research. The laboratory originally comprised four rooms, and later increased to eleven. Wundt and his associates were active in research, and much concerned with vision and other problems of sense perception. For Wundt, psychology was the study of experience; immediate experiencing – that is introspection – was its main method. His interest was in the normal, adult human being, who was required to introspect in accord with certain conventions which Wundt had formulated. Both the subject matter and the methods used were unduly restricted, but Wundt laid down the foundations of a new science, and men of many nationalities came to Germany to study under him. They returned to their own countries taking with them the methods of the new, experimental psychology.

Both in its pre-scientific period and in the years that followed Wundt, psychology has changed. It has extended its subject matter, modified its methods, and altered its points of emphasis. The statement by Professor Boring, a distinguished historian of the science, summarizes these changes. From the study of the 'soul' as it was for Plato and Aristotle, psychology became the study of 'mind' and the introspective analysis of 'states of consciousness'. Today it is often defined as the science of 'behaviour'. As time progressed the Wundtian conception of psychology as a kind of mental chemistry, and of the psychologist's task as analysing consciousness into component elements in accord with prescribed rules, ceased to dominate the field. The 'new psychologists' of Leipzig became the traditionalists, against whom a series of vigorous intellectual movements launched their attacks. Three of these movements were of special importance for the development of modern psychology. *Behaviourism* rejected introspection as a method and sought to exclude experience as subject matter. The behaviourists proposed to confine psychology to the study of observable behaviour, and thus make the subject a respectable representative of the natural sciences. This more limited programme had its positive side also; in fact behaviourism did much to enlarge the subject matter to include observation of human development, and the method of animal experimentation. A second movement, *Gestalt psychology*, made numerous positive contributions of its own, particularly to the understanding of visual perception. The Gestaltists did not oppose introspection as such, but encouraged the study of the mental life of people in general; they were opposed to Wundt's attempt to build a science out of data obtained from trained introspectionists. The third important movement was *psycho-analysis*, which stemmed from the genius of Sigmund Freud (1856–1939). This enlarged the subject matter to embrace not merely consciousness, but also the study of unconscious mental life. Psycho-analysis contributed to the understanding of the abnormal personality, and prominent among its contributions were the insights it provided into the subtlety and complexity of human motivation.

Together with these and other schools of thought may be noted an eclectic tradition, and two influential books by a leading American who belonged to no school. In *Contemporary Schools of Psychology*, Robert S. Woodworth provided a summary and assessment of these various reformist movements. The word 'contemporary' was appropriate in the 1930s when the book first appeared, but is exceedingly misleading today. More typical of psychology as it now exists than of any of the schools was Woodworth's own book, *Experimental Psychology*, which represented what he called 'the middle of the road'. This, and its later editions, has greatly affected the form and content of psychology as it is now understood and taught in modern universities. Woodworth's chapters reflect the typical subjects which interest psychologists themselves, for example human and animal learning, perception, thinking, remembering, emotion and motivation.

This present book is intended as a contribution to the main stream of psychology as defined by Woodworth, but exhibits also a number of deviations from it that will be made explicit. First, as the title suggests, it will be more than averagely receptive to the methods of introspection and the study of *subjective experience* as having a legitimate place in the methods and subject matter of psychology, despite the dogmas of early behaviourism. Secondly, it will be more concerned with the *phenomena of mental life* – whether experience or behaviour – than with theories and explanations about them. Thirdly, it will give additional weight to the contributions of psycho-analysis and to *unconscious mental life*. Justification for these three points of emphasis will emerge in chapters which follow. Brief reasons may be given here. As regards introspection there are many signs that psychologists are outgrowing the excesses of early behaviourism. This change is long overdue. Uncritical respect for the opinion that introspection should never be used has resulted in the wholly avoidable loss of valuable clues to the solution of significant problems. This book will not be concerned to defend 'introspectionism', the doctrine that introspection is the main method of psychology, a doctrine prominent in the early years of the science but now belonging only to its history. On the other hand, attention will be paid to experience, as well as behaviour, to the family of methods we call 'introspection', and to the need for psychologists to be alerted to their use.* The emphasis on phenomena, rather than on theories, has been mentioned. At the time when Darwin's evolution theory was formulated it was said that 'the storehouse of knowledge was fairly bursting for want of an embracing generalization'. This is by no means true of many of the fields of psychology to be discussed. Darwin's theory followed – among many other things – his five-year voyage with the *Beagle*, during which he kept voluminous notebooks on his observations of many things – geological, zoological, and botanical. In psychology today we need a generous injection of this spirit of the naturalist:

* As Mace (1950) has pointed out, introspection involves more than merely *having* an experience: it also involves *communicating it*. The difficulty, as he says, is communicating 'in a clear, correct, and illuminating way'.

concern with accurate description, classification, and naming where necessary. This is true of both behavioural and introspective phenomena. Many of these require adequate description, their very existence is often not widely appreciated, their incidence has not been scientifically established, and sometimes they have not even been named. Finally, to consider unconscious mental life: here are many issues of a subtle and complex kind. This is particularly evident in relation to the psychology of motivation. In this realm it is difficult to proceed far without taking account of the subtle, intuitive thinking and enormous volume of information which together constitute psycho-analysis in its modern form.

In the contemporary scene another aspect merits emphasis, and in its historical context. This is the considerable attention now being paid by modern research to 'cognitive processes', including the psychology of thinking, using the word 'thinking' in its broadest sense. The recent history and future of psychology were assessed in the 1960 presidential address to the American Psychological Association. The then president, Professor D. O. Hebb of McGill University, Canada, spoke on this theme under the title 'The American Revolution'. By this Hebb meant the revolution of psychological thinking in the period 1898–1938, to which American psychologists had made important contributions. During these years, Hebb argued, the foundations of scientific psychology were laid. The main subject matter studied was the learning process, and behaviourism – with its rejection of introspective report as a method – dominated methodology in this era. But, Hebb argued, like the political revolution of 1776 this new 'American Revolution' gave signs of occurring in two stages. Stage 1 produced a scientific understanding of *learning*. Stage 2 required a similar understanding of the psychology of *thinking*. The present book is very much concerned with stage 2 of the process to which Hebb refers, which, by the late 1960s, was now firmly under way. Of this two-phase revolution Hebb said, 'The first banished thought, imagery, volition, attention, and other seditious notions'. But, he added, 'the sedition of one period . . . may be the good sense of another.'

The most important problem for contemporary psychology,

Hebb argued, is to place thinking on a firm basis of scientific understanding. There are numerous signs that this problem is becoming central to modern research. Processes like reasoning, judgement, fantasy, and dreaming, together with the factors which underly both reasoning and imagining, are now being intensively studied. (Compare Harper *et al.*, 1964.) New techniques of investigation have helped, among them sensory deprivation experiments, computer simulation of thought processes, and ways of recording the physiological accompaniments of dreaming. Thus as early as 1960 Miller, Galanter, and Pribram argued that modern computers made possible 'subjective behaviourism', a doctrine to which they admit, without shame, they themselves subscribe. Rejection or neglect of difficult problems like those of thinking, imaging, and imagining, because they did not fit into the narrowly defined methodology of early behaviourism, is much less apparent in the 1960s. By 1964 Robert Holt had published his paper with the provocative title 'Imagery: The Return of the Ostracized', and by 1966 Jerome Singer had contributed his book *Daydreaming* with the sub-title 'An Introduction to the Experimental Study of Inner Experience'. Work of such psychologists as these illustrates a changed emphasis in, for example, Holt's use of sensory deprivation experiments, and Singer's use of the rapid eye movement technique in the study of both waking and sleeping human fantasy. As an impetus to what Hebb calls the 'second phase' of development of psychology have come new techniques of research, fresh ideas, and widespread rejection of behaviourist presuppositions which are no longer appropriate. This book will take account of these contemporary developments, and the place they are giving to subjective experience in psychology.

SUBJECTIVE EXPERIENCE

In different ways both Wundt and Freud were much concerned with introspection. At Wundt's laboratory students were trained to perform exercises of introspecting in accord with rules laid down by Wundt. Only after many such exercises had been performed were their introspective results regarded as suitable for publication. Freud and his associates likewise built up a body of theory on the basis of introspective data elicited by them, though with the use of the additional technique of free association. When free associating, in accord with the 'fundamental rule of analysis' the person being analysed was required to put into words everything that emerged to his awareness no matter how trivial or unimportant, or contrary to convention, it seemed to speak these thoughts.

Along with Wundt and Freud may be mentioned a third important pioneer: Sir Francis Galton (1822–1911). What interested Galton about introspection was the evidence it provided about the subject's personal equipment for thinking, remembering, and imagining. From Galton stems the area of the subject today called 'Differential Psychology': the investigation of individual differences. By questionnaire methods Galton obtained detailed information about mental imagery: differences people showed in their use of the 'mind's eye', and 'mind's ear', and other types of imagery for their previous perceptual experiences. Imagery differences will be discussed in more detail in later sections. Here we may note how, under the influence of behaviourism, this aspect of experience has been unjustifiably neglected. As Holt (1964) points out, a re-emergence of concern with this field came largely as a result of outside interests. Various problems of a practical kind involving engineering psychology 'and similarly hard-headed' branches of the discipline necessitated attention to imagery problems. Specifically Holt notes the confusions resulting from imagery processes which interfere with perception in such activities as high-altitude flying, driving on motorways, and exploring polar regions in Sno-cats and similar vehicles. People concerned with such activities have been troubled by the emergence of imagery into consciousness. We may be tempted to use the word 'hallucination' for such subjective interferences as these. Here, as Holt rightly points out, we are in danger of unjustifiably extending and carelessly misusing the word 'hallucination'. He himself chooses rather to distinguish between a number of different kinds of subjective phenomena and in this returns to Galton's approach: the making of an inventory of visual subjective phenomena ranging from incapacity for such experience at all to complete hallucination. In this area, Galton argued, we find a complete continuum when we investigate different human beings.

As Galton found, many people rely a great deal on their visual imagery, and have no difficulty in forming pictures in their 'mind's eye'. Others do not think and remember in this way at all. Recently I talked to a woman psychologist who, like Galton before her, had become interested in these imagery variations. The reason for her interest is worth recording: she herself was largely bereft of visual imagery but discovered one day that her husband was 'a great visualizer'. And she admitted that it had taken her twenty-five years of marriage to discover this important difference between his mental life and her own! Many people live their whole lives without being aware of such differences between themselves and their friends or relatives. And if they do discover that other people are different, their reactions to this discovery may be not surprise, but hostility and intolerance. On investigation today we find, as Galton found at the turn of this century, that the reaction 'but surely everybody is like me' is common among not only people who possess the more usual kinds of image life, but those who exhibit its rarities. In some individuals, and under certain circumstances, imagery of intense vividness may occur and may be mistaken for real perception. Holt refers to the jet pilot operating in cloud, and the radio operator who has to monitor his instruments under conditions of visual fatigue. Again, to cite an actual incident, a fatigued motorist at night may 'swerve to avoid a purely hallucinatory rabbit', or may in other cases hallucinate non-existent cars in his headlights coming towards him. In this field, however, the word 'hallucination' has been overworked: thus Holt lists no fewer than thirteen different types of imagery and related experiences. These phenomena in their variety will receive emphasis in this book as neglected but legitimate aspects of the subject matter of psychology.

Some variants of subjective experience outside imagery may be noted. One of these is the illusion of recognition which takes the form 'I feel as if I have lived through this before, though I know

Subjective Experience

I haven't'. This is one of a number of commonplace phenomena which people on occasion worry about, and may even be tempted to assess as abnormal. Yet, to take evidence of incidence from an investigation of my own: of a group of 182 university students investigated no fewer than 126, or 69 per cent, had experienced this illusion (which is called *déjà vu*). Despite its frequency individuals who have the experience are often reassured to discover it has a name and is quite a common phenomenon.

Commoner still is another phenomenon which lacks an established name: this is the subjective impression of 'falling' and 'waking up with a start' while dropping off to sleep. Investigation with the same group of students revealed that this was reported by 144, that is 75 per cent, of the individuals. For lack of an accepted name we shall provisionally call this *the falling experience*.

In addition to this and *déjà vu* may be mentioned a third phenomenon, which may be intrinsically more frightening, and in which the need for reassurance may be even more pressing. During the process of falling asleep many odd phenomena occur. Among these are the visual, auditory, or other types of imagery of quasi-hallucinatory vividness which some, but not all people, report. These phenomena, *hypnagogic images*, will be discussed fully in later chapters. The visual kinds of imagery have been likened to a succession of lantern slides: they occur most often with closed eyes, but may also occur open-eyed in a darkened room. The auditory types of images are very often of music or voices. Quite a number of subjects report actually getting up out of bed to investigate the radio they thought they had heard, or the telephone conversation which proved to be non-existent. With hypnagogic imagery we again encounter individual differences: some people have them and others apparently do not. Thus one individual who happens to be a child may exhibit to another, who happens to be its parent, what may seem to be a very odd form of mental life. Alternatively the imager may tell nobody about the experience, which becomes subject matter for silent brooding and worry. Thus the occurrence of these variations should be more widely known, as also the fact that they are perfectly harmless variations within the realm of the normal.

THE DESIRABILITY OF EMPATHY

In both outward behaviour and subjective experience, which together define our personalities, we start, as Somerset Maugham has put it, 'each one of us in the solitariness of our own minds'. Then, as time progresses and knowledge of other people enlarges, we come to realize the similarities and differences of our own personalities in relation to those around us. Such awareness, as it increases, extends our capacity for what the psychologist would call empathy. By *empathy* is meant an imaginative identification with another person of the kind which permits a fuller understanding of his mental life and his problems of adjustment. Empathy means understanding, and not necessarily siding with. We may empathize with a person whom we dislike, or with some formal opponent. Thus one may empathize with an opponent or enemy in activities which range from a game of chess to a military campaign, with the intention of defeating him, by anticipating what he will do next. Daily life provides many instances of failure of empathy introspectively noticeable in our own experience, or behaviourally observable in others. Thus we may wait in a queue muttering intolerantly about the excessively long time taken by the present occupant of the phone booth; a few minutes later, having gained possession of the telephone, we again catch ourselves muttering, this time about the impatience of people in the queue outside. And, as regards those two natural enemies of the modern world, it is remarkable how quickly the intolerant motorist will change into the intolerant pedestrian, simply by getting out of his car!

Many barriers to empathy stem from differences between people of age, sex, nationality, and personality. Difficulties of communication thus result from differences of, for example, custom and language between Britain and the United States. Thus in planning his American visit the Englishman is wise to remember that there is no such thing as a 'fortnight' in America; that proprietors of American restaurants may be polite but underneath shocked if mustard is ordered with steak; and that crossing a cheque invalidates it for an American bank, however usual this procedure may be in Britain. It may seem odd to the

Englishman in the United States to be told by notices 'Do not park on the pavement'. To the American 'pavement' means road, and thus the visitor's interpretation of the notice will be very different from what the notice is meant to convey. Differences which stem from nationality, like those which stem from age or personality, may provoke surprise and amusement. Until made explicit they may impede empathy and adequate communication.

Major purposes of this book will be to draw attention to the value of empathy, and to encourage empathy with people who differ from oneself. One formidable barrier to empathy separates the normal person from his understanding of the abnormal. Yet, even in severe mental illness – in psychosis – the patient may, in many important respects, be remarkably like other people. This was appreciated by the great mental hospital reformer Philippe Pinel, who lived at the time of the French Revolution. Pinel argued that the revolutionary slogans of 'Liberty, Equality, Fraternity' had implications for the mentally ill no less than for other people. By insisting on this, Pinel, in October 1793, was able to secure release from chains and other mechanical restraints of the patients of the Bicêtre Asylum in Paris. In his *Treatise on Insanity* Pinel used arguments which made sense to the men of his day. He pointed out that a despotic method of government may produce conformity, and brutality can produce the appearance of order and loyalty. This applies to the insane, no less than the sane. If, however, he is given a measure of liberty, the restrained patient will usually become less violent, and in some cases such liberation will remove violence altogether.

Reforms of a similar kind were needed equally in England, where as early as 1728 Daniel Defoe attacked the dreadful conditions which prevailed in private madhouses and urged that they should be 'suppressed at once'. Defoe added that if people are not mad when they go into 'these cursed houses' then soon after they are 'made so by the barbarous usage they there suffer' (Hunter and MacAlpine, 1963). Reforms, however, came slowly in Britain, as elsewhere. At Leicester one important reformer, Robert Gardner Hill, advocated completion of the work Pinel had begun. What Hill argued may be stated in his own words: 'I

23

assert in plain and distinct terms: that in a properly constructed building, with a sufficient number of suitable attendants, restraint is never necessary, never justifiable, and always injurious in all cases of lunacy whatsoever' (quoted by Hunter and MacAlpine, 1963). For his advocacy of this principle Gardner Hill was attacked as a visionary, as one who endangered the lives of the attendants, and even as a breaker of the fifth commandment. Yet over a period of six years at Leicester he reduced the number of patients put under mechanical restraint to zero. In institutions where this policy was followed there was no evidence of increased death rates among nurses and attendants.

These reforms are by no means complete, and in the world today we can find backward institutions where patients are tied to their beds or have their arms pinioned behind their backs, or where other such restraints are used. That this can occur at all, or has ever occurred, is evidence of the strict limitations of the capacity of the sane for understanding the mentally ill. Throughout history misconceptions, aggression born of fear, superstition and ignorance have been widespread. The sane have been slow to confront themselves with the thought: 'These people, though sick, are remarkably like ourselves in many important respects.' Much of this ignorance still remains. In *To Define True Madness* (Pelican, 1953), Yellowlees, a distinguished forensic psychiatrist, is vigorous in his condemnation not merely of the general public but also of people in official positions. He instances specifically the press, the churches, many medical men themselves, and lawyers and judges. This widespread ignorance is not merely a problem for those like Yellowlees who are concerned with communication about mental illness in court – a subject I shall discuss in a later chapter – but it also carries extra burdens for the mentally ill, and those interested in their treatment and care. In this area we encounter enormous resistance to empathy, and a widespread reluctance to accept available knowledge.

KNOWLEDGE, AND RESISTANCE TO ITS APPLICATION

Like other branches of science, psychology has both its pure and its applied aspects. Before mentioning some of these applications it is appropriate to emphasize the value of pure science as such. Knowledge pursued for its own sake may provide broader perspectives, and the applications which may in time follow are not necessarily immediately apparent. There is an apocryphal story about Michael Faraday and some demonstrations he once produced at a public lecture. The Prime Minister of the day happened to be present and remarked to him afterwards: 'Very interesting, Mr Faraday, but what is the *use* of it?' Faraday replied: 'Mr Prime Minister, one day you will be able to *tax* it!' And Faraday was right, for from these demonstrations emerged electricity.

Human attitudes, sentiments, and values are themselves an important area of subject matter for psychology. The way in which these produce resistance to change, and to the application of knowledge once it is available, presents problems in which the psychologist of today is exhibiting considerable interest. Some remarkable examples of resistance to the application of new technical knowledge can be found in military history, for example in the First Duke of Wellington's opposition to the substitution of rifles for smooth-bore muskets. Again, the appalling casualties of the American Civil War were very largely due to the retention of tactics appropriate to the earlier and less efficient musket, although the armies were in fact equipped with the newer and lethally accurate rifle. The history of the development and introduction of the tank into modern warfare presents some striking examples of human resistance and attitudinal rigidity. In 1916 when the tank was demonstrated to him Lord Kitchener assessed it as 'a pretty mechanical toy'. Winston Churchill had much to do with the development of the tank as a device for ending the stalemate of trench warfare in France. He placed an order for eighteen of these landships, and they were subsequently regularly referred to as 'Winston's folly'. As late as 1925 we find even the British Commander in Chief, Haig, able to say: 'Some enthusiasts today talk about the possibility of the horse becoming extinct, and prophesy that the aeroplane, the tank, and the motor car will supersede it in future wars.' This possibility did not impress the general; he went on: 'I feel sure that as time goes on you will find just as much use for the horse – the well-bred horse – as you have ever done in the past.' And with equal confidence he also assessed the machine-gun as 'a much over-rated weapon'. Unfortunately, as the Battle of Mons in the First World War showed regarding the machine-gun, and the whole of the Second World War showed as regards the tank, Haig was wrong in both his judgements. As we shall see, elsewhere and in many contexts, it is possible to feel absolutely sure and to be absolutely wrong. Irrational certainty, rigidity of thinking, and the slow process of changing attitudes interests psychology. Much scientific research of all kinds is wasted because even those prepared to pay for its being carried out are by no means always prepared to use it. Now to overcome this wastage is one of the most important problems to be overcome by modern psychology. Quite incredible delays can occur in the application of knowledge to daily living. Two examples may be taken from the context of road safety.

The dark-adapted human eye exhibits insensitivity to red, and this fact has been known to science for about a century and a half. In other words, red is perceived as black in twilight. The fact that pedestrians and cyclists who wear red on the roads at night are largely invisible against the surrounding darkness, and are thus inviting their own deaths, is by no means widely appreciated. Road safety posters may advise us to 'wear white at night': they might well advise us specifically not to wear red because of this well-established fact about the human eye. Nor are the general public alone in ignoring this long-established fact. Advertisements often use red against black, and the same is true even of road-safety posters themselves. One such poster reads: DRINK, DRIVE, DEATH. The first two words are in white against a black background, but 'death' appears as red against black. While all three words are visible in daylight the last word is invisible in twilight, during which time the poster conveys unintentionally the misleading encouragement to drink and drive.

Less well known are some interesting comparisons of pedestrians' judgements of their own visibility on the roads at night with what drivers see of them in their headlights. In 1940 two psychologists, Ferguson and Geddes, experimented on this problem, and their experiments revealed a widespread tendency for pedestrians to overestimate their visibility. Under the conditions used the range of clear visibility for the driver extended to 463 feet ahead of him; more than half the subjects, who were required to drop pegs in the road as they walked towards the car, dropped pegs indicating 'absolute certainty' outside this range. Some of the subjects dropped their absolute-certainty pegs as far as 500, 600, and even 700 feet away from the car. Here we encounter the phenomenon of being absolutely certain and absolutely wrong as well: there were many subjects, potential pedestrians, who judged themselves to be visible long before they were to a driver with good vision, seated behind the better-than-average headlights of the parked police car used in the experiment. This tendency to overestimate one's likelihood of being seen at night is probably unknown to most road users. Its discovery was a matter of surprise both to the psychologists and to the police authorities who cooperated in the study. Here we encounter a good instance of curious neglect of a research finding, published a quarter of a century ago, showing time lag in taking account of findings even when they are highly relevant to individual survival.

Progress has been made in the understanding of certain relations between communication of information and alteration of behaviour. This relationship is not always as simple as it is sometimes assumed. In 1956 Eunice Belbin reported some experiments on the effects of road-safety propaganda on children. She measured the ability of the children to recall the road-safety information imparted to them. But she also posted observers to watch how the behaviour of the children changed, for example in such matters as using pedestrian crossings. An interesting finding emerged: there was no positive relation between ability to recall information and alteration of behaviour. In fact, two contrasting types of reaction occurred. Some individuals were good at recalling what they had been told. Others, though poor at the recall tasks, used the information in their actual behaviour on the road. Belbin's experiment invites caution in making the assumption that ability to remember is – as it is often assumed to be – necessarily a good indication that what is remembered will be put into effective use.

Two conclusions emerge from the foregoing discussion. First, as we have seen, there is no reason why all research should be conducted with immediate application in mind. Secondly, nor is there any reason to assume, even when applications are obvious, that such applications will be made. With these two points in mind I shall take some illustrations of applied psychology, and mention also some areas of potential future application.

APPLICATIONS OF PSYCHOLOGY

The fields in which psychologists work are exceedingly numerous. Teachers of psychology are likely to be employed in university departments of psychology, education, and psychiatry, or less frequently in others like child health, anatomy, pharmacology, and tropical medicine. Those taught may include – as well as potential psychologists – such other groups as medical, law, and architecture students, industrialists, police and rehabilitation officers, and magistrates. Two of the most important areas of applied psychology are educational and clinical. In educational psychology employment is often by some Local Authority: work may include vocational guidance; intelligence, aptitude, attainment, and personality testing; and remedial education. In Soviet Russia 'defectology', the study of blindness, deafness, intellectual subnormality, speech defects, and other such problems, has emerged as a subject in its own right. Clinical psychologists must be distinguished from psychiatrists – the medical colleagues they work with – and are members of a team along with psychiatrists, psychiatric social workers, and psychiatric nurses.

One area of application in which psychologists in Britain have been influential is the prison service, and the relatively small group of men working in this field maintains exceedingly high standards. Much of their work involves feeding their results back into the system. One such psychologist has recently expressed the opinion that the last few years have seen more changes in British prisons than have probably occurred in the last two centuries. To these the prison psychologists have themselves made substantial contributions, not least in helping to train intelligent, humane, and realistic men and women as prison officers, from over 50,000 who apply annually for this work. Obviously here selection work is important, and in explaining selection procedures used one prison psychologist added, 'We are always on the look out for the bully, whom we rigidly exclude'.

The use of mental tests in selecting forms an important aspect of the work of many psychologists, including those concerned with 'occupational psychology', which has two aspects: the industrial and the armed forces sides. Often, however, psychologists have been invited to help with selection and have stayed to conduct experiments which have led to the redesign of the equipment used. Thus engineering psychology, the design of equipment in accord with the known attributes of the human user, is an important and growing branch of the subject. The modern aeroplane and the development of techniques for space research present many problems for the engineering psychologist's attention, but an example may be taken from a more everyday piece of equipment. Recent years have seen huge advances in the understanding of short-term memory: memory of the kind involved in, for example, holding a telephone number in mind while dialling. It has been established that the activity of dialling itself, together with the delays which ensue from operation of a dial, result in considerable interference with short-term remembering. Thus new types of telephone are being developed, and it has been shown that substantial decreases in the amount of wrong-number dialling can be achieved with some of these modified pieces of telephone equipment.

The work of the clinical psychologist has been mentioned: clinical psychologists work with the psychiatrist and assist him in his work of diagnosis, treatment, and prediction of the outcome of mental illness. Some clinics now also employ therapists who are not medically trained, but are psychologists rather than psychiatrists. These psychologist therapists collaborate closely with medical colleagues and also with social workers: not infrequently the changes of attitude the social worker can achieve in the home can be of extreme importance in assisting treatment of, for example, an intellectually subnormal, educationally back-ward, or emotionally disturbed child.

Work in other branches of medicine may be noted, for example in pharmacology, when in testing a new drug it may be helpful to apply well-established techniques of psychology to the measurement of animal behaviour in such activities as problem solving, resistance to stress, discrimination, and general activity. Similarly the behavioural studies of animal psychology have found a place in the somewhat parallel problems of tropical medicine. The behavioural effects of infection of animals can be studied in very much the same way as drug effects can be assessed.

A potentially important field of potential application is to general medicine itself. Of central concern to the physician is diagnosis: illnesses are diagnosed with the aid of sight, hearing, and touch, together with such extensions of human perceptual equipment as X-ray photography. In short, diagnosis involves perception, one of the central topics of psychology. An examina-tion of this important relation between diagnosis and perception was provided by Abercrombie (1960) when working in the Department of Anatomy at University College Hospital, Lon-don. Abercrombie was particularly interested in possibilities of human error, this being well illustrated by one study she men-tions involving X-ray photography. It concerned over a thousand radiographs that were assessed by five specialists as either positive or negative for tuberculosis. When reassessed by the same indi-viduals two months later, huge discrepancies emerged. Thus, for example, one specialist picked out 59 radiographs as positive on the first occasion, and 78 on the second. Abercrombie was particularly interested in techniques of instruction of medical students designed to minimize possibilities of such error. From her work it emerges that those kinds of perception we know as 'diagnosis' are subject to error, and that considerable variations between individuals occur. We need to know a great deal more about these variations, and these sources of error.

Several American universities now have courses in legal and criminal psychology: at Michigan State University, for instance, a thousand students take such a course every year. Several university departments in Britain give courses of instruction in relevant aspects of psychology to police officers, and at Sheffield courses including the subject have also been given to magistrates. Some American courts have for years had attached to them clinics in which remedial training is given to persistent driving offenders. What might be called 'forensic psychology' – applications of the methods and findings of the subject to problems of law – has a very important future. Thus one subsidiary aim of this book will be to draw attention to this underdeveloped field, in the hope of encouraging more interaction between psychologists and lawyers. Quite frequently in the United States, and more occasionally in Britain, the psychologist himself appears as an expert witness in court. Apart altogether from such practical activities, there are many problems of a research kind relating to perception, remembering, and communication in court. These issues will be discussed in a later chapter.

Quite apart from matters like military and aviation selection, and equipment design, warfare has brought many problems for the attention of psychologists. During the Second World War, for instance, teams of experts including artists, geographers and psychologists worked on the problems of penetration of camouflage by the study of photographs taken by allied aircraft. This work yielded, for example, information about the location of bases from which the Nazis intended to fire flying bombs: once detected these bases were effectively bombed by the Royal Air Force. It has been estimated that this delayed the appearance of the new weapon by a period of six months: a matter of considerable importance for both military and civilian morale. A different type of problem concerns the Far Eastern campaigns of the Americans, who became much disturbed by the fact that a large number of their own men, as prisoners of war, cooperated unduly with the enemy. The rather woolly concept of 'brain-washing' has been much misused in this connexion, and some far-fetched analogies between the treatment of these prisoners and Pavlov's researches into conditioned reflexes in the dog have been drawn. In what has been called 'brain-washing' we encounter the complexities of the process of altering human belief and behaviour. Technical psychology has a great deal more to contribute to the understanding of these personality changes than speculation about the resemblance of prisoners' behaviour to laboratory conditioning experiments. The American psychologists used the more effective, if more prosaic, method of interviewing former prisoners on return and collecting information from them about what had actually happened to them. Assistance of leading experts in the psychology of learning was obtained; for example Harlow with his colleagues conducted detailed interviews with returned prisoners. Techniques used by the captors were elicited, and one such technique may be described. If a prisoner is kept in solitary confinement his need for human company becomes acute, and this need can be exploited. It may be utilized by taking him from confinement to the company of an expert interrogator who then feeds him with propaganda he is ill equipped to resist. Thus – in the absence of any other information – a prisoner may come in time to believe, or half-believe, the propaganda imparted to him. He is rewarded for giving signs of such half-belief by the presence of other people, and by promises of reduction of discomfort and distress. In other instances it was discovered that extremely intensive programmes of instruction with slanted lectures on current events, lasting from four to five hours, were given to the prisoners in groups. They were then divided into smaller groups of 12–15 individuals for guided discussion. Other techniques included encouragement to inform on other prisoners who, when this happened, were not punished but encouraged to make public confessions of their fault. These techniques, when effective, had disastrous results on morale and on the readiness of any two prisoners to trust each other and band together for the purpose of resistance or escape. From the results of these investigations into what had happened to the men who collaborated unduly with the enemy, counter-training was given to other troops, and a code of conduct was drawn up as a basis of resistance to indoctrination. These counter-moves were based on a knowledge not only of personality and the learning process, but also on detailed information about the different types of pressures used. Such work involved the cooperation of the prisoners themselves with the psychologists and psychiatrists who participated.

A third illustration relates both to the aftermath of war, and to the legal and forensic field. After the Second World War, when the principal Nazis were tried at Nuremberg, psychologists were present both in court and out of it, and made detailed studies of the personalities of the accused. In his book *Nuremberg Diary* Gilbert, the principal American psychologist concerned, has provided a record of this information in detail. Gilbert, who has since been interested in forensic psychology of a more usual kind, had much greater opportunity to study the accused than occurs at most trials. A substantial amount of testing was conducted on the intelligence and personality traits of the Nazi leaders, and detailed interviews – at various important and stressful stages of the trial – were obtained. The valuable information elicited by these studies may be helpful in the prevention of another such war, but has relevance also to the understanding of the inhumanities that can occur in large-scale organizations. These were present in exaggerated form in Nazi Germany, but can occur anywhere when the men who issue orders are both geographically and mentally remote from the consequences of such orders. Thus individuals at different levels of a hierarchy have a variety of techniques of self-deception available to them, which serve to diminish their sense of responsibility and feeling of guilt about what happens. Some of these issues will be examined in a later chapter, when we come to discuss the various 'mechanisms of ego-defence' or processes of self-deception.

CONCLUSION

This chapter has sought to introduce psychology as the scientific discipline concerned with the study of experience and behaviour; a brief historical introduction has been given. It has also sought to make explicit the standpoint to be adopted in the chapters which follow, and to introduce some relevant ideas and concepts. As has been indicated, some emphasis will be given to topics which are again beginning to engage research attention in psychology after a period of unjustifiable neglect. As a whole this book will be concerned with what might be called 'psychological natural history' rather than with theories of psychology, and will attempt to indicate the diversity of phenomena which mental life exhibits. The early chapters will deal with this mainly in relation to *cognitive* mental life, that is with subjects like perception, imagery, thinking, and learning. Later chapters will deal more explicitly with *temperament*, and with topics like emotion and motivation.

CHAPTER TWO

Perception of the Outside World

There is no conception in a man's mind which hath not at
first, totally or by parts, been begotten upon the organs of
sense.
                                    THOMAS HOBBES

THE study of perception has been called 'the psychologists'
psychology'. There is much justification for this assessment.
Those who are beginning the study of the science probably do
not have questions about perception in mind. But if they sustain
this interest they will come to realize the fundamental importance
of the study of perception. Knowledge of reality, the material and
social environment to which adjustments have to be made, comes
from vision, hearing, touch, and other sensory channels. Science
depends upon 'observation', which is another name for perception; and science is on its guard against errors of observation
about which the psychology of perception has much to teach.
Medicine is concerned with 'diagnosis', another perceptual
activity conducted with the human sense organs and extensions
of these like the stethoscope, microscope, and X-ray photography. History and the law are preoccupied with the task of
establishing the facts about past events, and both human history
and legal testimony are products of perception and, at times,
misperception. Finally, as the quotation from Hobbes implies,
the raw materials of human thinking, remembering, and imagining are perceptual in their origins. These perceptions give rise to
daily preoccupations, plans, and ideas; they limit the products of
our thinking, and the extent of our imagining. Since thought
products often seem to be something more original than merely
recall of what we have previously perceived, it will be necessary
to examine more fully two different kinds of perceiving.

PRIMARY AND SECONDARY PERCEPTION

We make a great deal of use not merely of our own percepts, but
also of the communicated perceptions of others. In the absence

of an established terminology I shall speak of 'primary' and 'secondary' perception to elucidate this. Examples of primary perception would be seeing a human face, tasting a cup of coffee, hearing words spoken, and experiencing the pain of toothache. Instances of secondary perception would be looking at a picture of a face, listening to a sound recording, and reading or hearing a description – perhaps the lucid one given by Thomas de Quincey – of the pain of toothache. In what I have called secondary forms of perception there is communication of the information, through some intermediate process or person, about objects or events: the printed word, photography, pictures, and sound recordings have assumed considerable importance in the modern world. Thus secondary perception enormously enlarges the possibilities of human experience into the realm of the perceivings of others. It may also mislead us into accepting their misperceptions and imaginings. Through secondary perception we can gain information about geographically distant or historically remote people and events, and secondary perception provides an additional source of information for our own thinking. An interesting example concerns Coleridge's highly original thought product, his poem 'The Ancient Mariner'. When he wrote this poem, Coleridge had not even crossed the Channel. But he did possess an enormous amount of relevant material from having read widely about the voyages of early travellers and explorers. This secondary perception gave him access to the perceptions, and sometimes the imaginings, of Dampier, Cook and other early navigators. These became raw materials for his own thought product, his poem, whose sources have been traced by subsequent investigators. Outside the realms of literature, the processes of secondary perception are of great importance today with media like the film, radio, and television. These enlarge the raw materials of human thought products, and the possibilities of human thinking, by providing perceptual information about distant places, the historical past, and even the realm of the fictional and the imaginative.

THE SENSE ORGANS AND PERCEPTION

Sight, hearing, touch, taste, and smell represent the classical 'five senses'. These are five important channels of perceptual information. A modern classification of the sense organs allows for many more, in fact, three different types of sense organs: the extero-ceptors, interoceptors, and proprioceptors. We are least likely to overlook the *exteroceptors*, to which all of the classical five senses relate. The skin has other exteroceptors which, in addition to touch, give us information about heat, cold, and pain. *Intero-ceptors* are internal sense organs which give sensations that are prominent during strong motivation or emotional upset: the sinking feelings of the stomach which may accompany fear, and the pangs of hunger, are examples. *Proprioceptors* are located in the muscles and tendons, and give information about our body itself, and the position of its component limbs in space. In keeping in mind the sense organs other than the exteroceptors it is helpful to take account of psycho-analytic thought about percep-tion. Freud distinguished between the ego and the id. The ego is the aspect of the personality most modified by the external world and by external, exteroceptor perception. By contrast the id, conceived of by Freud as the seat of emotions and instinctive urges, may be thought of as closely connected with interoception, and the core of internal sensations associated with emotions and motivation. Following Freud, J. C. Flugel defines the ego as the perceptual centre of the personality: the aspect of the personality concerned with perception of the external world and adjust-ment to it. The ego, the part of ourselves we refer to when we say 'I', 'me', and 'mine', is intermediate between exterocep-tion from the outside world and interoception from within, as when for example 'I' perceive impulses which 'I' seek to resist.

The notion of the ego reminds us that the perceiver himself is part of the perceptual process. He is aware of himself as a physical object with spatially related parts whose positions are known to him not only through vision but also through pro-prioceptive perception. In this context we encounter the notion of the body image, or body schema. It was in 1908 that the neurologist A. Pick conceived of this idea that each person has a spatial impression of his own body, an impression in which the muscle sense organs play an obviously important part. In 1911 the neurologists Head and Holmes called this impression the body schema. This they defined as a standard against which, 'by means of perpetual alterations in positions, we are always building up a model of ourselves which constantly changes'. We use our body image in putting on our coat, in estimating whether an object is within our reach or not, and in locating our aches, pains, and other bodily sensations. Neurologists have been specially interested in the body image, but it has its importance elsewhere. Thus for example both introspection and observation reveal that people often use their body image as a sort of measuring rod, in giving assessments of the size of objects, for example when testifying as witnesses in court. In some preliminary studies of this J. Clarkson and I have found indications of how a person asked to assess the dimensions of standard objects like a pillar box or a telephone kiosk will employ his own body image. With some such objects that are not perceptually present at the time, we have found that errors of these assessments are significantly related to the height of the subject himself. The neurologist's interest in the body image stems from the fact that certain lesions of the central nervous system produce body image disturbances: an altered impression of the shape and size of the body, and its parts, as objects occupying space. There are many other circumstances such as fatigue, or the drowsy state before sleep, in which body-image changes can occur to the normal person. Many people while falling asleep have the impression that their body, or one of their limbs, has expanded or shrunk, or become distorted in one way or other. The stability or otherwise of the body image, and of extensions of one's own body including the vehicle one is driving, are of interest to engineering and aviation psychology. Thus body-image changes are reported during flights at high altitudes, or through cloud, and under conditions of monotony and fatigue in driving on a motorway. All these phenomena serve to remind us of the importance of proprioceptive perception, and of our own body as part of our perceptual environment.

Of central importance in understanding perception is the *stimulus*. Strictly speaking a stimulus is an energy change in the environment to which the appropriate sense organ is sensitive. More loosely we often refer to a light, a sound, or a pin prick as a stimulus to the visual, auditory, and pain receptors. We may note, however, the phenomenon of inadequate stimulation, when an inappropriate stimulus activates a sense organ. The best-known case of this is 'seeing stars' following a blow to the face which activates the optic receptors. A curious incident concerning this occurred in a nineteenth-century court case. A man had been attacked in the dark, but nevertheless claimed that he was able to recognize his assailant because the blow to his eye had created a sufficiently bright light to illuminate the darkness! As most readers will have observed for themselves, it is possible to obtain visual experiences of shapes and colours by the inadequate stimulation of pressure on the closed eyeball. Other instances of inadequate stimulation include paradoxical cold, which can be produced by electrical stimulation of the cold receptors of the surface of the skin. Thus a sense organ may be stimulated in one of two ways, by an adequate or an inadequate stimulus. The relevant principle in the case of inadequate stimulation is that the resulting experience depends on the sense organ activated and not on the stimulus. Thus for example in the case of para-doxical cold, provided a cold receptor is stimulated, no matter whether the stimulus is electrical, tactile, or of some other kind, the perception of cold occurs. Inadequate stimulation represents but one of many cases in which the perceptual experi-ence may deviate markedly from the sense data and stimulus situation.

Another phenomenon of this kind involves sensory adaptation: the decreased sensitivity of the receptor following continued stimulation. Adaptation may occur with vision, as when pro-longed inspection of a coloured surface leads to apparent loss of colour, a bleached appearance of the surface. The sense of smell, the olfactory sense, seems particularly susceptible to sensory adaptation: thus people who come to live in an area of thermal activity may be acutely aware of the sulphurous atmosphere, though this is hardly detectable to the permanent resident. As regards taste, the gustatory sense, the principle that eating garlic should be an all-or-nothing affair, that everybody should have it or nobody, recognizes the fact of sensory adaptation. Thus the state of the sense organ, including its adaptation, affects the resulting perceptual experience.

There may be a detectable aftermath of the stimulation of a sense organ called its after-sensation (or 'after-image'). The most familiar example is the dark patch one experiences after having looked at a bright light. Visual after-sensations of a variety of impressive kinds may be produced with simple materials: the essentials are sheets of coloured paper and good illumination. Coloured after-sensations are called positive when they occur in the same hue as the original stimulus, and negative when in the complementary hue. In the 'Franklin experiment', Benjamin Franklin demonstrated that positive after-sensations occur in a dark field, or with closed eyes, while negative after-sensations occur on bright surfaces with open eyes. To take an example, inspection of a well-illuminated red surface will give rise to a negative after-sensation of the complementary green if the eyes are switched to a white sheet. The size of the after-sensation can be altered: thus the complementary green may look small against a near-by surface, but larger if projected on to the wall of the room. After-sensations are not confined to the visual sense. In fact, in attempts to measure auditory acuity with an audiometer, auditory after-sensations can be a considerable nuisance. The after-sensation of the previous stimulus is sometimes confused with the next stimulus, and the subject 'hears' before there is anything to hear. After-sensations of movement can be produced following stimulation of the subject in a rotating chair. These may be positive, when the movement occurs in the same direction as the previous stimulation, or negative, when they occur in the opposite direction. It is, however, visual after-sensations that we most readily think of in this field. These should not be confused with visual memory images: after-sensations are a phenomenon which relate to the sense organ itself – in this case the eye – rather than to the brain.

DEFICIENCIES OF THE SENSE ORGAN

Most obvious of the sense-organ defects are blindness and deafness. It is not always appreciated that a man may be classified legally as blind or deaf without total absence of the sense of sight or hearing. Thus a man is legally accepted as blind if his sight is so extremely poor as to incapacitate him. There are, moreover, many blind people who have not been blind from birth, and who can thus use their memory of visual experiences. Visual memory images may be available to waking mental life after several decades, and such people may also, of course, have visual dreams.

There are a number of different kinds of colour blindness. Its commonest form is called deuteranopia, sometimes loosely referred to as 'green blindness'. In a well-defined instance of deuteranopia the person concerned has difficulties mainly with green: he will confuse dark greens with blacks, and have difficulty in making any differentiation between light greens and white. The second commonest form of colour blindness is protanopia (more loosely called 'red blindness'), which involves marked insensitivity to the reds. Thus a protanope typically finds it difficult or impossible to distinguish a well-defined red against a black background. He will sometimes exhibit surprise at the similarities other people say they notice between red and pink. To him the one is 'dark' and the other 'light'; his eye is markedly insensitive to the redness of hue on which, to the normal eye, their resemblance depends. There are other features of these two kinds of colour blindness, and it may be noted that the protanope and the deuteranope both tend to have difficulties with reds and greens. For practical purposes, colour blindness *is* protanopia and deuteranopia. Their incidence also shows a sex difference: they are found in about 4 per cent of men, and 0·4 per cent of women. There are also ethnic differences, incidence being lower among the inhabitants of certain of the islands of the Pacific. Very much less common are two forms of colour blindness which affect perception of blues and yellows. Even rarer is monochromatic vision, or total colour blindness, with an estimated incidence of 1 in 40,000 people. The vision of such people is limited to brightnesses – blacks, whites, and intervening greys – in terms of which what appear to other people as colours are all seen. In two cases of monochromatic vision which I have had opportunity to examine, the naming of colours was virtually random: it was based on the inadequate categories of 'light' and 'dark'. It is of interest to encounter an individual whose category for 'black' includes what other people would call 'red', who cannot distinguish a pink from a light blue, and who is perceptually unaware of any difference between yellow and light green. In addition to the well-defined cases of colour blindness, whether total as in these cases, or partial as in protanopia and deuteranopia, are the more commonly found instances of anomalous colour vision. It becomes a matter of definition how serious the colour-vision defect is to be before we are prepared to call it 'colour blindness'. Short of these well-defined cases we encounter gradations between the normal and colour blindness: such cases may be classified as protanomalous or deuteranomalous in accord with their kind of colour weakness.

Anosmia is a parallel defect of another sense mode, the olfactory sense. Smell blindness may be partial or total. There are, for example, individuals who are insensitive to the smell of vanilla, while for others violets have no smell. A temporary smell blindness may be produced by local application to the nasal cavity of cocaine, and it also occurs of course as an accompaniment of the common cold. A psychologist colleague, L. B. Birch, has provided me with an account of anosmia in himself which lasted for a period of eight years. This followed an air crash, and was later corrected by surgical operation to the septum of the nose. Of interest is his observation that his mental imagery for smells, ordinarily vivid, seemed to remain unimpaired. After restoration of his capacity for olfactory perception he was able to check up systematically on correspondences between the image and the percept, and he found that his imagery had remained reasonably accurate during the eight years.

Taste blindness, like anosmia, may result from injury. In one such case the taste blindness resulted from head injuries in a car accident. Despite recovery from this, the man concerned found himself with a generalized anosmia, and he reported rather ruefully on his resulting inability to distinguish between the tastes of whisky and of beer. Total taste blindness like this occurs. But what is usually called taste blindness is a highly specific, and genetically determined, phenomenon. In 1931 a chemist, A. L. Fox, discovered what has been described as one of the minor mysteries of the senses. There is a substance called P.T.C. (phenylthyocarbamide) which evokes two different taste reactions. The population of the world appears to divide itself into two categories: those for whom P.T.C. has a bitter, metallic taste and those for whom it is tasteless. This insensitivity to P.T.C., or 'taste blindness', is of interest to geneticists in that it has been found to be hereditary, and its genetics are to some extent understood. Studies with tasters and non-tasters have subsequently shown that the difference between them is relative rather than absolute. The taste-blind person can in fact taste P.T.C. but only at relatively high concentrations.

Pain-blindness is of interest to investigators of learning. Some individuals are born without a sense of pain, and pain blindness may also be acquired. The pain-blind individual lacks the opportunity other people have to learn to avoid many sources of injury, because of the absence of the usual warnings of pain. Such individuals often burn, cut, and mutilate themselves, thus testifying to what O. H. Mowrer has called 'the paradox of pain'. In many respects pain is obviously bad, but in others it is good as providing a system of early warning against serious injury.

Many instruments have been designed to compensate for sensory defects. These include humble but important devices like spectacles and hearing aids. Devices to assist the blind have been developed on the principle of echo-location, the auditory obstacle sense in which the bat is so proficient. Mention may also be made of the Moscow Institute of Defectology, where various other aids for the blind have been devised, for example one instrument which scans print, and translates the words into tactile signals sent to the finger tips of the blind reader. More generally, as Kenneth Craik pointed out some years ago, some of the most important developments of modern science have been devices which extended the scope of the human sense organs. Along with telescopes, microscopes, and radio may be noted radar with its capacity for penetrating fog, radio as used in astronomy to locate stars beyond even the range of telescope vision, and ultra-violet devices which reveal in the mineral world around us an impressive range of 'colours' to which human vision is insensitive.

Before continuing, the reader is invited to look at Figure 1, which relates to our next topic. His task is, following brief inspection of the figure, to make an assessment of the approximate age of the woman whose face is shown.

1. What is the approximate age of this woman?

SET AND PERCEPTION

In several experiments I have conducted with Figure 1, I have found that different individuals may give very different answers to this question.* Estimates of the age of the woman obtained from a group of 120 people appear in Figure 2. Some people are sure that it is an old woman, while others are equally sure that it is a young woman. It is of interest to find one person maintaining

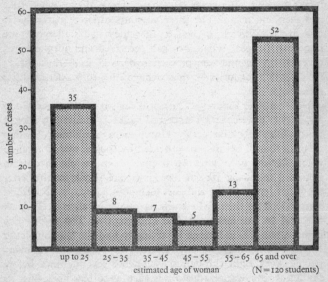

2. Estimations of age of woman in Figure 1.

that the face is of a woman under 21, while another person maintains with equal conviction that she is over 60! These alternative perceptions arise from the different mental sets with which subjects approach the task. Figure 1 is in fact ambiguous and permits two alternative perceptions. It illustrates both the

* I am indebted to my colleague Max Sime who suggested this experiment.

phenomenon of the reversible figure and the fact that perception is selective.

In relation to perception the term 'set' is used to refer to the tendency to perceive or notice some aspects of the available sense data and ignore others. Past experience, recent events, or spoken words may induce a set which exerts a marked influence on what we selectively perceive or fail to perceive. An unpublished experiment, conducted by James Drewery, illustrates this influence. He and two friends went away several days together, and afterwards all three wrote down what they had seen and heard. The three accounts differed markedly. It was in fact difficult to believe that they had undergone the same experiences. What they had perceived and not perceived revealed the mental sets of each – derived from their different learning histories – that defined the three personalities concerned.

Now consider Figure 3. The circles shown can be perceived in a variety of different ways in accord with sets induced by spoken words, like: 'Look for sixes', 'Group them in columns', 'Group them in fours'. Set may be provided by spoken words. Again a whole variety of different perceptions can be obtained from Figure 4 following spoken directions like 'Look for the letter x'. Other letters of the alphabet include H, L, N, Z, E, F, once we start to look for them. These sets have their parallels in everyday life, and set can make a person imperceptive. The reader may demonstrate this in himself by trying to find the one four-letter English word ending in –eny. There *is* one such word, yet many people work right through the alphabet several times before finding it; our learning history is such as to bias us against its discovery. Also of interest is the way in which events surrounding the publication of the unexpurgated edition of *Lady Chatterley's Lover* and the subsequent trial provided certain sets deriving from the concept of a 'four-letter word'. Thousands of words were written about 'four-letter words' at the time. Until my wife pointed it out, it certainly did not occur to me that 'love' is a four-letter word. And I suspect that others were made selectively imperceptive to this obvious fact, by the set induced by the 'Trial of Lady Chatterley'.

3. Perceptual set.

In Soviet Georgia there has developed one school of psychology which gives central importance to set. This tradition stems from the work of D. N. Uznadze (1886–1950), who remains an important influence on contemporary Soviet researches. In a typical experiment which Uznadze and his successors used, the subject is given two balls of wood, a large one in his right hand and a small one in his left. After several such presentations, two balls of equal size are placed in his hands. A contrast effect occurs: as a result of the set that has now been induced the one in the right hand is perceived as smaller than the one in the left. Variants of the experiment involve objects of equal weight, or tasks with a dynamometer which measures hand grip. In the dynamometer experiment the subject's left hand has to pull

47

4. Can you see the letter x? The letters E, N, and z? How many other letters can you see in this figure?

against a dynamometer with a heavy spring, while the right hand pulls against one with a light spring. Subsequently, as a result of the set induced, when he is given dynamometers of equal strength in both hands, he finds the task with the left easier than the task with the right, and his measured performance is better. Some other experiments conducted by this group of psychologists involve the production of sets by imagery rather than by previous perceptions: they will be discussed in a later chapter. In general a technique has emerged which has been found to differentiate between different types of personality, and which reveals some interesting differences in both the normal and the abnormal. Only a small amount of this research has as yet appeared in English; much of it remains untranslated in the original Georgian language.

Among techniques for research into personality differences, very much better known are the various tests of the projective type. One such test is the TAT or Thematic Apperception Test, which presents the subject with a series of twenty pictures, and requires him to make up a story about each. He has to say what is happening, what has led up to these events, and what is the eventual outcome. Materials used in the TAT, the Rorschach ink-blots, and other such tests are chosen for their ambiguity, and the possibilities they provide for a variety of different interpretations. The stimulus materials presented tend to be interpreted differently by different individuals, and thus reflect their learning history, personality traits, and emotional preoccupations. In short the responses given by the subject reveal the sets he has built up during his life history, and the influences these have upon his present perceptions. Under the heading of words like 'values', 'interests', and 'expectancies' we encounter the influences of set upon selective perceiving and perceptual performance outside the laboratory. To illustrate, it is recorded that the mountain men of the early American West could perform such feats as determine from an abandoned camp fire not only how many Indians had used it, but also whether they were Sioux, Blackfoot, Crow, or some other tribe. Such discriminations were often of vital importance in determining whether the Indians were friends or otherwise, and thus to personal survival. Occupational training, in for example the case of a police officer, is such as to provide him with the set, on seeing a motor car, to note and remember its registration number. Police officers have often commented to me on the absence of such a set in the general public – with rare exceptions – and the added difficulties such selective imperception creates for crime detection authorities.

THE GENERAL PSYCHOLOGY OF PERCEPTION

Earlier investigators of perception were – in the opinion of some of their later critics – somewhat too preoccupied with the 'general psychology' of perception. They sought to formulate principles which applied to human perceiving in general, and paid too little attention to individual differences which reflected the personality of the perceiver. These general principles are nevertheless important, and some of them may now be mentioned.

In one of the great classics of the subject, *Principles of Gestalt Psychology*, Kurt Koffka makes a useful distinction between the *geographical* or actual and *behavioural* or perceived qualities of the environment. We shall see in a later chapter that this distinction is very important when we discuss the psychology of emotion: people are provoked to emotion by their perception of events around them, and such perceptions may deviate markedly from reality. Thus we encounter people who are very frightened indeed because of a danger they perceive but which is not geographically present. Within the realm of perception Koffka's distinction is also important. An illusion may be defined as an instance in which there is considerable discrepancy between the behavioural and the geographical. Thus Figure 5 presents us with two geographically equal lines which are perceived as unequal. The figure shown is, in fact, a summation of two well-known effects, the Müller–Lyer illusion, and the horizontal–vertical illusion. Some remarkable effects can be produced with more complex materials. Consider first Figure 6, and then contrast the word LIFE with the same letters as they appear in Figure 7. The second set of letters achieves its non-vertical appearance from the 'twisted cord' nature of their structure, and from the setting in which they are placed. There are a number of variations of the twisted-cord illusion which were worked out by J. Fraser. The reader may wish to consult the original article (Fraser, 1908) in the *British Journal of Psychology* for its excellent illustrations of this illusion and its possible variations. One of these figures is shown on page 53 (Figure 8). It is difficult to believe that what is geographically present is in fact a series of concentric circles, so strong is the twisted cord illusion; we tend to perceive, instead, a spiral effect.

In these and other illusions we note a principle which has been much stressed by Koffka and the other Gestalt psychologists: what is perceived is very much dependent upon the total setting,

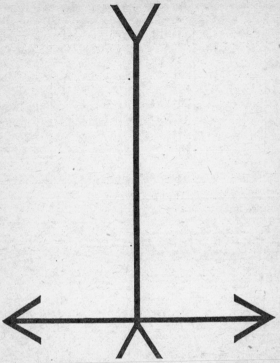

5. The horizontal and vertical lines are geographically equal.

the structure of which a sub-structure forms a part. This dependence of the perception on the setting can be illustrated from the perception of colour. Probably some of the most detailed and careful observations ever made of colour were those of the French scientist Michel Chevreul (1786–1889). Chevreul was originally invited to inspect the dyes used at the Gobelin tapestry factory in Paris, where complaints had been received about the drab appearance of many of the tapestries. It was suspected that the pigments must be defective. Chevreul found that in fact nothing was wrong with the dyes used; the drab appearances were purely perceptual effects that resulted from unfortunate choice of

6. The LIFE illusion, 1.

7. The LIFE illusion, 2. Contrast the appearance of the letters when shown against a different background.

adjacent hues. In fact Chevreul's book of 1835 contributes a great deal of our knowledge to the perception of colour. Among the many principles he formulates is the general one that every colour tends to modify the perception of surrounding objects in the direction of its own complementary colour. Thus, for example, a suitably chosen yellow looks most yellow when in close proximity to blue, and the blue looks bluest under these same circumstances. The perceived yellowness of the yellow is

8. Fraser's twisted cord illusion. A series of concentric circles is shown, but because of their background they do not appear to perception as circles.

a summation of its own hue plus the yellowness imparted to it by its adjacent complement. The blue is affected in a similar way.

From Chevreul, and other investigators, has stemmed our knowledge of simultaneous colour contrast: the effect of adjacent colours on the appearance of one another. From this may be distinguished successive colour contrast: the effects of previous coloured stimuli upon subsequent colours. Thus as Chevreul points out, whether simultaneously or successively perceived, complementary colours 'mutually improve, strengthen and purify each other'. His book – unfortunately a rarity today – provides some valuable suggestions that the future science of architectural psychology may well take account of. He points out some of the less happy effects which unfortunate choices of colour can have on the appearance of people through colour contrast. Thus, for example, on Chevreul's recommendations Paris theatre boxes were redecorated, because, as he showed, their original pink hangings imparted a 'more or less green' hue to the rosy complexions of the ladies who sat in them. The result was extremely unflattering! Blue, as Chevreul observed, is a very suitable colour for blond people in that the complementary orange which it imparts is pleasing to their appearance. Apart from his detailed observations, general principles, and recommendations, Chevreul also had much advice to give on the use of colour in the design of uniforms, in the lay-out of gardens of flowers, and in portrait painting.

The effects of the total setting upon our perception of shape and size, as well as of colour, may be noted. One effect of the placing of an area in relation to another area of equal size can be seen in an illusion which takes its name from Joseph Jastrow, one of the most original of the early experimentalists. In Jastrow's illusion (Figure 9), the two areas shown are geographically equal. The illusion becomes even more striking if two cards of these shapes are cut out and moved about. As we change the positions of the two, the one which was previously seen as the larger is now perceived as the smaller. Emphasis on how the setting will affect perception was only one of the points stressed by the Gestalt psychologists.

A *Gestalt*, the concept from which this school of investigators takes its name, is a whole with properties of its own in addition to those of its parts, *and* in which the nature of the whole determines the nature of the parts. In the field of auditory perception a tune is an example of an auditory Gestalt: we may play it in a different key in which all the component parts are different, but still perceive it as the same tune. Emphasis may be placed upon the second attribute of a Gestalt, and the extent to which the nature of the whole determines the nature of the parts. This is called the *strength of a Gestalt*. A number of principles which determine Gestalt strength have been formulated, for example the similarity and proximity of the parts to one another affect

54

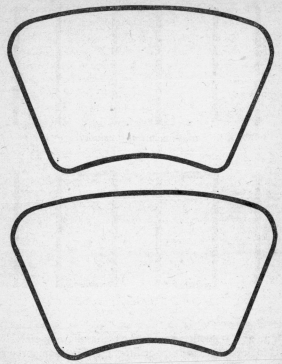

9. Jastrow's illusion. These two figures are geographically of equal size.

such strength. Consider for instance Figure 10 in which we can see how, in accord with the principle of proximity, the lines tend to be grouped together in three sets of pairs. Now consider Figure 11, in which we see this principle of proximity being overcome by another, which the Gestaltists call the principle of closure. A different grouping of the lines now results. Important among these Gestalt principles is the principle of pragnanz – the tendency for perception to exhibit a bias in the direction of simplicity and stability, and away from complexity and instability. In a later chapter we shall see that pragnanz is also important in the field of remembering.

10. Principle of proximity.

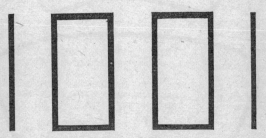

11. Closure overcoming proximity.

Of interest is another tendency which, following earlier work, the Gestalt psychologists tended to emphasize as important: the tendency we have to perceive in terms of figure and ground. Thus, for example, to return to Figure 1, our first impression may be of a young woman. When the reversal occurs and we see the old woman it is now the old woman, previously ground, who appears as figure. In a reversible figure what occurs is a figure-ground reversal, but we encounter the phenomenon elsewhere also. Thus maps provide an excellent illustration of the phenomenon: ordinarily it is land mass we perceive as figure, while sea mass forms the background as insignificant ground. For this reason people tend to be more familiar with the shape of Africa than, let us say, the shape of the Atlantic Ocean. Figure and ground effects are not confined to the visual, and indeed are very important in the auditory perception of speech. The noise level at a social gathering may be high, but despite this we are able to follow what is said to us, this standing out as figure against a ground of undifferentiated noise. Sometimes, with suitably chosen material, we can produce an auditory figure-ground reversal. Thus the words '. . . over run over run over . . .' spoken in a monotone by another person will produce reversals, and alternative perceptions of the words 'over-run' and 'run-over'. Reversals of auditory figure and ground may also on occasion spontaneously occur in, for example, what is called the cocktail-party phenomenon. We are, at a social gathering, listening to a person speaking to us when somebody in another part of the room speaks our own name. What has previously been ground now becomes figure. Much attention has been given by recent research to the study of the factors which select certain auditory stimuli as figure, and others as ground, and those which in this way give rise to the figure-ground reversal. A more detailed account of the enormous contribution of Gestalt theory and experimentation to the understanding of perception would be inappropriate in this volume. Many excellent studies in this field are readily available.

PERCEPTUAL CONSTANCY

The human organism exhibits a strong bias towards perceiving a stable environment around it: shape, size, colour, and other qualities are seen as relatively constant. As the psychologist J. Newson puts it, 'By and large physical objects in the world are constant, whereas conditions of observation are variable.' Human beings as a whole adjust to this fact, and the tendency to adjust in this way is called perceptual constancy. A number of specific constancy phenomena occur.

Colour constancy is the tendency for hues to retain their hue, and exhibit little change, despite markedly different conditions of observation. Our learning has enabled us to build up and retain a stable perception of the object's colour despite these changes. As the distinguished physiologist von Helmholtz has observed, our opportunities have been many to examine objects 'in full sunlight, in the blue light from the clear sky, the weak light of the clouded sky, and the reddish yellow light of the sinking sun'. Our learning from these opportunities is called *colour constancy*. Of related interest is brightness constancy, through which, for example, we perceive coal as black even in bright sunlight, and paper as white despite deep shadow. As measured by a photo-meter the coal may, in fact, be reflecting more light than the paper. Yet it is brightness constancy which determines our perception, and the coal is still perceived as black and the paper as white. A relatively neglected constancy phenomenon is *horizontal-vertical constancy*. However much we incline our head, vertical lines like telegraph poles remain vertical to our percep-tion, and horizontal surfaces remain horizontal. With our head rotated through 90 degrees and placed ear downwards on a table, the horizontal and the vertical still retain their usual appearance despite this markedly different condition of viewing. Size and shape also exhibit constancy. In *size constancy* objects are per-ceived as more similar to their actual sizes than their distance from us and the resulting small image on the retina would justify. Size constancy is encountered in, for example, the per-ception of a cinema screen from near the back of the theatre. The reader may be surprised if he attempts to verify this for himself: a quite small object, such as a cigarette packet, held near the eyes may be sufficient to blot out the screen despite its apparently large size. Similar phenomena occur in relation to size, shape, brightness, and colour. For example, because of shape constancy, shapes which vary enormously as they are moved about in terms of the image they actually cast on the retina exhibit much more minimal variations of perception.

A device for removing perceptual constancy is called a *reduc-tion screen*. A primitive reduction screen can be made by putting a pin through a card and looking through the peephole. Thus, for example, brightness constancy effects can be overcome by this device: the coal in bright sunlight, seen through the screen, will appear brighter than the paper in dark shadow. Again, two sur-faces whose brightness has been matched through a reduction screen may appear very different indeed in brightness to ordinary perception. The context in which they are placed here, as else-where, influences the percept. The effect of a reduction screen is to remove the surrounding cues upon which perceptual constancy depends. Similar effects can be produced in other ways. Thus a card painted to glow luminously in an otherwise dark room will be difficult to assess in terms of size and distance. Other objects have a known 'standard size' based on the perceptual norms we have built up through past experience. Thus a playing card, similarly prepared, will be perceived largely in terms of this previously established perceptual norm. As is well known to stage magicians, some interesting illusory perceptions can be produced against a black screen and with otherwise reduced perceptual cues, particularly if the expectancies of the audience are skilfully manipulated. Similar illusions are reported by explorers of polar regions, where monotonous white landscapes and absence of shadows and other cues as to depth and distance provide an excellent basis for misperception. Recent years have seen an upsurge of interest not merely in high-altitude flight, but also in space exploration. The perceptual difficulties of space explorers, and their adjustments to the unusual environments with which they have to deal, provide newer problems for the psychologist as investigator in this area.

Of interest also are unusual environments which have been constructed for the purposes of research into visual perception. Important among these have been the demonstrations constructed by Adelbert Ames, of which the best known is the distortion room. Illustrations of model distortion rooms, and of effects produced in them, appear in Professor M. D. Vernon's book on visual perception in this present series. In the Ames distortion room the arrangement is such that the learning history of the individual and his established mental sets bias him against accurate perception of what is geographically presented to him. Model or full-size distortion rooms are constructed to include misleading cues, so that objects which are geographically at different distances from the observer are perceived as at the same distance. The fact that they are at different distances is part of the explanation of why such objects appear as different in size. But this is only a partial explanation of the way in which objects appear to change size in different parts of the distortion room. We have already noted that there is a fundamental tendency underlying human perception towards perceptual constancy. This is an aspect of distortion-room phenomena which has received remarkably little comment. In terms of the perceptual constancies these effects of size change should *not* occur. An explanation is to be found in the fact that the Ames distortion room operates as an elaborate kind of reducing screen. Under normal circumstances in an ordinary environment, two objects of equal size but differing in their distance from the observer are perceived as approximately equal in size because of size constancy. This may be verified if two of the objects which look markedly different in size within the distortion room are placed at equivalent distances to those they have in the distortion room, but outside it. They now appear by no means as different in size as they do when observed in the room itself. Inside the room *both* their different distances from the observer *and* – equally important – the overcoming of size constancy which the room itself achieves are responsible for their markedly different appearances. The relationship of strange environments, whether naturally occurring ones of the kind we meet in polar exploration or high-altitude flying, or experimentally produced, to the constancy phenomena merits more research attention than it has, on the whole, received. An interesting generalization is made by the psychologist E. R. Hilgard in his discussion of these and other perceptual phenomena. He points out that under ordinary circumstances there is a strong tendency to perceive objects which maintain stability within a stable framework. Under certain circumstances – like these involving natural or experimentally created unusual environments – our perception of the object itself may conflict with our perception of a stable framework. In these circumstances we tend to perceive a perceptually stable framework, rather than a stable object. There are a number of other conditions which disturb perception, particularly size, shape, and colour constancy.

The following chapter will discuss the use of hallucinogenic drugs as a technique of psychological experimentation. The drugs most often employed have been mescaline, lysergic acid diethylamide, and psilocybin. The word 'hallucination' by no means embraces all the effects of these substances. One of their effects is on oddities of visual perception. Thus subjects who take part in experiments with them frequently report unusually vivid experiences of colour, or alarming changes in the shape or size of perceived objects. An interpretation of these happenings is that the drug disturbs the ordinary mechanisms of perception. Thus Gombrich suggested at a conference on the hallucinogenic drugs that a unitary explanation can be found by postulating a disturbance of perceptual constancy (Gombrich in Crocket *et al.* (eds.), 1963). In other words hallucinogenic drugs operate as a kind of reduction screen. Following this suggestion it is of interest to note that the subject of a hallucinogen experiment often reports that the objects he sees will exhibit alarming size changes. These might be explained as the result of an alteration between perception without size constancy and perception with size constancy: the result would certainly be marked size changes. Similar growth and shrinkage of environmental objects has been reported to me by some psychotic patients, and also by normal people under conditions of extreme fatigue following a long period of driving. Thus in January 1967 the motoring correspondent of the Sheffield *Star* deplored the lack of interest by British, as opposed to American, researchers in this field. As illustration he cites the case of a driver who, late at night, saw a pedestrian dash across the road. He braked hard before he realized nobody was there. These phenomena and the circumstances in which they occur merit careful and detailed research.

MCDOUGALL'S FIVE STAMPS EXPERIMENT

Certain rather puzzling phenomena of perception occur under conditions of hypnosis, and spontaneously in certain types of mental abnormality. An instance may be taken involving the neurosis of hysteria in which certain parts of the body may become anaesthetic to touch. Sometimes this takes the form of 'glove anaesthesia', when the area of the hand and wrist that would be covered by a glove loses tactile sensitivity. Glove anaesthesia may occur in hysteria, or may be experimentally produced in a normal person by hypnotism. If we now blindfold the subject we may touch the anaesthetic area, and adjacent non-anaesthetic areas of the hand and arm. The subject is requested to say yes if he feels it, and no if he doesn't. Curiously enough the blind-folded subject or patient will sometimes respond to a stimulus with 'no', thus indicating that he in some way 'perceives' in order to 'not perceive'. Parallel demonstrations involving visual perception may be conducted in the state of hypnosis.

The usual demonstration is to tell the hypnotized subject that a given person, Mr A, has left the room when in fact he stays. The subject is now asked to move about the room. Of this type of demonstration McDougall (1926) writes: 'It is obvious that in some sense he does perceive A, for in going about the room he avoids him, and also avoids looking directly at A.' Let us contrast this behaviour of the hypnotized subject with the behaviour of subjects who have been required in certain experiments, such as those of Orne (1962), to pretend to be hypnotized. In Orne's experiments, the simulating subjects, when told that a chair was no longer in the room, tended to bump into it. They gave as their reason for doing this that they were supposed not to see it, and walking around it would be an indication of seeing it. The hypnotized subjects behaved differently. When asked to walk about the room they avoided the chair and afterwards reported not seeing it but having seen 'an empty space'. These observations from experiments by McDougall and Orne suggest that a rather peculiar form of perceptual behaviour is going on. In some sense or other the subjects when hypnotized seemed both to 'perceive' and 'not perceive' the tabooed person or object.

A further experiment by McDougall (1926) provides additional information. His materials were five postage stamps, unused and of similar design; in Figure 12 the stamps are indicated by the letters A–E, and their positions indicated by numbers 1–5. The subject was put into a deep hypnotic trance and asked to point out the five stamps, which he did correctly. Next, two of the stamps were pointed out and the subject was told that when he opened his eyes they would no longer be there. In the diagram the two tabooed stamps are designated as B and D. On opening his eyes the subject, when asked, pointed to the remaining stamps A, C and E, and ignored the two taboo stamps. The subject's

McDougall's Five Stamps Experiment

first presentation

position   I   2   3   4   5

A   B   C   D   E

presented again in changed positions

position   I   2   3   4   5

B   C   D   E   A

12. McDougall's Five Stamps Experiment. Negative hallucination is given for the two stamps indicated. On the second presentation the positions of the stamps are changed. Which two stamps will the subject now fail to perceive?

eyes were again closed, and the positions of the stamps were changed. Now comes the crucial part of the experiment. To which of the stamps would he now point, and which would he ignore? Would he respond positionally, and ignore the stamps now occupying positions 2 and 4, or would he respond to the actual stamps, and ignore stamps B and D, despite their new positions? McDougall's finding was interesting. He reported that his subject still continued to ignore the two designated stamps, and continued to do so irrespective of where they were placed. In some way or other the subject appeared subconsciously to perceive these two stamps in order to ignore them. In other words McDougall found evidence which satisfied him that his subject was responding with two functionally different perceptual systems: it was necessary for system A to perceive, in order for system B to not perceive. He also found that later, when the subject was aroused from the state of hypnosis, the failure to see the stamps continued. McDougall took the subject's finger and guided it to touch first one of the stamps, and then the other, and in this way he restored their visibility.

An account may now be given of further experimentation into this rather paradoxical kind of perceptual behaviour. These experiments were conducted by H. Tonn and myself. We were not interested in how people in general act when hypnotized, or indeed in hypnosis itself, but in this aspect of perception. Our task was to discover whether it is possible to set up a situation in which two seemingly different perceptual systems are operating in the same person. We sought to repeat McDougall's five stamps experiment, and introduce some variations into it. Two subjects, both male American university students, were used; both were above average intelligence as measured by tests, and were aged twenty years. Subject 1 was given the post-hypnotic suggestion of amnesia: he was to remember nothing of the hypnotic session. Subject 2 was encouraged to recall everything he could about what had happened, and was interviewed in detail afterwards about his retrospections.

The first experiment, with subject 1, may be dealt with briefly. After he had been hypnotized we presented him with five unused stamps (American 1-cent stamps were employed) as in McDougall's experiment. Results obtained were negative, negative in the sense that we failed to replicate McDougall's result. When the stamps were put into their new positions the subject responded positionally, and not to the actual stamps. He now ignored the stamps occupying the previous positions of the taboo stamps, and saw the taboo stamps in their new positions. Having failed in a straight repetition to repeat McDougall's finding, we now introduced a number of easier perceptual tasks. For example we used five chessmen, the two tabooed objects being two bishops. The remaining chessmen were knight, castle, and queen. In other presentations we used five cigarette cartons of different designs, and other such objects which permitted easy discrimination. Of interest were the remarkably rigid perceptual performances that occurred. The subject continued to respond positionally even with these materials. In the concluding part of the experiment we used five coins, all of them American 1-cent pieces of the same design. All were presented 'heads' and all carried the facial profile of Abraham Lincoln. Two of the coins were, however, easy to distinguish from the others: they were bright and shining while the remaining three were dull and dark. The suggestion was given to the subject that he would 'not see' the two bright coins. He was now awakened from the hypnotic state. Then followed, as in McDougall's experiment, a persistence of the 'not seeing' response. This proved to be even more persistent than in McDougall's case. The experimenters picked up the coins and dropped them, and although the subject heard he still failed to see. They placed the coins in different positions in front of the subject, who remarked 'Do you enjoy moving empty spaces around?' One experimenter now placed the subject's finger on one of the coins. Unlike McDougall's subject, ours failed to see it. He said, 'Something's adhering but there's nothing there,' and then, 'That's an empty space.' Finally it was explained to him, very carefully, that he had been given a post-hypnotic suggestion not to see two of the coins. He was told that there were actually five, and not three, coins in front of him. He exhibited signs of surprise when, as he said, it 'gradually came into view, blurry at first but quite clearly after about a second'. The same procedure restored the second coin. Three things are of interest in this first experiment: (a) our failure to replicate McDougall's finding; (b) the rigid persistence of positional responses; (c) the post-hypnotic persistence of failure to see, despite auditory and tactile evidence.

In the second experiment it was decided to build up a perceptual set, working from easier to more difficult tasks of discrimination. We sought to train the subject to distinguish between individual items in the various sets of five objects we put in front of him. In presentation 1 five chessmen were used, a taboo being placed on perception of the two bishops. A positive response was obtained in the sense that the subject continued to ignore the bishops when they were placed in different positions. Presentations 2 and 3 were similar except that coins and playing cards were used; as before the perceptual tasks were easy, and as in presentation 1 we obtained positive responses. In presentation 4 the objects were five similarly designed postage stamps, but the task was made easy in that stamp margin paper was left at the top of the two tabooed stamps. A positive response was again obtained. In presentation 5 we used five stamps with no obvious basis of differentiation between them, as in the original McDougall experiment. On this occasion, with the aid of prior training, we sought to obtain a response to the objects themselves of the kind McDougall reported. In this we failed. When the taboo stamps were put into new positions the subject failed to ignore them, but ignored the stamps which now occupied their previous positions. We returned, in presentations 6 and 7, to further training with playing cards and coins. On presentation 8 we again presented the subject with the 'hard' stamps, and asked him to look at all five very closely. Stamps in positions 3 and 5 were now tabooed and, while the subject's eyes were closed, were now put into positions 1 and 4. *What now occurred was a positive response.* The subject now responded to the objects themselves and not positionally, and continued to 'not see' the tabooed stamps in their new positions. Presentations 9, 10, and 11 involved repetitions of this procedure, and again all elicited positive responses. The individual tabooed stamps were still 'not seen' and continued not to be seen wherever we put them. For the remaining part of the experiment it was decided to explore further the subject's perceptual performance. The difficult stamps were used throughout. On the first occasion the taboo stamps were presented at positions 1 and 5, with other stamps at positions 2, 3, and 4. All three of the non-taboo stamps were now removed and the subject was asked to point out the stamps he saw. He pointed to the three blank spaces, ignoring the actual but tabooed stamps at positions 1 and 5. On the second occasion the taboo stamps were first presented again at positions 1 and 5. Then another stamp was placed at position 5, the remaining taboo stamp being left at position 1. Other stamps were removed. When asked to point to the stamps he saw the subject pointed to the position 5 stamp, and to the vacant places at positions 2 and 4. He ignored the tabooed but actual stamp at position 1. A number of similar demonstrations were conducted, all showing that the subject was now able to differentiate which stamps not to see. Three responses were occurring: first, stamps visible to the experimenters were also visible to the subject; second, stamps visible to the experimenters were 'not seen' by the subject; and thirdly, stamps not visible to the experimenters were 'seen' by the subject.

In this second experiment the subject gave clear behavioural evidence both of differentiating between individual stamps despite the difficulty of this task, and of taking account of stamps 'not seen,' in order not to see them. Introspective reports later obtained accorded with these observational data. With reference to the chess pieces the subject said of the bishops, 'You told me they were disappearing and when I looked back they weren't there.' Of the 'easy' stamps with marginal paper attached to the tabooed ones he said that two of the stamps had 'little tabs' and 'you took them away'. In relation to the hard tasks with the stamps the subject reacted to the tabooed stamps as either 'a blank space' or in terms of 'you took them away'. Close questioning indicated that to introspective experience the tabooed stamps were not there. The subject also remarked spontaneously that the experimenters had 'taken different ones away' on different occasions, as was in fact the case.

In view of the rather remarkable feats of perceptual discrimination performed by this subject, following the training we had given him, we decided to conduct a control experiment with non-hypnotized subjects. In the main part of this control experiment the six subjects (five male and one female American university students aged 18–22) were first asked to look closely at the five stamps used. After two of these had been tabooed, their positions were changed. In only two cases out of twenty-three complicated re-presentations of the shifted stamps were the correct three 'seen' stamps designated. Both these correct trials were followed by failures, indicating that they were probably lucky guesses. Introspections were obtained. One subject just refused to believe that the stamps could be individually distinguished and didn't even try. Four subjects remarked that they could probably have been able to make the discrimination, but lacked the 'effort' or 'psychic energy' to put into the task. In this connexion of interest was a later spontaneous remark of the subject in experiment 2: he said that he wished he could put as much concentrative power into his study as he had put, while hypnotized, into the task with the stamps.

McDougall writes that 'any normal person can, by close inspection, discriminate and recognize one or two postage stamps among others'. It may be that some individuals are able to do this when not hypnotized, but our control experiment argues against McDougall's general statement and his use of the word 'any'.

McDougall himself interprets his original five stamps experiment in terms of personality dissociation. He writes that 'in order to describe the facts intelligibly we must no longer speak of B, the integrated personality, but rather of B1 and B2, B's two separately functioning parts'. We ourselves set out to investigate whether in this way two functionally different perceptual responses could be established in the same subject. We failed in a straight repetition in the first experiment, but in the second experiment – following training in a series of easier perceptual tasks – succeeded in this. One final aspect of the experiment may be mentioned. We were not entirely convinced of the logical tightness of McDougall's argument. Presented with five objects A, B, and C with X and Y tabooed, we cannot conclude that the subject necessarily ignores X and Y because he perceives them. Could he not, instead, have seen and recognized A, B and C, there being no taboo against such recognition? Thus as a subsidiary part of the experiment we used two taboo coins, together with three others. We then added eight new ones, and finally thirteen new ones. If, as proved to be the case, the subject continued to ignore the X and Y coins in their new positions this would seem to exclude any possibility that he performed this task except by 'seeing' them. In other words it was necessary to see these two coins in order to not see them.

SYNAESTHETIC EXPERIENCES

From perception itself we turn to one interesting linkage between perception and those 'revived percepts' we call mental imagery; in this connexion we encounter the phenomenon of synaesthesia. Synaesthesia involves a rather peculiar break-down of the barriers we ordinarily recognize between our different modes of perceptual experience. Learning plays an important part in perception, as we have already seen, for example in connexion with its influences upon expectancy and perceptual set. Another thing we learn is differentiation between our different sense modes, and distinction between the information that comes from the eyes, ears, and other sensory channels. In certain individuals, and under certain circumstances, these differentiations break down. Imagery of one mode may intrude upon perception in another mode, the language of one sense is used for percepts of another, or we lose insight into which of the senses our information comes from.

Our vocabulary and concepts are not always equal to the task of communication about perceptual experience. This is true even of vision, as can be seen daily in the police courts with cases involving road accidents: the complex spatial relationships involved do not always lend themselves to verbal descriptions of an accurate kind. These difficulties of communication are obviously more acute with other senses like, for example, taste and smell. Sometimes we encounter resort to language from another sense department in attempts to communicate.

The term 'synaesthetic description' has been used elsewhere (Simpson and McKellar, 1955) for attempts to solve the problem of communication in this way. Language of other sense modes is quite often used even with visual percepts, as when we refer to a bright colour as 'loud', and use other terms like 'harmony and discord' and 'warmth and cold' in relation to colours or colour combinations. Synaesthetic descriptions may be used more metaphorically as in, for example, the rather cynical description of television as 'chewing gum for the eyes'! We also find them used even in scientific texts, as when one standard text-book, discussing a series of experiments on smell, uses numerous words relating to other sense departments including: 'light and heavy', 'rough and soft', 'sharp', 'small', 'bright', and 'dull'. Often, however, the language is a little strained, even if we are able to understand the communication. Thus we may sympathize with the unfortunate who had to remain sitting on bare boards for so long that, as he afterwards declared, he 'could taste the wood'. Synaesthetic descriptions may be idiosyncratic, but there are also many such descriptions embedded in the conventionalized usages of our language, as when we speak of a 'rich velvety voice', describe one wine as 'smooth' and another 'rough', or refer to a noise as 'penetrating'.

Associative learning obviously underlies some kinds of synaesthetic descriptions. We expect foods tasting of lemon to be yellow in colour, and raspberry-flavoured food to be red, while the word 'orange' itself refers to both a colour and a taste. In one unpublished investigation the psychologist H. H. Ferguson conducted an interesting experiment which testified to the strength of these associations. He made a number of edible jellies which defied the usual conventions: thus the orange-flavoured jelly was coloured red and the raspberry-flavoured one was yellow. A series of jellies of these kinds were given to a group of subjects, a majority of whom tasted not in accord with the flavours actually present but in accord with their expectancies deriving from the colours. In connexion with set and expectancy we have already noted the researches conducted by one of the pioneers of contemporary Soviet psychology, D. N. Uznadze at Tbilisi in Georgia. Uznadze was also interested in possible regularities of connexion between the visual and auditory senses. He constructed drawings of a number of complex shapes, and presented his subjects with a list of invented words which they were required to assign to these various shapes. He found considerable agreements in the resulting matchings. Unfortunately Uznadze's original designs are not readily available, and indeed much of the subsequent work he has inspired is very inadequately known in the Western world. But these early studies influenced better-known investigators, such as the Gestalt psychologist Wolfgang Kohler. The kinds of shapes reproduced by Kohler appear in Figure 13. The task is to assign one of two words to each of the figures. Which is 'maluma' and which is 'takete'? Sometimes when showing the Kohler figures to a class I have pointed to the sharp, jagged figure and said, 'This, of course, is maluma'. The protests that follow are evidence of the inappropriateness for most people of such an association between the visual and the auditory.

An investigation following the work of Uznadze and Kohler was conducted by R. Davis in 1961. His subjects lived in a remote

13. Which is 'maluma', and which is 'takete'?

part of Africa; they were Swahili speakers, and their contact
with Europeans and European languages was minimal; their
village was cut off from the outside world by an 8,000-foot
mountain range and a lake that was seldom crossed. Children of
the tribe were given two figures similar to those used by Kohler,
and the names 'ulooma' and 'takete' to assign to them. The same
regularities of association occurred. In a further study Davis
obtained similar results from English children, from both
London and rural areas.

Synaesthesia may be distinguished from synaesthetic description and uses of language. This is a phenomenon of mental life which some, but not all, people exhibit. Its discovery has often been wrongly attributed to Galton, despite the fact that Galton is explicit in making reference to earlier work. The first recorded case – that of the brothers Nussbaumer – was published in 1873. Eugene Bleuler was himself subject to synaesthesia, and in 1892 together with Lehmann reported an investigation of 600 individuals, 12 per cent of whom exhibited the phenomenon. The term synaesthesia was introduced by Millet in the following year. Its commonest form is called 'chromaesthesia', or coloured hearing, and involves the tendency to experience imagery of colour on hearing music or other sounds. More generally, synaesthesia occurs when a stimulus of one sense mode evokes mental imagery of another mode, as readily as of its own. A typical instance from one of my subjects may be quoted: 'When hearing music I visualize shapes and colours, and if I hear the same music again I "see" roughly the same shapes in roughly the same shade of colour.' As a spontaneous phenomenon and a characteristic of the mental life of certain individuals, synaesthesia is overwhelmingly most often of this kind: visual imagery evoked by auditory perception. Various investigations subsequent to that of Bleuler, including several of my own, give the incidence of this kind of synaesthesia as about 20 per cent of people. Synaesthesia may be not merely a feature of the thinking of such individuals, but may also form the basis of attempts by them to communicate with others. Such attempts are not always successful. Resort to synaesthetic uses of language is not, in itself, sufficient evidence that the person who attempts to communicate in this way is himself subject to synaesthesia. Thus I shall follow the convention suggested above and retain a distinction between synaesthesia proper, and mere synaesthetic description.

The two components of synaesthesia are imagery and perception of two different sense modes. A simple definition would be 'imagery of one sense mode aroused by sensations of another mode'. In terms of this definition it may be seen that many different types of synaesthesia are theoretically possible. In 1955 my colleague Lorna Simpson and I suggested a convention involving use of two hyphenated words to specify these different types of synaesthesia, for example visual-auditory, visual-tactile, auditory-gustatory. We suggested always using the first word to denote the imagery, and the second word to denote the perceptual component. Thus visual-auditory synaesthesia – the commonest type – is different from auditory-visual synaesthesia: the latter would involve auditory imagery in response to some visual stimulus. This is uncommon as true synaesthesia, though we often resort to conventional synaesthetic metaphors of this kind, as when we describe a colour as 'loud' or even say that it 'shrieks at us'. To illustrate some of the other types of synaesthesia we might take the case of one of my present colleagues who regularly experiences olfactory-auditory synaesthesia: when he hears the 'Blue Danube Waltz' he experiences 'a fairly distinctive olfactory image of the smell of leather'. He explains this by associative learning, past experience of skating rinks at which he had many opportunities to associate this music with this pervasive smell. Some synaesthesias appear, as in this case, to have a definite basis in learning. Others suggest a break-down of the clear distinctions between the different categories of sensory information which we ordinarily make. This seems to occur under the influence of certain drugs, for example hashish. In an experiment with hashish one subject reported an instance of gustatory-auditory synaesthesia. On listening to music he had definite taste imagery: the notes, he explained, 'had a rich taste, none too sweet'. In a story by Sax Rohmer we encounter synaesthesia being experienced by two of the central characters who are overcome by the fumes of hashish in a perfume blender's workshop. They 'hear' the perfumes which 'speak' to them in voices which differ in accord with their different olfactory qualities (auditory-olfactory synaesthesia); in addition they 'see' the sounds spoken by the perfume blender. In this latter instance we encounter the common visual-auditory synaesthesia, though apparently with hallucinatory vividness. Some spontaneous cases of synaesthesia reported by C. S. Myers, an earlier investigator, also give evidence that on occasion the imagery component of a synaesthesia can assume the vividness of a hallucination.

The use of hallucinogenic drugs like mescaline and lysergic

acid diethylamide (or LSD) has been mentioned. Such experiments produce many interesting phenomena which are not easy to describe in words. It was in connexion with a series of experiments with mescaline that Lorna Simpson and I first decided to use the two-word convention in attempting to specify the possible types of synaesthesia. Apart from the visual-auditory kind, which is relatively common, other types of synaesthesia rarely occur in spontaneous form. Many different types of synaesthesia occur in experiments with mescaline, and also with LSD, though our experimental experience with this second drug is more limited. Thus the various subjects who took part in our series of mescaline experiments were quite often confronted with synaesthesia for the first time in their lives. While visual-auditory synaesthesia occurred often, it was not the only one. Thus two different subjects under rather similar circumstances, namely ascending in a lift after lunch when returning to the laboratory, experienced synaesthetic visual imagery in response to this kinaesthetic perception. One subject described the imagery of shapes and colours as 'like a fountain', and the other as 'like a firework display'. The first subject added that the feeling of ascending in the lift and its imagery accompaniment was like being caught in a fountain, and being shot off the top of it. She added, 'The water was coloured and the sunlight was shining through the water.' Another subject, who normally experiences tactile imagery on hearing music, experienced an intensification of this tactile-auditory synaesthesia with mescaline. A fourth subject, who also had tactile synaesthesias during the experiment, remarked, 'My hands didn't stop feeling all day.' Attempts were made to investigate the influence of different kinds of stimuli on visual-auditory synaesthesia by presenting the subject with standard recordings of notes of known frequency. In response to this one subject's report may be quoted. He said he experienced 'a rather trivial intrusion of a jet of colour upon the primarily uncontrolled imagery of a really impressive kind that was going on. The jet of colour appeared in the field nearest the actual location of the microphone from which the noises came'. In another experiment the subject heard the experimenters talking in the next room, and responded with visual-auditory synaesthesia.

Their voices were heard very softly – to his strongly synaesthetic thinking they were 'very small' – and he experienced a 'microscopic kind of imagery' of a visual kind in response to this. A characteristic of hallucinogenic drug experiments with mescaline and similar substances is their tendency to produce subjective experiences which are in practice very difficult to describe in words. One huge category of experiences of this kind proved to be synaesthesia, including synaesthesia in some of its more unusual forms.

The rarer types of synaesthesia can sometimes be found spontaneously in certain individuals. Russian psychologists have, as we have seen, exhibited a long-standing interest in intersensory phenomena, and one such psychologist, A. R. Luria, has reported an interesting case. The subject studied was a Moscow journalist who had strong taste imagery both for sounds and for visual experiences: he experienced both gustatory-visual and gustatory-auditory synaesthesias. To illustrate, on one occasion when asked if he could find his way back home from the laboratory he said that this provided no difficulty. His landmarks were unusual and included, for example, 'a briny-tasting fence'. Mention of this case came to the attention of a Scottish school teacher, who wrote to me in the following terms: 'I was rather surprised to find that you found it difficult to find people who tasted, or rather had a sensation of taste, on hearing a sound. . . . I have always had this sensation.' She explained how the sound made by the sharp blow of a hammer on metal gave her one kind of taste image, and how the noise it made against wood or against earth gave her equally vivid but different taste images. Both the Moscow journalist and the school teacher, who shared this unusual variant of synaesthesia, had always believed till they were investigated that their kind of subjective experience was universal.

It is, however, mainly in connexion with hallucinogenic drugs like mescaline that we encounter the rarer forms of synaesthesia. That lysergic acid diethylamide has similar hallucination-producing effects was discovered, accidentally, by the chemist Albert Hofmann in 1943 at his laboratory in Basle, Switzerland. Of some interest are Hofmann's laboratory notes following this discovery, which are quoted in translation from their original German: 'All acoustic perceptions, like the noise of a passing car, were translated into visual sensations, so that every tone and noise elicited a correspondingly coloured picture, changing kaleidoscopically in its shape and colour.' In this description we may now recognize the phenomenon of synaesthesia, in its most common visual-auditory form, which also occurs spontaneously in the mental life of some people, but remains unknown to others. This and some of the rarer forms of the same experience may now be experimentally produced in the laboratory. Synaesthesia itself represents a connecting link between perception, with which we have been concerned, and imagery and related subjective processes, to be discussed in chapters to follow.

CHAPTER THREE

A-Thinking and R-Thinking

I don't invent it, really do not, but 'see' it and write it down.
CHARLES DICKENS

THE word 'thinking' comes from everyday speech. It is ambiguous, and refers to a number of different activities including
reasoning, imagining, and remembering. Remembering will be
discussed in a later chapter. In this I shall be concerned with
thinking in its wider sense, including not only reasoning and
problem solving, but also fantasy, waking and sleeping forms of
imagery, and the processes of imagining. For convenience I shall
speak about 'thought products' as a brief way of referring to such
end products of human thought as poetry and novels, paintings
and plays, scientific theories, and inventions. Thus the statement
by Dickens which heads this chapter referred to his thought
products, his novels, and how he composed them. Dickens, who
has quite a lot to say about how he worked, is here referring to his
use of subjective experiences rather than perceptual information.
He seems to have made considerable use of mental imagery, both
visual and auditory, as raw materials. Other authors, for example
Robert Louis Stevenson, have used their dreams. Thus in one
chapter of *Across the Plains* Stevenson tells how he experienced
dreams in which 'little people' made up his stories for him, and
all that was left for him to do was to record them on paper, 'pay
the registration' on the letter containing his manuscript, and
send it in. An instance of this was part of the plot of *Dr Jekyll and
Mr Hyde*, of which Stevenson says: 'For two days I went about
racking my brains for a plot of any sort; and on the second night
I dreamed the scene at the window, and a scene afterwards split
in two, in which Hyde, pursued for some crime, took the powder
and underwent the change.' To this Stevenson adds: 'All the
rest was made awake, and consciously.' Others who have used
their dreams in this way have included Kafka, who kept extensive

records in dream notebooks, and Lewis Carroll. Lewis Carroll found his dreams such a fruitful source of raw material that he invented a special device, 'a nyctograph' as he called it, for recording them. In contrast are other authors who draw on their perceptions of the external world rather than on waking or sleeping fantasy. Thus Keats, in his poem 'The Eve of St Agnes', made very detailed use of his observations of the furniture and decorations of Stansted House, near Chichester. Conan Doyle built his fictional character Sherlock Holmes round the appearance and personality of the surgeon Charles Bell, while another immortal character, Billy Bunter, was constructed by his author Charles Hamilton ('Frank Richards') as a composite figure from four people he actually knew.

A-THINKING AND R-THINKING

One of the greatest students of the schizophrenic psychoses was Eugene Bleuler (1857–1939). From Bleuler, in his attempts to describe the phenomena of schizophrenia, stems the term 'autism'. By autism he meant the kind of thinking which is fantasy-dominated, self-generated, and uncorrected by reference to external reality. The term *A-thinking* will be used, following Bleuler, to refer to one huge category of thinking to include fantasy, dreams and nightmares, visionary activity, hypnagogic imaging, hallucination, and the like. Thus we have seen that writers like Dickens and Stevenson have used A-thinking, their waking or sleeping fantasies, as raw materials for socially valued thought products. With A-thinking may be contrasted what I have called *R-thinking*. This is thinking of the kind that is prominent in sane, adult wakefulness, in its most logical, realistic, and prejudice-free moments. R-thinking is taken to include realistic appraisal in terms of the evidence, critical evaluation, and logical inference of the valid kind.

Some years ago (1957) I developed the thesis that it is from the interplay of A-thinking and R-thinking processes that useful thought products emerge. This view was criticized by R. C. Oldfield, a leading British psychologist, on the grounds that I had gratuitously identified R-thinking with two different things: valid logical reasoning, and taking account of the relevant evidence. These criticisms add something of substance. It is certainly necessary to remind ourselves that logically sound inferences can proceed from false premises: in fact this is a characteristic feature of the forms of thinking we encounter in psychosis when delusion is prominent, notably in paranoia (see Chapter 12). Again, there are also some interesting cases in which sound conclusions have been reached by inferences which would not have withstood the scrutiny of a logician. That processes not adequately covered by the terms A-thinking and R-thinking may also be involved, and that this dichotomy oversimplifies the interaction between A- and R-thinking reminds us, however inadequately, of the importance of interplay. The interplay is more complex than I originally suggested, but the A-thinking and R-thinking dichotomy draws attention to certain of its aspects.

The same interaction seems to underlie those socially useful thought products we regard as scientific, no less than those we call works of art. As the chemist Kekulé wrote, 'Let us beware of publishing our dreams before they have been tested by our waking intelligence.' Kekulé's statement is the more interesting in that he himself was responsible for a major advance in scientific theory, as the result of a subject matter of A-thinking. The theory of the benzene ring emerged to Kekulé from two occasions on which he engaged in half-asleep imaging. On the first of these occasions he was dozing on top of a bus: 'Suddenly the atoms danced before my eyes . . . and all whirled round in a ring. I noticed that the larger ones would form a chain dragging smaller ones along at both ends.' At this point of his hypnagogic imaging Kekulé was awakened by the conductor calling 'Clapham Road'. The imagery was resumed on a later occasion, or rather resumed itself because it was strikingly autonomous, and was in no sense consciously thought up by Kekulé himself. Kekulé was working in his study, began to doze, and similar imagery returned. Of interest, in view of his own emphasis on the necessity for testing by waking intelligence, is what Kekulé did next. He reports: 'This time also I spent the rest of the night working out the consequences of the hypothesis.' The benzene-ring theory which emerged resulted from an interaction of this subsequent R-thinking with the previous A-thinking. Critical, evaluative activity was necessary as well as half-awake fantasy to the emergence of the thought product. Moreover, also relevant is the fact that the solution to the problem emerged to a mind well stocked with relevant information. Undoubtedly A-thinking was a necessary factor, but it was the A-thinking of a trained scientist equipped with past knowledge of relevance to the solution. Another scientist who was interested in how his own original thinking took place was Galton, who employs the metaphor of a 'presence chamber' in which full consciousness holds court, and 'an antechamber full of more or less allied ideas'. And Galton is careful to add that effective thinking depends on 'large attendance in the antechamber' of ideas germane to the problem in hand.

Charles Darwin is another scientist of stature whose thought has received careful investigation in recent years. At a symposium on 'Creativity and the Growth of Concepts' the psychologist H. E. Gruber presented an account of his detailed study of Darwin. If we wish to explain a given thought product – whether poem or scientific theory – the question arises: at what point are we prepared to allow our curiosity to rest? It is not an adequate account of the origins of Darwin's evolutionary theory to say that it arose merely because – as is well known – he had read the famous article by Malthus on population. Gruber attempts a much more thorough account, and he pays particular attention to Darwin's activities during his five-year voyage on the *Beagle*. In this period Darwin kept voluminous notebooks of observations on matters geological, botanical, and zoological. 'I must begin with a good body of facts,' he wrote, and his methods exemplify his remark. There was, in Darwin's case, the large attendance in the antechamber, to which Galton refers, of relevant external perceptual information. Moreover, as Gruber shows, Darwin did not confine himself to perception but used his powers of imagery and 'tried to picture' the appearance of the country under other circumstances. Elsewhere Darwin wrote explicitly about his own excellent capacity for visual imagery. Of interest also is the process whereby a system of relations observed in one context may be applied to another subject matter for the solution of a different problem. Thus not only the Malthus essay was of significance to Darwin's theory, but so also were the observations he made while on the *Beagle* of how coral reefs appeared to be formed. In May 1837 Darwin read papers about coral formation to meetings of the Geological Society, and it was in July the same year that he opened his first notebooks on 'transmutation of species'. In their subject matter Darwin's two theories are different but, as Gruber is able to show, there is a detailed formal similarity between them. In Darwin's better-known later thought product, his natural selection evolutionary theory, we see the results of an interaction: an interaction of primary and secondary perception, of imagery with contemporary perception, and of earlier attempts at building a theory with later ones. Words like 'creativity' and 'originality' can create confusion if we fall into the habit of regarding them as traits rather than as words: they are simple names for highly complex processes of interaction. One part of this interaction is the interplay between A-thinking and R-thinking.

SENSORY DEPRIVATION EXPERIMENTS

An additional, and powerful, technique for investigating subjective processes of the A-thinking kind – together with certain aspects of perception also – appeared in 1954. This was developed at McGill University in Canada and is associated with D. O. Hebb and his associates. Its origins are two-fold. Hebb as a leading theorist had for theoretical reasons become interested in the effects of monotony on learned behaviour. At the same time, Hebb was later able to reveal, a great deal of 'dismay' was being felt at the kind of 'confessions' that were being produced by techniques of the kind that are now often referred to as 'brainwashing'. Through the experiments conducted at McGill it was hoped to learn something about how prisoners in an environment carefully manipulated by their captors could become susceptible to propaganda and prone to make confessions.

The original experiments at McGill, by Bexton, Heron, and

Scott in 1954, made use of student volunteers. Each subject was experimentally subjected to conditions which limited his visual, auditory, tactile, and other sensory input. He was placed in a lighted, comfortable, semi-soundproof cubicle, and wore translucent glasses which transmitted a diffuse light but prevented pattern vision. In addition, gloves with cardboard cuffs were worn to limit tactile perception, and he lay against a U-shaped foam rubber pillow which, together with the masking noise of the air-conditioner, limited auditory input. A two-way speaker permitted communication with the experimenter. Food was given, and the subject went to the toilet on request by himself. He was asked to undergo these conditions of visual, auditory, and tactile deprivation for as long as he could; usually this amounted to 2–3 days.

The general effects of this limiting of perceptual input can be summarized. The effect was greatly to reduce R-thinking, and to stimulate A-thinking processes. As one subsequent investigator in this field was later to put it, the result was 'emergence into awareness of thinking usually found in dreams, psychosis, and artistic creation'. During the original McGill experiments twenty-nine subjects were tested, and twenty-five of them reported what the experimenters called 'hallucinations'. For some of these experiences a more neutral term like mental imagery would seem more appropriate. Visual effects were prominent, and one of the subjects became convinced that the experimenters were projecting pictures on to his goggles. The experimenters describe the visualizations as ranging from the simple to the more complex: ranging from dots and lines, through geometrical figures, to objects, and finally scenes. Emphasis is placed by the investigators on the autonomy of these visualizations: they were something the subject experienced rather than in any way consciously thought up. One of my favourites among the more complex images took the form of 'a procession of squirrels with sacks over their shoulders, marching purposefully across a snowfield'. Other phenomena included disturbances of the subject's body schema, which he frequently reported as having changed in size or shape.

Many investigators began to experiment elsewhere, and various modifications of technique were used. Thus J. A. Vernon (1963) at Princeton conducted 'dark cell' experiments, in a light-proof and sound-proof room. Under these conditions, curiously enough, fewer intrusions of A-thinking processes of the imagery-hallucination kind occurred than with the more partial deprivation used at McGill. Of a series of twelve subjects investigated by Vernon, none visualized integrated, complex scenes, though one 'saw' a coin on the floor, and another 'saw' the edge of a sandwich glow. Many such investigations have now been conducted with sensory deprivation techniques of various kinds. Sometimes the visual experiences which occur are strikingly detailed. For example in one experiment the subject hallucinated a newspaper, three-dimensionally, and saw on it the name 'Fred' clearly visible. Sometimes a subject has exhibited considerable fear at what he saw, as in one case when a subject hallucinated a creature with a long and slender body and many legs. On occasion the visualizations reflected characteristics of the subject himself. Thus in one such experiment a subject who was a psychology graduate hallucinated a Rorschach Test card in a blacked-out window of the room; another subject, a medical student, in the same window saw an X-ray of the stomach of an ulcer patient.

Among the more interesting of the later experiments were those conducted by J. T. Shurley at Oklahoma City, in which subjects were floated in water and wore a specially fitted helmet. None of the twelve subjects used was able to endure these floating experiments for more than six hours (it will be remembered that original McGill experiments lasted 2–3 days). Every subject had some form of mental imagery. Shurley reports 'all gradations of phenomenon', and explicitly mentions waking daydreams, sleeping dreams, hypnagogic visualizations, and hallucinations. Some of the experiences were short-lived but contained great detail, for example 'a head in terracotta resembling a Mayan or Aztec image with gold ear-rings, and scowling'. Other images lasted longer, like 'golden toadstools standing in bright sunlight' in full colour, and three-dimensional. This subject was able to recall the image with sufficient clarity to paint it several months later. Autoscopic hallucination, in which the subject has a hallucination of himself, is comparatively rare. One of Shurley's subjects reported an a-typical autoscopic hallucination. She hallucinated herself as a spoon in a glass of tea, and 'woke' to find she was moving her left foot in a circle like a spoon in the act of stirring. Rich imagery, visual, auditory, kinaesthetic, and olfactory, was typical of all subjects in these water-immersion experiments. Among other techniques may be mentioned those which employ relatively short periods of sensory deprivation. Thus for example at Sheffield University, Loxley (1962) found that much of the imagery and many of the body image changes and other phenomena could be produced with periods of deprivation of no more than one hour.

The general effect of sensory deprivation, by whichever of these techniques is used, seems to be to release A-thinking processes. Resemblances of phenomena to those of the half-awake, hypnagogic state – to be discussed below – have often been noted. If the subjects have often noted this resemblance, experimenters have themselves on occasion noted a resemblance of the sensory deprivation phenomena to two other situations: psycho-analytic treatment and aviation piloting. As in psycho-analysis we encounter the couch, the relaxed state, and the instruction to report everything. Similarly, the subject resembles a pilot immobile in his seat while flying, with, in straight and level flying, relatively nothing to do, and with a monotonous horizon, particularly at high altitudes. Thus Vernon, in reporting his results and explaining his interest in sensory deprivation experiments, mentions not only the Korean War but also space flight. Apart altogether from the monotony of the unusual environment encountered in space research, we find oddities of experience associated with orthodox aviation. Body-image changes may occur, as may visual effects resulting from loss – in cloud flying – of the more usual reference points. West (1962) refers to kinaesthetic hallucinations of 'buffeting' of the plane which may occur during monotonous flights, and the fact that jet pilots have nicknamed this hallucination 'the clicks'. From a series of cases reported by Bennett (in West, 1962) may be taken one illustration of the relevance for aviation of sensory deprivation experiments. The pilot was flying his plane at 40,000 feet; there was haze over the ground, and the horizon was indistinct.

Suddenly he felt detached from his surroundings and had the strong impression that the aircraft had one wing down. He corrected for this, without checking on his instruments, and as the plane was in fact flying straight and level went into a spiral dive. Fortunately he was able to pull out of this in time. This is but one of many such cases, and, as we have seen in an earlier chapter, similar oddities of subjective experience can also seriously impede adjustment to reality in motorway driving. Probably a substantial number of motorway accidents can be attributed to these intrusions of A-thinking processes under conditions of monotony, though as yet we lack adequate information on this important issue.

HALLUCINOGENIC SUBSTANCES

The work of Prentiss and Morgan late last century opened up another technique for the study of A-thinking processes: experimentation with hallucinogenic drugs. The value of this type of study, and the serious scientific purposes behind it, merit restatement the more because of the dubious and irresponsible uses to which hallucinogenic drugs have sometimes been put in recent years.

Hallucinogenic substances have both their scientific and their pre-scientific history. Their pre-scientific origins are often traced to the Aztecs of the American continent, but there are other aspects to this history also. In medieval Europe of interest is the fact that witches' 'potions' were taken by mouth, and that the people concerned were often skilled in the use of drugs and poisons of botanical origin. Barnett (1965) concludes, 'It would seem that pharmacology offers a firm basis for explaining some of the unusual as well as the usual features of the witch-cult.' Certain of the substances used, like belladonna and henbane, are today recognized as having hallucinogenic properties. Of special interest is a hallucinogen called bufotenin that chemically closely resembles the hormone serotonin (a hormone which plays an important part in normal brain functioning). Bufotenin was first extracted by scientists from the skin of toads – a fact of some interest in connexion with the traditional witches' brew – but can also be obtained from the cahobe bean of the Caribbean Islands. Both European and voodoo witchcraft seem to have made use of this hallucinogen, as well as others from readily available plants. All this throws some light upon the improbable and impossible events associated with magic and witchcraft. The category of 'the supernatural' is complex, resistant to any single naturalistic explanation. But one aspect of such an explanation may be found in these close associations with hallucination-producing substances. In hallucination, as in dreams, all things including the impossible can seem to happen.

The New World also had its hallucinogens. The Aztecs, like the Greeks, inherited much from previous civilizations of Mexico, Mayan, Zapotec, and Toltec. Allowing for possibly earlier origin in pre-Aztec culture, the Aztecs themselves possessed three main hallucinogens: peyotl, teonanacatl, and ololiuqui. Twentieth-century research (Cerlotti, 1963) has revealed the botanical sources of these three Aztec hallucinogens to yield respectively mescaline, psilocybin, and lysergic acid diethylamide. These comprise the three best known, and most studied, of the modern hallucinogens. Mescaline was first obtained from a small cactus botanically known as *Anhalonium lewinii* (or *Lophophora williamsi*). This plant – sometimes known as the 'dumpling cactus' – grows in the vicinity of the Mexican border of the United States, in the lower valley of the Rio Grande. To avoid a common confusion it should be noted that mescaline has no connexion whatsoever with the mescal plant, a succulent, not a cactus, and a species of Agave, which is widely distributed in the American South-west. The other two main hallucinogens are known to modern science through the work of the chemist Albert Hofmann, of the Sandoz Laboratories, Basle. Mention has already been made of Hofmann's subjective experiences, including marked synaesthesia, on the occasion of his discovery of the hallucinogenic properties of lysergic acid diethylamide (LSD). The usual source of this is ergot of rye, the fungus *Claviceps purpurea*. The third of the best-known hallucinogens, psilocybin, was isolated by Hofmann in 1958, its source being one of the American mushrooms, *Psilocybe mexicana heim*. Later Hofmann investigated yet another botanical source of hallucinogens known to the Aztecs, ololiuqui, and found at least two hallucinogens in it: one of these was, again, LSD. This he isolated from the seeds of an American plant of the convolvulus family, *Rivea corymboxa*. These represent but a few of the known hallucinogens, and there are many others of, for example, mushroom origin. Boyd and Roberts (1963) have drawn attention to the contradictions and confusions to be found in the literature of mushrooms. They report an incident in the life of Gordon Wasson, who was later to become known for his studies of 'sacred mushroom' ceremonies in Southern Mexico. In 1927, Wasson, while on honeymoon with his Russian wife Tina, encountered a clump of what were to him 'nasty toadstools'. His Russian wife, with her different cultural background, greeted them with enthusiasm, filled her handkerchief, and took them home to cook. Boyd and Roberts report two versions of the story: in one she 'ate them alone'; in the other – it being after all a honeymoon – the couple ate them together. The incident represents an initially inexpert reaction, in a man later to become an expert, similar to that to be found in many people. Confusions and deaths occur over mushroom edibility, cultural differences pronounce differently on edibility, and there is also much confusion as between 'hallucinogenic' and 'poisonous'.

Religious ceremonies involving both peyote (mescaline) and hallucinogenic mushrooms have continued among the Indians of Mexico, and adjacent American States like Arizona and New Mexico, up to modern times. Wasson, who has studied such ceremonies in Mexico, describes such events as essentially religious ceremonies, and in no sense any kind of orgy. Peyote-taking among the Navajo, Pueblo, and other modern American Indians is similarly a calm and dignified ritual. This opinion has been firmly and repeatedly expressed by anthropologists, psychiatrists, psychologists, and others who have witnessed the ceremonies. In the case of peyote the ceremonies begin late in the evening and last through the night, during which time as many as 50 mescal buttons – the dried tops of the cactus – are taken, though 12 to 20 are more usual numbers. These mescal buttons have something of the appearance and size of dried apricots and might well be mistaken for 'sacred mushrooms', though these, as we have seen, are of a different botanical origin. The survival of peyote-taking has features of additional interest in the emergence of a vigorous Indian religious movement which had its beginnings about 1870, and was formally established at Oklahoma in 1918. The Native American Church of North America, as it is now called, is a powerful body. It is associated with a strong religious movement of a distinctively Indian kind. Issues concerning this ceremonial taking of peyote have concerned both Federal and State authorities. The church has a membership of Indians from as far apart as Canada, New Mexico, and Oklahoma, and it has been very effective in legally preserving this Indian right.

The first scientific experiments with the hallucinogens were those of Prentiss and Morgan (1895). They were followed by those of Weir Mitchell (1896), who incidentally produced some of the best recorded introspective reports on the effects of the drug. Klüver's monograph of 1928 helped to stimulate interest, as did the later discovery by Hofmann in 1943 of the very similar properties of lysergic acid diethylamide. Since in recent years these and other hallucinogens have been irresponsibly used it is appropriate to restate the reasons for serious scientific interest in them, two of which seem important. On the one hand these substances produce a variety of altered mental states, and phenomena such as hallucination, synaesthesia, thought disturbances, and vivid visual imagery. Some of these states and phenomena have been thought to overlap with those of psychosis. In other words, from a 'model psychosis' produced by experimental means it has been thought that something might be learned about the phenomena of naturally occurring psychosis. As Osmond and Smythies (1952) put it, 'Mescaline produces every single major symptom of acute schizophrenia, though not always to the same degree.' A second and different reason for the study of the hallucinogens later emerged. Because of the chemical composition of these substances it seems probable that a fuller understanding of their biochemical activity may throw light upon the biochemical abnormalities believed to be responsible for schizophrenia and other functional psychoses. Thus it seems that continued serious scientific investigation of this family of substances may contribute to the understanding of not only the phenomena, but also the causation, of serious mental illness.

In 1952, some years after the first period of research, a new discovery was made about mescaline. Examination of its structural formula revealed that it closely resembled the hormone adrenaline. The investigators concerned, Osmond and Smythies, published their hypothesis: that some 'M substance', chemically similar to mescaline but – like adrenaline – naturally occurring in the body, might be responsible for schizophrenia. Because of the chemical resemblance between mescaline and adrenaline the investigators postulated that this M substance might be a break-down product of adrenaline. These observations gave birth to one important school of biochemical research into the psychoses, and in recent years chemical variants of mescaline have been intensively investigated. Of necessity animal rather than human experiments have had to be conducted with many of these substances. An alternative theory, associated particularly with the work of D. W. Woolley (1962), concerns the hormone serotonin (5–hydroxytriptamine), which is found in the human body in the hypothalamus and basic ganglia: the large nerve centres, and the part of the brain most involved in emotion. Woolley's hypothesis is that in schizophrenia and certain other psychoses there is an interference with the functioning of serotonin, which – as an essential metabolite – is necessary to normal brain functioning. Woolley's 'lock and key' analogy is helpful in explaining his position, which involves the idea of interference with the action of a metabolite by an antimetabolite. The turning of the key – by the metabolite (serotonin) – normally opens the lock and sets in motion the normal chain of biochemical events. If, however, we have the wrong key – presence of the anti-metabolite – shaped sufficiently like the real key to permit insertion in the keyhole, but because of slight differences from the real key unable to turn the lock, then the door to normal metabolism is not opened. In other words the antimetabolite displaces the essential metabolite and prevents its action on the central nervous system. Of interest is the fact that LSD is an antimetabolite to serotonin, as are harmine, yohimbine, psilocybin, and many of the hallucinogens. Also noteworthy is the resemblance of certain of these substances to drugs that have proved effective in the treatment of the psychoses. In this connexion it is interesting that from another plant, the Indian vine *Rauwolfia serpentina,* one of these psychiatric drugs, reserpine, was first isolated. This very closely resembles the hallucinogen yohimbine, and in fact Woolley describes reserpine – one of the most valuable of the psychiatric drugs – as (chemically) 'a more complicated yohimbine'.

The various hallucinogens mentioned all have a close chemical resemblance to one another, and also to the hormone serotonin, which, as we have seen, plays its part in normal brain functioning. More detailed discussion of these issues is outside our present concern, though from what has been summarized it will be apparent that further researches in this field may have some significant contributions to make to the understanding of psychoses in general or schizophrenia in particular, as a product of disturbed body chemistry.

From theoretical concern with the biochemistry of mental illness we may return to the psychological phenomena produced by this family of substances. With mescaline, LSD, psilocybin, and other hallucinogens of this type, some striking alterations of mental life can be produced. The term 'hallucination' is too narrow to cover the wide variety of phenomena encountered. In general terms it may be said that the effect of these substances is to intensify A–thinking processes, and to diminish the influences of R-thinking. It is more appropriate to speak of 'visual imagery' than 'hallucination' for certain of the most characteristic phenomena encountered, though hallucinations proper undoubtedly occur. The opinion of two of the leading investigators in this field may be noted on this point. Woolley writes: 'Perhaps too much attention has been given to hallucinations. . . . If one looks only for hallucinations he may miss a great deal that is relevant.' Smythies remarks that 'more attention should be paid' to the relationships between the hallucinogenic drugs and thinking. He adds: 'There is no word to describe "interference with thinking" drugs. This kind of evidence is really extremely important.' It may be added that there is little doubt that the hallucinogens may produce, and sometimes amplify and caricature, some of the most characteristic phenomena of abnormal, psychotic, thinking. This aspect of their study has received too little attention.

As one early investigator, Havelock Ellis, put it, 'Mescaline produces a saturnalia of the specific senses and principally an orgy of vision.' What Havelock Ellis says of mescaline applies also to LSD and psilocybin, whose effects are virtually identical. In the visual phenomena encountered – images, hallucinations, and pseudo-hallucinations, certain regularities occur. A major contribution to their understanding was made by H. Klüver (1928), who found evidence for what he called 'form constants' in these visualizations, spirals, webs, lattices, and arabesques being recurrent appearances. For the subject himself, among the most striking phenomena are the upsurge of vivid visual images, which many investigators have independently likened to imagery of the hypnagogic state. Such images are characteristically vivid in colour and highly original in content. Havelock Ellis reports that they 'never resembled familiar objects' and describes them as 'constantly approaching, yet constantly eluding, the semblance of known objects'. The imagery is often extremely beautiful, and as with hypnagogic imagery subjects frequently deplore their inability to paint or otherwise record it. Another feature of the images and hallucinations is their tendency to intrude upon the tasks of hard thinking that the experimenters may require of the subject.

My own research interest in these substances has been primarily in the light they throw upon the phenomena of thinking. The relevance of the phenomena produced to the thought processes of normal people becomes more apparent once we recognize that much 'normal' thinking is also unimpressive if measured by the standards of rationality and realism. It is less common than we sometimes realize to find the normal adult thinking with one eye focused on the evidence, and with both ears closed to the whisperings of emotion and prejudice. Thinking in its most adult, logical, and prejudice-free moments exhibits, among others, three features: constraint by accurate perceptual observation, use of naturalistic modes of description and explanation, and confinement to logical rather than merely associative connexions. The hallucinogenic drugs provide one way of investigating interferences with accurate perceptual observation, resort to other than naturalistic modes of description and explanation, and associative rather than logical connexions between ideas. Thus they permit us to study phenomena of abnormal thinking, deviations from the more usual kinds of normal thinking, and normal thinking itself. Among deviations from usual kinds of thinking may be mentioned thinking of a synaesthetic kind: instances of synaesthesia produced in such experiments have already been considered (Chapter 2). Leaving aside pathological kinds of thinking resembling those of the psychotic, we may next turn to phenomena produced by the hallucinogens that have led to their assessment as 'mystical'.

Investigation of mystical thinking, as of other forms of thinking, is a legitimate subject for psychology. The main classic in this field is William James's *The Varieties of Religious Experience* (1902). James also wrote about similar phenomena of an experimentally produced kind when he discussed the effects of nitrous oxide on thinking (James, 1897). Substances like mescaline can in certain people produce mystical reactions that resemble those reported by James with nitrous oxide. It may be emphasized that not all subjects exhibit these responses: for example in some experiments with mescaline we were not able to produce in our subjects anything remotely resembling a mystical thought, no matter how hard we tried to provoke it. That other investigators have found similar individual variations is evident from the research literature as a whole. Quite obviously situational factors may encourage such reactions: in ceremonial uses of peyote, 'sacred mushrooms', and other agents by American Indians we might expect such mystical responses to be more frequent, and more prominent. In our own experiments my colleagues and I observed a number of instances of the phenomenon of '*presque vu*'. This is the feeling of being on the edge of grasping some very important truth: a similar awareness of almost, but not quite, achieving such insight is prominent in mystical writings. Of interest also was another phenomenon, a strong impression of 'significance', and sometimes of 'certainty'. Both the significance and the certainty impressed the experimenters as being somewhat free floating. The subject was in a state to feel certain about 'something', or to recognize that 'something' was extremely significant. He seemed to seize upon available subject matter – perhaps images, hallucinations, awareness of an altered sense of passage of time – and attach these feelings to it. In other words the feelings appeared to be primary, and the things to which they were attached secondary. Again, hallucinogens can produce strong elation, an elation of the kind we nicknamed 'feelings of self plus'. The subject might think, or say, that the experimenters were incredibly naïve, and inadequate recipients of the great wisdom he would like to be able to impart. As one subject in an experiment with psilocybin remarked, 'It was like a gnat asking you to describe things in terms *it* could understand.' He added, 'You would laugh, and spray it with flit' (Breslaw in Ebin (ed.), 1961). The questions we asked as experimenters, and the tests we administered in our own mescaline and LSD experiments, provoked similar reactions on many occasions. Sometimes the response of the subject was more subtle, in that he himself felt inadequate and unworthy of the enlarged and mystical vision of things that had been granted him. This interesting blend of grandiosity and humility was expressed by one subject as like being on top of a hill, seeing a beautiful sunset, and trying to describe it to others. This subject, like several others, expressed the wish that he as a person had greater talents with which to communicate.

If a given individual is personally disposed to react mystically, then in the phenomena themselves there are some excellent materials to work with. To begin with, the visual imagery may itself be of striking beauty, and of a kind not easily describable in words. From my own knowledge of the research literature I would assess Weir Mitchell as having been the most successful at communication. His experiences included 'miles and miles of rippled purples, half transparent and of ineffable beauty'. Havelock Ellis found himself seeming to gaze into a hollow vessel 'on whose polished concave mother of pearl surface the hues were constantly changing'. On another occasion he saw 'a vast field of golden jewels, studded with red and green stones', and again the imagery exhibited movement and change.

Granted imagery of this kind, subjects who lack the ability to paint, to write poetry, or to use words which convey subtlety and complexity may become preoccupied with the ineffability of the experience. This sense of ineffability, which William James held to be one of the defining characteristics of mystical experience, can be prominent in the reactions of certain subjects. Also of interest are the phenomena relating to time, which may themselves evoke mystical forms of thinking. Subjects may react to the experimenter's request to perform an act of judgement such as a time estimate in a way which seems to external observation crude and slipshod. The subject himself, introspectively and retrospectively, may react differently. In one of our experiments the subject, when asked to make an estimate of a time interval, replied, 'Anything I can think of seems wildly improbable.' When we insisted, she presented no fewer than three verbal estimates: 'fifteen minutes', 'two to three seconds', and 'seven minutes'. When we went over the sound recordings later with this subject, she said, 'At that point I could have agreed that there were any number of times you mentioned.' Throughout the experiment on the subject of time, as on other subjects, this person reacted in a strongly mystical way. The complexities that surround the scientific study of time estimation will be discussed, as such, in Chapter 6.

A final point to be made about mystical kinds of thinking with hallucinogen drugs relates to what seems to be a partial awareness on the part of the subject that he and the experimenters are at cross purposes. To the subject it is a matter of irritation to be dragged from his contemplation of exceedingly beautiful imagery, or meditation on some mystical insight, to perform some seemingly trivial task for the experimenters. As one of our subjects put it, 'What to you is text is for me footnotes; and what is footnotes for you is text for me.' There are many ways in which subjective experiences, and thus the context within which thinking occurs, are altered for the subject. Under these conditions the temptation to resort to forms of thought and communication which closely resemble those of spontaneous 'mystical' thinking can be a strong one.

Three main influences may be noted in the hallucinogenic

experiment. First is the drug itself; second, the personality of the subject; and third, the situation. As regards the drug: mescaline, LSD, psilocybin and several of the other hallucinogens seem to be essentially similar in their effects on people in general. Differences are also noticeable. Thus the active dose of LSD is tiny by contrast with that of the other two drugs. The effects of psilocybin are more short-lived than those of the other two, and last about five hours; one hallucinogen, DET (N.N. diethyltryptamine), produces essentially similar reactions lasting three hours; another, DMT (N.N. dimethyltryptamine), has effects which last for only about one hour. The second factor is the personality of the subject. Given a hallucinogen, as we have seen some people react mystically, others will respond in a persecutory way suggestive of paranoia, while others again may produce a hypomania or a depression. These personality differences have not on the whole been adequately stressed in the research literature. The third factor is the situation in which the drug is taken. An American Indian religious ceremony may predispose to mystical responses, just as a laboratory experiment in a medical school may discourage these and help to evoke others. All three factors, drug, personality of subject, and situation, will interact, and what is available to observation, and introspection, will vary accordingly. In a later section I shall examine another aspect of hallucinogen research: its use in producing a 'model psychosis' and, as such, providing data of interest in the understanding of the natural psychoses.

THE THINKING OF SLEEP

Freud conceives of dreams as nothing more than a particular kind of thinking made possible by the conditions of sleep. He argues that dreams are an attempt by the dreamer to grapple with his emotional preoccupations and solve his problems. That sleeping mental life should be concerned with this activity is, for Freud, no more mysterious than the fact that wakefulness should be similarly employed. Dreaming is, however, an activity in which R-thinking plays a minimal part: its resemblances in wakefulness are to be found to reverie, daydreaming, and fantasy rather than to reasoning and scientific judgement. This difference between dreaming and typical R-thinking is well summarized by another historically important psychologist, William McDougall: 'In dreaming we regress to a lower, more primitive form of thinking which tends to be conducted mainly in the form of, and by the aid of, visual images rather than by the aid of words.' This regressive, typical A-thinking character of dreams is emphasized by many investigators and theorists. Some of these theories may be summarized, as each serves to alert us to certain features of the phenomenon of the dream.

The *wish-fulfilment theory* of Freud has many facets to it. These are well illustrated in one particular dream with which he became acquainted while formulating the theory. It concerned a medical student called Pepi who had difficulty in waking up in the mornings. One day sleep seemed particularly sweet to Pepi. His landlady called from his bedroom door, 'Wake up, Herr Pepi, it's time to go to the hospital.' In response to this stimulus Pepi had a dream. He was lying in bed in a ward of the hospital, and there was a card over the bed on which was written: 'Pepi, H., Medical student, age 22'. Thus Pepi had found a solution in fantasy to his problem, a pictorial version of his saying to himself, 'Since I'm already in hospital there's no need for me to get up and go there.' And so he went on sleeping. Pepi's dream illustrates several characteristics of dreaming, and Freud's way of viewing it. First, it will be seen that the motivation underlying the dream is a wish, and the content of the dream the fulfilment of that wish. Secondly, the dream performs the function of protecting sleep and permitting it to continue. Thirdly, the typically visual nature of the dream is apparent: it is an affair of visual imagery, not of verbal thinking. Fourthly, we can see how an external stimulus – the landlady's voice – can affect the content of the dream. As Freud puts it, 'The sensory stimuli which reach us during sleep may well become sources of dreams.'

Concern with this fourth, perceptual, aspect of dreams has given rise to an alternative theory that T. H. Pear has called the *stimulus theory* of dreaming. In fact the stimulus theory was held by many of Freud's predecessors in this field. One such investigator illustrated it with a dream of his own, in which he was climbing Mount Etna, and the ground became intolerably hot. He awoke to find he was lying with his feet on the hot-water bottle! One of the important investigators of the dream before Freud, L. F. Maury, defended this theory. Maury himself was responsible for the much-quoted French Revolution dream. In this he found himself in the midst of the Reign of Terror, and was brought before the tribunal, condemned, and led to the place of execution. The blade of the guillotine fell and he awoke to find that the top of the bed had fallen and struck his cervical vertebrae in just the place where the guillotine would have struck. Maury, and others after him, argued that this dream provided evidence that dreams can occur instantaneously. Freud opposed this notion, and later researches with the rapid eye movements (REM) technique – which permits dreams to be timed – indicate that he was correct in this opposition. Freud was also critical of the stimulus theory itself, which seemed to him to exaggerate the importance of just one aspect of dreaming. In his criticisms he referred to Hildebrandt, an earlier investigator who had, like Maury, defended the theory. Hildebrandt had found evidence for the stimulus theory in many dreams of his own evoked by the stimulus of his alarm clock. But why, Freud asked, should the same stimulus evoke different dreams on different occasions? Things other than the stimulus itself need to be considered to explain this. Thus Freud himself set up a theory which was concerned to link together this stimulus aspect, the protection of sleep function, and wish fulfilment.

The *conflict theory* of W. H. R. Rivers (1923) places emphasis on another aspect of dreams. Rivers saw dreams not as wish fulfilments but rather as attempts, in sleep, to solve the conflicts which trouble waking life. The emotional tone of the dream depends on the extent to which this activity is successful: where there is marked failure to solve the problem an anxiety dream occurs or, in extreme instances, a nightmare. Rivers saw the wish-fulfilment theory as too simple a formulation to fit all cases, and attempted a more general theory. He also rejected Freud's conception of dreams as a product of censorship. For Freud the dreams of children tend to be simple wish fulfilments, but those of adults tend to be disguised wish fulfilments: the disguising process Freud explained in terms of repressing forces which he called dream mechanisms. Rivers took the alternative view that the apparent distortion is the product of regression rather than of censorship. Dreams are attempts to solve the problems of waking life, but they are attempts made at a lower and more primitive level of mental functioning. It may be noted that Freud himself recognized a category of dreams which do not readily fit the wish-fulfilment criteria: these he called anxiety dreams. It is helpful to have these two points of emphasis as representing two extreme categories into which dreams can be classified. Some dreams are pleasant wish fulfilments of the kind emphasized by Freud; others are anxious and fit in more with the idea of conflict dreams which Rivers was led to stress. Some dreams can be fitted into either type of theory. An example may be taken from the work of an investigator of children's dreams, C. W. Kimmins. A child reported a dream in which 'a robber came to our house and broke all the cups'. It emerged that the boy had himself broken a cup and was frightened that his mother would find out: if a robber came and broke *all* the cups then she would never know that he had broken one of them. Such a dream could be interpreted either as a wish fulfilment on Freud's theory, or as a fantasy solution to a waking problem in the way Rivers would have interpreted it.

Kimmins himself (1937) may be taken as an example of an early contributor to the dream inventory approach. His original work was done with thousands of dreams from children of both sexes, representing different age groups and special categories such as the blind, the deaf, and the delinquent. From the works of Kimmins and others it is possible to answer a question that naturally occurs about dreaming and blindness: do people blind from birth ever have visual dreams? In brief the answer is 'no', though it must be remembered that there are many kinds of legally accepted blindness, not all of which involve total absence of sight. It appears that, in the case of total blindness occurring before the age of 5 years, visual imagery in dreaming does not occur. If blindness occurs after about 7 years of age there may be visual dreaming, which can persist for many decades after loss of sight. Between 5 and 7 years much depends upon individual differences, and the amount of development that has occurred in the child in question. In typical dreams visual imagery predominates. Kimmins gives examples from the blind of non-visual dreams. One boy, aged fifteen, dreamed that the school was on fire. Bells rang over all the building, and a master came to tell the boys to get dressed and keep calm. The fire brigade came, and asked the children to help them hold the water pipes. In the dream there are images of auditory, tactile, and kinaesthetic kinds, but not visual images. Dream inventories are of value in enabling a variety of questions to be answered that cannot readily be dealt with through the dream theory approach. A leading contemporary representative of the inventory is Calvin S. Hall who has accumulated and cross-indexed some 10,000 dreams. On sex differences Hall's records reveal that there is a significantly greater tendency for women to report dreams in colour than men. In general the majority of dreams reported are without colour, though in one sample of 3,000 dreams analysed coloured imagery occurred in 29 per cent. Differences in the content of dreams have also been studied: for example the records show that men dream about males about twice as often as about females, while women dream about males and females more or less equally. On the theoretical side Hall inclines to the Rivers type of theory. In dreams, he says, we deal with 'our problems and predicaments, our fears and hopes'. Elsewhere Hall develops somewhat the same view as Freud – that there is no particular mystery about dreams. He writes, 'The continuity between waking thought and dreaming is firmly established', and adds that psychologists 'are now studying dreaming in order to understand normal cognitive processes'.

Some of the questions surrounding dreaming appeared, until relatively recent decades, to be unanswerable. Does everybody dream? How long do dreams last? How many dreams occur in a typical night's sleep? Are there sex differences in dreaming? Do the people who don't report dreams not have them, or do they forget them? These kinds of questions can now be scientifically studied. In 1939 there appeared Nathaniel Kleitman's book *Sleep and Wakefulness*, and 1963 saw its reappearance in a new and enlarged edition. This later volume reflects the enormous advances in the scientific understanding of the dream made in this period, and Kleitman himself is closely associated with the most important of these. This was the discovery of recordable, physiological accompaniments of dreaming. In 1953 Aserinsky and Kleitman, followed in 1957 by Dement and Kleitman, reported their studies of characteristic eye movements which occur during some phases of sleep. These rapid eye movements or REMS could be objectively recorded by a standard technique which was evolved, and through the closed eyelid of the sleeper. Most important, the occurrence of a period of REMS seemed to be closely associated with dreaming. If wakened during such a period the sleeper tended to report a dream, if wakened a few minutes after he tended to report fragments of a dream, and if wakened fifteen or so minutes after the REMS he tended to report no dreaming. Thus it would seem that we should distinguish not between dreamers and non-dreamers, but between what Kleitman calls 'recallers' and 'non-recallers'. There has emerged strong evidence that most dreams are lost through forgetting, and that people who say they do not have dreams forget them rather than don't have them.

It may be objected that the only really convincing evidence that a person has had a dream is his introspective, or rather retrospective, report to that effect. Yet the evidence using REMS and other criteria – such as certain changes of the EEG or brain rhythms – of an externally observable accompaniment of dreaming is striking. If we accept these REMS and other criteria as adequate, then it becomes possible to answer many hitherto insoluble questions about dreaming. The evidence suggests two different kinds of sleep which, for want of an established terminology, I shall call X and Y. At first there occurs a period of Y sleep without rapid eye movements, followed by periods of X sleep during which the REMS – and presumably dreaming – occur. The X and Y sleep alternate during the night, and in general the periods of X (or REM) sleep increase in duration as the night progresses. With the EEG, the REM, and other observable recordings – for example changes of muscle potential – it is possible to perform controlled observations and even experiments upon the sleeper. On the one hand we can study the effect of systematically depriving the sleeper of dreams by waking him; then follows a period of initial Y-sleep, and a further waking before x-sleep gets under way. We can study the length of time taken for dreams to occur, and the effects of external stimulation upon dreaming in accord with the stimulus theory. A fuller account of work in this field is to be found in Oswald (1966) in the Pelican series. Perhaps most interesting of all is the possibility of extending the use of the REM technique to the study of waking thinking, for example imagery, problem solving, fantasy and imagining, and hallucination. This aspect of development will be discussed in the next chapter, with particular reference to advances made by investigators at the City University of New York.

BETWEEN WAKEFULNESS AND SLEEP

The imagery which may accompany the process of falling asleep has aroused the curiosity of many thinkers, including four of the most important investigators of the dream: Maury, Freud, Rivers, and Kleitman. Aristotle has left some of the first recorded references to it, and one of its earliest appearances in literature is in Chaucer's *The House of Fame*. In the fifth century Macrobius distinguished among the five types of dream he differentiated a kind which occurs when we are not fully asleep, and believe ourselves to be awake. Later followed the comments of two sixteenth-century bishops, an introspective report in a letter by the philosopher Spinoza, and the first data-collecting investigation, which was by Johannes Müller on Berlin university students. Eventually in 1848 Alfred Maury named the phenomenon '*hypnagogic imagery*'.

Maury himself was a regular hypnagogic imager. He records seeing in the dark grotesque and unfamiliar faces, with peculiar hair styles, that pestered him with remarkable persistence while he was trying to get to sleep. Of importance is Maury's recording of the fact that his servant also had the experiences, though his mother did not: in other words some people do, and some people do not, report the phenomenon. I shall return to the matter of incidence below, and first describe the characteristics of the imagery. It may be visual, auditory, or of some other kind, and if visual may occur either with closed eyes, or open-eyed in a darkened bedroom. Content may be reproductive of the events of the day, or seemingly strange and foreign to the personality. Such content may be pleasing, frightening, worrying, or amusing, and the imager, as in dreams, has little control over appearance, departure, and content of the imagery. On investigation it emerges that many people who are subject to the imagery fail to notice it until they are alerted to its occurrence; there are some investigators like Oswald (1962) who regard the imagery as possibly universal. They would view the distinction between those who report it and those who deny its occurrence as parallel to that between Kleitman's recallers and non-recallers of dreams. Incidence may now be examined in terms of those who report the phenomenon.

The world seems to divide itself into two categories of people: those who report hypnagogic imagery, and those who say they do not know the experience. If we add together visual, auditory, and other modes of hypnagogic imagery, the imagers seem to outnumber the non-imagers: investigations by colleagues and myself yielded an incidence of 63 per cent of subjects who had experienced at least one such image. This incidence is supported by Owens (1963) who found it reported by 77 of 100 subjects studied. As between the visual and auditory kinds of imagery – undoubtedly the commonest kinds – the relative incidence is a matter of dispute. Our own studies found auditory imagery to be commoner than visual, being reported by 43 per cent as opposed to 34 per cent of subjects. But in another study Owens (1963) found a higher incidence of visual than of auditory imagery. These different findings may depend on the sample of people investigated. Oswald inclines to the view that the visual kind of imagery is perhaps more likely to be overlooked as commonplace, compared with such happenings as hearing a loud voice abruptly speaking a phrase in the privacy of one's bedroom. The auditory imagery can certainly be very striking indeed, and sharp distinctions between it and auditory hallucinations are not easy to draw. Many of our own subjects – in several investigations – reported confusion with real perceptions. As regards regularity of occurrence, F. E. Leaning (1925) in a very comprehensive investigation found that 55 per cent of one group of hypnagogic imagers had the experience regularly or nightly.

The visual kind of imagery sometimes assumes – as it did in Maury's own case – the form of faces in the dark. Frequently the faces are of people unknown: 'no face ever resembled an acquaintance' is a representative comment. Landscapes are another common item of content, and these also can often be strangely original. The imagery may seem strange in other ways; for example objects may be seen from peculiar angles. Thus one subject said, 'The viewpoint is at an angle from above them, almost as if I were hanging from the ceiling', while another saw 'a windmill from below looking up'. Imagers were often impressed by the strange juxtapositions of objects and unusual clarity of detail which often leads them to liken the experience to surrealist painting. 'Objects arranged in unusual ways, being most like paintings by Dali' is a representative comment. On occasion I have found it possible to tape-record and time the imagery. Duration varies: thus one subject had a vision of an alligator lasting two and a half minutes, and a pencil shape lasting eighteen seconds. Sometimes the imagery changes exceedingly rapidly; one subject reported, 'I had a peep and it passed.' Many subjects commented on the unusual qualities of colour and lighting, and among descriptive phrases that have been recorded are 'strange luminosity', 'glow of the setting sun', and 'sparks of gold speckles across them'. Henslow reported to Galton the brilliance of the cut glass, and gold and silver filigree ornaments, which he saw.

In one investigation my colleague and I (McKellar and Simpson, 1954) were interested to find how visual hypnagogic imagery differed from dreams. Obviously the two phenomena shade into one another, and in intermediate cases classification becomes an arbitrary matter. We asked our subjects how they knew they were awake and not asleep. Among the reasons given were: being able to have other perceptions at the same time (for example, engage in conversation), being able to have separate thoughts, and being able to open eyes, close them again, and then resume the imagery. On one occasion when I was tape-recording a drowsy hypnagogic imager it was possible to induce the person concerned to form an ordinary memory image which remained separate and did not blend with the hypnagogic experience. Once, when I was tape-recording myself, I actually found it possible to get out of bed and work the recorder – a rather primitive one which had to be wound up – and then close my eyes and continue the imagery, which remained uninterrupted even by these actions. A further distinction between dream and hypnagogic visualizations is suggested by Leaning, who says: 'In dreams the dreamer is part of all the scenes and doings, but in the hypnagogic state he is a beholder only.' The imagery is strongly autonomous and, as Leaning says, exhibits a tendency 'neither to be commanded nor invited'. The author of the imagery seems to be very much in the position of an observer.

The content of auditory imagery is most often music or voices. Imagery may also be tactile, as in the case of one of my subjects who reported touching and having to remove a hypnagogically imaged snake from the bed. The imagery may be composite, as when for example imagery of temperature like the warmth of the sun accompanies some visualized scene. Rather rare are hyp-nagogic pains, though I have encountered isolated cases and two instances of hypnagogically imaged electric shocks. Sometimes visual imagery may accompany the common falling-asleep experience of seeming to fall or float.

People react differently to hypnagogic imagery. For some it is a matter of interest and even amusement, while for others it is anxiety-provoking or even an occasion for terror. The fact that some people have (or remember) the imagery and others do not may be of considerable importance. The imager may be a child, and the one who lacks the experience some adult from whom he seeks reassurance. Recently I talked to a mother about the night terrors of her small son. The boy himself was too terrified to tell his parents why he became so frightened. I had my suspicions. These were confirmed when I saw the child, who told me about the ugly and frightening faces which grimaced at him in his darkened bedroom. In return I told him about the kind I had had at his age, of a distinctly terrifying witch flying through the air on a broomstick in front of my bed. Moreover, I emphasized that more than half the people investigated had experiences of these kinds, though not everybody. This matter-of-fact interest in the details of a 'normal' rather than an 'abnormal' variety of experience seemed to be reassuring to the child and, I suspect, to the mother also. Those adults who themselves have hypnagogic imagery frequently need reassurance that the phenomena are very common indeed, and that science has a name for them.

In considering the stimulus theory of dreams it has been noted how perceptual stimulation may give rise to dream imagery. Similarly such stimulation may evoke imagery in the hypnagogic state. A good instance of this concerned one subject who, having a bad cold, was breathing heavily as he settled down to sleep. He had a visual and auditory hypnagogic image of a motor car with engine trouble: the noise of the engine was distinctly unhealthy. As he listened to it he became aware that the chugging of the car's engine was in fact his own laboured breathing. Sometimes these linkages between perceptual stimulation and hypnagogic imagery can be of a synaesthetic kind. A good illustration, involving visual-auditory synaesthesia, occurred while one would-be sleeper lay in bed but was interrupted while drifting off to sleep by intermittent bursts of conversation from the flat below. He experienced a clear visual image of an evening view of a tall, modern, building with many windows. The lights of these windows went on and off, and the 'on' periods coincided with the intermittent auditory stimuli from the room below. Synaesthesia does seem to occur both in hypnagogic states and during dreams, though on the whole rather rarely.

From these experiences F. W. H. Myers distinguished *hypnopompic imagery*, which he defined as 'persistence of some dream image into the first moments of waking'. If a distinction is made between these and the falling-asleep kind of image, then hypnopompic images appear to be less common. Thus in one study Owens (1963) found it in 51 of 100 subjects who yielded an incidence of hypnagogic imagery as high as 77. Some of the instances of hypnopompic imagery fit in well with the definition given by Myers. As one of my subjects reports, 'When I begin to wake up I seem to see something out of the last dream I had. . . . For example if I dreamt about cars I'll wake up seeing a car across the room.' Like the falling-asleep kind of imagery the hypnopompic kind can be emotionally disturbing, as in the case of the unfortunate who 'used to waken under a vast vault of contemptuous and spiteful faces'. The relation of hypnopompic images of this kind to the night terrors of children merits more attention than it has received. Another kind of image tends to be anticipatory in character, and may give rise to some odd confusions with reality. A very striking instance was told to me by one young married couple. The wife went to sleep ready to get up early and serve her husband his breakfast in good time for him to catch his plane. The following morning she 'got up', 'made breakfast', and was 'seeing him off'. Then she realized that she had in fact done none of these things: her husband – who had had to get his own breakfast – was saying good-bye to his hypnopompic-imaging wife in the bedroom before he departed! Many subjects reported illusory impressions of similar kinds involving getting up, washing, dressing, and then realizing that they were still waking up: having performed all these acts in fantasy it was necessary now to perform them in reality. Thus hypnopompic images, like dreams, may protect the sleeper from full wakefulness. There are, as with hypnagogic phenomena, waking-up images of other than visual and auditory kinds. A good illustration was contributed by one correspondent – a woman physician – who reported: 'I was dreaming I was toasting bread, and awoke quite quickly to smell toast burning. . . . I arose to check whether I had left the oven on, but I had not.' Yet another kind of hypnopompic image lends itself to supernatural interpretation, as when the sleeper wakens to 'see' a shadowy figure dressed in the garments of a former age. Some 'apparitions' appear to be of this hypnopompic kind.

One curious phenomenon of the between wakefulness and sleep period has been noted by various investigators. As it lacks an established name I shall call it *hypnopompic speech*. A good example of the schizophrenic-like verbalizations which can occur during drowsiness was a young woman who awoke to find herself murmuring 'Put the pink pyjamas in the salad'. Singer (1966) refers to frequent occasions on which, following arousal from sleep, he found himself making some incomprehensible remark to his wife. His explanation is that such thoughts or statements are evoked by a dream from which the sleeper is awakening. The observations of A. Mintz (1948) suggest that hypnopompic speech is not invariably related to dreams, but rather to a loosening of the thought processes of a kind reminiscent of schizophrenia. A good illustration, given by Mintz, concerned the young wife who on waking up remarked to her husband (who was already up), 'Light the towel.' As he did not appear to comprehend her wishes she repeated this demand with some anger. Eventually it emerged that this statement meant 'raise the window shade'. The translation given by Mintz is that lighting means light, and a towel and a window shade are the same shape. The presence of a distorted kind of sense, underlying the apparent nonsense of the words spoken, is evident also in a piece of hypnopompic speech involving myself. While I was still waking up my wife asked me to tell her the time and I said: 'I'll rub together two clocks and tell you.' Free association immediately afterwards yielded the following interpretation. There were a clock and my wristlet watch on the table at my side of the bed, and the designs of both are less than perfect – as is often the case with modern watches and clocks – for reading the time, when drowsy, without making a mistake. So, very reasonably, I proposed to ensure accuracy and – having looked at both – assess the time. Also relevant, as a background thought, was the idea of boy scouts making fires by rubbing together two sticks, and the joke – which I rather like – about making fires by 'rubbing two boy scouts together'. Thus interpreted there appeared to be some meaning underneath my odd remark. As Mintz has put it, 'Schizophrenic thinking is within the behaviour repertoire of the normal individual.' In the two instances taken there is no particular reference to a dream. What occurred seemed to be thinking of a lower and more primitive kind, in response to words spoken to the waking sleeper.

Craik (1966) in a posthumously published paper gives many instances of 'the confused trains of thought' which occur while falling asleep or waking. Thus on one occasion when told that it was time to get up for breakfast he replied that he was 'bound to get up at the right time because the sand was bound to divide at the place the ashes were'. His retrospections revealed he had been dreaming about work in an iron foundry in which the layer of ashes between the two halves of the sand mould ensured opening at the right place. Confusion had occurred between iron casting and getting up and 'that seemed a good enough reason, although all the concrete details were irrelevant and wrong, and in normal consciousness I would have realized their irrelevancy'. Craik observes that to the sleepy consciousness each idea arouses an idea which is relevant to the immediately preceding idea but not to the whole context. He likens the mental processes concerned to the activity of an inefficient secretary who cannot file papers correctly because she cannot grasp the principle of classification.

One of the earliest observers of these odd forms of speech was Schjelderup-Ebbe in 1923. Phenomena reported by him relate to the hypnagogic rather than the hypnopompic state. He made systematic observations on himself by interrupting his process of falling asleep, and writing down what he happened to be thinking about. An instance from Schjelderup-Ebbe is 'seven young men who gave all their poison claws to poison-princesses'. This, and numerous other statements recorded by him, seemed at the time to be meaningful, though nonsensical afterwards.

These hypnagogic and hypnopompic verbalizations may, as we have seen, be overtly spoken – and perhaps elicited by the speech of another person – or subvocally thought, as in Schjelderup–Ebbe's case. Perhaps related to them are the visual images which sometimes occur in the drowsy state, of print which appears in jumbled form usually accompanied by the *presque vu* experience of almost, but not quite, being able to read it. Anyway a number of bizarre forms of verbalization are reported in states adjacent to sleep, which many observers find strongly reminiscent of schizophrenic utterances. These, along with the imagery of these states, may provide yet a further basis for empathy by the normal person with the thought processes of the psychotic.

THERE ARE MANY KINDS OF THINKING

The distinction which has been made between A-thinking and R-thinking reminds us of the varied forms of mental activity which 'thinking' embraces. Those thought products which we find useful tend, as I have argued elsewhere more fully (McKellar 1957; 1963), to be of composite origin. They arise from the interplay of different kinds of thinking. Thus we may distinguish *creative thinking* from *critical thinking*: creative thinking performs the tasks of an author in that it provides a subject matter of fresh and new ideas, while critical thinking performs the functions of an editor in evaluating and revising these ideas. Alternatively we may distinguish between two kinds of thinking which emerge from the work of J. P. Guilford and his associates: *convergent thinking* and *divergent thinking*. Guilford's work concerned the education process, and will be examined more fully in a later chapter. He was led to make a distinction between convergent thinking, as the kind of thinking which orthodox intelligence tests measure, and divergent thinking, which is involved in innovation, revision of the known, and imaginative excursions of thought into the realm of the possible. In making this distinction Guilford sought to correct what he saw as the over-preoccupation of psychology with the study of *more intelligent v. less intelligent* forms of thinking. In this we find a distinction which broadly differentiates man from the lower animals, adults from children, and individuals from one another. But as a later investigator, Torrance, following Guilford, has written, 'The traditional measure of I.Q. taps only a few of man's thinking abilities.' Moreover, in the developmental field, investigators like Piaget have been interested in differences between *adult thinking* and *childhood thinking*. These differences, Piaget has shown, are more than merely those of intelligence: the differences are qualitative and not merely quantitative. Other important researches into the developmental psychology of thinking have emerged from contemporary Soviet researches, and will be examined in a later chapter in connexion with the problems of the learner.

This chapter has noted some of the differences of thinking

which occur in the waking, sleeping, and hypnagogic states. It has examined some of the manifestations of A-thinking that can be experimentally produced with hallucinogenic drugs and conditions of sensory deprivation. One goal of such investigation is to illuminate more clearly differences between normal and abnormal thinking activity: some further aspects of this problem will be examined later in relation to the abnormal personality. In the chapter which follows more detailed attention will be given to normal, waking thinking, with particular reference to the mental imagery which plays its part in thought, remembering, and imagining.

CHAPTER FOUR

Mental Imagery

> I am one of those persons whose normal waking life is almost totally free from sensory imagery, either visual, auditory, tactile, or of any other kind.
>
> W. H. R. RIVERS

TWO functions may be associated with vision, hearing, touch, and the other sense departments: that of perceiving, and that of imaging. In addition to being able to perceive, we possess subjective forms of 'seeing', 'hearing', or otherwise cognizing objects, persons, and situations that are not perceptually present at the time. As William McDougall expresses it, 'We seem to experience in a faint, thin, ghostlike fashion, the sensory qualities on which we rely in perception.' A more formal definition of a mental image is provided in Warren's *Dictionary of Psychology*: 'an experience which reproduces or copies in part, and with some degree of sensory realism, a previous perceptual experience in the absence of the original sensory stimulation.' This definition applies more especially to imagery of one of two main kinds, namely memory imagery. Also to be noted are imagination images – presumably products of rearranged previous perception – whose resemblance to these sources in past experience may be less convincing than their apparent originality. The psychologist's use of the word 'image' differs from that of the literary critic, who in using a phrase like 'the imagery of Shakespeare' merely means the allusions made by the poet. Yet poets and writers themselves have quite often made explicit use of visual and other forms of imagery in the psychologist's sense. Thus Wordsworth refers to 'that inward eye' which, he says, 'is the bliss of solitude', and in his sonnet 'To Sleep' writes about his use of a series of visual and auditory images in an attempt to induce sleep.

> A flock of sheep that leisurely pass by,
> One after one; the sound of rain, and bees
> Murmuring; the fall of rivers, winds and seas,
> Smooth fields, white sheets of water and pure sky . . .

Mental Imagery

THE PHENOMENA OF IMAGERY

The words 'image' and 'imagery' refer to a whole family of phenomena which we encounter in wakefulness, in dreams, and in the hypnagogic state. Imagery is not necessarily visual. Though capacity for both the visual and the auditory is found in most people, there are other possibilities. Thus one subject, not capable of visual or auditory thinking, reports leading 'a rather drab image life'. He adds: 'However, I can make myself taste imaginary food, and can even add spice to it to see what it "tastes" like.' Dreaming and hypnagogic imaging have already been discussed, but we find imagery of a large variety of other kinds. It may accompany – as in Wordsworth's case – attempted acts of recall, efforts at planning and thinking out a problem, spontaneous problem solving in the form of 'flashes of insight'. Imagery may be a component of idiosyncrasies of individual experience like synaesthesia, and of others such as colour association and diagram forming. It may also assume quasi-abnormal forms, as in visual, auditory, and other types of hallucination. It may vary widely; for example in its visual forms it may be flat or three-dimensional, coloured or achromatic. It may provide panoramic views or close-up detail, sometimes even to the extent of print which the imager can 'read'. In one kind of experience – the immediate memory image – the detail may provide a person with additional information of a kind he failed to notice during the immediately preceding perception. Memory imagery may also help retention, and many people admit to having a kind of mental blackboard on which they can record and retain visual information. One such person reported that he could retain 'sharp visual images of Latin prose or mathematical equations for twenty-four hours or so'. Imaging may assist remembering, though it can sometimes impede it, while its relations to thinking seem to vary greatly from one individual to another. Some people report that they think from image to image; others like Rivers assert that they think without it; others again describe their imagery as an epiphenomenon to their thinking, its relation being similar to that of the illustrations of a book to the text.

Some of the variations of imagery to be found may be illustrated from within a single occupational group, nineteen police officers, whose imagery I investigated. All had available to them both the visual and the auditory kind. A representative comment on the value of such imagery may be quoted from one: 'A police officer has a great advantage if he can imagine what someone looks like from a written description, or if he can form a picture in his mind from a plan or a sketch.' Every officer but one considered visual imagery desirable in his work, and fourteen of them considered it essential. Fifteen reported being able to visualize three-dimensionally. A number of the subjects stressed the desirability of having a good range of imagery, 'the more kinds the better'. Some stressed the value of imagery for smell and temperature, specifically in relation to the early detection of fires.

Policemen are not the only occupational group who regard possession of visual imagery of reasonable strength as desirable or essential. A second such group I have investigated was of professional anatomists in one University Department of Anatomy. These proved to be good visualizers. Asked to define the kind of imagery necessary to their work they tended to stress also the importance of being able to visualize three-dimensionally. Not irrelevant either are the problems of the learner with such a subject. In a study at Liverpool University A. C. Owens (1963) investigated students learning anatomy, and found that those who were poor at visual thinking and remembering tended to have difficulties with the subject. Studies of my own with individual students accord with this. Many such students have told how they encountered additional problems with, for example, pictures and diagrams which they had to code into words in order to remember. One such person told in detail of her problems with dissection. She said: 'I was all right with the simpler organisms but became a little baffled when we got to frogs and crayfish. I just couldn't remember what was inside them.' For reasons stemming from her almost total absence of visual imagery she gave up medical studies for another career. The other end of the visual imagery scale is represented by a man who had unusual advantages in biological science from his imagery.

Professionally he was a pathologist, and he found that he was able to 'go over' the post-mortems of the day and 'notice' detail he had overlooked at the time; this he was able to accomplish at home afterwards from his unusually stable and vivid visual imagery.

Memory and imagination images should not be confused with those aftermaths of perception known as 'after-sensations' (sometimes called 'after-images') which were discussed in Chapter 2. At an early date one of the pioneers of modern psychology, Fechner (1801–87), who was interested in both after-sensations and mental images, differentiated the two in some detail. William James (1890) subsequently pointed out another difference. It is possible to change the size of after-sensations by projection; if projected on to a distant screen they appear larger, while if projected on to a near one they appear smaller. James added: 'No such change takes place in mental pictures.' Fechner's interest in mental imagery proper has often passed unnoticed. He noted wide individual differences of imagery and added, 'It would be interesting to work up the subject statistically' (James, 1890). It was, however, left to a later investigator to take up this field and this suggested approach. The first major study of mental imagery variations was that of Sir Francis Galton (1822–1911), and his book of 1883 still represents the best introduction. (See also selections from Galton in Semeonoff, 1966.) He sought to introduce quantification into this field, and following a questionnaire investigation placed reports of imagery on a 100-point scale of vividness. This scale embraced three larger categories in which the 'faculty' was high, mediocre, and low. At the top end of the scale were subjects who described their imagery as possessing a vividness and clarity comparable to that of the original percept. Others, at the lower end of the scale, described their capacity for imagery as 'zero' or 'non-existent'. These studies revealed enormous variations not only in the dimension of vividness, but also – in the case of visual imagery – in colour and capacity for dimensional visualization. There were, moreover, great variations in the relative strength and predominance of the different sense modes.

Galton has often been accused of introducing an imagery

typology: the division of people into visiles, audiles, and motiles; but this typology was a later development for which he was not responsible. It probably dates from the year 1886 and a book review in the journal *Mind*, in which J. Jacobs wrote, while reviewing a book by Alfred Binet, 'This division of men into visiles, audiles, motiles and indifferents, as we may respectively call them, is of great interest and importance.' This grossly oversimplifying typology has, on the contrary, been a serious impediment to subsequent thought and research. Burt (1949) has criticized this 'theory of imaginal types', and the period during which children and adults were wrongly thought to be classifiable into sharply separated groups. He writes that the 'so-called mental types are not clear-cut classes; they are extreme instances of minor tendencies which may vary in almost every degree'. Galton was far too careful an investigator, and too subtle a thinker, to make this mistake, which represents too crude a formulation to embrace the variations of imagery he himself found. As Burt has subsequently shown, there is not an inverse relation between vividness of one kind of imagery and vividness of others. Factorial studies have shown a positive, not an inverse relation: a general factor 'for vividness of imagery of every kind'. Nor is vividness the only dimension of interest in relation to mental imagery. Elsewhere I have tried to show the complexity of the relation between imagery and thought by examination of one particular case, a linguist interested in pronunciation of the spoken word. In this instance composite imagery, and the well-integrated use of visual imagery (e.g. phonetic script), auditory imagery, and motor imagery (imagined movement of tongue and speech organs), played their part in disciplined thought (McKellar, 1965). Variations of imagery, and their relations to occupation, can involve more complex phenomena than we may at first envisage.

As regards general trends, rather than specific cases, I have elsewhere (McKellar, 1965) reported on a study of three dimensions of imagery variation; these variations render meaningless any attempt at a single typology. People may differ in range of imagery, predominant kind of imagery, and relative strength of imagery. In terms of range or repertoire of available imagery, of a group of 500 subjects (representing a variety of occupations) 97 per cent reported having visual imagery available to them; 92 per cent reported availability of auditory imagery also. More than half the subjects had a range of imagery which included movement, touch, taste, smell, and pain, and nearly half had imagery for temperature as well. In terms of predominant kind – that is the imagery most relied on in thinking, remembering, and imagining – as we might expect, the visual mode tended to be the most common. Of the subjects 83 per cent reported this, while 26 per cent reported predominance of auditory imagery. Among the 500 people studied there were none in whom the other kinds of imagery predominated. In other investigations I have encountered such individuals, for example, some for whom taste and smell were predominant modes. It is a problem for future research whether other kinds of imagery predominance are highly represented in certain occupations: tea and wine tasting and perfume chemistry are obvious examples. And perhaps, among athletes, motor imagery might achieve predominance. On the other hand these other forms of imagery were readily available to a large proportion of the subjects, sometimes being available with reasonable strength and vividness. The third aspect investigated was vividness. It is, for example, possible for a person's imagery range to embrace a number of image modes, but such imagery to be available only in weak and fragmentary form. To illustrate from a psychologist who has worked intensively in this field, T. H. Pear says of himself, 'My world of memory is nearly always silent'; he adds that his auditory imagery, though not absent, is of but slight intensity. With this may be contrasted one of my subjects – who is incidentally bereft of visual imagery – who describes his auditory imagery as 'almost phonetic'. This enables him to image music 'as detailed as the original performance . . . sometimes so loud as to "roar" and "deafen"'. To turn from illustration to quantification: of my 500 subjects 86 per cent reported visual and 69 per cent reported auditory imagery as either 'strong' or 'reasonably strong'. Ratings of the other modes were 32 per cent for movement and touch, 25 per cent for smell, 22 per cent for taste, 16 per cent for pain, and 10 per cent for temperature.

The dimensions studied represent only three of the ways in which imagery can vary. Aspects like controlled *v.* autonomous imagery, flexibility, and – in the case of visual imagery – colour and dimensionality were not given detailed investigation. Yet even in terms of the above data we cannot readily speak of visiles, audiles, and motiles. A given person may have good imagery in all three modes, and in terms of predominant kind the 'motile' imager did not exist at all within the sample of 500 people studied. Good imagery in one mode tends to be directly rather than inversely related to goodness of imagery in others. Moreover facility in moving easily, and appropriately, from one image mode to another may be very much more important in effective thinking than mere vividness of imagery. Rather than to attempt to type people it seems better to look at the imagery of a person in terms of a profile of traits including the traits of range, predominance, and relative strength.

AUTONOMOUS AND CONTROLLED IMAGERY

Faced with the diversity of imagery phenomena it is desirable to attempt some form of classification, for example in terms of the predominance of one or other kind of image mode, or in terms of strength and stability of the imagery. A third, and rather fundamental, basis of classifying imagery may be made in terms of a distinction suggested by Gordon (1962) between 'autonomous' and 'controlled' imagery. Autonomous images occur and depart without the volition of their author, and their content is something over which he lacks voluntary control. Such imagery is typical of dreams, and also of the hypnagogic state. Thus one of the subjects of Galton's earlier study in relation to his own hypnagogic imaging described himself as 'a mere spectator' and 'in no way concerned with the getting-up of the performance'. Controlled imagery is called up, dismissed, and manipulated by the imager himself. Some individuals are able to make considerable use of controlled imagery in their waking thinking, though such imagery appears to be rare in dreaming. An illustration of its use in wakefulness may be taken from one subject, a keen photographer who reports ability 'to visualize the finished product at which I am working' and being thus able 'to manipulate the variables under my control – lighting, viewpoint, exposure, and development -- in order to secure the nearest possible approach to the ideal'.

Both autonomous and controlled imagery may play their part in the creation of socially valued thought products. Thus we have seen, in the realm of science, how Kekulé used his autonomously occurring hypnagogicimagery as subject matter for the benzene-ring concept which heralded a major advance in organic chemistry. In art we find many instances of the use of dreams or other autonomous imagery as raw materials, an illustration being Max Ernst, who employed hypnagogic imagery in his surrealist paintings. Agnew's investigations (1922) of auditory imagery in connexion with music throw further light upon Gordon's distinction. Agnew's subjects were 200 musicians belonging to a music teachers' association, and she also used biographical material about the great composers. In terms both of strength and also control of their imagery, the music teachers proved superior to a group taken from the general population. They were also superior to a second control group used, consisting of professional psychologists. Among the subjects was one – a psychologist, not a musician – whose difficulties in performing some of the tasks set by Agnew illustrate the relevance of autonomy and control of imagery to the occupational issue. Agnew required him to form an auditory image of a piano playing a particular tune. He failed, and his failure is instructive. He reported being able to form an auditory-motor image of his own voice singing the tune. Moreover he was twice able to seat people at the piano in his mind's eye but 'I could not get the faintest image of a piano note'! Information of a biographical kind revealed that some of the composers had considerable control over their imagery. Others used autonomous imagery: thus Berlioz often composed from his dream imagery, and Wagner at least once used hypnagogic imagery as source material.

As we saw in the previous chapter, autonomous imagery is very characteristic not only of dreaming and the hypnagogic state, but also of the kinds of imaging that occur in hallucinogenic and sensory deprivation experiments. It is likewise typical of the kinds of imaging we call hallucination. An understanding of the autonomous processes that occur spontaneously in the normal, or that can be experimentally produced in normal subjects by appropriate techniques, may assist normal people to empathize more completely with the strongly autonomous happenings in the mental life of the psychotic.

HALLUCINATION

A sharp distinction between mental imagery and hallucination is not, in practice, always easy to draw. Thus Galton was led by his researches to write: 'I have a sufficient variety of cases to prove the continuity between all forms of visualization, beginning with an almost total absence of it, and ending with a complete hallucination.' Hallucination, whether visual, auditory, or of some other kind, is traditionally associated with mental abnormality. This is a misconception. Obviously visual hallucination, and less readily hallucination of other kinds, can be experimentally produced in normal people with hallucinogenic drugs or other appropriate agents. Moreover one very large investigation 'The Census of Hallucinations', showed that just under 10 per cent of the thousands of people studied had experienced at least one hallucination during their lives. This figure explicitly excludes hypnagogic phenomena and others of a marginal kind that we might be tempted to classify as hallucination (Sidgwick, 1894).

A small investigation of my own on a group of 500 normal people found no fewer than 125 who had experienced a hallucination. Some of the visual hallucinations related to early life, and some had religious content, for example 'seeing an angel in church during the service', and 'in early adolescence I saw God (conventional white robed man with beard) . . . and the devil, equally conventional'. Others were auditory, frequently of voices speaking and one of 'sounds of a dog known to be dead'. Tactile hallucinations, for example 'feeling a tap on the shoulder' were also reported by some subjects, together with hallucination of smell, such as the 'smell of food cooking when nothing to account for it'. One interesting category noted earlier is motoring hallucinations, sometimes visual, but also auditory, as when one fatigued motorist 'heard' his companion speak when nothing had in fact been said.

Of particular interest, whether they occur spontaneously to normal people or to psychotics, are hallucinations of probable as opposed to improbable events. Thus one subject hallucinated an aeroplane crash, and many hallucinated speech from people who had said nothing. One recovered psychotic patient, Lang, has written about such hallucinations in detail. Thus on one occasion Lang, while playing cards, heard his partner bid three clubs. It is obviously extremely difficult, even when a patient has insight into the fact that he is hallucinated, to retain this insight in such instances, which obviously may be very disruptive of personal relations. In this connexion, from hallucination proper may be distinguished what is sometimes called 'pseudo-hallucination'. This involves a projected perceptual-like image, but one in which the person concerned recognizes the subjective nature of the occurrence. If this distinction is made, pseudo-hallucination is extremely common in experiments with hallucinogenic drugs. Also common in such experiments is what might be called 'hallucinatory movement of stationary objects'. For example an object may move, may pulsate around its normal shape, may seem to 'melt and drip like dripping wax', or be seen as though through a pool of rippling water. Another category of what a psychologist might call 'hallucination' is not assessed as such by the subject, who may interpret it as an apparition, a ghost of some deceased person, or otherwise supernaturally. Many phenomena, including what we might prefer to call hypnopompic and hypnagogic imagery, or hallucinations, are on occasion given such interpretation by a subject with appropriate beliefs. Of interest is the fact that we also encounter remarkably similar phenomena in people who have different beliefs, and who thus prefer to interpret them naturalistically.

Two rare forms of hallucination may be noted. One of these is the autoscopic hallucination in which the subject 'sees' himself. Such hallucinations seem to occur on occasion to normal people under conditions of extreme stress. Rawcliffe (1952) gives the case of a tank officer blown up by a mine who became conscious of floating through the air while looking down at his own body lying injured. This hallucination represents an instance of a perceptualization of the man's realization of what had happened to him. The second type of rare hallucination to be noted is negative as opposed to positive hallucination, in which the subject omits from his perception some aspect of the environment which is perceptually present. Negative hallucinations appear to be uncommon among hallucinations of both a spontaneously occurring and an experimentally produced kind. Two instances of negative hallucination are reported by Steinberg (1956) from her experiments with nitrous oxide. Following administration of the gas in one of these cases, 'the surface of the table at which the subject was sitting disappeared, and only the pencil and paper remained, "suspended in mid air".' Later the same person experienced another negative hallucination. A third person was standing in the room during the experiment, and the subject reported that 'only a pair of legs remained; the upper part of the body had disappeared, and the wall was visible behind'. It is, however, in experiments involving the state of hypnosis that we are most likely to encounter negative hallucination. The five stamps experiment discussed in Chapter 2 exemplifies hypnotically induced experiences of this kind. Two other instances may be noted. In one of these (reported by Dorcus, 1956) a conditioned response was established in the subject to the lighting up of a lamp. The conditioned response failed to occur when hypnotic blindness to the lighted lamp was induced. An auditory equivalent of this was contributed by Erickson (1938), when a conditioned withdrawal response was established to the sound of a buzzer. The two subjects used were then given the hypnotic suggestion that they had become deaf; their conditioned withdrawal responses ceased, but returned when the hypnotic deafness was removed.

In the five stamps experiment we noted that more perceptual activity seemed to be going on than the subject was consciously aware of: we may, if we like, say that the subject was exhibiting subconscious perceptual activity as well as perceiving consciously. Morton Prince sought to explain hallucination along somewhat similar lines, as involving an emergence into consciousness of imagery belonging to 'subconscious thought'. As Morton Prince conceived it, two streams of thinking are going on at the same time, and some of the imagery from the second stream enters consciousness in the form of hallucinatory activity. An idea formulated by Stekel may help in the understanding of this aspect of hallucination. As Stekel puts it, 'We never have single thoughts but always many, an entire polyphony of which speech expresses but one melody; the other voices and the counterpoint remain hidden.' Sometimes we are introspectively aware of concurrent trains of thought, which may suddenly surprise us by their intrusions into the focus of conscious attention in the form of imagery. We may be able to notice secondary processes which intrude as imagery. This type of intrusion seems to occur in visual hypnagogic imagery in which we unexpectedly become aware of images which seem quite unrelated to what we have been thinking about. On the whole it remains difficult for the normal person to empathize with the psychotic in his hallucinations. But the normal person may find the beginnings of an understanding in his introspective awareness of how his own thought products can emerge unexpectedly, and even surprise him by their content.

EIDETIC IMAGERY

Imagery of an unusually vivid and stable kind, which may on occasion submit itself to being projected by the imager into his environment, has been called eidetic. True eidetic imagery is assessed as rare in adults, but provides us with a label we can extend or make specific in accord with our preferences. Although Galton observed the phenomena, important researches and the name 'eidetic' are associated with E. R. Jaensch. Jaensch contended that 'rudimentary forms of eidetic imagery could be found to exist in most, probably all, children'. Later investigators such as Peck and Hodges, confirm Jaensch's estimate of incidence at about 60 per cent of children, and about 6 per cent of adults. Illustrations of such imagery can be taken from the researches of Klüver, who with one subject exposed a picture for 30 seconds: it showed a small Negro boy taking refuge in a tree from a crocodile. From his image alone the subject was able to give the number of teeth in the crocodile's mouth, an exceedingly minute detail in the picture shown. Another of Klüver's subjects, three months after being shown a picture for 30 seconds, was able to put up a quite remarkable performance from his image. The original included three dogs, and various human figures. Three months later the subject was able to report correctly such things as that the dog on the left had its mouth open, and that only two of the dogs had collars. It must be stressed that eidetic imagery is not invariably correct in its reproductions, and may share with other imagery the quality of providing vivid but inaccurate detail.

Eidetic imagery is not always visual. Thus for example the psychologist Titchener appears to have had auditory imagery of this kind: he could never settle down to think or read without an accompaniment of musical sound in which, he tells us, 'the woodwind instruments predominated'. It is a matter of definition what we are, and are not, prepared to call eidetic imagery. Many people when questioned assert their ability to 'read' from their imagery of the printed pages of books: this ability is certainly reported as commoner than would be suggested by the usually accepted incidence of the rarity of adult eidetic imagery. Vivid imagery falling short of the eidetic is not uncommon, and is often of value to the person concerned in a variety of ways. Thus one subject, an engineer, who is representative of many, reports his ability to 'draw a diagram and sometimes form a working model and watch it' in his imagery. Many artists use their unusually vivid and stable imagery, and one, representative of several, reports 'I often work from images which just appear without any attempt to call any image up . . . often in the form of a complete painting or sculpture.' Not all visual artists appear to work in this way, though some do seem to use this method, elegantly expressed by a child reported by Roger Fry as describing his way of drawing in these terms: 'First I think, and then I draws a line round my thinks'!

Another category of vivid imagers are those who are able to 'turn on' their auditory imagery when they need it. A representative case is the person who said, 'I often "hear" music and frequently alleviate boredom by "playing" an opera record with my mind's ear.' There is also the case of Charles Hamilton, better known as 'Frank Richards' – the creator of Billy Bunter and Greyfriars School – who used his own visual and auditory imagery to play games of chess with himself while engaged in long and boring conferences with an unusually talkative publisher. A former colleague, a physics lecturer, told me of how when at school he and a similarly gifted pupil used regularly to play games of chess on an imaged board which they projected on to the school blackboard in class. When I tested him as an adult he proved capable of manipulating his imagery sufficiently to play a game of 'fox and geese' through imagery alone. Eventually when his opponent got lost and withdrew he was able to give correctly the position on the board of all the pieces. Many people prove, on investigation, capable of playing through imagery at least a simpler game like noughts and crosses, though imagery chess seems to require the eidetic or near-eidetic imager.

VERBAL IMAGERY

Some individuals assert that words either play an important part in their thinking or replace imagery altogether. Thus one leading psychologist, Sir Cyril Burt, describes his own mental life as 'like a broadcast debate, with the voices of conscience, my friends and myself, all arguing together in the twilight'. Burt reports that his verbal imagery is auditory, that he 'hears' these words. The concept of 'verbal imagery' may be misleading if we do not take account of its ambiguity. Some people, like Burt, use auditory imagery. Others mentally visualize such words, and these visualizations may vary a lot among themselves: in print, in one's own handwriting, and in colour. Others again have motor imagery of themselves speaking the words, or motor imagery of other kinds; for example, 'my fingers mentally type them out'. One verbalizer, whose imagery is auditory, reports a voice which accompanies his thinking and writing; he adds that if the reasoning becomes difficult the voice becomes 'a vague muttering'. There are others again who deny that the words through which they think, remember, and imagine are imaged at all. As one such person puts it: 'I find my words rising mysteriously from some dark filing system, in groups or singly: a little unnerving when I do not really know where or how they come.' As we can see, people differ in the extent to which words play a part in their mental life, and the term 'verbal imagery' covers a variety of different forms.

IMAGERY VARIATIONS

Certain variants of imagery such as those of the hypnagogic, hypnopompic, and eidetic kinds have been noted. Mention has also been made of synaesthesia, in which a perceptual experience in one sense department is accompanied by imagery in another (Chapter 2). These represent only a few of the many variations of mental imagery to which some people are subject. Among the phenomena to which Galton drew attention were number forms, and in 1880 he wrote an article in *Nature* about them giving several illustrations. This led to an influx of correspondence from number-formers; thus one science master at Cheltenham College sent Galton a detailed account of his own case, and of other cases from among his pupils. Number forms comprise a regular tendency to think of numbers through imagery in some spatially arranged way. Sometimes these regular imaged forms are three-dimensional, and they may also be coloured. Galton (1883) reproduces many instances of diagrams drawn by number-formers of their own imagery idiosyncrasy. Thus one of his subjects always mentally 'saw' numbers 'in the shape of a horse-shoe', another reported that numbers 'from 1 to 20 lie on a level plane, but from 20 they slope up to 100 at an angle of about 25 degrees', while others imaged numbers with different combinations of lines and curves. It also emerged that there are people who experience date forms: similar spatial visual imagery of a regular kind for dates, and the passage of time. At a later date the psychologist Pear suggested the generic term 'diagram forms' for number forms, date forms, and other such phenomena. Members of this general category mentioned by Pear are imaged forms for algebra, piano notes, and the Ten Commandments. One of his subjects reported no fewer than 30 diagram forms of different kinds. Some of these can be of considerable complexity. Investigators differ slightly in the incidence they give for diagram forms. Pear (1922) found an incidence of 6·7 per cent in a group of 525 people he questioned. My own researches (McKellar, 1957) place the incidence at 7·69 per cent. Certain of the aspects of diagram-forming that relate to time are discussed in Chapter 6.

Very much commoner than number forms are the experiences that have been called colour associations. My own studies suggest their occurrence in about 20 per cent of people. In these there is a strong tendency to associate colour imagery with numbers, days of the week, months of the year, names, or other things. Colour associations, in my own subjects, proved to be commonest for months of the year and days of the week. They also occurred for numbers, names, seasons, and letters of the alphabet. There was a marked sex difference, the experience being considerably more common in women than in men. Colour associations can give rise to some interesting difficulties of communication. An example was provided by a correspondent to the *Listener* (11 April 1963) who explained that he had always associated numbers with colours. Thus '10', for example, was a deep rust colour, 'the colour of strong tea'. This writer reported the difficulties he encountered when he attempted to communicate with others in these terms. Thus he remembered telling somebody at the age of six that his brother 'liked "ten tea"', and also the exasperation of being accused of talking nonsense! The most important thing about these variations of mental life is the fact that some people have them and others do not. Only too readily can perfectly innocent variants of normal subjective experience give rise to intolerance, reproof, and a sense of guilt and isolation. Thus from the standpoint of mental health it is important that we recognize them, name them when they lack names, and insist that they are variants of the normal.

LATER INVESTIGATIONS OF IMAGERY

Following Galton, many psychologists devoted themselves to the task of developing 'objective' tests of imagery. Thus some compared learning by ear with learning by eye, in this way hoping to establish differences between visual and auditory imagers. Others used a distraction method, assuming that the visual imager would be more affected by visual distractions, the auditory by auditory distractions. Others again used designs which the subject was required to look at and later copy. In his *Experimental Psychology* Robert Woodworth has provided an interesting summary of these attempts, and their repeated failure, of which he says, 'The causes of their break-down furnish a valuable psychological study'. One source of difficulty has been the assumption that vividness of imagery matters most: for certain purposes other attributes of imagery such as range and flexibility may be more important. Another difficulty has stemmed from the very great interest which Galton himself showed, and encouraged others to show, in relations of imagery to remembering. A distinction should perhaps be made between memory imagery and thinking imagery: good imagery – for example of a visual kind – as regards recall and reproduction is not itself a guarantee of good imagery of a kind that can be manipulated in a task of eductive thinking. This distinction between mere reproduction and thinking is of importance if we are going to correlate introspective reports of goodness of imagery with performance in tasks involving spatial performance. We need to correlate:

(a) verbal reports of goodness of visual recall with performance in tasks of visual recall;

(b) verbal reports of goodness of visual reasoning with performance in tasks of visual reasoning.

Earlier investigators sometimes made the mistake of attempting to correlate items under (a) with items under (b), for example introspective reports of goodness of recall with performance in tasks of visual reasoning. There is no particular reason why such correlations should be high. To illustrate: on one occasion I was with a 'good visualizer' who looked into a shop window and saw a dress which she liked, and declared her intention to make for herself. I suggested making a sketch, but she said this was not necessary: her memory imagery was quite adequate. The same person – who was undoubtedly good at visual remembering – when subsequently asked to manipulate her visual imagery in tasks involving visual reasoning performed badly: she asserted correctly that she was no good at such tasks, but was good at visual remembering. Good capacity for visual reasoning may accompany good visual remembering, but does not necessarily do so.

In 1935 the psychologist A. A. H. El Koussy conducted a research involving administering a number of spatial tasks to male children aged 11 to 13. He found evidence for 'a group factor running through the whole field of spatial perception'. This he called the k-factor, which he said 'receives a ready psychological explanation in terms of visual imagery'. Tasks measuring El Koussy's k-factor included memory for designs, pattern perception, fitting of shapes and similar items. His own interpretation favours the view that the k-factor involves the ability to utilize spatial imagery. The history of the k-factor since this date has been complex, and contradictory findings have emerged. In this field it would seem important not only to keep in mind differences between spatial thinking and spatial remembering, but also the strong evidence that has emerged that short-term memory and long-term memory seem to operate differently. A leading American investigator, J. P. Guilford, has found evidence for factors comprising visual and auditory remembering, and these Guilford explicitly relates to the early imagery studies of Galton. Such factors correspond to item (a) above, and its equivalent in the auditory field. It may be argued that they do not necessarily involve visual and auditory reasoning. Of interest is the work of P. E. Barratt (1953), who has provided evidence of the composite character of capacity for visualization. He administered twenty-three spatial tasks and obtained from his subjects ratings of the extent to which the tasks involved visual imagery. Three factors emerged from subsequent mathematical treatment of the results, these being a factor of spatial manipulation, a factor of shape recognition, and a factor of spatial reasoning. Spatial manipulation involved capacity to manipulate visually and was found to involve visual imagery more than the other tasks (it seems to resemble (b) above). Studies of this factorial kind may help to elucidate some of the problems involved in relating subjective assessments of visual and other kinds of imagery with performance in actual tasks.

Thinking and remembering and imagining may all involve somewhat different components of imagery. Imagery in its relation more especially to imagining has been studied in detail at the City University of New York by Singer and Antrobus (1963). They found 'daydreaming' to be composite, and report seven distinct patterns from their factorial studies. Among these components are frequency of daydreaming, self-recriminatory daydreaming, objective reflection about inner experience, neurotic and egocentric fantasy, and autistic daydreaming. In terms of relations of imagery to imagining, in the sense of waking fantasy, a person may score highly on one of these variables without scoring highly on others. There is good evidence for the view that the word 'imagining', like the words 'thinking' and 'remembering', is commonly applied to not one but a number of different processes. This evidence is of distinct importance to the future progress of imagery research.

One important line of investigation is the pursuit of physiological or otherwise objectively recordable accompaniments of imagery. In 1943 Golla, Hutton, and Grey Walter began studies of relations between imagery and the electrical rhythm of the brain as recorded by the electroencephalogram (or E.E.G.). Such studies have continued into recent years in relation to both sleeping and waking imagery. We have already noted the discovery in 1953 by Aserinsky and Kleitman of characteristic eye movements or REMS which occur during sleep and appear to accompany dreaming. As early as 1903 C. S. Moore had sought to relate eye movements to waking imagery, but he was limited by having to base his observations on the movement of the pupil against the closed eyelid. Development of the dream REM technique by Kleitman and his associates provided better techniques. These allowed actual recording of both horizontal and vertical eye movements, accompanying EEG measurements, together with recordings of changes of muscle potential. Now emerged the possibility of using the REM and associated techniques in the study of waking imagery. Thus in 1964 Singer, working with John and Judith Antrobus, turned to studies of eye movements both during daydreaming itself and following the instruction to break off a daydream. They found that increased recordable

REMs accompanied breaking off having an image. The eye movements were increased by the instruction to engage in acts of hard thinking as opposed to passive fantasy. In general the REMs were more marked with closed than with open eyes. There were extremely well defined, and recordable, eye movements accompanying tasks of following moving objects in imagery. One such task involved visualizing and following the movements of a game of tennis seen from the net.

These investigators were thus able to apply the REM technique to the study of what Singer calls 'internalized forms of looking behaviour'. His view of visual imaging is that overt responses are 'miniaturized' and overt eye movements are 'gradually reduced to brief spurts of horizontal or vertical eye movements' (Singer, 1966). The techniques of Singer, Antrobus, and Antrobus and their findings merit attention. They seem to point the way to powerful techniques for the study of the otherwise 'subjective' processes of imagery in waking thinking and daydreaming. The subjects were fitted with horizontal and vertical electrical ocularogram recording apparatus, and in the course of time they habituated to these electrodes above, and to the side of, their eyes. In the first period they were merely instructed to keep their eyes open and lie in a relaxed position. Later, as time passed, they were questioned in detail about their thinking and perceptual activity. Answers were tape-recorded, and the recorded introspections were rated by independent judges. In the second period subjects were asked to image scenes, make arithmetical calculations, and perform other tasks. Thirdly they were asked to engage in a daydream involving the fulfilment of a secret wish, 'one you haven't told people'. Fourthly they were asked to begin a daydream, and then suppress it as if they were attempting to prevent someone from reading their thoughts. It will be remembered that in dream studies with the REM technique it is the occurrence of dreams that tends to be associated with the REM periods. In these studies of wakefulness the investigators found that visual imaging was associated with minimal eye movement, while attention to external perceptual details was associated with much more ocular motility (Singer, 1966). Of particular interest are the tasks involving suppression of fantasy, at which times eye movements were extremely numerous. By contrast, during daydreams about their secret wishes, very little eye movement occurred. These results on the whole contrast with those found on sleeping persons. Of interest in this connexion is a finding by Judith Antrobus – who has also been interested in conventional dreaming and REMs – that persistent non-recallers of dreams showed more REMs than did frequent recallers (Antrobus, 1962). Thus there seems to be reason to associate recordable REM activity with processes of the suppression and inhibition kind. Perhaps more important than any specific findings is the development of the REM technique itself, and the exploration of its possibilities for the study of imagery in thinking, controlled imaging, and free fantasy. The REM technique which has contributed so much to the understanding of dreaming is likely to have much to contribute to our knowledge of waking imagery, in the various forms in which it occurs.

A different line of research which looks very promising is less concerned with the recordable accompaniments of imagery than with its recordable effects on behaviour. In this connexion we encounter the phenomenon of mental practice. Mental practice is defined by Richardson (1965) as 'the symbolic rehearsal of a physical activity in the absence of any gross muscular movements'. It is exemplified in athletic training in which the athlete is instructed by his coach to think over the movements before performing them. In 1939 Perry investigated the possibilities of improving physical performance in a series of standard tasks, by requiring his subjects to think through the appropriate actions. He obtained positive results. Further work by Vandell, Davis, and Clugston (1943) may be taken to illustrate the method. Three groups of schoolboys were used, the task used being basketball throwing. Group 1 were given no practice, but after twenty days showed a 2 per cent improvement. Group 2 were practised in ball throwing and achieved a 41 per cent improvement after twenty days. The third group were given no overt practice, but were required to 'practise' by imagining themselves carrying out the tasks during the intervening days: this group showed a 43 per cent improvement. A subsequent study by Start and

Richardson (1965) provided evidence that the greatest improvement in a mentally practised task occurred with subjects who possessed imagery which was both vivid and controlled. The least improvement occurred in subjects who possessed vivid, uncontrolled imagery. Richardson, who makes explicit reference elsewhere to Gordon's distinction between controlled and autonomous (uncontrolled) imagery, and to Gordon's test for measuring this, thus supports the notion that this variable as well as mere vividness of imagery may be of importance. Richardson (1965) has developed the theory that capacity to form images of the required movements may be a central feature of mental practice, a phenomenon which – whatever its theoretical explanation – appears to have been effectively demonstrated. He suggests lines of future research in this field. Thus is spaced mental practice more effective than massed practice, or is mental practice with intervening periods of overt physical practice the best strategy for achieving optimum results?

Another line of research concerns the influences of imagery upon perception. Work on this problem has emerged under the influence of the tradition established by Uznadze in Georgia. As was noted in a previous chapter this tradition has been concerned with the influences of set on perception, as when for example wooden balls of equal size are perceived as unequal because of previously established sets. Natadze (1960) extended this study into imagery, arguing that human beings have an ability 'to act not only in conformity with an actual situation but an imaginary one as well'. Thus, in a modification of the wooden balls experiment, the subject was required to imagine himself holding two balls of unequal size. This imaging task was repeated fifteen times. Then two balls of equal size were actually put into his hands: a majority of the subjects experienced the contrast illusion, in this case as a result of contrast between the previously imaged experience and the present perceptual one. Natadze confirmed his finding that previous imagery can in this way affect perception with other tactile and kinaesthetic tasks involving size and weight. Together with the discovery of the phenomenon of mental practice through the apparent use of imagery, what might be called the 'Natadze phenomenon' – the influence of imagery on perception and judgement – opens up further lines of interesting research in this field.

Of interest in the experimental study of visual imagery of the autonomous kind are photopic stimulation images. The phenomena were discovered in 1823 by J. E. Purkinje, and have been intensively studied in more recent years by Smythies (1959, 1959a, 1960). Conditions for their investigation involve an intermittently flashing light (a stroboscope may be used) which is projected from the back on to a ground glass screen. Subjects sitting in front of such a screen see, of course, complex patterns as a result of the stroboscopic flashes. They may also experience phenomena strongly reminiscent of the imagery encountered in hypnagogic imagery, or in hallucinogenic or sensory deprivation experiments. Smythies (1959) found certain differences in the phenomena which occurred with stimulation of one as opposed to both eyes. He studied thirty-five subjects using a procedure involving exposure of both eyes, and exposure of each eye separately. Seven different types of phenomena are described by him. These comprised amorphous 'oily swells' of colour, particular small objects (e.g. 'pond life . . . germs under a microscope wriggling madly'), stationary patterns, watery patterns, design patterns (like Victorian wallpaper), animate patterns, and full scenes. Two of the subjects reported a continual stream of fully formed scenes which one – from the odd sequence of the images – described as 'like a badly cut film'. Smythies found that these stroboscopic images differed among individual subjects, and that individual imagery patterns remained stable for the same subject over extended periods of time. He likens the imagery to that encountered in the autonomous visual images of mescaline experiments. A subsequent investigation by Freeman and Marks replicated the Smythies experiments and reveals imagery which ranged from simple lines and dots to objects of the real world and – though in one case only – an integrated scene. These investigators draw attention to the over-all characteristics of the imagery as exhibiting autonomy (in most cases), irrelevance to the thoughts of the subjects, originality, and brief duration. They conclude that these are four of the five characteristics that have been reported in mescaline, hypnagogic, and sensory deprivation imagery. The fifth characteristic, unnatural vividness of colour, was noticeable with some but not all of the subjects. In connexion with this observation it might be stressed that oddities of colour and lighting, though they do occur with some hypnagogic images of the visual kind, are not invariably present (Ardis and McKellar, 1956). It may further be added that the visual imagery of mescaline, to which Freeman and Marks make explicit references, is also remarkably similar to that encountered with LSD on the one hand and psilocybin on the other. The use of stroboscopic experiments to produce these photic stimulation images provides us with yet another technique of research, and a remarkably convenient one at that. Implicit in the work of Smythies is the idea of a close resemblance of the imagery thus produced to the imagery occurring in hallucinogen experiments. Ardis and McKellar have examined in detail the similarity of mescaline and hypnagogic imagery. Freeman and Marks have noted the strong similarities in the imagery occurring in all four types of situation: hypnagogic, sensory deprivation, hallucinogen and stroboscopic. Earlier we noted the form constants to which Klüver drew attention. The recurrence of these form constants in a large variety of circumstances has been noted by Klüver himself (1942), and by subsequent investigators.

THE RETURN OF THE OSTRACIZED

In one very important paper Robert Holt (1964) asks us to envisage a man lying on a bed in a darkened room who 'sees' patterns and geometrical designs followed by animal and human faces. This man exhibits all signs of loss of touch with external reality, and absorption in his fantasy material. What do we as psychologists make of him? Is it the onset of a psychosis? Is he merely a subject in an experiment of either the sensory deprivation or the hallucinogen kind? Or is he a member of that half of mankind who are subject to hypnagogic imagery experiences? Holt draws attention to the extent to which psychology has, until recent years, exhibited ignorance about such phenomena. This, he argues, is not surprising in view of the absence of adequate discussion, or even mention, of such phenomena in standard texts. Nor is it surprising that 'in the jumble of available terminology a few concepts glittered attractively', and in particular the term 'hallucination' came in for 'a great deal of overuse and misuse'. In his paper Holt relates how imagery came to be ostracized from psychology, how there has followed a return of the ostracized in recent years, and why we should examine these processes more carefully. In particular he makes a plea for a more adequate phenomenological study of the realm of mental imagery.

Among the phenomena – he explicitly excludes after-sensations – Holt lists twelve kinds. Among them are dreams, eidetic and hypnagogic images, synaesthesias, thought imagery, hallucination proper, and pseudo-hallucinations (in which the person recognizes the subjective nature of the phenomenon). This list could be amplified. There is, I suspect, some justification for the distinction between hypnagogic and hypnopompic imagery, and there may well be reason – as I have suggested – to distinguish between the kinds of imagery that accompany memory and recall, on the one hand, and those which assist the thinking out of problems. The distinction that Gordon makes between autonomous and controlled imagery may well be a fundamental one that enables us to recognize two major families of imagery. Many additions might be made to Holt's own list of phenomena, but he has himself made an important step in the right direction. To misuse the word 'hallucination', and to extend this word unduly, is a source of confusion, and an impediment to effective communication and research. Perhaps, as Hebb has suggested, thinking will form the central topic of the second phase of the development of scientific psychology. Should this prove to be the case it is both desirable and inevitable that psychologists should themselves become more sophisticated about the terminology they use, and more alerted to the family of phenomena subsumed under the name 'mental imagery'.

CHAPTER FIVE

Remembering and Human Testimony

Remembrance becomes personal mythology.
WILHELM STERN

To establish what happened about a past event may be a matter of extreme difficulty. This difficulty arises not only from forgetting, but also from misremembering: from what Stern called the 'personal mythology' aspect of remembrance. We may be tempted to think of remembering as like the retention of information on a blank sheet in ink which gradually fades – as we forget – with the passage of time. A more appropriate analogy is the one used by Hunter in his book *Memory* in the Pelican Psychology Series. Hunter likens remembering and forgetting rather to a filing system. As new information comes in through sight, hearing, and other perceptual channels, it is stored into appropriate categories; these categories themselves have been built up out of past perceptual experience. This analogy with a filing system may be taken a stage further: in remembering, as in many office filing systems, information may be lost but later found. Moreover, as additional information comes in to be stored, the filing system itself is altered and refined: it becomes necessary to reorganize the file headings, to subdivide categories, and to reclassify.

A process of this kind can be studied introspectively in oneself. Consider, for instance, how when reading a second book on a new subject the earlier book provides a system of knowledge, a frame of reference for both retaining and understanding the new information. Such a system of knowledge, or organization of past experience which provides a kind of mental filing system, has been called a 'schema' by Sir Frederick Bartlett (1932), one of the most important investigators of the memory process. It is in terms of such a scheme that newly perceived information is comprehended and stored. Schemata may be subject to reorganizations, during which the information stored may be lost temporarily or more permanently. And both our schemata themselves, and the information, possess autonomy: they may coalesce, interact, and blot out one another. It is in terms of these processes of internal activity, rather than of passive recording and fading away, that contemporary psychologists tend to view both forgetting and the misrememberings that distort testimony for past events.

REMEMBERING AND PASSAGE OF TIME

Several important relations hold between retention of information and passage of time. Most obvious of these is loss of information, as expressed in a curve of forgetting. Hermann Ebbinghaus (1850–1909) was the important pioneer in this field and, working on himself as subject, contributed the basis of our modern knowledge of the forgetting process. He used as his materials nonsense syllables – three-letter words with two consonants and a vowel between them – and with some 2,000 of these meaningless words he set out to study retention. From experiments on himself with nonsense syllables, he found that approximately half the syllables learned are lost in the first half-hour, two thirds are forgotten in the next eight hours, and four fifths are lost in a month. Certain circumstances delay the forgetting process, such as overlearning. If learning is carried out beyond the point of perfect performance the nonsense syllables or other materials are said to be overlearned. Another circumstance which delays forgetting is the intervention of a period of sleep, which permits the learning to age and consolidate, without interference by new learning. The relation between the ageing of learning and the retention of information is an important one. Two principles concerning this relation were formulated by A. Jost, a student of Ebbinghaus. *Jost's Laws* deal with the superiority of old learning over more recent learning. The laws state that: if two pieces of learning are of the same strength but different ages, (a) the newer learning fades more readily than the older, and (b) further learning activity increases the strength of the older more readily than of the newer. Thus the intervention of sleep, or a rest period is of advantage to retention. It is not only that it permits the learner to rest, but also that it allows consolidation and ageing without interference by new material. Thus numerous standard experiments have shown the superiority of spaced learning – learning with the insertion of rest periods – over massed learning. Such experiments have their practical application to study and other tasks involving learning. If we wish to retain the information it may be better to work for two hours, and then allow a ten- to fifteen-minute rest period, rather than to work continuously for three or four hours. 'A poor memory' is often a matter of bad habits of learning, and in general, better strategies of learning can be adopted by making use of the principle of allowing learning to age without interference. This can be achieved in a variety of ways, as may be seen from the classic experiment of Jenkins and Dallenbach (1924) using sleep, and more recently the work of Summerfield and Steinberg (1957) in which a depressant drug was used to reduce such interference.

It does not inevitably happen that the elapse of time will result in poorer remembering. Researches have revealed an effect of an opposite kind, known as the phenomenon of reminiscence. An introspective account of reminiscence is provided by the remark: 'I didn't remember it before, but I do now.' When reminiscence takes place information not available at time A becomes available later, namely at time B. The phenomenon is well illustrated in an experiment performed by Curran and Schilder (1937) involving what might be called a procedure of 'saturation'. The subjects were required to learn some verbal material, and immediately afterwards to recall it. The first recall was followed by a second, a third, a fourth, and so on until the subject became exhausted or refused to cooperate further. Examination of this series of instances of recall showed the experimenters that they were not dealing with a simple process of fading. Instead they found evidence of reorganizations of the memory traces. Again and again there emerged, in the later recalls, words, phrases, and information not available in the earlier ones. In other words, each recall tended to bring to light different aspects of the original remembering. The experimenters concluded that 'the trace remains constant', and that 'every recall brings different sides of the trace into appearance'.

The experiment of Curran and Schilder, and the phenomenon of reminiscence, are of some importance to testimony in courts of law. In a major case a witness may make a statement to a police officer on the spot, another at the police station soon afterwards, a third in the magistrates' court, and a fourth to a higher court three months or more afterwards. Forgetting may occur, but so also may reminiscence. Honest testimony may be quite wrongly assessed as 'a thought-up story'. Police and legal authorities, and laymen jurists, need to be alerted to the fact of reminiscence and the ways in which it may give rise to discrepancies between different acts of recall.

The process of recalling our own dreams provides us with an introspective awareness of some of the complexities of the remembering. On one occasion we may be aware, on return to wakefulness, of both the fact of having dreamed and the content of the dream. On another we may be aware of dreams 'slipping from memory' during the waking-up process. On a third occasion, on waking we may be quite aware of having dreamed but be unable to recall any of the dream's content. Or yet again we may wake up having forgotten both the fact and the content of a dream, and later some incident during the day will evoke memory for the fact of having dreamed, and perhaps fragments of the content also. Recent researches on the dream associated with Kleitman and Dement, discussed elsewhere, reveal that most human dreams are forgotten, though – as we have seen – such forgetting may be partial and is not necessarily permanent. In all the phenomena that surround remembering and forgetting we find evidence that blocking as well as fading may be important. But from forgetting itself we may now turn to some of the very interesting forms of misremembering that also occur to complicate testimony about past events.

ESTABLISHING THE FACTS ABOUT PAST EVENTS

All 'facts' are perceived facts, and every reported event a re-membered event. Perceiving is, as we have seen, selective in its inclusions and omissions; and remembering, as Stern points out, readily becomes personal mythology. A given human being has a personality which is largely determined by the learning history he has had: this has equipped him with a repertoire of mental sets and schemata that influence his testimony. His acts of remembering can thus become complex blends of fact and imagining or, as H. G. Wells once put it, 'the forceps of our minds are clumsy things and crush the truth a little in the course of taking hold of it'.

Even before Wundt had established the first major psychological laboratory at Leipzig, William James had set aside a small room at Harvard for psychological experiments. In 1892 he invited the German psychologist Hugo Munsterburg to take charge of this, now greatly enlarged, laboratory. Munsterburg represented a different attitude to psychology from that of Wundt and was much interested in practical matters. He has been called, with some justification, 'the father of applied psychology'. And one area of applied psychology that greatly interested Munsterburg was human testimony. Munsterburg's book *On the Witness Stand* lays the foundations of legal and forensic psychology, and in it he relates numerous laboratory experiments designed to throw light on human behaviour in courts of law.

Associated with Munsterburg was Wilhelm Stern, another highly original, and today somewhat neglected, pioneer. Stern, in the early years of this century, brought the processes of rumour and hearsay into the psychological laboratory. This type of experiment has since become traditional and is today known as *serial reproduction*. Stern's own account of his pioneer experiments merit the attention of contemporary investigators (Stern, 1939). A serial reproduction experiment is concerned with the effects of social transmission upon information. The first subject, A, is given material to look at or read; he writes his report and passes this to B; B writes his, and passes it to C, and so on. The material thus transmitted may be either visual or verbal. In one experiment in which I used both, an original that began as a passage of philosophy was by the end of the serial reproduction process a painting of a Bacchanalian revel!

A different type of experiment with which Stern also did important pioneer work is called *repeated reproduction*. For example in one study Stern presented his subjects with pictures and after an interval of forty-five seconds required them to report what they had seen. Later, at intervals of time, they were again and again asked to report on the pictures. Stern thus studied how, with the passage of weeks, errors and misrememberings increased. Repeated reproduction experiments have distinct relevance to human testimony in the witness stand. On a recent occasion in court, I heard one witness being questioned in detail – five months after the events in question – on such subjects as whether the smell of gun-smoke was stronger in the kitchen than in the living-room! But interrogation introduces additional sources of error into memory for past events. Another early investigator, Borst, in 1904 found only 2 per cent of errorless narratives in a series of 250 reports. The percentage of errorless narratives dropped to only 0·5 per cent when question and answer was introduced. Another investigation conducted by Pear and Wyatt in 1914 studied the testimony of children. Their general finding was that such testimony was reasonably reliable only when given spontaneously. This was true with both normal and intellectually subnormal children. And with the children of low intelligence, under interrogation, the number of incorrect replies actually exceeded the number of correct ones.

The processes by which people deceive themselves – the mechanisms of ego-defence – are discussed in a later chapter. Two of these mechanisms, denial and repression, are of importance in selective remembering. Denial represents one important source of omission. It implies not perceiving, and thus not remembering, what one is strongly motivated not to perceive: 'there are none so blind as those who *will* not see.' The word 'see' may be taken to include being selectively blind, selectively deaf, or otherwise imperceptive to information because of contrary motivation. Repression bears the same relation to remembering as denial does to perceiving. It refers to a process of blockage as a result of contrary motivation. Freud in discussing repression points to two situations in which the excuse 'I forgot' is not likely to be accepted: love and war. The soldier must not forget what he is ordered to do; the suitor who tells his beloved that he 'forgot' is likely to be informed – with some heat – that a year ago he would not have done so. In both cases the implication is that the motivation of the offender is faulty, and he is to be blamed for his forgetting. Freud's two concepts provide important linkages between self-deception and the remembering process.

In serial and repeated reproduction experiments we find many instances of denial. But we also find an important source of distortion of testimony in a process of an opposite kind which Bartlett (1932) has called invention: addition of material not in the original. To illustrate, on one occasion I was invited to a formal ball which I did not attend, but I loaned a collar stud to an acquaintance. Later in the evening he and several others called on me, and another member of the party said, 'I hear you loaned x your dress suit.' The process whereby a collar stud becomes – through serial reproduction – a whole suit of clothes nicely illustrates the process of invention. Along with invention, among other aspects of misremembering Bartlett mentions dramatization. There is a tendency for the good story to improve in the telling. Many of the distortions that occur may be summarized in a general principle, stemming from the work of the Gestalt psychologists: the principle of pragnanz. This pervades human remembering no less than human perceiving. It involves a tendency for bias to operate in the direction of the simpler and the stabler, and away from the complex and more unstable. Abbreviation, dramatization, and oversimplification are typical manifestations of the pragnanz principle.

Using the method of repeated reproduction Kay (1955) studied the errors that occurred. These were remarkably persistent. From the first reproduction onwards there emerged a stable form which 'though far from accurate was persistently maintained'. Errors tended to recur in exactly the same form even when, in the experiments, subjects were given opportunity to amend them by re-acquaintance with the original. Bartlett (1932) had been interested in what he called 'unstable items': the items in serial and repeated reproduction tasks most subject to error, omission, and distortion. Proper names, foreign words, and numbers are good examples of unstable items; about these, whether in the psychological laboratory or outside it, human remembering tends to be notoriously unreliable. Also interesting among unstable items are the temporal order of events, and spatial relations, indeed anything about which precise information may be needed. Such information is likely to be of importance in courts of law, for example in motoring cases. The unstable item character of spatial relations may be illustrated from a serial reproduction experiment of my own. The original material was a picture which showed a man in the middle distance and a woman in the foreground. The man had his back to the woman. In this we see the difficulty – which the subjects experienced – of expressing complex spatial relations in words, and of answering questions about them. The description of the woman as being 'behind the man' was, though true in a sense, also misleading. The same experiment also illustrated the principle of pragnanz. In the picture the man was leaning across a team of horses with a ploughed field in front of him. But the concept of 'a man, horses, and a ploughed field but without a plough' – no plough was shown in the picture – is an unstable one. Soon in the serial reproduction process the interpretation 'a man ploughing a field' was made, and all subjects but the first believed there to have been a plough shown in the picture. Inference may give rise to invention, in Bartlett's sense, as in this case. Such an inference was not justified by the picture itself: some other agricultural implement – a disc or a roller – might well have been in use on the ploughed field. But, in the experiment, the subjects invented and interpreted; in brief – following the principle of pragnanz – they went beyond the evidence presented.

SERIAL REPRODUCTION AND EVERYDAY LIFE

Hearsay, taking such forms as rumour, gossip, atrocity stories, and stereotyped misconceptions, represents the process of serial reproduction in daily life. Two leading American psychologists, Allport and Postman, in discussing rumour relate it to two things: the importance of the events to the individuals concerned, and the ambiguity of the evidence. In other words strong emotions (or emotional habits) and ignorance are two factors liable to generate rumour. Both tend to be prominent accompaniments of active warfare. In this connexion of interest is one of the things done by Winston Churchill after becoming Prime Minister during the Second World War. He outlawed hearsay concerning himself. The Chief of the General Staff and the Secretary of the Cabinet were informed very plainly by Churchill that he would accept no responsibility whatsoever for what anybody *said* he wanted done. He indicated that his decisions would always be communicated in writing, and never verbally through others. In making this sensible arrangement Churchill may have been influenced by the rumours which were a prominent feature of the First World War. In the early period of this war, stories swept through allied countries about atrocities committed by Germans against Belgian civilians. At the same time fictitious atrocity stories about what Belgian people were doing to German soldiers were sweeping through Germany! In both cases deliberate propaganda – distortions of the truth and plain lying – seems to have been involved. But the processes of the serial reproduction of everyday life, in an atmosphere of ignorance and strong emotion, also played their part.

One unhappy effect of the fictions of the First World War was the cynicism they had bred in good time for the Second. This cynicism, 'it's all propaganda', assisted self-deceptions of the denial and repression kind. A great many people simply did not believe the incredible cruelties actually perpetrated by the Nazis. Moreover similar ego-defences operated even in the Nazi leaders themselves. In his study of the Nuremberg trial the principal American psychologist who tested and interviewed the accused, G. M. Gilbert, records how these defences were finally penetrated. He reports that some of the accused, when confronted with films and other evidence of what had happened in extermination camps, actually wept in the court room, or shortly after they had left it. One of them covered his eyes, another closed his eyes and looked away, a third blinked his eyes trying to stifle tears, another wept. After the showing of the film one Nazi leader, shaking with sobs, declared: 'No power in heaven or earth will erase this shame from my country: not in generations – not in centuries.' Because denial is such a powerful self-deceptive process it may be, as in this case, difficult to penetrate. For Dachau Camp was not far from Munich, and Ravensbrück was close to Berlin itself. Even among those who had responsibility for the events that happened there and in similar places were many who exhibited the 'blindness' of those who 'will not see'.

In a smaller way, but none the less definitely, serial reproduction and ego-defensive activity contribute their legacy of avoidable suffering in daily life. The prominent place which serial reproduction plays in the outside world may be contrasted with the attempts to exclude it from courts of law. British law is vigilant as regards hearsay evidence. Moreover it proceeds on the principle that innocence exists unless, and until, guilt is proved. The serial reproduction of everyday life operates, at times, on a different principle: guilt is to be presumed until innocence can be established. Lynch law, witchcraft trials – at a time when the law was less careful – and 'witch-hunting' in the various forms it has later assumed are all indications of the need to study, understand, and control everyday serial reproduction. People working close to the law quite often express concern. One leading forensic scientist has expressed to me his opinion that gossip is probably responsible not merely for suffering, but for more actual deaths (suicides) than are 'teenage thugs'. Individuals responsible for malicious gossip are difficult to detect, and, some may feel, penalties following detection are far from adequate. Some examples of the content of everyday serial reproductions of this kind that I have myself collected include accusations of drug addiction, bankruptcy, homosexuality, criminal activities, dismissal from employment for impropriety, and even the practice of black magic, without any foundations in fact. The effects of rumour and gossip of these kinds upon individuals who are victims of it merit study. Accusations can be extremely difficult to disprove, and the 'innocent till proved guilty' principle of the law courts seems a sound one. Difficulties about the alternative 'no smoke without fire' principle are several. Both smoke and fire can be invented; they can also be hallucinated; and serial reproduction can transmute mole hills into substantial mountains.

F

In ordinary speech good stories improve in the telling. Moreover in everyday life people are, to some extent, competing with one another for the attention of their listeners. In this, at times very competitive activity, a speaker is frequently tempted to hold attention in such informal conversations by devices of the 'I know something you don't know' kind. Along with this may go exaggeration and dramatization, together with a certain amount of invention: these are features of serial reproduction in daily life no less than in the laboratory.

In connexion with more formalized systems of communication – such as those involving the press and other mass media – the concept of 'the gatekeeper' has been introduced (Schramm, 1960). Gatekeeper activity is characteristic of certain chains of communication in which a given person has the right to say whether a given message will be recorded and retransmitted. Along this chain may be a series of people who have the right either to open the gate or to close it to any message. This is exemplified in newspapers. The first gatekeeper is the observer himself, equipped as he is with his own tendencies to selective perception; next we encounter the reporter who talks to this source of news; next is the editor who decides whether to publish, and how to slant publication. The process may not be complete even then, as other gatekeepers we know as news agencies may be involved in saying 'yes' or 'no' to the transmission of information from local newspapers to national or international forms of publication. Overall policies and individual personalities may exert their influences in these decisions to transmit, or not to transmit, the information further along the information chain. A kind of gatekeeper function is also to be found, performed by a judge or a magistrate, in courts of law during jury trials, in which the jury may be told which information is to be considered, and which ignored as inadmissible evidence, in coming to their decision. Remarkably little is known about the effect of evidence, which has been 'heard' but officially assessed as inadmissible, upon human judgement in such situations. This is but one of the fields for future research on the frontier between psychology and law.

Courts of law are busy places, and newspapers are limited by available space. The pressures for brevity that result may make for inaccuracy by the omission of essential qualifying phrases. Numbers, time estimations, and any form of quantification represent a major kind of 'unstable item', highly susceptible to omission or distortion. In the case of both courts of law and newspaper reporting, strong influences towards brevity and relevance may greatly impair the accuracy of the communication process. Many people express irritation on reading in the press something they are alleged to have said, because of these omissions and distortions. Similarly, in a small investigation of people who had been witnesses in court, I found many with a deep sense of irritation and frustration. Although aware of having spoken only the truth, they were also aware of not having been allowed to speak the whole truth. Because of this widespread problem – which any individual may unexpectedly find himself having to face – I quote one experienced court witness, a pathologist, and his advice on this matter. If court examination puts a witness in this position it is appropriate for him to say: 'I cannot answer that question, as asked, without misleading the court.' Unless the witness is merely seeking an excuse to be long-winded or irrelevant, the court is likely to react reasonably and allow him to explain his testimony.

One neglected aspect of the serial reproduction of everyday life may now be noted. Man is not the only victim of this process. Other species have, on occasion, become victims of the human tendency, in communication, to confuse fantasy with fact. Some interesting examples relate to the desert country of the American South-west. Here, as elsewhere, many harmless snakes suffer persecution either because they are snakes – and as such are killed on sight – or because of an unfortunate superficial resemblance to some poisonous species. There are, throughout the world, some 2,000 species of snake, and fewer than 200 of these are harmful to a normal, healthy man. But the snake is not alone in this. In Arizona the harmless gecko lizard is frequently killed because it is often mistaken for the young of the gila monster. About the gila monster itself – a poisonous reptile found in the American South-west – there are many inaccurate legends. It does not spit poison, nor is its breath poisonous – though this is widely believed; only its bite is poisonous. And even here we encounter both fiction and fact. The bite of this particular creature is venomous to man provided he is persistent enough to insert his finger into the exceedingly small mouth of the lizard. On the other hand it seems that in this case, as with many other animals, there is much confusion between venom and infection. There is good reason to believe that other factors contributed to the death of some of the thirty or so people recorded as deaths 'because of the bite of the gila monster'.

Perhaps most interesting of all is the case of the American Tarantula spider. The name 'tarantula' originated in southern Italy where in the fifteenth century there occurred an epidemic supposedly resulting from the bite of a particular spider, *Lycosa tarantula*; the victims were affected by convulsions and an irresistible impulse to dance (hence the Neapolitan dance the tarantella). Later on immigrants brought to the New World a fear of spider bites, and the name 'tarantula'. This name they applied to the large, hairy, and ferocious-looking spiders of the family *Aviculariidae*, or 'bird-eating' spiders. These interesting creatures – whose life span is, incidentally, ten to twenty years – inhabit the southern and south-western part of the United States. Their zoological name is itself misleading – they are not bird-eating; and most of the legends about them are even more so. Novelists have contributed to the undeserved reputation of this creature, which fictional villains are wont to put on the chest of the sleeping hero with obvious intent. When I visited the South-west I was anxious to see a tarantula: the creature which, I had been told, springs distances of six feet, and inflicts a bite which causes a long and lingering death. My efforts were at first unsuccessful, and I learned from the head of the adjacent zoology department, 'Sorry, we haven't one at the moment. The last we had went to school with Dr S's children'! The allegedly ferocious killer had in fact gone to school and had been passed round from hand to hand by the children. They are quite often kept by children, and make docile and even affectionate pets. The stories about the American tarantula are mostly products of human imagination, a statement which is supported by detailed study (e.g. Baerg, 1958). Like other wild creatures, the spider will bite if molested. Such bites may of course become infected, and here again we encounter the common confusion between infection and venom. The poison of the tarantula of the United States lies very largely in the reputation given to it by frightened, gossipy man. A plea may be made that animal reputations – as indeed human reputations – should not be accepted on hearsay. Many creatures are needlessly destroyed – and some of them face extermination – for no good reason. The case of the American tarantula affords yet another reason why we should check the facts before we accept hearsay. Bad reputations are easily acquired, and by no means easily lost, because of the serial reproduction of everyday life.

A later chapter will discuss emotions like fear, and emotional habits such as sentiments and prejudices. An attempt to assess the influence of these upon testimony, whether in the court room or elsewhere, is made by Allport and Postman (1947). They point out that distortions are particularly likely to occur, for example in rumour and gossip, when the content of the message is of emotional importance to those who take part in the communication process. Thus serial reproduction may assume aggressive, sexual, sadistic, and wish-fulfilment flavour from the emotional life of the participants. A habitual gossip-monger can project his own envy, jealousy, or unsatisfactory sexual adjustment into his inventions and dramatizations about the doings of other people. In war-time he may project his aggressive and sadistic fantasies on to the enemy. Elsewhere Allport has developed the idea that rumour and gossip perform ego-defensive functions, and protect their author against emotions in himself that would be unacceptable if faced directly. Of particular interest in this connexion is the emotion of indignation, which combines a sense of righteousness with a socially permitted expression of hostility and aggression. This emotion commonly receives expression in the correspondence columns of newspapers in the utterances of advocates of corporal punishment. It was also prominent in newspaper columns at the time of the events in Britain that have come to be called the 'Profumo Affair'. To refer to correspondence of the day, of some interest is a comment by a writer to *The Times* who was impressed by the fact that, for many individuals, 'the contemplation of other people's moral inferiority has an exhilarating effect similar to that of drinking champagne'. But, he added, there is a difference, since champagne's effects are transitory, while 'the satisfied elation produced by condemning other people may be mistaken for the genuine power of goodness'. Since it has also, on occasion, been mistaken for a religious virtue it is appropriate to add that Christianity at least has been both emphatic and persistent in condemning pride and self-righteousness as the opposite of virtue.

In 1938 L. F. Richardson, in a very original paper, produced a theory of mental epidemics. These he likens to epidemics of disease. Richardson was himself primarily interested in the spread of war-fever, and I have discussed his analysis elsewhere (McKellar, 1952). But his concepts also have application to the serial reproductions of everyday life. His idea is that various categories of people interact with one another in this process of flow of unverified information. There are the 'susceptibles': in this instance the gullible people inclined to accept unverified talk. Then there are the 'carriers': the gossip-mongers who habitually pass on the disease as rapidly as possible to the susceptibles they meet. Their influence is minimal on a third category of people, those who are 'resistants' and who thus form barriers to the spread of disease, rumour, or gossip. A fourth category in this interaction are those who have 'acquired immunity', perhaps through contact with victims of the present or of previous epidemics. In the case of rumour they may have acquired their immunity through education, for example experience of war-time notices of the 'careless talk costs lives' sort. Finally on Richardson's analysis – as in my application of it to the serial reproduction of everyday life – there is a fifth category to be considered in the equation, the victims themselves: those who have been injured or have perhaps died as a result of the epidemic. We have seen how such forms of serial reproduction as gossip can result in the unnecessary killing of harmless animals; my forensic informant draws attention to human deaths that can, and do, also occur. We need to study this process, and in the case of rumour and scandal much can be done to check the epidemic by the resistants and those with acquired immunity. These comprise individuals whose values, sentiments, and principles make them prepared to act as barriers to the spread of unverified information.

BIAS AND HUMAN TESTIMONY

In accord with a generalization formulated by A. F. Shand, sentiments like love and hatred, dislike and respect, carry with them their relative ethics. We readily pass adverse moral judgement on those we already dislike, and are equipped with perceptual sets which lead us selectively to notice justification for such judgements. We are selectively perceptive to the vices of enemies, just as we are selectively imperceptive to the faults of friends; we are imperceptive to the virtues of those we dislike, and if there are ethically respectable motives behind their actions tend not to notice them. In these ways bias arising from sentiments can exert influence on testimony in courts of law, influences which fall short of the telling of deliberate lies. Thus a lawyer friend tells me that one of his biggest problems with clients is to prepare them for what they are going to hear in court when witnesses for the other side tell their story. If not prepared in this way the client may find it difficult to resist the impulse to interrupt proceedings as he listens to what seems to him a conglomeration of distortions, half-truths, and downright lies. Thus his own lawyer has to tell him in advance: 'These people will be telling the truth as they believe it to be.' Conflicting witnesses may be equally certain about their evidence. Certainty of conviction may be a comfortable feeling to have, but it is a dubious guide to truth. Thus equally confident but contradictory statements may be made on important issues like the speed of a car. In one such case the numerous witnesses who observed the accident varied in their assessments from 'under 25 m.p.h.' to 'it was doing 70'. Bias is not the only reason for such enormous discrepancies as these. As we have seen, previous events which provide the context, and perhaps such factors as size of the vehicle, may also affect judgement on such occasions.

The influence of values, sentiments, and bias on testimony

may be illustrated from newspaper reporting of certain events that occurred in 1947. The winter of that year saw a fuel crisis which induced the Government to adopt emergency measures including cutting off coal and electricity supplies. Thus more or less everybody was affected, not least the Londoner. As part of a study I made at the time, I attempted an analysis of the leading articles – all were about the crisis – of every available newspaper published in London on one particular day. In general these articles followed closely the political policy of the paper in each case. The extreme Conservative papers blamed the then Labour Government, and demanded the resignation of the Minister of Fuel and Power. Less extreme Right-wing papers merely blamed the Government. Politically central papers tended to the view that, although errors of judgement were involved, the severely cold weather was, in part, unpredictable. One independent Left-wing paper published recipes for meals which didn't have to be cooked, and stressed obligations to make adjustments to the unfortunate realities. An official Labour paper blamed the previous Conservative Government, and the extreme Left blamed the 'capitalist system'! The same events gave rise to a remarkable diversity of newspaper reactions, and estimations of cause: the opinions of individuals studied tended closely to resemble the opinions expressed in their preferred newspaper.

Even when attempts are made to be accurate and careful, serial reproduction effects may not be entirely absent. Thus in a journal article – which, ironically, was about this testimony problem – I once referred to 'the late Dr A.' when the man in question was in fact alive and well. But the rumour of his death – towards which I had myself been gullible – was so widespread that several people had been invited to write his obituary. A striking case concerned a lecturer in biochemistry who was about to lecture to a class of students: for one of his illustrations he had occasion to look up the figure for the percentage of iron in haemoglobin. His textbook gave the figure of ·0335, but his experimental data suggested this couldn't be right. So he omitted reference to it, and after his lecture looked up several other textbooks. The next five also gave the figure ·0335, but the sixth gave ·335, which was, in fact, correct. A systematic study of many textbooks revealed that fewer than half of them were correct. The mistake of the others suggests the serial reproduction process. Perhaps in the act of copying '·335' had become '0·335', and then '·0335'. In this or some other way, presumably some early textbook writer or his printer had invented the unwanted additional 'o' and others had copied the error. The instance reveals two other features of serial reproduction: first, how it is possible to 'confirm' false information, and secondly, that even scientific texts may not be free from errors of this kind. And if they can occur within the context of science, vigilance against such errors in everyday life seems doubly necessary.

A largely underdeveloped area of study awaits the attention of those interested in the frontier dividing psychology and history. Ward (1949) has opened up one such set of problems. He obtained a series of coins dating back to the fourth century B.C., and introduced by Philip of Macedon. During history these had been copied by neighbouring tribes, and the designs spread across Europe through France and Belgium to England. Ward obtained representative coins showing these changes, and conducted experiments employing serial reproduction methods, starting with the originals. The laboratory studies yielded very similar changes by the serial reproduction process to those that had occurred in actual historical transmission.

PERSONALITY AND MEMORY

During one symposium on remembering Neil Miller suggested a small exercise to his hearers. It was to try to remember a number he spoke to them, the number being 149218627231416. Set in this way the task is beyond most people. But, Miller suggested, it becomes easier if the facts that (a) 1492 was the date that Columbus set sail, (b) 186272 is the speed of light, and (c) 31416 is Pi are given. Miller was seeking to illustrate how meaning, and the grouping of data, assist remembering. Let us consider his illustration more fully. The additional information he subsequently provided might well help certain people, but not others: for example an American, with some knowledge of physics, who remembered his geometry. Thus, for a fifteen-digit number I should have myself preferred to remember, for example, 106618483142857, 1066 for obvious reasons, 1848 because I am a New Zealander and that is the date of the founding of the city I was born in, and 3142857 because that was the value of Pi that I learned at school. It is probable that a person who is not an American, an Englishman or a New Zealander, and who is uninterested in geometry and history, would not find it easier to remember either Miller's number or my own. Obviously cultural differences are involved in what it is easy or hard to remember. But in addition, if the human personality can be conceived of as the product of its learning history during its own individual life span, so also are personality differences.

Freud's theory of remembering, and the hypothesis that we tend to forget what is unpleasing to us, have given rise to a great deal of research. For the light it throws upon the influence of personality on remembering much of it has proved inconclusive. But there are other aspects which have been greatly neglected, not least the influence of interest on remembering. As we will see in a later chapter strong pro and con attitudes towards an issue are indications of emotional concern and ego involvement, and not of indifference. Because of this we cannot conclude that a group of atheists and a group of religious people would necessarily differ in their memory for words relating to religion. Both groups, because the issues are of interest to them, might well remember better than a group of people for whom religion is a matter of apathy and indifference. Much experimentation of this kind needs to be done, to establish how and in what ways interests affect the selectivity of human remembering.

A great deal of work has gone in recent years into the study of how 'functional' factors, including personality, emotion, and social norms, affect perceiving. Other investigations have sought to link learning with personality, to show for example that extraverts are slower in conditioning than introverts. Equivalent work on memory largely awaits future research. From the work of Bartlett and others on serial reproduction we know something about 'unstable items', the elements of content most liable to omission or distortion. Very limited is our knowledge of the relation between these and personality differences. Burt (1921) in serial reproduction studies with children distinguished two types of response: 'the positivist', which involved a brief, unadorned précis, and 'the imaginative', involving embellishment, dramatization, and elaboration. These two trends are illustrated in one experiment in which I took part. A group of us sat in a room and watched an interview that was taking place, through a one-way screen. Each observer was then required to write a report on what had occurred. The reports tended to be of two kinds: those we might call descriptive, and those we might call interpretive. Descriptive reporting confined itself to what was observed: it was objective in the sense of being factual and without overtones. Interpretive reporting involved injections of opinion and inference into the testimony, and in general tended to be misleading in that different personalities interpreted differently. Experiments I have conducted with police officers reveal a tendency in them to resist interpretive reporting. There is all the difference in the world between the testimony 'I didn't see it' and the assertion 'it wasn't there'. Similarly courts tend to prefer the testimony 'the car carried an L-plate' to the testimony 'it was a learner driver', as the second inference doesn't necessarily follow from the first observation. The enormous differences between individuals as between descriptive and interpretive remembering, and their relations to measurable personality differences, largely await investigation. They may be illustrated from one testimony experiment in which I showed the subjects an engraving portraying a crowd scene, and after an interval asked for an interpretation of what was going on. Interpretations ranged from 'a riot' and 'an orgy' to 'the reading of the Bible at a prayer meeting'. The picture used was, in fact, a Hogarth engraving of a party conducted before a political election. Yet complex as the picture was it was remarkably simple by contrast with, for example, testimony involving memory about temporal matters of the 'who hit who first' kind. Certain relations between personality and temporal estimation have, however, been established, and will be discussed in the following chapter.

CHAPTER SIX

Adjustment to Time

A day full of excitement is said to pass 'ere we know it'. On the contrary a day full of waiting, of unsatisfied desire for change, will seem a small eternity. WILLIAM JAMES

SOME personalities find it more difficult than others to adjust to reality: psychiatrists and clinical psychologists may be professionally involved in helping them to make these adjustments. What does 'reality' mean in this context? Three of the aspects of adjustment involved would seem to be space, money, and time. Thus not only the psychotic but others also may, on occasion, make dangerous maladjustments to spatial reality, as when a fatigued motorist at night swerves to avoid a hallucinated pedestrian. Again a deluded, intellectually subnormal, or excessively elated patient may allow himself inadequate margins of safety in his dealings with money. Time is the third of these aspects of reality to which adjustments, also involving margins of safety, have to be made. Despite the enormous importance of such adjustments, sometimes even to the individual's survival, very little has been scientifically established. Almost a century of research has yielded remarkably little solid information, and many text-books of psychology, including some of the best, omit all reference to the subject.

One reason for this lack of progress may be stated briefly. The problems of the relations of time to experience and behaviour are extremely complex. They are confusingly difficult, and disarmingly so, in that they often appear to be simple when they are not. The subject is complicated at almost every point both by ambiguous terminology and by the temptation to make assumptions of an unjustified kind. This chapter will discuss three aspects of the psychology of time. First come *subjective phenomena* that we are aware of through introspection; secondly *behavioural phenomena* like, for example, performances in tasks of time estimation;

thirdly there are *social phenomena* which comprise the norms and conventions, and the cultural variations these show, that concern human thinking about time.

SUBJECTIVE PHENOMENA

During a pleasant, interesting day, 'time flies'. When monotony reigns and we are bored, as William James puts it, 'the while seems long'. But here we meet the first of the complexities that surround time: in retrospect these relations are reversed. The enjoyable holiday which felt all too brief in the passing seems, when we look back on it, to have 'lasted an age'. Yet the succession of dull days, during which time dragged, seems, in retrospect to have occupied little time. This reversal in retrospect is only one of several strange phenomena that accompany the subjective experience of time.

Many factors influence our impressions of the passage of time. Anaesthetics and drugs may have the effect of altering the apparent speed at which time passes. Thus Steinberg (1955) in her experiments with nitrous oxide found that, of 40 subjects, 26 reported speeded-up, and 14 reported slowed-down, passage of time. Steinberg, like other investigators, also found that these subjective impressions bear no simple relation to actual performance in tasks of time estimation. In other words it is necessary to distinguish such subjective phenomena of introspection from behavioural performance in such tasks. As we have seen, William James associates the impression of speeded-up time with pleasurable excitement, and slowed-down time with boredom. It does not, however, follow that the slow passage of time is necessarily associated with unpleasantness. Illustration may be taken from one experiment with mescaline in which I acted as subject. This substance resembles nitrous oxide in that it may produce marked disturbances in the impression of passage of time. Some hours after being given the drug the experimenters recorded this introspection: 'Time passes very slowly, and has passed slowly all day – slowly and pleasantly – no need to hurry or worry about anything – plenty of time for it.' At another stage of the experiment the subject communicated his satisfaction at possessing a 'huge reservoir of time'. Such instances as this provide a corrective against the automatic assumption that the illusorily slow passage of time is associated with the unpleasant. Moreover the rapid passage of time may itself be far from pleasant. Perhaps, as Cohen (1958) argues, the hands of the dentist's clock move slowly for us when we are in the dentist's chair. On the other hand, before we entered the surgery the hands of the clock in the same dentist's waiting-room may have seemed to move very fast indeed. This fact is also unpleasing to us. And the association of pain with the slow passage of time, which Cohen assumes, does not necessarily hold. In her book on the psychology of time, Sturt (1925) collated evidence then available from studies with experimentally induced pain, and found no evidence for any such tendency. In fact the reverse seemed to occur: subjects – at least with experimentally induced pain – tended to experience a speeded-up rather than slowed-down passage of time. Relations of subjective impressions of the tempo of time to pleasure on the one hand, and displeasure and pain on the other, seem to be complex, and not simple, as is sometimes supposed.

Passage of time has been the subject of much comment in literature. Rosalind in *As you Like It* notes that 'time travels in divers paces with divers persons', and that it may trot, amble, gallop, and stand still. In everyday life there is little doubt that time can move with exasperating slowness, or quite unreasonable speed. Representative of this awareness is the comment of one rather talkative woman who remarked, 'When I'm on the telephone three minutes is no time! I've never said what I want to say.' Baudelaire called the clock 'a sinister, terrifying, insatiable god'. This wish for liberation from clockwork time was realized in Samuel Butler's *Erewhon*, where the possession of a watch was an offence punishable by imprisonment. Some people never wear watches, and one such person, one of my subjects, when told about *Erewhon* remarked: 'I think that's excellent: I wish it applied today!' This young woman had a regular, vivid, and coloured visual image of time as 'a great monster that is always chasing me'; she added that the monster was 'dark brown, prehistoric type, somewhat like a buffalo', and that she never had enough time for the things she wanted to do. Some people like this, for whom time passes too fast, wear a watch but keep it several minutes ahead of actual time, and thus manage not to be late for appointments. Only one of my subjects produced the opposite kind of behaviour and in this resembled Lenin, who regularly kept his watch ten minutes slow! People may exhibit in fantasy their wish that clocks would behave variably and sometimes run faster, sometimes slower. This fantasy is echoed in a popular song which proposed 'a bargain with Father Time', an arrangement that he will 'hurry through each week-day and, on Sunday, slow down for me'.

Relation of days of the week to time was investigated in the 1930s by Israeli. He found, with a group of American university students, that Monday was overwhelmingly the least preferred day. The most preferred was not Sunday but Saturday, followed by Friday. In 1965 I repeated Israeli's study, again with a group of American students. My subjects gave their first preference to Friday, then Saturday: they agreed with Israeli's subjects in exhibiting a marked distaste for Monday. There were no significant sex differences in this second investigation, though the women students showed somewhat greater variability than the men.

One oddity of subjectively experienced time is the illusion of slow motion. This I first noticed in myself when, as passenger in a motor accident, I had the impression that the car turned over in slow motion. Subsequent inquiry has elicited many descriptions of accidents in which the people involved reported a similar phenomenon. There are many circumstances in which the subject's impressions of time are seriously out of gear with the progress of the clock. Cohen gives a rather striking instance from a mescaline experiment, during which the subject rose from his chair and walked across the room. To the observers his movements appeared feverishly accelerated. He himself had the impression that the events around him, and his own movements, were occurring in slow motion. Such a hiatus between subjective experience and objective reality can result in peculiarities of the problems of adjustment in subjects who have taken a hallucinogenic drug. Normally a speaker is able to make reasonably accurate assessments of how long an interval he is allowing between the words he is speaking, and how long has elapsed since the last word he spoke. Insight into this may deteriorate with mescaline, and communication with the experimenters may deteriorate because of this somewhat unusual problem which the speaker faces. Moreover, to external observation the subject's speech may be speeded up, slowed down, or normal. Oddities of this kind have sometimes been observed in psychotic patients also.

A somewhat related phenomenon can also occur in model psychosis experiments with mescaline, and again is observable in some deluded psychotic patients. I have discussed it more fully elsewhere (1957) and called it 'The time discontinuity phenomenon'. An illustration may be taken from one mescaline experiment in which I was myself the subject. I was invited to play a game of chess with an experimenter, a mathematician with whom I had previously played. Objective recording of my behaviour during the game was 'subject's attention was repeatedly redirected to the game with some difficulty'. This observation hardly does justice to the alarming events accompanying the game as I experienced it. My opponent's face appeared to be constantly changing shape, one effect of the drug, but this was less disturbing than the game itself. Every now and then I would look at the pieces to discover I had lost my queen, then my bishop, and then both my castles. These pieces I would see no longer on the board but standing by the side of it: presumably they had been taken by my opponent. Now in these circumstances two things are important: first, I was aware that I was taking part in a scientific experiment, and had been given a substantial dose of mescaline; secondly, I knew my opponent, had played with him before, and had no reason to think of him as likely to cheat. Yet I had no memory at all of losing my pieces. One could see how easily under other circumstances the interpretation of being cheated, or 'persecuted', might have been placed on the sudden and unexplained events, the loss of these chess pieces. Several psychotic patients with delusions of a persecutory kind, subsequently interviewed, provided evidence of experiences of time discontinuity resembling those which occurred in the experiment mentioned. Blank periods – periods of brief amnesia –

can occur, but events do happen in them even though the subject has no awareness of them. The result can be alarming impressions of objects and people appearing and disappearing in different places, rather than moving about in the way we would see them do so with normal and continuous experience of the passage of time. Uncaused, unexplained, and frighteningly unexpected events provide excellent subject-matter for delusions, including the delusion that these happenings result from the activities of one's 'persecutors'.

Another substance which can markedly derange the sense of time is alcohol, and the disturbance seems to be particularly acute in respect of *order of succession of events*. The inability of a person suspected of being intoxicated to give an accurate account of events in the right sequence is, in fact, quite often used as a clinical test of being drunk. These effects can be experimentally simulated with mescaline, and some other interesting phenomena regarding the order of events are also reported. I refer in particular to certain happenings reported by Christopher Mayhew M.P. in a paper to a conference on hallucinogenic drugs in 1963. Subjectively Mayhew experienced things happening in an impossible sequence, for example 'events at half past three *before* events at three o'clock'! And on one occasion he found himself observing with interest first himself stirring the sugar into his cup of tea, and *then* the tea being poured into his cup! Many odd things in addition to illusions of speeded-up and slowed-down time can occur during hallucinogen experiments. They are sufficient to justify the frequent comment by subjects that 'time is behaving in strange ways'.

We cannot assume that similar conditions will produce the same effects on different individuals, or even on the same individual on different occasions. Nor can we assume that a given drug or anaesthetic will invariably produce a given experience such as 'time flies' rather than 'time drags': we have already seen that with nitrous oxide some people experienced the one, and some experienced the other. What is apparent is that chemical interference may seriously interfere with the realism of the subject's adjustment to external events: that is it may disorientate him in relation to time. In a series of laboratory experiments with alcohol in which medical students were subjects, it was evident that alcohol has a marked tendency to disrupt temporal behaviour. The errors of adjustment to reality thus produced – and thus the margins of safety the individual is likely to allow himself – in our subjects occurred either way.

Another source of disorientation in relation to time is oxygen lack, and too little is known about it in view of its importance in aviation. One air force pilot, who had taken part in an experiment on the effects of anoxia conducted in a decompression chamber, told me that he and other pilots had frequently noted disturbances in their adjustment to time. Of himself he reported that he had noted in previous experiences in the decompression chamber 'complete loss of sense of time . . . able to recount events but not their sequence or when'. It is now suspected that a good proportion of accidents in the First World War – before anoxia effects were understood – probably resulted from this cause. If this was the case, disturbed time estimation and resulting lack of realism in allowance of margins of error may well have made a substantial contribution. Relations between oxygen-lack effects and temporal adjustment are still little understood, and even in these days of pressure cabins merit full investigation.

Another subjective phenomenon relates to the effects of ageing on the impression of more long-term passage of time. A piece of admittedly indifferent, anonymous doggerel poetry I once encountered sums up admirably this relation:

> When as a child I laughed and wept, time crept,
> When as a youth I dreamed and talked, time walked;
> When I became a full-grown man, time ran;
> And later as I older grew, time flew.

That increase of age has this over-all effect on the experience of the flow of time has often been noted. There are, however, within this life-process many unevennesses. Most of us are familiar with how specific situational factors, at whatever stage of life they occur, can in this uneven way disrupt our adjustments to actual clock time. But the over-all trend seems to be a clear-cut one as a person passes from youth, through maturity, to age. These different impressions of the speed of the passage of time at different ages may have an important bearing on the phenomenon of the conflict between the younger and the older generations. It may help to explain why the young are inclined to regard the older as slow in getting things done, while the older accuse the young of excessive impatience. Thus, in an office, some item waiting to be dealt with in the older man's in-tray may seem to him to wait only a short time. To his younger subordinate, for whom weeks and months are on the whole experienced as longer, it may seem to wait a very long time indeed. Thus empathy and communication between the younger and the older may suffer considerably when time is involved.

The felt speed of the passage of time is but one of the things on which a person will rely if asked to make a serious judgement about how long has, in fact, elapsed. In everyday life, outside the laboratory, there are many clues in addition to these subjective impressions: watches and clocks, the position of the sun, hunger and thirst, signs of the rush hour in the streets, and light and darkness. In laboratory experiments these additional clues are often artificially removed. Yet even in such experiments investigators have sometimes required their subjects to make not one, but two judgements: how long do they *feel* has elapsed, and how long do they *judge* has elapsed. Under certain circumstances the subject may be acutely aware of a discrepancy between felt time and judged time. This sense of discrepancy, noticeable in ordinary experiments, may become extremely acute and give rise to a number of quaint phenomena in studies with such substances as nitrous oxide and hallucinogenic drugs, and in sensory deprivation experiments. Thus for example the two times phenomenon may occur. A subject asked to make an estimate may with perfect sincerity and seriousness ask, 'Which kind of time?' He may add, 'By your time it was ten minutes, but by mine it was half an hour.' The first judgement seems to be a somewhat colourful expression of judged time, the second of felt time. And during hallucinogen experiments in particular as we have seen the subject may become even more colourful, and tempted to rather mystical ways of communicating. He may for example assert that throughout the day of the experiment he has been living on 'a different time scale' from that of the experimenters. Very similar phenomena have been reported in nitrous-oxide experiments. In either case we may encounter a subject who is disposed to adopt a cryptic, knowing, and sometimes rather mystical distinction between 'time' (ordinary clock time), and 'Time' (something he feels to be different). I remember one such subject who noticed that the experimenters had carelessly left him with his watch and then asked him to make time estimations. He remarked, 'My watch is still on my arm, but that is irrelevant: I'm trying to assess *Time*'!

BEHAVIOURAL PHENOMENA OF TIME ESTIMATION

Of interest in performances in tasks of time estimation are the marked individual differences which occur. These differences are of considerable importance to courts of law and the testimony of witnesses; matters involving time provide some of the most unreliable evidence with which courts have to deal. To illustrate, in 1964 there occurred a smash-and-grab raid in central London in which £250,000 of jewellery was stolen from a shop. There were many witnesses to the raid. Their estimates of the time taken by the raiders ranged from forty seconds to six minutes! Most unfortunately a court of law, when it is not confronted with such an obvious indication as this of the unreliability of human witnesses, is often inclined to treat the rough time estimate of a witness as though it were recorded by a stopwatch. Courts thus often impale themselves on pseudo-problems of their own creation by their readiness to accept whatever time estimations witnesses happen, or are induced, to make. Testimony about time is, of course, unreliable in other aspects too, for example in the assessment of the temporal order of events.

Similar individual variations can readily be demonstrated in laboratory tasks of time estimation. Illustration may be taken from one small study. The subjects, fifteen university students, were set a routine task, being interrupted at intervals and asked to estimate the time since the task had begun. For a total clock time of 260 seconds the average of their estimates was 398 seconds: in other words the group as a whole produced an average positive error of 138 seconds in their verbal estimations. Individuals in their estimations of the clock time of 260 seconds varied widely, and ranged from 98 to 720 seconds. The study mentioned illustrates the 'method of verbal estimation', one of the standard techniques for the laboratory investigation of time. Similar variations between individuals can be elicited by other methods, for example the 'method of production'. In this the experimenter decides on a time interval, say a minute, starts the subject estimating, and asks him to stop when the subject thinks a minute has elapsed. This involves a different task from that of verbal estimation: essentially the method of production studies the concept the subject has for the time interval specified. These concepts vary greatly. Thus, in the case of a minute I have found that some subjects estimate this as being completed when only 15 seconds of clock time have elapsed; others estimate their minute at a clock time of 90 seconds or more. Some of the circumstances which appear to affect time estimation performance may now be mentioned.

One of the best modern studies was by J. C. Loehlin (1959). This provided evidence of four factors underlying the verbal estimation of time: (1) an interest *v.* boredom factor: the more bored subjects tended to give longer estimates; (2) a filled time *v.* empty time factor: longer estimates tended to occur with filled than with empty time; (3) a repetition factor: estimates of the second of two periods of a repeated activity tended to be shorter; (4) an activity *v.* passivity factor: periods of passivity are estimated as longer than those of activity.

Loehlin's factorial study stands out in a field whose research literature is confusing to read, and in which reviews of researches conducted are often unhelpful. The literature is difficult precisely because it contains many statements like 'so-and-so's overestimated time'. Careful reading of the original test – review articles with their omissions and abbreviations are best avoided – reveals the following (1) the method of obtaining verbal estimates of elapsed time intervals was used; (2) by 'overestimation' is meant overestimation of the amount of time that has passed, i.e. underestimation of actual time intervals; (3) time intervals of the order of minutes (not seconds, half-hours, or hours) were used; (4) the writer finds support for his conclusion in an earlier investigation by somebody else: on examination this proves to have been conducted with another method – the method of production – and the ambiguities of the word 'overestimation' become particularly acute when these two methods are compared. In the end it emerges that the earlier investigator had in fact shown that so-and-so's 'underestimate' of time was an 'overestimate' in the terminology of the more recent investigator. And further it appears that this other investigator has used time intervals (which are not quoted by the present investigator) of a quite different order of magnitude, namely from 0.5 to 5 seconds. The comparability of the two investigations, and indeed the meaningfulness of either, are very much open to question.

The above example is by no means unrepresentative of a literature which – with some wholly admirable exceptions – is a confusing blend of terminological, methodological, and factual problems. Thus professional psychologists resemble laymen when they discuss time-estimation problems, in that the symbol of their thinking often becomes the reversible figure. Reversals of thought often occur, with the frequent apology, 'Sorry, of course I've got it wrong; it's the other way round!' Among areas in which unjustified assumptions tend to be made, in both spoken and written communications, may be mentioned: first, relations between the subjective phenomena of experience, and performance in actual tasks of time estimation. Thus systematic researches have failed to reveal the relations we might anticipate between either 'time flies' or 'time drags' and any systematic direction of error of estimations. Secondly, a variety of different tasks have been used in experiments on time estimation. From performance in one such task we cannot predict how a person will react in another of the tasks; knowledge of the reliability and validity of the alternative methods is extremely scanty; and the relation of laboratory experiments to time-estimating behaviour in daily life – for example crossing the road – remains largely uninvestigated. Thirdly, the order of magnitude of the time interval used is important. In surveying the research literature Loehlin found little evidence of any consistent direction of error as between small, medium, and large intervals of time. Nor is this surprising. There seems no reason to assume that a person who has – perhaps as a photographer – developed skill in estimating with accuracy intervals of the order of seconds is necessarily going to be good at estimating intervals of the order of several minutes, half-hours, or hours. This may be the case, but we simply do not know. Yet this is precisely the type of assumption that has often been made.

A major impediment to progress in this field has been an unfortunate generalization based on the early work of Vierordt in the nineteenth century. 'Vierordt's principle' – sometimes dignified with the name of a 'law' – has often been stated in the form: 'overestimation is associated with short intervals of time, and underestimation with long intervals.' Few generalizations could be more misleading. Vierordt worked with very small time intervals ranging from fractions of seconds to seconds: 'short' and 'long' should be interpreted in these terms. His principle may still, despite many contrary findings, have some relevance to the understanding of time estimations of these small magnitudes. If taken to apply to time estimating of other magnitudes the principle is highly misleading. People build up frames of reference for seconds, for minutes, for half-hours, and for hours. Social, developmental, and personality differences may have substantial effects on these frames of reference for these different magnitudes. It would not be surprising if these influences operated differently at different magnitudes. A further source of confusion is the implication of Vierordt's principle that there is a point at which 'overestimation' changes to 'underestimation': this Vierordt called 'the indifference interval'. Much effort has gone into the pursuit of this nebulous entity. It is perhaps a sign that investigators are returning to more profitable pursuits that one more recent survey article differs from its predecessors: it omits all reference to Vierordt's principle and the indifference interval.

As regards the unfortunate words 'overestimation' and 'underestimation', Woodrow in 1951 expressed the opinion that these terms 'need careful definition'. This is an understatement. In communicating about time estimation these words – probably the two most commonly used words in time-estimation research – are best avoided altogether. They are not merely ambiguous, but may in fact convey opposite meanings to different people.

Running short of time is not unlike running short of petrol. In such circumstances the motorist in question may be said to have 'underestimated' (the petrol he has used) or 'overestimated' (the amount he thinks he has left). Similarly a person who misses his train 'underestimates' the progress of time on his way to catch it, and 'overestimates' the time he has left to catch it. It would seem better to express the facts in some other way, for example by saying – whether with reference to petrol or to time – that the traveller has allowed himself 'an insufficient margin'. Alternatively we may say he has committed a 'negative error' of estimation, defining negative error as less than clock time; or a 'positive error', defining 'positive' as greater than clock time.

An experiment of my own may be quoted to illustrate this terminology. It concerned the effects of oxygen lack on verbal estimations of elapsed time. Subjects were asked to make verbal estimates both under control conditions at ground level, and under conditions in a decompression chamber which simulated an altitude of 15,000 feet without oxygen. Estimates were of the order of fractions of minutes, and minutes. The results are interesting, and their interest lies in both the magnitude and the direction of error. Paradoxically the magnitude of the average error of the group was smaller under conditions of oxygen lack than at ground level. Estimates were more accurate. But the direction of the error changed from being a larger positive error at ground level to being a small but negative error at 15,000 feet. The experiment is offered merely as an illustration. More work would be needed to relate it to practical matters such as running out of time and fuel at the controls of a plane. But the error which occurred, however small, was, it will be noted, an error on the wrong side. Its result would be an inadequate margin of safety, and in many activities involving everyday life's time estimations 'a miss is as good as a mile'. Both magnitude and direction of error would merit examination in this whole field, and it is suggested that the terms 'positive' and 'negative' error, to indicate direction, are less confusing than the terms 'over-estimation' and 'underestimation'.

If we return from laboratory experiments and their findings to everyday life we encounter complex problems involving time and movement of objects, as when for example a motorist or a pedestrian tries to adjust his behaviour to reality. Consider a motorist who is trying to overtake another vehicle, and is making estimations. Let us try to express this in the terminology of overestimation–underestimation. If he underestimates his own speed and the distance he will travel in a given time, or overestimates the time he has to travel that distance, he may run into the car ahead of him. If he overestimates its speed or underestimates the time it will take to travel a given distance, he may do likewise. Moreover there may be a third vehicle approaching him from the other direction, and if in overtaking the car ahead he underestimates the speed of the approaching car, underestimates the time he will take to reach a certain point, or overestimates his own speed he may collide with this third vehicle. Spatial and temporal relations between the three cars concerned are complex enough. It seems best to specify them as simply and unambiguously as possible. A person who runs into another vehicle, or who has missed his train, has allowed himself an inadequate margin of safety. As regards his time estimation he may have made a negative error, in that his estimated time is smaller than the clock time actually needed for an adequate margin of safety.

From terminology we return to other investigations of recent years. One important research programme has been conducted at Stockholm University by Marianne Frankenheuser (1959). She relates estimation of time to perception and remembering. She confines the term 'perception of time' to the experience of brief time intervals, grasped as one perceptual unit, and relatively unaffected by memory. By contrast 'retention of time' she uses to denote the experience in retrospect of longer time intervals assumed to be affected by memory. By getting her subjects to tap or count at an estimated rate of one per second, she obtained a measure of present time estimates. Subjects were then required to estimate verbally the time which had elapsed. By this 'method of present and past time estimation' she found that estimates of past time were smaller than both clock time and the present time estimates on which they were based. This result was predicted on the assumption that the relation between time perceived and time retained is analogous to the relation between perception and retention. Less is ordinarily remembered than is perceived. Thus Frankenheuser studied the factors affecting perception of time and subsequently those affecting retention of time. Present time estimates were found to be larger when, for example, a metronome was beating at a fast rate than when it was beating at a slow rate. Other effects of the stimulus background were studied, such as the intensity of background noise. Estimates of time intervals were made when these intervals were terminated by an electric shock. Results showed larger estimations of retained time. Effects of various drugs were also studied, and in more detail, by this method. Nitrous oxide, for example, was found mainly to affect retention rather than perception of time. In all Frankenheuser conducted a programme of thirteen experiments which opened up some new and hitherto uninvestigated problems arising from her decision to relate the little-understood problem of time estimation to the better-known fields of perception and remembering.

THE SOCIAL AND PERSONALITY PSYCHOLOGY OF TIME

Variations are to be found between different human societies in the conventions they have developed for thinking about and measuring time. The Greeks had their myth about the Three Fates in relation to the passage of time during the human life-span: Clotho spun the web of life, Lachesis twisted it, and Atropos cut it off at the appropriate span with her shears. The Romans reckoned their time forwards and backwards from the Ides and Calends of the month. We have twelve months to our year, while the Navajo Indians of the American South-west have thirteen. Many spatial devices have been constructed to assist thinking about the measurement of time, not merely the clock and the pendulum, but also the sundial, the marked candle, and the hour-glass. Other than visual ways of measuring time have, on occasion, been developed. Thus anthropologists have recorded that the Andaman Islanders had an 'odour calendar': the succession of odours as different flowers came into bloom during the year was used as a way of marking the passage of time. Plants may be employed in place of the clock no less than for the calendar. Fraisse (1964) records that the botanist Linnaeus evolved a 'floral clock', a collection of flowers that opened their blooms at different times of the day. In connexion with such floral clocks may be noted the chicory plant (*Cichorium intybus*), which opens its blue flowers regularly, and at different times from the yellow flowers of the evening primrose (*Oenothera biennis*). An interplanting of the two will produce interesting effects, both the beginnings of a floral clock and a change of colour from blue to yellow at different times.

Apart from botanical aids, man himself is equipped with one category of motives, the appetites like hunger and the sleep need, which assist his adjustments to time. These are not accurate enough for modern urban requirements, though such accuracy is not yet the norm everywhere in the world. As regards the American continent, a former Commissioner of Indian Affairs refers to the 'more spacious' sense of time of the American Indians, and is much in sympathy with their emancipation from the 'clock-mindedness' of the European and white American with their 'clock-work time'. Much depends on differences between urban and rural life. Thus, like the Navajo Indian farmer, the Scottish ploughman of the Highlands may need only two times: 'yoken time' and 'loosen time': the times he yokes up his horses and begins, and the time he loosens them from their harness and concludes his work. But the city dweller needs more precise temporal categories. On the whole, the clock and the calendar have tended to assume precedence among modern man's ways of thinking about and adjusting to time.

The anthropologist Erickson suggested the value of an approach to different societies in terms of the individual's time goals: how far ahead is the time span with which he is concerned. John Cohen (1958) makes the suggestion that subcultural differences in such a temporal horizon may be related to the system by which wages are paid. Weekly wages and monthly salaries are likely to have differing effects of a very practical kind upon the planning of the individual household and thus upon the temporal horizon of its members. Le Shan (1952) conducted an investigation into different socio-economic strata of the United States in terms of their different time spans. In lower-lower groups he found a limited span, an absence of regular meal hours, and a tendency for each member of the family to eat – if food was available – when hungry. In upper-lower, middle, and lower-upper groups the evidence suggested much longer tension-tolerance sequences. Members of these groups would plan for years ahead, and as regards food behaviour they would wait 'until a watch shows it is time to eat'. The upper-upper class groups gave evidence of seeing themselves as part of a sequence of generations. Their temporal horizon extended backwards as well as for-wards, and food behaviour would be at conventional hours estab-lished by traditions of the past. Other work by Le Shan revealed that these differences of temporal horizon reflected themselves in the performances of children of these three groups when they were asked to tell a story. In general Le Shan regards the habits of child rearing and child feeding of these groups as major in-fluences upon the temporal horizons that children are likely to develop. Children of the lower-lower class group, reared in an environment in which 'major changes in their lives often occur suddenly and unpredictably', fail to develop systems of control, and also have unduly restricted temporal horizons.

Numerous studies have been conducted with a view to show-ing that different personality types behave differently in tasks of time estimation. Investigations with short intervals of time of the order of seconds and minutes have proved inconclusive. Perhaps more promising is the approach to these differences in terms of longer intervals. As illustration may be mentioned one study by Orme (1969), who worked with intervals of the order of 20–30 minutes. He avoided the artificiality of many time-estimation investigations by arranging his tasks so that the subjects were unaware that they were later going to be asked to estimate elapsed time. With intervals of 30 minutes the normal group made a negative error, and on average verbally estimated this 30 minutes as 25. Psychopaths, hysterics, and intellectual defectives gave longer estimates than the controls; schizophrenics, de-pressed patients, and anxiety-state neurotic patients gave shorter estimates. The same order merged in a confirmatory study by Orme in which he used intervals of 20 minutes. Results obtained were clear-cut, and large groups were used in both the 30-minute and the confirmatory 20-minute study. There was no evidence of sex differences in either the controls or the clinical groups used.

In individual variations between normal people in how they think about time, a study conducted by myself revealed – as might be expected – a predominance of imagery for conventional clocks and watches and, with longer periods, calendars. Other imagery reflected non-visual aspects of our culture, for example the announcer's voice reporting the time over the radio, and even a boxing referee counting! Some other interesting variants of imagery may be mentioned:

Historical personages dying in sequence; a corridor through which one walks backwards so that the past is before and the future ahead; movement of a long ribbon; a mental picture of sun, moon, and stars; a winged chariot hurrying; and the week being imaged as a track with each day divided from its neighbour by a small hurdle.

Some of the subjects reported conventional date forms: regular spatial images – sometimes three-dimensional and sometimes coloured – of lines, angles, and curves representing the week, month, seasons, or sequence of the years. One subject wrote no less than thirteen pages – illustrated with sketches – about his own complex system of date forms for almost every conceivable aspect of time. In addition to date forms, and even more commonly, colour associations were reported. As illustration may be instanced one American girl who at eight years had the following colour associations for days and months:

DAYS		MONTHS	
Sunday	white	January	red
Monday	brown	February	orange
Tuesday	purple	March	grey
Wednesday	yellow	April	silver
Thursday	blue	May	green
Friday	white, black, pink	June	black
Saturday	silver, gold, copper	July	blue
		August	pink
		September	lime

In this case the months October, November, and December had no colour associations, but were associated with other regular imagery: pumpkins, turkeys, and gifts respectively. The parents recorded certain additional associations of the child. Thus Tuesday's purple arose 'because Joseph wore purple on the first Christmas day'; Wednesday's yellow was associated with the sun; and Thursday, the child's favourite day, was associated with blue, the child's favourite colour. The association not of colours but of other imagery with days of the week is also common, though seemingly less so than colour association. Many subjects reported spatial imagery for time of the sort that reflected literary influences which they were often able to specify, like rivers which 'flowed', and 'footsteps' in the sand. Others again reported scenes or landscapes.

Frames of reference, with or without associated imagery, relating to time have presumably to be learned. Language itself can provide difficulties of communication between those who, through learning, have acquired different concepts. This applies even between British and American speakers of English. Thus the concept of 'a fortnight' is meaningless to many Americans, as is 'Boxing Day'. The Englishman for his part fails to make the American's distinction – a useful one – between 'Monday *till* Friday' and 'Monday *through* Friday'. As between languages other difficulties occur. For example a German or a Dutchman will say in his language 'half ten', meaning 9.30, while the term 'half ten' as used in England is interpreted to mean 10.30. Other difficulties occur when, for example, a German is learning to speak English. We have developed the linguistic habit of omitting the word 'minutes' in such expressions as 'five past' and 'ten past', but confine this omission to the 'fives' and the 'tens'. A frequent error of the German speaker of English is his tendency to extend this and to employ such expressions as 'twelve past', or 'fourteen past'. There are numerous other regularities of error in specifying time of which these are but examples, awaiting fuller investigation by students of the learning process in association with students of linguistics.

Acquisition of a temporal vocabulary is, on the whole, a later rather than an earlier part of the child's learning process. The time categories of the child are at first crude ones, but become more sophisticated with increased experience and age. Binet's scale of intelligence tests requires the child by the age of 6 years to know morning from afternoon; by 9 years to know day of the week, month, day of the month, and year; and by 10 to know all the names of the months. These norms relate to the child of average intelligence – an intelligence quotient of 100; obviously better performances can be expected of the intellectually superior child. Early studies by Oakden and Sturt in 1920 provide evidence of the slowness with which a temporal vocabulary is nevertheless acquired. Of interest are their findings in one experiment in which elementary school children were asked to place characters of history in chronological order. Many children exhibited a kind of egocentricity, using a time scale provided by their own life: that is, they placed the characters and events not in chronological order, but in the order in which they had first learned of them! Representative of many was the child who reported: 'I put Robin Hood first because I heard of him in infant school, and I heard of King Alfred in the first form.' Some over-all trends are to be seen in another study by the same investigators in which children were asked to place the following in chronological order: 'Attila lived in 438 A.D.; Philip of Spain lived in 1585 A.D.; Nero lived in Rome 50 A.D.' At age 8 half the children could perform the task correctly. By 10 years 67 per cent were correct; at 12 there were 85 per cent correct; by 13 96 per cent gave the correct response. Errors which frequently occurred are instructive and teach us something about the kind of difficulties children can encounter over time, e.g. 'Philip came first because his number is bigger', and 'Nero lived fifty years ago' (Sturt, 1925). Detailed studies of general trends, and of regularities of error, would provide some valuable information both for the teacher of elementary history and for the student of childhood thinking more generally.

Different ideas of time intrude upon the teaching–learning situation, not merely in the school but also in the university. Age differences may intrude, as when a university teacher may say to a class 'You will remember so-and-so', and then have the belated insight that his audience were not even born when the events in question happened! Of interest is the coalescence into a rather undifferentiated category of 'the past' in the mind of the learner of what, to the teacher, are temporally distinct events. Thus, for example, first-year university students today can show some marked confusion of the events of the First and Second World Wars. And cultural differences may provoke communication problems also: the British visitor to the United States, for example, is well advised to remember that the Americans have had four wars, not two. Loose references to 'the last war' are likely to confuse: the visitor may mean the Second World War, but be interpreted to mean Korea or Vietnam. Many under-investigated issues surround the ways in which people of different age and national groups relate events to their categories of the past.

Individual people behave as though each had an 'internal clock' with which he records, adjusts, and maladjusts to time. These internal clocks exhibit some of the properties of external clocks we have all known. They may run too fast, or too slow, they may stop and deceptively start again, and they may be affected by outward events. Among external factors which affect their accuracy are stress and emotional excitement. The psychologist Schonbach has suggested the principle that the greater the motivation to reach a goal the greater the estimation of the amount of time spent in the barrier situation en route to that goal. This principle is nicely illustrated in the diary of a soldier spending days waiting under fire during the Gallipoli campaign: 'Tomorrow never comes, and yesterday seems years ago.' On the other hand the opposite response may occur in battle and its accompanying emotional excitement, as in the case of one soldier actively engaged in fighting during a day of the Battle of the Somme. The fighting began at 9 a.m. and ended with the going down of the sun. The soldier recorded his surprise on seeing the sun go down: 'The operations seemed to me to last say half an hour – nay, perhaps hardly so much.' One factor which seems to differentiate these two reactions, and thus the fastness or slowness of one's 'internal clock', would seem to be the extent to which one is *either* attending to time *or* absorbed in the events. The second reaction is seen in the case of a researcher who was being orally examined for his doctorate degree. His thesis had been concerned with time estimation, and one of his findings had been that anxiety results in negative errors in estimating elapsed time. During the examination one examiner suddenly asked: 'How long have we been questioning you for?' The candidate replied, 'Forty minutes.' In fact, the clock time had been sixty-five minutes. On the reasonable assumption that candidates who want their doctorates are likely to be anxious while being examined for them, this candidate's own behaviour admirably supported the thesis he was upholding. Afterwards, in discussion, he told me that – being fully aware that anxiety reduced elapsed time estimates – he had tried to compensate for this tendency. He had made a negative error of twenty-five minutes all the same!

The oral examination mentioned represents one occasion on which everyday behaviour agreed with systematic research findings. On the whole, however, too little has been ascertained about how relations established by laboratory research also hold in daily life. A large number of important adjustments of behaviour to temporal reality remain largely uninvestigated. Among them may be noted crossing the road in safety, overtaking another car, catching one's train, and allowing sufficient time to get one's car or plane back home in safety. Marked individual differences of behaviour have been demonstrated in the field of margins of safety by David Katz, and specifically in relation to road-crossing behaviour by John Cohen. On the other hand we still know too little of the states of mind, situation, and types of personality that make for negative and positive errors of time estimation.

In conclusion, let us empathize with two relevant states of mind in the context of daily life. Absorption in events seems to go with negative error; attention to the passage of time seems to go with positive errors. We make negative errors when we burn the toast we are making, when we get lost in the conversation and allow our coffee to get cold, and when we think we have time to get home but night overtakes us. By contrast, we commit positive errors when making tea and meditating on the proverb 'the watched kettle never boils' or when in listening to a dull lecture a surreptitious glance at our watch provokes the regretful 'It's earlier than I thought'. As a whole the negative type of error seems more undesirable and even, on occasion, disastrous to survival. It is this which accompanies such maladjustments as missing one's train, holding a grenade too long before throwing it, and being overtaken by night in the mountains far from shelter. Nevertheless too big margins of time, like too narrow ones, can on occasion be maladaptive. They may likewise be dangerous to survival: for example a grenade thrown too soon may be thrown back. Absence of error altogether, rather than direction of error, may in certain circumstances be essential. A rich field of investigation awaits future researchers. Although undeservedly neglected temporal adjustment is important for many reasons, both theoretical and practical.

CHAPTER SEVEN

The Teacher and the Learner

The process whereby one individual enables another to learn something more quickly than he would on the basis of his own trial and error.

Student's definition of Teaching,
quoted by O. H. MOWRER

THIS chapter will be mainly concerned with the learner as a person rather than with theories of learning. Many psychologists have been concerned, and for many decades, with the learning process and with formulating theories about it. This preoccupation has on occasion given rise to neglect of the relevant aspects of differential psychology: the study of the individual as thinker, perceiver, and learner. In Chapter 1 attention was paid to the influence of Robert Woodworth on psychology, taking Woodworth as a major theorist and investigator who contributed substantially to the mainstream of the subject's development. Woodworth himself gave, and encouraged others to give, emphasis to the study of processes like perceiving, thinking, and learning. This field of interest remains important, and wholly legitimate, but it comprises only one part of the subject matter of psychology. Developmental study on the one hand and the investigation of individual differences on the other, are also important. Moreover as McClelland (1955) has put it, psychology is legitimately 'interested in what goes on in people's heads'. And as McClelland sees it this study of mental content collapsed for various reasons: partly under the influence of early behaviourism, partly because 'introspectionism' – the too-exclusive concern with introspection and nothing else – came to a dead end, and partly because of an over-preoccupation with '-ing' words like 'learning', 'perceiving', 'remembering', and 'thinking'. It is argued that we should today study both process variables (like learning and perceiving) and content variables (what people learn, and think about). Thus, in this chapter, the learner as a person and what he learns will receive emphasis, and both 'process' and 'content' will be examined.

Earlier chapters have examined some of the characteristics of the thinking and remembering which individuals exhibit, and accompanying variations of imagery. Similarly, variations are to be found between individuals as learners. But before turning to these, it will be appropriate to make a distinction between two different but important uses of the '-ing' word 'learning' itself.

TYPE A AND TYPE B LEARNING

Type A learning will be taken to refer to what occurs when an individual learns, in the sense of acquiring new information or a skill: for example he learns a new subject like economics, or learns to drive a car. To achieve this he gathers up information, stores the information in a disciplined way, and develops a system of knowledge or skills available for subsequent use. The curriculum of a school or university is directly concerned with type A learning.

Type B learning is something broader and more general. It is, in McClelland's terminology, the process variable that has concerned theorists of the learning process. It might be defined as 'modification of the organism's behaviour by the events of its life history'. In this broader sense, type B learning is probably the most central topic of psychology. It is important in all branches: in understanding how organisms adapt to their material environment, how they learn the social norms of the groups of which they accept membership, and how the individual develops as a personality as a result of the experiences he undergoes. Thus general and experimental psychologists have sought to formulate an overall theory of learning. Social psychologists have studied imitation and suggestion in the acquisition of social norms. And personality psychologists have stressed the importance of the first five years of life and its accompanying learning in the shaping of the individual personality. Moreover, as Freud was able to show, not all events which affect subsequent behaviour are necessarily available to conscious recall afterwards: some may be repressed, or actively forgotten, but may nevertheless exert profound influence. Moreover, whether accompanied by remembering or not, much early learning appears to be so profoundly influential as to be largely irreversible. An illustration may be taken from the case of the publisher Victor Gollancz, who as a child, reared in an orthodox Jewish home, learned the taboo against having meat and milk in close proximity. In his biography Gollancz tells how, even at an advanced age – and many years after having abandoned the Jewish faith – this learning persisted. His early learning history still ensured extreme discomfort for him in such situations as having lunch with a person who ordered a steak and a glass of milk. This extreme persistence of early learning is important in understanding much social and individual behaviour. Hebb (1949) puts it in the form of a question: 'How can we hope to construct a theory of learning from the data of maturity alone?' The emotional habits that result from type B learning may be of considerable importance in the teaching–learning situation.

Educational psychologists have naturally been much interested in curriculum-based, or type A, learning. Very rightly they have not confined their attention to it. Thus in discussing the educationally backward child Sir Cyril Burt has examined the influence of such factors as inefficient teaching and resulting hostilities to authority, discouraging conditions in the home, and adherence to the norms of the neighbourhood. Similarly Burt has elsewhere paid considerable attention to such aspects of type B learning as a given child's punishment history. The teacher's problem may depend very much on whether he is dealing with an under-punished, over-punished, or inconsistently punished child.

Many psychologists have, however, been primarily interested in type B learning, and with the construction of an over-all theory about the learning process. Often they have drawn heavily upon animal laboratory experiments. Among such theorists have been some who sought to explain all learning in terms of the principles governing conditioning as elucidated by Pavlov, or some extension of these. Others produced alternatives to the Pavlovian kind of theory. Twenty or thirty years ago saw the emergence of a number of rival theories of learning. An admirable summary of these was provided by Hilgard in 1948, though it does not do justice to the contemporary scene. This work provided what

Hebb (1960) has assessed as 'an outstanding contribution to psychology'. The contribution was made, however, under the influence of a methodology which, as Hebb says, 'banished thought, imagery, volition, attention', and related notions as not fit subject matter for science. These exclusions perhaps explain why attempts to apply animal laboratory studies of learning (type B) to the classroom were, on the whole, less than successful. Teachers reacted with an initial intolerance, and an eventual boredom, to repeated attempts of this kind by major learning theorists: in the meanwhile they continued to employ *ad hoc* notions of their own. To them, learning theory was as irrelevant to the problems of learning which concerned them as was Wundt's kind of introspectionism to the problems of personality adjustment which interested Freud. Recent years have seen what is to the teacher a more relevant development, as exemplified by one of Hilgard's later publications in which learning is dealt with in its direct relation to the curriculum (Hilgard, 1964). Other psychologists, notable among them Mowrer, have attempted to apply extensions of learning theory – closely related in this instance to conceptions derived from psycho-analysis – to the study of normal personality, and the understanding of mental abnormality.

Within the same period a rather different development occurred in Soviet Russia. In this the individual learner's problems in attempting to master a specific curriculum have been given central emphasis. Thus the Russians interested themselves and their research in what I have called type A learning, for example in how best to instruct the learner in mathematics and physics. They were concerned to study ways of bridging the gap between theory and practice: for example in studying how people can be taught to use their knowledge of physics in tasks of practical engineering. Much attention was paid to the slow learner, and how to overcome his difficulties. As illustration of this interest in type A learning we may consider some of the work of the Soviet investigator E. A. Fleshner. He was concerned with how, in developing an understanding of scientific physics, the learner has first to abandon his pre-scientific concepts. Thus initially the concept of 'weight' is too narrow, and applies in the learner's thinking only to objects he has himself weighed. He has to learn a more abstract awareness of weight as a property of all physical objects, and Fleshner found that even by 12–13 years the child still has difficulty in grasping such concepts at the appropriate and scientifically necessary level of abstraction.

It would be misleading to imply that psychologists elsewhere have been uninterested in type A learning of this kind; on the contrary they have made some important contributions. Nevertheless the basic orientation of the Soviet psychologists has been different, and their total rejection of mental testing as a method resulted in the vigorous development of a different kind of educational psychology: one which diverges from educational psychology as we know it in Britain. Moreover a substantial number of the ablest and most influential of the Russian psychologists have been interested in curriculum learning: this has not been so true of Britain, America, and elsewhere. Thus the Russian investigations have resulted in a re-examination of familiar problems of the learner from a refreshingly different standpoint. Such studies have revealed an extreme reluctance to explain unsuccessful learning in terms of a difference of ability or intelligence. The Soviet antagonism to mental testing goes too far for most British or American psychologists, but may in itself prove a useful corrective. Fortunately much of the work is now becoming more readily available in translation. The interaction with other psychological work is likely to be valuable, while much Soviet research has some direct relevance to problems of school and university teaching–learning situations.

The conception of the unsuccessful learner as an individual who has for some reason failed to build up a system of knowledge and skills necessary to mastering the curriculum which confronts him is one which fits in well with certain other trends in contemporary psychology. A more direct approach to the learner and his problems has become apparent in the work, over recent years, of Skinner, a leading learning theorist. Skinner has in fact become a major investigator of techniques of type A learning, and his influence has been considerable. One aspect of that influence has been his contribution to programmed instruction, and the use of teaching machines.

PROGRAMMED LEARNING

Teaching machines date from a device developed in 1925 by Sydney L. Pressey. In the following year Pressey published a paper on 'a simple apparatus which gives tests and scores – and teaches'. This apparatus presented the learner with a series of questions, a choice of four answers to each, and four keys to press. If the learner chose the right answer and pressed the appropriate key, the next question would appear; if he chose the wrong one the original question remained. By 1927 Pressey had produced a more elaborate machine, which also recorded items to which a wrong answer had been made on previous runs through the programme. From these early beginnings developed the method of programmed learning, to which Skinner made subsequent important contributions.

On the basis of principles derived from his earlier researches with animals – rats and pigeons – Skinner proceeded to the study of human learning. In a systematic way he developed the full implications of the idea of building up the desired knowledge or skill step by step. Since Pressey others have worked with programmed learning, but characteristic of Skinner's approach is the presentation of the items of information in very small units. These items are so designed as to be easily assimilated, and wherever possible the programme itself prompts the learner in the direction of the correct answer. The aim is to render mistakes improbable. The programmed information may be presented in a variety of ways, through teaching machines of different kinds or through the specially designed books now known as 'programmed texts'. Programmes now exist in a huge variety of fields, ranging from spelling and English grammar to subjects like accountancy, statistics, and psychiatry. Programmed learning is particularly suitable for subjects like foreign languages and mathematics. Other investigators, for example N. A. Crowder, reject Skinner's use of small units of information. Although error is more probable time is saved by the alternative method, which involves presentation of the material in larger units. Leaving aside such techniques as these, we may now consider some of their advantages for the learner and the teacher.

First, programmed learning provides a convenient and automatic feedback of information from the learner to the teacher. The teacher is brought face to face with the kind of errors which occur, and with which of them are most likely to occur; thus he is enabled to modify his programme in the light of this information. Secondly, in making his own knowledge explicit by preparing and revising his programme, the teacher gains a new orientation towards his subject matter. He acquires new mental sets, becomes more aware of imperfections in his own systems of knowledge, and more alerted to his aims. Thirdly, a learner with a teaching machine can settle down to grapple with and master some inadequacy, such as inability to spell. He can struggle with this alone, and go over the programme again and again if necessary, without the overtones of embarrassment he might feel with a human teacher. Fourthly, the learner is able to work at his own speed, and in this the situation has advantages over the ordinary classroom, in which all learners have to work at the same pace.

The value of programmed instruction as an aid to conventional teaching is fairly obvious. It has its uses with complex material, but also with learning of the more elementary kind. One application of it has been to the overcoming of problems of widespread illiteracy in countries which also have teacher shortages. Thus the United Nations has established programmed-instruction centres to deal with basic education problems in Africa, Asia, and Latin America. Perhaps most interesting of all is the reaction of many teachers themselves, as subject-matter experts, who have collaborated with a psychologist and written and tested their own programme. Very often indeed such teachers have been impressed by the way programme writing has reorientated them to the teaching process, and alerted them to the learning problems of the individual.

THE INDIVIDUAL LEARNER

In 1963 a group of psychologists took part in a symposium, 'The Teacher and the Learner'. One speaker, L. B. Birch, editor of the *British Journal of Educational Psychology*, contributed a striking instance of the importance of individual differences. A group of secondary-school children were being taught to swim the crawl stroke, and – as often happens in learning this stroke – some were having difficulty with their breathing rhythm. Five were finding this particularly difficult, but a very simple solution was found with three of them: they were asked to turn their heads to the left rather than the right. The swimming instructor, though doubtless aware that there are both left-handed and right-handed people, did not appreciate the relevance of this fact to the learning situation. By ignoring this variation between learners, he had created difficulties where none need have been.

There are many possibilities for problems to occur in the teaching–learning situation because of failures of empathy. Even unusually good powers of retention may create misunderstandings, as in the case of one of my subjects who records: 'When I was a schoolgirl my mother used to tell me to "study", and since I had read the lesson and knew it I simply didn't understand what she meant. *She* seemed to think that one learned by a process of iteration she called "studying".' Information of help in understanding some of the variations of remembering has emerged from detailed studies of individuals with remarkable powers of calculation, such as Professor Aitken of Edinburgh University. The psychologist Hunter, who has studied Professor Aitken, reports his subject's ability, when a schoolboy, to square numbers like 57,586 in his head in two seconds. Testing of him as an adult revealed the ability to repeat twenty more digits – presented at the rate of five a second – both forwards and backwards. Many of Professor Aitken's performances in mathematical calculation defy our ordinary powers of empathy, though Hunter was able to unravel one aspect of the explanation. Our usual distinction between thinking and recall breaks down. Thus if an ordinary person is given the sum 4×8, he will reply '32', this being a simple act of recall from his memory of the multiplication table. But with, as in this case, a man who knows the multiplication table up to 100×100, and all squares up to 1000×1000, the contribution of memory to acts of calculation is proportionately greater. An answer to the sum '97×71' comes automatically, and memory likewise contributes answers to much more forbidding kinds of arithmetic than this. Such individuals as Professor Aitken, and another mathematical calculator who has been studied, Mr Klein – who learned most of the Amsterdam telephone directory on one occasion for fun – help us a little to appreciate other cases in which difficulties arise because of the learner's unusual memory powers. Two instances of this may be taken. One university student was brought before a disciplinary committee and accused of cheating in an examination: close inspection of his script had revealed an unreasonably accurate coincidence as between it and the text-book. Only an independent test revealed that this remarkable performance was the result of eidetic imagery, and not of copying from the book. In another instance a subject told me how, during a chemistry examination at the age of fifteen, he had 'opened' the pages of his chemistry book and 'copied out' the formula for nitric acid. These acts had occurred not in fact but in visual imagery only, yet he reported feeling enormously guilty about it at the time. While a good many people say they are able to 'read' from their imagery of pages of books, for most people acts of recall involve more hard work than this. Some allowance may have to be made for individuals who lack appropriate imagery for certain kinds of remembering, for instance one subject who reported of himself: 'Meditating, reasoning, remembering, imagination are manifested as a voice in my head. I cannot picture even a diagram in my mind, and have to draw it.'

Many classrooms have known the intellectually dull individual who can readily arouse the exasperation of the teacher, and become the butt of the other pupils. Such people may later find employment, and I shall take one instance to illustrate their problems in the work situation; the girl in question I shall call 'Bertha'. She worked in a factory and after repeated failures elsewhere ended up in the packing department. The reactions of the other women may be summarized in the comment of one: 'What on earth have they sent her to us for? She slows us all down, and she can't remember even the simplest things we tell her.' As the girl fumbled to put the jars into the boxes – an exceedingly monotonous task – she was overheard to say: 'This *is* interesting work, and people are *so* nice to you.' In fact the other workers had spent much of the day telling her to 'get a move on', and making faces at her behind her back. Finally something of a social bridge was achieved by a student working at the factory who realized the need of explaining to Bertha over and over again what she had to do. The girl remarked, 'Everybody thinks I'm daft, but I'm not really, you know, if only they'd tell me what to do.' She herself had little insight into the fact of how very many times, by ordinary standards, she needed the instructions repeated. Finally Bertha was accepted by the others and taken by them into their social group. The observations related – and recorded by the student who was working in the factory at the time – indicate, perhaps better than general statements, how the day-to-day problems of the intellectually dull person are increased by their troubles over social isolation and acceptance by the group. Much more is known today than formerly about methods of training dull learners so that they can earn a living. Intellectual differences between people may be admitted, but they may become a focus for inter-personal difficulties as well.

THE ACQUISITION OF SYSTEMS OF KNOWLEDGE

Various words have been used for the process through which new information is acquired, assimilated, and integrated with information already possessed. Early thinkers like Leibnitz and Herbart, and pioneer experimentalists like Wundt, spoke of a process of 'apperception'. Later Bartlett working on the psychology of remembering talked about building up a 'schema', and as we have seen Hunter likens remembering to establishing and using a 'mental filing system'. Hebb was interested in the relevant accompanying physiological processes which he conceived of in terms of what he called 'cell assemblies' and 'phase sequences'. We have seen that earlier and contemporary Soviet psychologists such as Vigotski on the one hand and Slavina on the other have also been very much concerned with this activity. Whichever of these terminologies we use, undoubtedly the establishment of a system of knowledge is central to the process we call educating. In this connexion we encounter the trait of suggestibility and the process of suggestion. Suggestion has been defined by Cantril as 'acceptance of a frame of reference without intervention of the critical thought processes'. Some relations between this process of uncritical acceptance and the goals of the education process will be examined.

One of Cantril's own investigations (Cantril, 1940) is of considerable interest in this connexion: the 'Invasion from Mars' study. A play, based on an H. G. Wells novel, and depicting an invasion from Mars, was broadcast on 30 October 1938 in New Jersey. Many listeners tuned in late and believed the broadcast to be an account of real events: to use Cantril's central concept, they interpreted what they heard in terms of the 'frames of reference' they possessed. Thus some, at a time soon after the Munich crisis, believed it to be an invasion of America by Nazi Germany. Others, with a frame of reference fed by space fiction and popular science, actually accepted it as a Martian attack. Others again, with pessimistic religious views, were only too ready to accept it as the end of the world. These and other interpretations often found support from additional perceptions which accompanied attempts to check up. Thus some listeners tuned in to another station, heard church music, and concluded that people had gone into church to await the end! The fact that many turned on their radios late and missed some of the more fantastic events helped to create panic, as did the use of local place names in the New Jersey area. Of interest is one young American I interviewed years later, who had heard the broadcast. He was in Taos, New Mexico, at the time, and as a child felt exceedingly remote from New Jersey, and untroubled by the information that 'the enemy' were crossing the Hudson River near New York. Others, however, in Princeton, were disturbed to hear about enemy advances upon some town near by that they knew. Cantril and his colleagues conducted a subsequent research, and sought to discover differences between those who believed the broadcast to be a report of real events, and those who were able to assess it as 'only a play'. The amount of formal education subjects had received did not differentiate the two groups. Some kinds of education had had the effect of increasing suggestibility rather than reducing it. Thus in the play prominent astronomers and other prestige-full people were quoted and interviewed. Moreover we develop the habit of accepting much of what is communicated to us by radio announcers, and a radio announcer was a central character in the play.

In case any reader feels the Americans of the New Jersey area were as a group excessively suggestible on this occasion, another event may be mentioned. It will be remembered how in Britain, some years ago, many listeners exhibited their own suggestibility by accepting uncritically one April 1st broadcast by Richard Dimbleby about the excellent quality of the year's spaghetti crop, which, he reported, he had seen growing in the fields of Italy! There is a difference between people which makes some of them over-receptive to information, and others unwilling to accept stories about Martian invasions and spaghetti crops. Some people suspend their judgement in the face of reports and continue to do so until they have made some realistic external check. The personality of the individual, the situation he is placed in, and the subject matter concerned all affect suggestibility, and the presence or absence of critical thought. In the invasion from Mars study Cantril found that prominent among the people who realized it was a play were those whose past learning had led them to develop systematic knowledge, or realistically tested frames of reference. In the absence of these it is difficult for discriminations to be made between fact and fiction. It would seem to be a major goal of education in general, and higher education in particular, to develop such standards of judgement.

Gullibility, and susceptibility to suggestion, are to be found in people in relation to matters on which they lack these adequate systems of knowledge. Mere possession of information may not be enough, as the 'little learning . . .' quotation reminds us. In some, as yet little understood, way, the educated, wise, or well-informed person possesses a way of using his existing knowledge to sift new information, to evaluate it and make it his own, and to generate further thought from it. This activity, as A. L. Pressey has put it, is not 'so crude a process as accretions of bit learnings stuck on by reinforcements'. In this Pressey is rebelling against one prominent kind of learning theory as inadequate to cope with the educational process. An important part of what I have called type A, or curriculum-mastering, learning, involves something additional: a teacher seeks to assist the learner to acquire an integrated system of knowledge which enables him to think for himself critically, and also creatively, in relation to the subject taught. The end product of this is illustrated in the doubtless apocryphal story of the biology professor whose students one night tried to frighten him. They built a monster which they pushed through the doorway of the sleeping professor's bedroom. He woke up and looked at the creature, and murmured 'claws, carnivorous; horns, herbivorous: doesn't exist', then closed his eyes and went back to sleep. Possession of an adequate system of knowledge about his subject liberated him from gullibility and fear. Likewise professional astronomers, or laymen with an educated attitude towards scientific matters, do not exhibit much suggestibility about invasions from Mars. They may, however, be suggestible towards other matters about which they lack adequate systems of knowledge. To be a scientist is no guarantee that one will think in a consistently scientific way about all subject matters. Thus the names of men distinguished in other fields have regularly been advanced as instances of believers in 'psychical' phenomena. Perhaps the most relevant experts in relation to some of these alleged happenings are not scientists but professional stage magicians, who possess highly sophisticated frames of reference in relation to what can be achieved by naturalistic means in this field.

Radio, television, the printed word, and other mass media contribute enormously to the information received by the modern learner. He receives a constant bombardment through the influences of secondary perception. It is not, in practice, always possible to make observations for oneself, and much of the information that comes to us through our sensory channels is in this way indirect, and has to be taken on trust. We may contrast modern man living in a highly educated and advanced society with people of former times, or those living in underdeveloped countries. Even today we find cultures and subcultures in which books are rare, radio is not available, and literacy is limited. Such areas produce individuals who have to rely for their information largely on their own perceptions and thought, and the limited amount of information they gain from talking to others they meet. Areas of this kind are to be found even in or near highly developed countries like Britain and the United States: one may instance the peasant villages of Ireland, and the Navajo Indian reservations of Arizona. The availability of at least written language, and the ability to read it, are so pervasive that we are inclined to overlook their influence and advantages. Without written language, and books as a source of secondary perception, it is difficult to achieve such highly sophisticated systems of knowledge as those we call science, law, and history. Yet even in relatively recent times we encounter instances of the emergence of written languages, instances which will serve to remind us of the enormous enrichment this provides for the learner.

One such event occurred in the early nineteenth century and involved the work of a highly gifted man, the American Indian Sequoyah. The Cherokees to whom he belonged possessed spoken but no written language, and missionaries had come to teach them English. Sequoyah himself knew no English, but was interested in this activity. He obtained primers for the teaching of the language and used them for his own purpose, which was the development of an alphabet and a grammar for a written form of Cherokee. What he was trying to do in putting marks on paper was not understood by many of his neighbours, but was interpreted by them in terms of their more usual frames of reference. He was suspected of witchcraft and forced to leave Cherokee country for Arkansas. But by 1821 he had accomplished his task: he had constructed a language of 86 graphemes or written characters and rules for their use. This he was able, in less than a month, to teach to his six-year-old daughter. A test was conducted for the benefit of his sceptical fellow tribesmen. The child was sent three miles away, and Sequoyah asked for a message to her which he then wrote down and had sent. The child now demonstrated one powerful advantage of written language as a means of communication at a distance, by translating Sequoyah's graphemes into phonemes, or units of spoken language. Cherokee was the first of the American Indian languages to achieve this written form, and in the events that followed we can see some of the advantages that we ordinarily take for granted. One of these was immediately used by the missionaries. When the Bible had been translated into the new language it became easier for it to be taught in this way than by the laborious alternative of teaching all the Cherokees to read written English. In a relatively short time the Indians of this area learned to read and write Sequoyah's graphemes: they were now able for the first time to send letters to people in distant parts of the country. Then followed the printing of a newspaper: the emergence of an important mass medium. A written Cherokee literature, and history, was now possible for the first time: it became possible to deal with historically and geographically remote events, and more abstract ideas. Not least important was the establishment of a formal system of recorded law. In case the example taken seems too remote it is perhaps helpful to remind ourselves, in an England where literacy and inexpensive paperbacks are both widely available, of this same country at the time of the Civil War. Although we do have recorded history of this period only a minority of people in this country could read and write, and as in some parts of North Africa today, if a letter had to be sent it was necessary to employ the services of a professional letter writer. In England then, as is still the case in many countries today, people were severely handicapped in their mental horizons by their illiteracy. Their knowledge was thus largely limited to what they themselves had seen, heard, or otherwise perceived.

Civilized man is very much concerned with symbols that represent objects, events, and relationships. Learning of the curriculum-mastering kind may involve, in its initial stages, acquisition of the ability to write and speak words and numbers. Later the learning situation is concerned with what, in the absence of an alternative term, might be called 'language' in its broadest sense. This comprises more than merely symbols, but symbols with an accompanying 'grammar' or system of pre-established rules for their use. In an interesting account of the characteristics of human as opposed to animal thinking and learning von Bertalanffy (1956) explains how these systems of symbols as it were 'acquire a life of their own'. The symbols that comprise mathematics, languages, or musical notation convey, he argues, more than merely the information in the individual symbols, because of these pre-established rules. It becomes possible to make predictions, to consider alternatives, and to explore new relations.

With a system like algebra, in which Xs and Ys can stand for any quality or relation whatsoever, with one like the atomic theory or another like Roman law, our possibilities of thought become highly abstract and greatly enlarged. The Linnaean system with its concepts of species, genera, families, and classes permits classification of newly discovered creatures or plants in an orderly way. Other such 'languages' include the structural formulae of chemistry, the established mathematical symbols and conventions which make computer science possible, and symbolic logic. As von Bertalanffy sees it, science itself results from the ability, at which man excels, to employ symbols and their accompanying grammar to formulate new hypotheses, and test them. We do well to remind ourselves that when we speak about learning in the learner–teacher relationship we are very largely concerned with a subject matter of this kind. As we have already seen, Soviet educational psychologists have been much preoccupied with investigation of how best to teach people to learn this kind of activity. Similarly the programmed-learning movement has found its greatest strengths with programmes which cater for this distinctively human kind of learning, with mastery of mathematical systems, foreign languages, and scientific principles. Even in the case of primarily motor learning – learning to drive a car, or to master an athletic skill – symbolic activities of these kinds may play an important part. In universities, and even in schools, it is this kind of learning that has an essentially central place.

Difficulties of the learner may be examined in the light of this. A given learner's problems with a new subject matter may stem from his lack of understanding of the symbols through which this knowledge has to be acquired. This applies with ordinary language as when additional difficulties are encountered because a learner's first language is not English. An illustration may be taken in the case of the foreign student who was greatly troubled by the two words 'instincts' and 'insects'. On one occasion I encountered a colleague struggling with the difficulties of this learner over one chapter of a text-book. As the chapter concerned dealt mainly with 'the instincts of insects' the confusions of the learner, and ultimately of the teacher also, had to be heard to be believed. Subtle versions of this kind of problem can be encountered with complex subject matter when the learner either lacks the vocabulary needed, or has not fully mastered the rules for its use. Many such difficulties can arise in teaching–learning situations of communities in which bilingualism prevails. To give some indications of these I quote the observations of one young psychologist of Spanish-American descent. Although he was initially Spanish-speaking he has himself been able to overcome the problem to which he refers, though very naturally remains interested in the issues. He reports that in New Mexico, in the American South-west, the Spanish-American will first learn Spanish in the home, and 'then at the age of six he is cast into a completely new environment, namely the school where only English is used'. My informant says, 'In his zeal to learn the new language he will forsake the old language, the process being encouraged by his parents, until finally many Spanish-American children do not know how to speak in Spanish.' He adds: 'Maybe eventually it will no longer be necessary for this writer to speak to his younger brothers and sisters in English – while speaking to his mother and father in Spanish – which is a situation we find in many Spanish-American homes today.' Further problems arise with bilingualism, as they do with the Spanish–American, when the language learned in the home has the advantage of primacy, while the other as the language of the educational process has greater social prestige. Moreover it may be noted that different languages may involve different concepts and associations, even when the words imply quantification. Thus, to compare British and American usages of 'English', we encounter the Englishman's 'a pint of pure water weights a pound and a quarter', and the American's 'a pint weights a pound, the whole world around'! Similarly British and American usages differ in a confusing way in relation to such concepts as a gallon, a penny, a billion, and a game of football. These cultural differences may help to amplify the more subtle differences of a subcultural kind which may arise as between school or university and home.

Elsewhere (1965) I have discussed in detail some of the barriers to learning which result from the conflicting standards of the home and the teaching–learning situation. These difficulties may be considerable when, as for the Spanish-American, the language of education is not that of the home. But it may apply more generally also, as when the schooling and education of the learner exceed that of his parents. His use of words, his pronunciation, his concepts, and his systems of knowledge become increasingly different from those of the home. If the parents have themselves sided with education, and made sacrifices to achieve it for their child, their awareness of these differences may result in hostility and resentment. Relatives who are over-ready to label the different forms of behaviour and speech as 'getting big ideas' or 'being stuck up' do not always help. The attempts of the learner himself to read, or otherwise pursue his studies, may often provide excellent subject matter for labelling as 'being lazy', by those who do not understand, or are motivated trouble-makers. Education is very likely indeed to enrich the conceptual life of the learner, thus to create additional barriers and stimulate ambivalences already present. Moreover it is the case with higher education that it creates specialized knowledge, and resulting precision and refinement of thinking. Questions of a seemingly simple kind asked by the layman – as is only too apparent with specialists who act as witnesses in courts of law – are often either meaningless to the expert, or impossible for him to answer. A specialist may devote a lifetime of study to building up a system of knowledge about a field whose very existence is largely unknown to his close relatives of an earlier generation. This can create enormous problems for the learner in the teaching–learner situation. Communication between the older and the younger is difficult enough in any case, and acquisition of systems of knowledge is one thing that may occur to increase the barrier.

INTELLECTUAL DIFFERENCES AND INTELLECTUAL DEVELOPMENT

Intelligence testing had originally the very practical aim of educational classification. In 1905 its pioneers, Alfred Binet and Théophile Simon, evolved their test for measuring the abilities of Paris school children. They sought a method of classification involving 'questions fixed in advance' which, as they say, did not suffer in its validity 'from the bad digestion or bad humour of the examiner'. It merits emphasis that the problems used in the test were based on Binet's extensive observations of children's thought and behaviour in classrooms. As is well known the method involved assessment of the child's mental age by its success in solving problems which became increasingly difficult for later age groups. Terman, who revised the test, added a concept suggested by Wilhelm Stern, that of 'intelligence quotient', this being the ratio between mental age and chronological age. Good accounts of the development of intelligence theory and technique are readily available, for example in the comprehensive collection of papers edited by Jenkins and Paterson (1961).

A second important advance in the understanding of intelligence and thinking came with the Swiss psychologist Piaget. Piaget was himself associated with the early Binet–Simon work, but he was less interested in whether a child could 'pass' a given test or sub-test than in the kind of errors he made. In this Piaget found one powerful way of studying the development of thinking under the influence of development and increased experience. His over-all finding has been that the child is not just intellectually inferior to the adult, but is also different in his ways of thinking. Thus with the passage of time, which allows both intellectual maturation and increased learning, the child develops a better ability to deal with such concepts as number, cause and effect, and greater levels of abstraction. Thus the notion that objects retain their shape and do not change, as they appear to do from different points of perspective, needs to be learned. The realization that it is possible to make an assumption which is contrary to the observable facts, and explore its possibilities, is a product of sophistication and experience. It is also essential to some of the higher forms of adult thinking. After a somewhat undue time lag the work of Piaget on the developmental psychology of thinking became known in Britain and the United States. Less well known are parallel developments in Soviet psychology, and the influence of Piaget himself on this work. An illustration may be taken from the researches of the contemporary Soviet investigator P. I. Galperin, to illustrate how developmental studies of intellectual life are being applied to teaching.

Galperin, following a line of thought which has also been explored by Piaget, is interested in how activities occur first at the level of overt action, but are later mastered by the child to become part of his ideational mental life. This development can provide a guide for the instructional methods of the teacher. Galperin takes as an example learning arithmetic (see Simon, 1957). First the teacher demonstrates the action and gets the child interested in the relevant materials. Second follows mastery of the operation using objects: by counting the objects the child discovers the concreted content of the action for himself. Thirdly, the child speaks aloud while it counts with the aid of the objects: thus the action becomes a verbal activity. Fourthly the activity is transferred to the mental plane: the child is taught to count in a whisper, and then sub-vocally, so that, as Galperin says, 'it is really not an action any longer but a flow of concepts about it.' Finally, the action is abbreviated and consolidated, and with the dropping out of any unnecessary accompaniments it becomes fully automatic.

Procedures of this kind are used widely today. They may be used either in ordinary education or with problem learners in remedial teaching. Thus in the United States, for example, Bruner (1964) reports on experiments involving overt operations with a balancing beam and rings which have been used to teach quadratic equations. The time lag in the spread of Piaget's work has been noted. Studies similar to those of Piaget that have been going on for many years in Soviet Russia are slowly becoming known in the Western world. Whether the relevant researches stem from Switzerland, Russia, England, America, or elsewhere, it is becoming apparent that the intellectual development of the child progresses through a series of stages, with consolidation of one followed by progress to the next. The growing body of knowledge about such development has important implications for the school curriculum. Differences which divide younger child from older child, and child from adult, are not merely quantitative, but also qualitative. Realization of this, and its full implications, is of considerable importance to both parent and teacher.

Educational psychology has traditionally placed emphasis on the phenomenon of transfer of training: early learning interacts with later learning. A given task may be interfered with by one's earlier habits, as is familiar to the motorist who learned to drive on the left and has to adjust to driving on the right. This is an instance of negative transfer. Positive transfer occurs when the earlier learning assists rather than inhibits the later learning.

The study of positive transfer has received considerable impetus from the work of Harlow as a leading animal investigator. Harlow's central concept is learning set. A learning set is an organized system of habits which is built up from learning tasks of a particular kind, and which assists learning in similar tasks. Thus in the course of his life an individual builds up a repertoire of learning sets. Working at first with monkeys, Harlow was led to reject the sharp distinction many previous learning theorists had made between insightful and trial-and-error learning. He found that his subjects would at first solve the problems set by trial and error. Later they progressed to greater efficiency with problems of a similar kind, and exhibited insight. Thus trial and error on the one hand, and insight on the other, were found to be merely different phases of one long, continuous learning process. Subsequent experiments with human infants revealed the same story as with animal subjects. The child's learning contributed to a learning set for problems of a similar kind, and marked its progress towards a learning set, or increased repertoire of learning sets. Thus under the heading of learning set we encounter the old problem of transfer of training in a new framework, and one vigorous area of both animal experimentation and experimental child psychology.

Both teachers, whether in schools or universities or elsewhere, and educational psychologists have frequently experienced an awareness that their efforts are not always encouraging to the originality of those they teach. Thus Thurstone (1952), writing as a university teacher, distinguished two types of student: those who were creative, and those who merely developed critical ability as a result of their teaching. He went on to suggest that sometimes we are inclined to confuse scholarship with mere 'intellectual docility'. This line of thought has led to some important advances in the study of the learner. Important work has stemmed from a presidential address to the American Psychological Association in 1950 by J. P. Guilford on creativity. Guilford was led to make a distinction between what he called *convergent and divergent thinking*. He equated convergent thinking with the kind of thinking that orthodox intelligence tests measure: its best measures are problems which have a single, conventionally accepted, right answer. Divergent thinking is different. It is concerned with innovation, with the solution of problems in which originality, flexibility, and minimum dependence on known information are involved. Using the techniques of factor analysis Guilford and his associates have thus sought both to analyse 'intelligence' into its components, and to perform a similar analysis of 'creativity'. From his factorial studies Guilford (1959) arrives at the finding that there are about fifty known factors underlying the cognitive mental life of the individual. These he subdivides into: those concerned with the discovery and recognition of information, those concerned with the use of such information, and those concerned with evaluating and making judgements on what we know, remember, and produce. Progress has been made in designing and validating tests for measurement in all three of these fields. Much research has followed. One important investigation by Getzels and Jackson (1962) offers some quantitative support for Thurstone's earlier observations about two types of learner. Working with school children they made a systematic comparison between those who scored highly on 'intelligence' tests, and those who scored highly on tests of 'creativity'. The high creativity scorers gave evidence of much deviation from the norm of teacher's expectations and classroom approval, and showed interestingly original thought products in contrast to the conventionalized productions of the 'intelligence' group. Getzels and Jackson argue that more should be done to encourage the activities, and improve the morale, of the original and non-conformist thinker in the classroom. A note of caution may be sounded. It may well be that what needs most of all to be sought out and encouraged is not either 'intelligence' or 'creativity', but some combination of both. A group of individuals of this kind was not included in the Getzels and Jackson study. As Burt has put it, 'Creativity without general intelligence produces nothing of interest or value.' High originality may involve something more than intelligence, and certain aspects of this 'something other' – granted that good intelligence is also present – seem to have been elucidated by Guilford and his associates. We may note also Getzels and Jackson again for their general conclusion, that we should seek out and foster, in all ways possible, desirable cognitive traits of *all* kinds. The classrooms they studied appeared not to do this. Traits measured by conventional intelligence tests do not, as Guilford's work has shown, embrace all such traits.

Recent years have seen an enormous growth of interest in the psychology of what has come to be called 'creativity'. There is, as we have seen, reason for caution in view of the enormous amount of research which is going on. Thus Mednick (1963) sees it necessary to make a distinction between 'originality' and 'creativity'. He points out that the number 7,363,474 is 'quite an original answer' to the problem of adding $12 + 12$, and much 'originality' is to be found in the productions of psychotic patients. But creativity involves originality which is in some way or other useful; it is originality upon which some additional requirements have been imposed. More recently N. H. Mackworth (1965) draws attention to wider issues: the forms of thinking which it is desirable to seek out and encourage nationally through the education system. The distinction he makes is between problem-solving and problem-finding. He argues that 'problem-finding is the more important', that today 'problem-finders are scarce and are going to be more in demand as the years go by'. In support he refers to C. P. Snow, whose experience in this matter has been considerable in that he was prominently involved in the reallocation of scientists in Britain during the Second World War. A further reason for the increased importance of the problem-finder is the emergence of the computer with its potential problem-solving power. Thus Mackworth draws attention to the case of the mathematician Wang, who was able to design a programme for a computer which enabled it to solve 350 theorems from the first thirteen chapters of *Principia Mathematica*. It took just under eight seconds! Computers are better than men as problem-solvers, but markedly inferior as problem-finders.

The two types of mental activity in the human thinker may be seen in terms of the activity of a computer. Problem-solving involves the selection and use of an existing programme ('set of mental rules') from an existing set of programmes. Problem-finding, however, involves being able to detect the need for a new programme from a comparison of existing programmes and expected future programmes. These contributions point the way to certain desirable forms of thinking, somewhat obscured by the all-embracing concept of 'creativity', which it seems desirable to seek out and in all ways encourage in the education system. As we have seen vigorous work on this issue is being conducted elsewhere, by Soviet educational psychologists.

EMOTIONAL PROBLEMS AND THE LEARNER

One teacher described at a course I was conducting at an American University Summer School the *dramatis personae* of her own classroom. There were 26 children, ages ranged from 9 to 10 years; 17 of them had what she assessed as emotional problems. Fictitious names will be used. One dominant boy was Ted: his influence was considerable and his father was in prison. George was a product of culture conflict, and came from an Anglo-Japanese home. Bill had been brain-damaged at birth, and was 'easily led', being under the influence of Ted and four other children whom the teacher described as 'having no home super-vision'. Mildred and Susan had another kind of problem: they gave much evidence of resentment by being displaced by new baby sisters; these two girls often regressed to baby talk. Henry had been abandoned, had no home of his own, and was a ward of the State: he was a large and belligerent boy. Stephen and Ann both had divorced parents, and gave much evidence of feeling themselves to be unwanted. Albert was a victim of parental smothering love, and addicted to lying. Bert had a long history of physical illnesses, and also a father whose intense ambitions for the boy kept him under perpetual strain. Woody had been adopted, and adopted into an excessively strict and puritanical home. Two of the other boys were seriously out of parental control: this the teacher attributed to the effects of unwise over-indulgence. Of interest are two of the other children who exhibited no signs of emotional problems: one was a Negro girl, and the other a Navajo Indian boy. This particular class illustrates the range of problems which can confront teachers in respect of the emotional life of their pupils. As my informant – who was perhaps more unfortunate than most teachers – pointed out, 'And all in one room.'

What is a teacher prepared to assess as an emotional problem? On this there has been much investigation. The researches of Wickman in 1938 on teachers in elementary schools provides a beginning. These teachers found that more 'problems' arose with boys than with girls, and the problems most often mentioned related to behaviour in the school situation. Most often mentioned were whispering (74 per cent), inattention (59 per cent), and carelessness in work (44 per cent). The investigator concluded that 'the personal problems of the child seem to be subordinated to the problems in teaching and classroom management'. Of interest are subsequent investigations which have listed 'problems' relating to the child, and which have sought the assessment of the seriousness of these problems by teachers on the one hand and psychologists, psychiatrists, and social workers on the other. In general this mental hygiene group tended to rate more seriously problems involving withdrawal and silent misery; the teachers by contrast rated more highly problems involving heterosexual activities, dishonesty, and disobedience. A study in 1959 by Porter used the sentence completion technique. He asked various groups to complete sentences like: 'I think the child who continually steals should . . .', and 'I think the child who is always late should . . .'. The responses obtained he classified on a scale ranging from 'take punitive measures' to 'praise or encourage', and 'study him and find cause'. Behaviour for which punitive reponses were most frequent comprized: showing off, bullying, and disobedience. Responses of senior high-school pupils showed a frequent inclination to use punitive measures; these were less common among university students, and less common still with experienced teachers. There would seem to be evidence of a tendency for the older and more experienced teachers – at least in America, where the researches mentioned were conducted – to move towards more mental-hygiene-type methods like 'study the child and seek to understand'. Of interest is a judgement made by the woman psychologist Lois Murphy on the basis of a longitudinal study of problem children, 252 in all, investigated over a period of fourteen years. (At the end of the period 224 children remained, a high figure and itself a tribute to the investigator.) Lois Murphy finds abundant evidence that normal children have problems: tantrums, fears, and jealousies reached a peak at about 4 to 4½ years when they occurred in more than 50 per cent of cases, and then decreased. She concludes that certain problems are to be expected, and given time many such problems are outgrown: this is a healthy reassurance to the worried adult.

In the *dramatis personae* of her classroom as described by the American summer school teacher we encountered instances of children who were problems because of unwise parental indulgence. Sometimes parental weakness and stupidity of this kind is rationalized in terms of the magic formula, 'Psychologists say . . .' or 'but psychiatrists advise'. In this connexion may be noted a vigorous objection by Melitta Schmideberg (1959), who writing as a New York psycho-analyst relates some of the cases she has had to handle. As illustration I take the case of Mrs A and Jimmy. Mrs A had read all the books, and had tried to bring up Jimmy in accord with 'the best psychiatric advice'. Her resulting tribulations are instructive. At 3 years of age Jimmy was sent to a progressive nursery school, from which at 4 he was expelled. This was followed by a period at a still more progressive school which seems, by ordinary standards, to have permitted quite unusual licence. At this school the children were so wild that the grandfather was unable to go and fetch Jimmy after lessons for fear of a heart attack. Jimmy seems to have stood out even at this school: the bus driver for instance refused to drive the bus if Jimmy was on it. At 6 Jimmy was asked to leave. Schmideberg brings out the contributions of the mother towards reinforcement of Jimmy's behaviour; for example when Jimmy kicked another child from its bicycle she would take him upstairs and read him a story. She had been told that a fit of temper needs to be taken very seriously, and handled as carefully as an epileptic fit. Psychiatry and psychology have too often been blamed quite unjustifiably for excesses of this kind. In the examples taken we have Schmideberg as a psycho-analyst testifying that she has to devote a considerable amount of her work to undoing the harm done by the unwise indulgence of parents who believe themselves to be acting in accord with psychological advice. As Schmideberg says of another of her cases, it was necessary for her to point out to the parents concerned that because of their total avoidance of any form of reproof or punishment of the almost incredibly unruly child, and because they overpraised continually and overwhelmed the child with presents, they 'soon would not even have the means of bribing her'. In the end, Schmideberg reports, her arguments proved successful and by the time the child was four 'as a result of my efforts the mother began to lead a reasonably normal life'.

If psychologists 'say' anything on the matter of child upbringing, they are apt to be found stressing the importance of different circumstances, and of individual differences of personality. They are likely also to be found making reference to specific investigations. An illustration of this more typical approach is to be found in, for example, the work, reported in 1947, of Jenkins and Glickman, who classified the three main types of personality most commonly encountered in child-guidance clinics. They distinguished: first, the unsocialized aggressive child; secondly, the socialized delinquent; and third, the over-inhibited child. The unsocialized aggressive individual tended to exhibit violence, destructiveness, and cruelty, with apparent absence of a sense of guilt. Such children tended to come from an atmosphere of parental rejection: the kind of home in which the child was made to feel unwanted. Statistical evidence revealed that maternal rejection and the illness of the mother during pregnancy were both prominent in the background of such children. The socialized delinquents held membership of a delinquent group, they participated in, rather than led, anti-social activities, and showed loyalty to their gang. Children of this category had experienced some early socialization in the home, but subsequent neglect. These children were found to be more like the non-delinquent school population than the other two groups, but bad companionship was a major characteristic. Parental neglect rather than parental rejection was distinctive of them, and they tended to find their significant social activities and emotional ties not in the home but among companions. The over-inhibited child represented a different type of problem. Typically he was shy, sensitive, and submissive, with strong feelings of inferiority of the kind to which Adler drew attention. From a discouraging home of an unduly restrictive kind – with perhaps a cold father and a domineering mother – he had come to habits of excessive over-conformity.

These studies and others like them have sought to show how different home background, and influences outside the home, can produce different kinds of personality. If we know the recipe for different forms of undesirable behaviour we can much better see how to understand it, and how to put it right.

Very important throughout the teaching–learning situation is the attribute to which Adler paid particular attention: the sense of inferiority. Adler regarded feelings of inferiority as a universal human phenomenon. He explained them from the universal experience of being first a child, and surrounded by larger, more powerful and abler adults. Various reactions are possible. One child may be crushed by it, discouraged, typically under-confident, and regularly an under-performer. A second may over-compensate, be noisy and demanding, and in all respects apparently the reverse of inferior. Yet, as Adler sees him, such a child is exhibiting – in disguised form – its need for encouragement and improved morale. Some physical attribute – like being too tall, or too short, or having pimples or freckles – may increase a child's sense of isolation, and resulting feeling of inferiority. Another child, rightly or wrongly, may feel rejected and unwanted and develop excessive under-confidence for psychological rather than physical reasons. To Adler's thought on this problem may be added the concept, from orthodox psycho-analysis, of 'restriction of the ego'. Each person limits his aspirations in certain ways, being emotionally involved with his successes and failures in some activities, but indifferent to his achievements in others. As with adults, much of the behaviour of children in relation to morale and inferiority feelings can be seen in terms of the individual's habits of ego restriction.

A teacher himself may make substantial contributions to the inferiority feelings and difficulties of the learner. Some teachers exhibit an excessive tendency to put labels on a child's behaviour, and potential. An illustration is the case of one person who, as an adult, remained quite unable to sing in tune. His disheartening experiences as a learner at school are perhaps not irrelevant. His teacher represented a somewhat extreme instance of those who view pupils not as potential learners but as personifications of fixed abilities. When weekly singing classes were held, he divided the pupils into those who 'could sing' and those who 'could not'. The morale of the second group – which included the person under discussion – was not helped by a further habit of the teacher to use the labels 'the sheep' and 'the goats'. After the division of the class into the singers and the non-singers, those who 'could sing' then sang each week, and subsequently took part in the school concert. The others sat restlessly in class, and did nothing: no attempt whatsoever was made to teach these rejected pupils.

Very different is the approach to the same problem of one Soviet psychologist, A. N. Leontiev, who investigated a group of school children assessed by their music teachers as tone deaf. Leontiev used an oscilloscope which displayed in visual form on a screen in front of the children both the note they produced and the note they were trying to produce. In one experiment, after ten lessons, all members of an allegedly 'tone deaf' class were taught by this method to sing in tune.

CONCLUSION

Over-concern with 'the book' has been, on occasion, a major impediment to the imaginative, humane, and realistic handling of young people by adults. Thus in the past, and sometimes even now, the Bible has been used as though it were a text-book on child upbringing and discipline. The resulting excesses of moralized human cruelty, for example about 'original sin' and childhood, are unimpressive testimony for the adult's capacity for intelligence, empathy, or common sense. After misusing the Bible in this way, human unreason readily seized upon other books as a substitute for effort to achieve real understanding of the child. Authors of books are not always to be blamed for the excesses of rigid and uncritical disciples. For example, in New Zealand, the work of Sir Truby King gave rise to a system of child care with exceedingly high standards, and made infant mortality in that country amongst the lowest in the world. But 'the book' on which these reforms were based had its irrational by-products. There were parents who did not dare to feed their infant who was making its hunger plainly apparent to any impartial bystander, until the time interval required by the book's feeding schedule had elapsed. Such unfortunate children were fed in a way that was determined by fixed schedules on which their parents had developed an unhealthy emotional dependence: the screamings of an obviously hungry child were ignored.

Psycho-analysis began as a revolt against rigidity and self-deception. It was later itself to provide rationalizations for the intellectually lazy, and subject matter for the excesses of unwise adult permissiveness. The cases quoted by Schmideberg provide illustrations. Words like repression, inhibition, and insecurity only too often became a devaluated currency whose small residue of meaning was remote from anything Freud actually taught. It is in this context that the psycho-analyst Theodore Reik quotes an old German proverb: 'With the formation of a system the talking of nonsense begins.' Psycho-analytic terminology if misunderstood – in the way the word 'repression' for instance has been misunderstood – invites the talking of nonsense. Many over-anxious, unwise, and hypochondriacal adults have succumbed to the temptation. In 1946 there emerged yet another source of raw materials for use in impeding adult–child understanding, and again the author is not to be blamed. In that year appeared Dr Benjamin Spock's book *The Common Sense of Baby and Child Care*. The word 'common sense', present in Dr Spock's title, was remarkably absent in many forms of 'Spockism'. (Of parallel interest is Freud's remark to Reik which Reik quotes: 'Me, I am not a Freudian!') Dr Spock has himself referred ruefully to the excesses committed in his name. These included the discipleship of one mother who kept a copy of Spock in the living-room, a second in the bedroom, a third in the bathroom; she was thinking of acquiring another for the upstairs hall! Among the many serious barriers to effective empathy in the adult–child and teaching–learning relationships may be mentioned 'the book' in the various forms in which this misuse of the printed word has manifested itself. It is also unfortunate that psychology as a branch of science has so often been blamed for these misunderstandings. Psychology has, in fact, much to contribute, and not least through its understanding of the self-deceptions or ego-defences which can operate in various ways like taking refuge in the printed word. Its relations to the teacher–learner situation are complex, not simple. In the United States, Soviet Russia, Britain, Switzerland, and elsewhere, it has pursued some important, if different, lines of inquiry. To the study of basic problems it brings its varied techniques of experimentation, observation, mental measurement, and introspection, in a broad approach to the problems of the learner.

CHAPTER EIGHT

Emotions and Emotional Habits

> Every emotion has a potential disinterestedness, so far as
> among the stimuli which excite it are some which excite
> it on behalf of another individual instead of on behalf of
> oneself.
>
> A. F. SHAND

THIS chapter will have a historical emphasis. My justification
for this is that some of the more powerful and interesting ideas
about emotion stem from the past rather than more recent years.
'The greatest psychologist since Aristotle' was William Mc-
Dougall's assessment of Freud. In this opinion, apart from its
recognition of Freud's genius, is also implicit a judgement of the
lean years that divided Ancient Greece from twentieth-century
Vienna. A beginning will be made with one criticism, I think a
fundamental one, that has been made of Freud's thought.

Alexander Shand, who was first secretary of the British Psychological Society, had substantial contributions to make to the
understanding of emotion. From Shand came a somewhat unexpected, seemingly paradoxical, criticism of Freudian thought:
the psycho-analysts have, Shand argued, paid too little attention
to the *analysis* of human emotion. Thus Freud himself writes in
an extremely loose way about 'love': sometimes it is an instinct,
sometimes an emotion, and sometimes an emotional habit of the
kind Shand would call a sentiment. This tendency in Freud received little approval from Shand, himself a scholarly, sensitive,
and above all subtle thinker about the complexities of emotion.
Professor T. H. Pear, who knew Shand as a person, has recorded,
with obvious respect for Shand both as a psychologist and as
secretary-organizer of the early dinners of the newly formed
Society, 'Shand always spoke of the different emotions as if they
had different vintages and bouquets.' Shand's thought on emotion is important precisely because of his scholarship. He took up
the idea from John Stuart Mill, and set out to collate the observa-

tions and thoughts of past thinkers about the psychology of emotion. His major work, *The Foundations of Character*, records this survey, and in it Shand formulates no fewer than 144 principles about emotion. One of these, which we might call Shand's 'principle of disinterestedness', heads this chapter. The book as a whole reflects two aspects of Shand's contribution: first, an examination of relations between emotion and motivation; secondly, a distinction between emotion itself and emotional habits.

SENTIMENTS AS EMOTIONAL HABITS

Typical of the emotions are joy, sorrow, fear, and anger. From these Shand distinguishes sentiments, for example love and hate, liking and disliking, respect and contempt. This distinction between emotion and sentiment squares with the phenomena of experience. When influenced by an emotion like anger a person is acutely aware of the object of his emotion, and of the circumstances which provoked the emotion. In this he differs from, for example, a person who has a sentiment of hate: hate like love is a habitual response to an object, involving a disposition to respond which persists even when one is not thinking of the object of the sentiment. More strictly speaking, a sentiment is not merely a disposition, but a system of dispositions which give rise to a number of different emotional reactions to the object. As Heider (1958) has put it in more recent years, the sentiment is a connecting link, and 'different situations give rise to different actions and feelings that in some way are appropriate to the sentiment'.

The characteristic of sentiments as being complex systems of dispositions applies both to positive or pro sentiments and negative or con sentiments. Positive sentiments are characterized by their tendency to lead to sympathetic emotions towards the object. The presence of this object gives rise to pleasure and the emotion of joy; the absence of the object is an occasion for sorrow and regret; if the object is threatened or injured, the sentiment results in sympathetic fear or anger on behalf of the object. By contrast, sentiments like dislike and hate result in antipathetic emotions. The presence of the object results in displeasure and regret; its absence is an occasion for pleasure; the object's well-being may result in sorrow; and anger is only too readily experienced against, rather than on behalf of, the object. Thus, Shand argues, we can analyse sentiments as involving a system of dispositions to respond emotionally in a variety of ways, in a variety of circumstances involving the object. Important among the emotions concerned are four: joy and sorrow, fear and anger. But this is not the whole story: we do not have one sentiment, but many, and these sentiments interact. Important among the other sentiments are those which involve our feelings of right and wrong, ought and ought not: these are the moral sentiments. Thus because of our moral sentiments we may not feel joyful and pleased at the injury or misfortune of our enemy: we may feel guilty if we catch ourselves beginning to feel such pleasure. Thus the moral sentiments restrain our reactions from the excesses of sympathetic and antipathetic emotion.

Another factor to be considered is to be found in Shand's principle of relative ethics of sentiments. This principle is recognized in the proverbial saying 'all's fair in love and war'. In other words, our sentiments – whether pro or con – carry with them an ethic of their own, and this permits us to limit the guilt we feel when we indulge our loves and hates. One aspect of an investigation I conducted into negative sentiments may serve to illustrate this notion of relative ethics. It emerged that the subjects concerned tended to attribute moral inferiority to the object of their hostile sentiment. Of 30 subjects, 25 asserted that the object was ethically inferior to themselves, 3 said the object was 'both good and bad', and only 2 were prepared to describe the object as 'good'. Instances of the ethical traits attributed to the object of hostility included spitefulness, dishonesty, selfishness, and being 'stuck up' and 'rough and ill-mannered'. At times this ethical inferiority was asserted very strongly: in one case the object was described as 'the smallest and most mean and contemptible person I encountered in my adolescence'. This tendency, which emerged in my own investigation, to argue that the object was morally inferior is in accord with Shand's principle of relative ethics. The subject thus feels liberated from restraint in his actions towards the other person, and from guilt over his hostility or hatred.

Sentiments as Emotional Habits

Shand (1922) defined a sentiment as 'a system of emotional dispositions having different conative tendencies, connected with a common object and subordinated to a common end'. Following Shand's introduction of the concept at an earlier date, psychologists in Britain tended to make considerable use of it. Foremost among such psychologists was McDougall, who developed a theory of human motivation in terms of two concepts: instincts or innate conative tendencies, and sentiments or acquired conative tendencies. From this early period there emerged a classification of sentiments into three broad categories: concrete particular (e.g. love or dislike of a specific person), concrete general (e.g. hatred of cats), and abstract (e.g. respect for integrity). Among the abstract sentiments are moral sentiments, which we have seen are our habitual ways of feeling about concepts like right and wrong, good and evil, justice and injustice.

We may also classify sentiments as pro (liking, loving, respecting), and con (hating, disliking, and holding in contempt). But we owe it to Freud that we are today more fully aware of the ambivalence of emotional habits: a person may have both positive and negative feelings towards the object of a sentiment. The notion of ambivalence stems from Freud, though was of course recognized before him, in for example that period when cynical and witty Frenchmen competed with one another in designing maxims about human nature. Most famous of these are the *Maxims* of La Rochefoucauld, which bear witness to ambivalence in human sentiments, as in his well-known saying, 'In the misfortunes of our dearest friends we find something not entirely displeasing to us'. From time to time people express in wit their awareness that 'love' may contain considerable ambivalence. To take a more recent example, the cartoonist Jules Feiffer has advised us: 'We should love our enemies; love is too dangerous an emotion to use on our friends.' But love is not an emotion, it is a sentiment, and an exceedingly complex one. As we have seen, it can be a strongly ambivalent sentiment, carrying with it tendencies to both sympathetic and antipathetic emotion. The lover loves, but may also feel twinges of resentment for the power the loved one has over him. Similarly the hater hates, but what is predominantly a hostile sentiment may also be ambivalent in that he experiences an accompanying pity for his enemy. Freud himself does not make use of the notion of sentiments, and it was not Freud but Sir Cyril Burt who adopted explicitly the extreme position: all sentiments are ambivalent. This is an interesting hypothesis for further investigation. Certainly there is much evidence that people can lack considerable insight into their own sentiments. Aspects of sentiments may undergo repression, and the holder of a sentiment may be largely unaware of either the intensity of the emotion, or the ambivalence of that emotion, locked up in the sentiment. The word love, as ordinarily used, certainly covers a multitude of different emotional habits.

In one sense the opposite of love is not hatred, but the opposite of both love and hatred is indifference. We are emotionally involved – as Muzafer Sherif would put it, 'ego involved' – with certain people, types of people, and abstractions. Others are a matter of indifference. The early Quakers used the term 'concern', and they themselves exhibited concern with such matters as slavery, poverty, and cruelty. This emotional concern, or preoccupation of people with one another, is observable in everyday inter-personal relations. We notice it, for example, in the lovers' quarrel which is said to be 'love's renewing'. What seems to happen is that through time hostility builds up between two people who are intensely emotionally concerned with each other. Some provocation results in a quarrel which drains away the ambivalence of the relationship, and then love in relatively undiluted form remains. During such a quarrel either party may slam the door and make an exit while expressing the wish never to see the other person again. This statement is not to be taken at its face value: manifestly it is a statement of indifference, but latently it is clearly something else, and an indication of continued emotional preoccupation. Freud has found a basis of understanding other inter-personal phenomena from the study of the behaviour of people in love. Somewhat similar to the lovers' quarrel are occurrences which may happen during analysis when transference – an emotional dependence of the patient on the analyst – has developed. Transference tends to be highly ambivalent. At times the positive aspect of transference may be uppermost, while at others the hostility may be most apparent and may give rise to emotional outbursts. Similar instances of intense emotional preoccupation are to be found in sentiments people build up in relation to subjects like politics and religion. The enthusiastic atheist and the enthusiastic religious fanatic are both noticeably similar in that they manifest the opposite of an indifference towards religion. The content of the two sentiments may be different, but the form and emotional intensity may be remarkably similar in both cases. One insightful study of emotional dependence together with ambivalence has been provided by Ibsen in his play *Emperor and Galilean*. As a dramatic production, which partially reflects historical events, it deals with the Emperor Julian the Apostate. It tells of Julian's early conversion to Christianity, his subsequent rejection of it, and his continuing emotional preoccupation with it throughout. As is often observable in the person who rejects something very strongly, so Julian gives much evidence of his hostility to those who show indifference. Other more recent writers have dealt with manifestations of ambivalence. Thus Somerset Maugham's short story *Sanitorium* concerns two tubercular patients who are always having quarrels. Then one of them dies. The survivor is overcome with distress, and shows the deep loss he now feels because of his obvious emotional dependence on his object of hostility. At a very much earlier date the philosopher Hume discussed this aspect of inter-personal relations. Hume pointed out that we are as emotionally linked to those we profess to hate as to those we profess to love. In both cases the welfare of the other person is a matter of considerable concern to us.

OTHER EMOTIONAL HABITS

Sentiments comprise only one category of emotional habits, though an important one. They organize emotional experience, and its behavioural manifestations, in relation to such important matters as religion, politics, ethics, and the people and institutions with which we are concerned. As Cantril has said, we can understand a great deal about, for example, human conflict from a study of the groups and institutions with which people identify themselves. Another important category of emotional habits is prejudices. Like sentiments, prejudices can be classified as pro and con; and we can also classify them in terms of degree of emotional intensity. Anti-semitism and colour prejudice may be taken as typical examples of emotional habits. Both have been intensively studied by psychologists.

In considering negative or con prejudices it is important to take account of the fact that not all hostile habitual reactions are necessarily prejudices. The Jewish survivor of a Nazi concentration camp with a hostility to the S.S. or the Gestapo cannot realistically be diagnosed as having a prejudice. But, by contrast, a habitual hostility to all Germans would be a prejudice, the sub-type of prejudice that manifests over-generalization. We are at times apt to forget that most of the inmates of concentration camps were in fact Germans. Hostile sentiments towards whole populations, e.g. whole national groups, will be taken as prejudices. Hostile sentiments based on grounds which would seem reasonable adjustments to reality to an impartial observer – for example hostility of the Jew to the Nazis, of the American Negro to the Ku Klux Klan, or the South African Negro to the present South African Government – will be regarded as not necessarily prejudices.

With this in mind, a distinction may be drawn between two kinds of prejudices. These I have discussed elsewhere as *primary prejudices and secondary prejudices* (McKellar, 1952). Primary prejudices are those based on first-hand experience of the people concerned. It is no use saying to the holder of a primary prejudice, 'You don't know these people'. His answer is 'Yes I do'. But it is appropriate to say to him, 'Aren't you over-generalizing on the basis of your own unhappy experience?' If attempts are made to remove primary prejudices, and are to be successful, this fact of over-generalization must be established to the satisfaction of the prejudiced person. Secondary prejudices are of a different kind. Such prejudices were exemplified in a study of New Zealand university students, many of whom had prejudices against Turks. Inquiry revealed that none of them was aware of ever having met a Turk! Their prejudice they had picked up at second hand, perhaps on the basis of stories relating to Armenian massacres by Turks. (Once I met an Armenian, and his anti-Turkish sentiment was of quite a different kind, approximating to what I have called primary prejudice.) In the case of secondary prejudices, it *is* appropriate to argue, 'You don't know anything about these people' or 'Why not meet some before you rush to conclusions?' As a hypothesis for future investigation I would offer the suggestion that primary and secondary prejudices tend to differ in their effects on behaviour. Primary prejudices are the kind most likely to lead to violent behaviour, lynching, atrocity, and other forms of group pathology. Secondary prejudices tend to be dislikes rather than hatreds, or even something of weaker emotional intensity. They often express themselves in such forms as 'I am not against Xs, *but . . .*'. Secondary prejudice of this kind is an exceedingly widespread phenomenon, but is socially less dangerous than primary prejudice so far as law and order are concerned.

On the whole, prejudices differ from sentiments in being somewhat along the scale towards another kind of emotional habit, namely *complexes*. The term complex has been widely misused but seems a legitimate word to apply to emotional preoccupations of a kind which shade into the pathological. As Pear has observed, psychology needs the two words sentiment and complex to refer respectively to the 'tidy' and 'untidy' organizations of emotional life. Sentiments on the whole give rise to relatively consistent behaviour, and behaviour of a kind we are, on the whole, prepared rationally to defend. Thus we may intellectually justify our political, religious, and moral sentiments: we defend our friends, and argue that we are perfectly right in disliking our enemies. Complexes, on the whole, we tend to apologize for, rather than rationally defend; 'I can't help it but . . .' is more the typical reaction. And complexes, for example, excessive emotional preoccupation with inferiority feelings, with guilt, with sex, or with specific but irrational fears, on the whole give rise to more uncoordinated forms of behaviour. The manifestations of fear, guilt, and inferiority called complexes may be hedged round with ego-defences. But as organizations of emotional life, complexes typically differ from sentiments.

Prejudices have some of this all or nothing character that complexes show. This seems to be particularly the case with prejudices of the primary kind. Sharp distinctions cannot always readily be drawn, so we may conclude our discussion by suggesting a scale of emotional habits: this seems to range from typical sentiments, through typical prejudices, to typical complexes. All such emotional habits seem to affect our emotional threshold, our readiness to experience emotion in circumstances relating to the object of the habit.

THE EMOTIONS

It is difficult for human beings to think unemotionally about emotion. The same may be said of some psychologists in their attempts to approach emotion in an objective, impartial, and cognitive way. Thus William James (1842–1910) writes scathingly of previous studies. He remarks that he would as soon read through verbal descriptions of the shape of the rocks of a New Hampshire farm as again toil through the psychological literature on emotion. Following William James comes J. B. Watson who, after referring to 'James's barren but graceful formulation' – William James's own theory of emotion – then adds that if anyone thinks that the psychology of emotion has become more exciting since this judgement was passed 'let him try to read McDougall's *Social Psychology* and Shand's work on the sentiments'. To these judgements, which have gone on record, I shall add my own. The contemporary absence of serious scientific study of fear, anger, and other major emotions is a sad commentary upon the stultifying limitation which Watsonian behaviourism imposed upon psychology; this, even today, psychology has not yet fully outgrown. Of interest in this connexion is a judgement made in 1939 by M. M. Desai: 'An exhaustive historical treatment of any particular emotion has not been, to the knowledge of the present writer, undertaken at all.' Desai (1939) himself contributed an account of the history of ideas – together with a series of experiments – on one particular emotion: he chose surprise. Since that date historical treatments of the emotions of anger (McKellar, 1949) and of fear (Garwood, 1961) have been contributed. These and other studies do something to fill the gap referred to by Desai.

Another unsatisfactory feature of the psychology of emotion was mentioned recently by a speaker at a conference of the American Psychological Association. He had conducted a documentary analysis of chapters on emotion in psychology textbooks. And he had found an excessive tendency for exaggerated attention to be given to 'negative emotions', such as fear, anger, and hatred; by contrast, 'positive emotions' like joy, love, and amusement had received scant attention. While we may query this psychologist's neglect of Shand's fundamentally important distinction between sentiments – like love and hate – and emotions, his general point stands. This gives me some justification for beginning with one highly positive emotion, amusement, and the related activity of laughter.

There are many theories of laughter, and each serves to highlight one or other aspect of the phenomena involved. Thomas Hobbes argued that it is the task of a theory to tie facts into bundles. His own theory of laughter provides a tidy bundle of instances of laughter provocation of one particular kind. The Hobbes *sudden glory theory* is that laughter is a response to an awareness of sudden glory in ourselves, provoked by perception of the misfortunes and infirmities of others. This theory – one-sided as it is – is particularly concerned with the important problem of the circumstances which provoke emotion: in this instance, amusement. Situations which provide an awareness of our own superiority to others, or – Hobbes is prepared to add – of our superiority to ourselves on a former occasion, may result in laughter. But to go further into the question of provocation it is helpful to follow a traditional distinction made between wit, humour, and the comic. There is something typically verbal about *wit*; and puns, repartee, and other forms of wit tend to exhibit both brevity and elegance. *Humour* is characteristically represented by jokes, and in these content and meaning are important rather than mere verbal form. *The comic* is largely behavioural, and slapstick comedy is a typical instance of it.

Freud's theory is primarily concerned with wit. There are, he argues, two kinds: harmless wit, and tendency wit. Harmless wit provokes pleasure and amusement from an appreciation of the elegance of the words used, and from an economy of effort resulting from, among other things, brevity. Tendency wit is different in that it has a further component, namely a playing with some taboo. Prominent among these are the taboos on open manifestations of aggression, sexual allusion, and blasphemy. Flugel (1954) has developed Freudian thought on this point, and produces a skilful analysis of the complexity of tendency wit. The joker laughs at the embarrassment of his hearer, and for scoring off him by leading him astray and depriving him of the satisfaction of openly violating the taboo; the hearer laughs at being relieved of the embarrassment of having to refer to the tabooed act; and both laugh at their unavowed understanding of the inner meaning. Some good examples of tendency wit involving the taboo on open and direct expression of aggression are to be found in the retorts of accomplished public speakers to hecklers. There appears to be a continuum from tendency wit, through thinly disguised hostility, up to overt verbal attack. The story is well known, but will serve as illustration, of the *soi-disant vigilante* wishing to intrude on the affairs of others – in this case a rather plain woman who during the First World War asked the youth: 'Young man, why aren't you in the armed services?' She met the retort: 'Madame, same reason you are not in a beauty chorus, physically unfit!' Here the hostility is so thinly veiled as hardly to count as wit. But in typical tendency wit the hostility is masked by elegant choice of phrase in which the taboo is not too openly violated. There are many marginal categories in which verbal cruelty may play its part, as in the case of the lecturer who caught a young woman student making up her face during his class. He commented acidly, 'Madame, the boudoir and not the lecture room is the place to remedy the omissions of nature, and the ravages of time.' In other cases the element of hostility may be more slight, as when Lord Birkenhead said of a famous statesman, 'He devoted the best years of his life to the preparation of his impromptu speeches.' Wit is an intellectual kind of activity; it is inclined to provoke a smile rather than uncontrollable laughter; and, because it is frequently closely associated with hostility, it may often give offence.

A leading British psychologist, R. H. Thouless (1935), has some important comments to make on Freud's theory of wit, and on laughter provocation more generally. He emphasizes the importance of the social situation. Thus the same joke, with underlying sexual implications, may provoke laughter in a circle of men, embarrassment with tendency to laugh if told in mixed company, and neither laughter nor embarrassment if told to a group of psycho-analysts. The point made by Thouless is well illustrated in *Camille* – as portrayed visually by Greta Garbo rather than in the original Dumas novel – when Marguerite Gautier asks her beloved why he does not laugh at X's jokes, which are being told at a meal. To this Armand replies that he knows all X's jokes, in fact he told X most of them himself, and, knowing them, he does not regard them as appropriate to the dinner-table of the woman he loves. As Thouless stresses, this importance of situational factors in laughter provocation has been considerably neglected. And of course the joker himself may make mistakes, wedding speeches providing not infrequent evidence of this. Not for nothing, even today, do friends and relatives of the bride and groom sit on opposite sides of the church. And the 'best man' – though no longer armed – is there to protect the groom. In the speeches which follow at the wedding reception the threshold for laughter is low; it is easily provoked, but ambivalence and hostility between the families is often also near threshold. The joke which oversteps the knife-edge between humour and aggression may not only provoke anger, but also give rise to enduring sentiments of dislike and hatred. Ambivalence towards bride and groom may also express itself; this seems to be particularly so of weddings in Scotland, where the bridegroom especially is the target of joking aggression – sometimes resulting in physical injury – at the hands of his 'friends'. Other societies manifest apparent awareness, or at least take counter-measures, in view of the aggression and ambivalence of the wedding situation. Thus among the Navajo – the largest group of American Indians – only the relatives of the groom, and not those of the bride, are allowed entry to the hogan where the wedding takes place. The humour of weddings in its relation to ambivalence repays more detailed study in both our own and other societies.

McDougall's theory of laughter draws attention to some important kinds of humour. McDougall argues that it is at the minor misfortunes of other people, and of ourselves, that we tend to laugh. We laugh so that we are not constantly depressed by such happenings. Thus, for McDougall, laughter is what Freud might have called a reaction formation: it has an important compensatory function. Its prototype is that remarkable achievement of evolution, rueful laughter, in which we laugh at ourselves. McDougall's theory draws attention to the affinities between laughter and pathos which many great humorists have explored. An interesting example – mentioned by Allport – was the comedian who lost all his money in a financial disaster, wrote a screamingly funny play about it, and thus regained his fortune.

Bergson's theory relates primarily to the comic. Bergson argues that we are provoked to laughter when we encounter 'something mechanical encrusted upon the living'. The pompous man slipping on a banana skin is the prototype of the Bergsonian category of the laughable. Despite his dignity, his wish to assert his superiority over other men and the superiority of the animate over the living, it is gravitation which takes over. The comic may also assume verbal forms in which ludicrous visual imagery of improbable happenings seems to contribute to our amusement. Some fashions of the day, for example the elephant jokes of recent years, illustrate this: for example, 'How do elephants get down from trees?' The answer is, of course, 'They stand on a leaf and wait till autumn'. But more typically perhaps, the comic is perceptually visible, rather than imaged. Examples are to be found in the antics of clowns, or in the performance of the skilled man who clowns some activity like skating or diving. Similarly in *Monsieur Verdoux* we find Charlie Chaplin falling from the drawing-room sofa, but ending upright on the floor with his unspilled cup of tea still in his hand. In these cases laughter seems to involve something more than amusement at mechanical and rigid behaviour. There appears to be an element of appreciation of the underlying skill without which the apparently clumsy behaviour could not have occurred.

There are other theories of laughter, and many insightful observations have been made about amusement. The Dutch psychologist Heymens finds the essence of laughter provocation in 'bewilderment succeeded by illumination'. Herbert Spencer stresses the part of expression of emotion no longer required: the laughter of fear, and the laughter of relief are instances of this kind. The Japanese philosopher Kagawa stresses the mentally healthy aspect of laughter, and the ways it can operate to undermine both stern-faced tyranny and fanaticism. The philosopher Spinoza makes an important distinction between merriment, as the laughter of joy, and ridicule, as the laughter of hatred. And many have adopted a view of laughter compatible with McDougall's theory. 'Our sincerest laughter with some pain is fraught', wrote Shelley, and to this a recent French thinker adds, 'Laughter is a defence against anguish'.

Examination of these views must inevitably support an eclectic theory. A cure-all is called a 'panacea'. It has been suggested that an 'explain-all' needs a name: one name that has been suggested is a 'panachreston'. In a field in which thoughtful men have differed for over a thousand years, we are unlikely to find a 'panachreston' for laughter. As regards laughter provocation, the methods of factorial study have helped to clarify some of the main categories of the laughable. In one such study Andrews (1943) found six major categories: (1) derision-superiority, reminiscent of the Hobbes kind of theory; (2) reactions to debauchery, reminiscent of Freud's tendency wit; (3) subtlety, the intellectual element, prominent in harmless wit; (4) the sexual, again as in tendency wit; and (5) the ridiculous, suggestive of the Bergson kind of theory, and of the standpoint represented by Heymens. Much research needs to be done on the respective appeal of these and other categories of the laughable, in different social groups, at different ages of development, and to different types of personality.

THE EMOTION OF ANGER

The parallel problem of what provokes the emotion arises with anger. As regards emotional provocation, whether to anger, fear, surprise, or joy, an important point emerges. A person is provoked to emotion by the situation as he perceives it, not necessarily by the situation as it really is. Thus, for example, many people are provoked to anger by what they perceive as an insult when no insult is, geographically speaking, present. We may call such people unduly sensitive, or perhaps 'somewhat paranoid', in their proneness to unjustified emotional upset.

An investigation of my own was concerned with, among other things, the circumstances which tend to provoke anger. Findings were based on two categories of data: an introspective analysis involving detailed recording of every instance of my own anger over a period of some weeks; and, in case mine happened to be atypical, analysis of instances of anger collected systematically from groups of other people. From these studies two rather different kinds of anger-provoking situations emerged. First, what I called *need situations*: these involved a thwarting of the individual in his pursuit of his various goals. His various needs were in some way prevented from expressing themselves. Second were what I called *personality situations*: these were circumstances in which the individual felt himself to be the subject of attack, injury, or humiliation, or of some other onslaught on his personality. The personality situations, in accord with Shand's principle of disinterested emotion (quoted at the head of this chapter), may be taken to include onslaughts not merely on the individual as such, but also upon his values, or upon people with whom he was emotionally preoccupied. A woman may be provoked to anger by a 'personality situation' because her child, her husband, or even her choice of clothing is in some way threatened. A man may be provoked to anger in defence of some institution of which he accepts membership, or in defence of his dog or some aspect of his property.

A distinction between 'need' and 'personality' sources of provocation seems a useful one, and takes us further into the understanding of both anger and hostile sentiments. Need situations on the whole were found to provoke warm-blooded anger, anger of short duration, and anger directed towards brushing aside the obstacle. Personality situations tended rather to provoke a cold kind of anger, and with it a tendency to malice and revenge. Such anger was found, on investigation, to be of longer duration, and it might also give rise to the development of hostile sentiments including dislike and hatred. In a study of hostile sentiments as such, on no occasion did these seem to have arisen without personality provocation as a component. Need situations, while they might provoke anger, did not seem to give rise to enduring hostile sentiments. It also emerged that the kinds of anger resulting from the two different kinds of situation differed somewhat in their aims. This may be illustrated by a situation that readers, like myself, may have experienced: that of missing a train because time did not permit buying a ticket, and because the official at the barrier prevented entry to the platform without it. If in such circumstances one brushes past, overcomes the obstacle, and catches the train, one may be manifesting an obstacle-removing kind of anger, likely to be short-lived. If, however, one is prevented by the official and also insulted by him, the resulting anger may be cold and revengeful. Such anger may motivate one to go and complain to the stationmaster about his officious subordinate, and one may turn aside from one's other goals to do this. In more extreme anger provocations of the personality situation kind, I encountered almost unbelievable heights of malice and revengefulness. The people studied often wished to hurt, to humiliate the object of their anger, and one realized the need for the limits imposed by the Mosaic admonition of 'an eye for an eye'. Physical pain inflicted by another, physical injury, and humiliation represent three manifestations of this kind of provocation. Their result – if the influence of moral sentiments does not intervene – tends to be motivation to inflict something similar upon the object of the anger, or hostile sentiment. Much anger is, however, of the need situation kind, and bereft of this kind of motivation. The extent to which the person concerned subjectively feels 'frustrated' seems to be an important factor in this kind of anger. But inspection of the situations which in fact provoke people to anger did not support an all-embracing explanation of anger in terms simply of frustration and thwarting.

A study was also attempted of how people expressed the anger which they experienced. Overwhelmingly the commonest reaction was to do and say nothing. Fantasy and imagery might occur, but the subject did not express the anger outwardly in any way. Overt expressions of anger, much rarer, usually took a verbal form. Very rarely indeed, in the subjects studied, who were adults living in the London area, was physical aggression resorted to. When it occurred it tended to be displaced, its target being something from which retaliation was improbable or impossible: such targets included inanimate objects and animals. A third type of reaction was interesting, and might be called 'delayed expression'. The subject frequently sought out some friend or other audience whom he expected to be sympathetic, and told him of the situation. The purpose of this seemed to be to induce sympathetic anger in the audience: not merely his sympathy but also his own anger seemed to be required. On occasion my subjects were thwarted in this aim: the audience would either be uninterested, or take the other side. A common reaction in these circumstances seems to be, again, displacement: the subject reacts against the audience in his disappointment, and blames him for his failure to assume the expected role of sympathetic listener. The thwarting of such expectations can certainly give rise either to displacement of the original unexpressed emotion, or to additional anger.

Some investigators, notably I. D. Suttie in his book *The Origins of Love and Hate* (also published by Penguin), go so far as to place central emphasis on thwarted love as the main cause of aggression, hostile sentiments, and anger. As David Hume observed at an earlier period, if positive emotional habits turn to negative ones they can be of high intensity. Moreover, Hume suggests, the intensity of the resulting hostile sentiments tends to be proportionate to that of the original positive one. Supporting evidence for this view is to be found in the bitterness with which civil wars are fought, the malice we encounter in many family quarrels, and in many relations between former friends. But Suttie's conception of thwarted love as the basis of hostility and hatred more generally cannot be upheld. Many intense dislikes and hatreds are provoked because the person hated has been a humiliator. A number of the subjects in my own investigation developed strong negative sentiments towards some person who had caused them physical pain; it seems nonsensical to maintain that the victim hates his torturer because of frustrated love. Indeed one wonders whether martyrs have not achieved consolation in their sufferings – John Knox as a galley slave is a case in point

– by their theological conviction of an after-life of even worse sufferings to come to their persecutors. Many of the manifestations of hostile sentiments seem to set limits on the theory of frustrated love as a general explanation.

In transition from the emotion of anger to that of fear we encounter another of Shand's principles, one which links aggression with fear. Shand's principle holds: 'Fear, though it may be forced into aggression, tries to achieve its aim without aggression.' The aim of fear is, if possible, withdrawal from the source of provocation. Only if escape is blocked does it result in aggression and attack upon the provocation. This principle would seem particularly relevant to human dealings with animals. There is abundant evidence that many animals are dangerous when, and only when, they are barred from the escape they would very much prefer. Under such circumstances aggression – aggression provoked by fear rather than anger – becomes highly predictable. Animal psychologists, naturalists, and others have frequently commented on the remarkable tendency to irrational behaviour, and inappropriate emotional responses, man can show in his relations with animals. One such investigator, H. Hediger, reminds us that 'wild animal' should never be confused with 'beast of prey': a freshly caught hare or an antelope is a wild animal, and some but not all wild animals are predators. As Hediger points out, if an animal escapes from a zoo or a circus the reactions of the public tend to be activated by their stereotypes. Even escaping predatory animals should not be confused with dangerous absconding criminals: their activities are concerned with unhindered flight, and not with devouring the first human being they meet. Many valuable animals have been senselessly destroyed because of failure to appreciate these facts, and lack of application of the principle formulated by Shand, quoted above: fear may result in aggression if escape reactions are thwarted.

THE EMOTION OF FEAR

Fear is, as we have seen, closely associated with the flight reaction. Of interest in this connexion is the knowledge which has been built up by Hediger and other animal investigators of the escape distances of different species. If the escape distance – which may be measured in feet and inches – is invaded the animal will take flight. Examples, from Hediger, of average escape distances include 80 yards for the African buffalo, and 150 yards for the giraffe. Environmental circumstances may affect escape distances; thus, for example, in Albert National Park the escape distance for the buffalo is only 15 yards, and for the elephant about 50 yards. In general the escape distances of large animals are large, and of small animals, small: thus a lizard may be approached to a distance of a few yards, while the crocodile makes off at fifty. When we tame an animal we in effect reduce its escape distance to zero. Interference with escape reactions may, as we have seen, lead to aggression. This fact may be used – and is used – in controlling animal reactions, for example by the circus trainer. Here we encounter Hediger's own considerable interest in animal training: the trainer may invade the escape distance of the animal, and bar its course of flight, and thus manipulate its movements and place the animal where he wants it. With a knowledge of the escape distances of the species or individual concerned, a trainer may systematically invade and withdraw from these distances and place obstacles between himself and the animal. As Hediger remarks: 'It often looks as if the trainer were pulling or pushing the animal to the desired spot by invisible wires.' To accomplish this, to make the animal withdraw or advance, it is not necessary to invade the critical distances in person; such invasion may be achieved by some extension of the man such as his stick or cloak.

Like other typical emotions such as anger, fear is a provoked reaction: whether it occurs or not depends upon certain circumstances which may or may not occur in the environment. In civilized society under normal conditions fear seems to occur less often than anger: this has been verified by a number of investigators, including myself, at least in the case of themselves. Hebb has developed the most interesting thesis that man is the most emotional of all animals, but his proneness to emotional upset is to a large extent hidden by the barriers to emotional provocation he erects. Such barriers seem to be particularly effective in relation to the fear emotion. And in this connexion we encounter another interesting idea, contributed by Graham Wallas some decades ago: the theory of the baulked disposition. Wallas argues that man misses the opportunities, which civilized society denies him, to experience emotions like fear. He may thus become restless and unhappy and seek opportunities to experience emotion. It is to this motive Wallas would attribute such happenings as the readiness of small boys to play 'last across the road' in front of passing cars, the willingness of people to pay money at fairs to go on roller coasters and other devices which provoke fear, and at least part of the motivation of the mountaineer. All these circumstances give people opportunity to experience emotions they would not otherwise readily have. If there is such a motive it is of some interest and would repay fuller investigation. At any rate society seems, on the whole, relatively efficient in setting up conventions and other barriers which greatly limit opportunities for the experiencing of strong emotions.

More than most thinkers of the past, the philosopher Thomas Hobbes (1588–1679) placed emphasis on fear as basic to the life of man, and to the foundation of human society. Hobbes, writing of an England in which many very real dangers were abroad, drew attention to the widespread fears people have of their fellow men: they ride armed, they lock their doors, and they lock up their property. Fear of one's fellow men, fear of nature, and superstitious fear of invisible forces are, on Hobbes's view, characteristic of man; and society is organized to limit these fear-provoking situations.

From such general observations let us turn to studies that have been made of what people actually fear. At the end of the nineteenth-century G. Stanley Hall used a questionnaire technique by which he studied some 700 people in respect of their fears. In all he obtained a list of 6,456 fears. The commonest objects of fears were thunderstorms and reptiles. Elsewhere we have noted the enormously widespread fear of reptiles – especially snakes – which results in the destruction of many harmless animals: another manifestation of the close association fear can have with aggressive and destructive behaviour. Hall, like many subsequent investigators, found evidence of sex differences and incidentally supports the widespread belief that women are more afraid of mice than men are. In studies of boys and girls, he found that the boys exceeded the girls in fear of water, heights, and their own personal shyness; the girls exceeded the boys in fear of electrical storms, fears of rats and mice, fears of blood, and fears of the end of the world. That sex differences continue to exist in the objects and events that arouse fear is supported by the much later investigations of Garwood (1961), who has made a comprehensive study of the fear emotion. Garwood used both questionnaires and essay-writing procedures. As regards sex differences in his investigation, and a repetition of it a year later with a second group, he found evidence of far more tendency for girls to report fears involving harm from other people, than boys. Other differences were found in accord with age and with socioeconomic background. Garwood's general conclusion as regards provocation is that the emotion results from dangers, or believed dangers, about which the individual concerned doubts his own adequacy of response. In connexion with fear, as with anger, it may be stressed that what is important as provocation is the situation as perceived by the subject: this may, of course, differ markedly from the situation as it – geographically speaking – in fact is.

War-time has brought, very naturally, an interest in problems of fear. Indeed a major source of controversy between the orthodox psycho-analysts and others arose during and after the First World War. Many psychiatrists in this period were convinced by what seemed to them the obvious fact that many soldiers exhibited psychiatric break-down as a result of fear: the more complex formulations of the psycho-analysts failed to impress them. Important among these critics was W. H. R. Rivers, who was led to make a distinction between the kinds of break-down he observed in private soldiers and officers. The soldiers – under conditions of trench warfare – tended to produce neurotic reactions of the hysteria kind (discussed in a later chapter), while the officers, precluded from exhibiting or even admitting their fear to themselves, tended rather to anxiety neurosis. Circumstances of war change, and it is interesting to note that hysteria was a relatively uncommon phenomenon in the Second World

War, while anxiety reactions became relatively more common. A major study of the Second World War was by S. A. Stouffer and his colleagues, *The American Soldier*. Stouffer was interested in which weapons used against them the soldiers concerned found the most fear-provoking. These findings support Garwood's contention that a sense of helplessness, and uncertainty about one's own ability to cope, plays a central place in fear provocation. Being bombed from the air figured prominently in these assessments, a representative reaction being 'it's right on top of you before you know it's coming'. Also of interest was the widespread fear of weapons creating noise – dive bombing, shell fire, and other such things being mentioned by subjects, who would often reiterate their own felt sense of helplessness.

Fear of the supernatural has, throughout history, been an important factor; moreover it has often resulted in aggressive reactions on the part of the frightened, throughout history. In ancient Babylon, the plague together with floods and other climatic disturbances were frequently attributed to the activity of malevolent magicians. In Rome, the early Christians, whose actions it was believed had angered the gods, were often blamed for similar misfortunes: 'the Tiber overflows: the Christians to the lions!' Christianity itself, in its turn, seems often to have confused the gods of the pagan religions which it displaced with demons, and the supporters of these religions, with witchcraft. During the fourteenth century, when the Black Death spread across Europe, malevolent witchcraft was widely regarded as responsible. Moreover anti-Semitism also took on a demonological flavour, and many thousands of Jews were massacred as a result. The successes of individuals were sometimes attributed to magic, for example in the case of Cardinal Wolsey: a contemporary, Sir Richard Neville, approached an Oxford astrologer and requested him to make him a ring like the one the Cardinal wore so that he too would enjoy the high favour and position achieved by Wolsey. Even at a much later date King James I wrote his own book, indicating his very real belief in witchcraft. At times when men, well educated by the standards of the day, and even kings, accepted witchcraft, it is not surprising that the common man could share these fears. Today it is difficult to estimate the numbers who suffered in the resulting persecutions, and the retaliatory aggression against the presumed witch; but some illustrations may be given. Thus in 1596 no fewer than 600 people are reported as having been burned as witches by order of the Bishop of Geneva. In Sweden, during one day 23 adults and 15 children were executed.

At such times, perverted men whom we would today diagnose as 'psychopaths with sadistic inclinations' came to the fore. Thus in England there arose the profession of witch-hunter. Among the best known of these was the seventeenth-century Matthew Hopkins, who charged a fee of 20 shillings for each town he investigated for witchcraft. Financial profit was one factor in such a calling, but detailed records leave little doubt that delight in the suffering of individuals thus accused – a delight which could be enjoyed in a socially accepted way – was another powerful motive. Some people received institutional support for their actions, the most notorious being the two Dominican priests Johann Sprenger and Heinrich Kramer, who were appointed by Pope Innocent VIII to carry out witch-hunting in Germany. These two men were responsible for one of the most evil books ever written, the *Malleus Maleficarum*, that was to become the text-book of the witch-hunter. This classified various types of witch, produced theological justifications for moralized sadism, and laid down methods of securing confessions.

One of the prominent victims of this period, and of organized human aggression fed by fear, was the abnormal personality. Humane treatment of psychosis was seriously impeded by demonology and fear of witchcraft; many schizophrenics and other psychotics were tortured and executed in this grim period of history. And in this period too we encounter vigorous onslaughts by reformers – many of them medically trained – who sought to combat the superstitious fear of the age, and its exploitation by those who, however sincere, used it for their own purposes. The demonological conception of mental illness and the fear of possession by evil spirits are unfortunately not dead in backward communities, though they seldom find support through the machinery of law. Exceptions occur from time to time. Of interest are some exceptions from more recent times.

Writing in the 1920s, Lévy Brühl gives an illustration of how, in Africa, envy and jealousy have on occasion assumed a demonological flavour. If, in some parts of West Africa, two friends go fishing and one secures a better haul than the other, the more fortunate is likely to be accused of having invoked the aid of evil spirits. At about the same time, in the American South-west, which was greatly affected by the drought of 1922, religious controversy gave rise to dispute in which accusations and counter-accusations involving the supernatural played a part. In the pueblo of Taos, New Mexico, members of the growing Peyote (mescaline) cult were accused of – let us remember the Christians of Ancient Rome – having angered the gods, and thus prevented rain. Conflict between the Peyote cult and others in the pueblo reached a climax in 1936, and culminated in a hearing before a Senate Committee on Indian Affairs. A deputy law enforcement officer, displaying his Federal badge and gun, had invaded a Peyote meeting, and had later sat as prosecutor and judge. Imprisonment and fines were imposed on members of the peyote group – later to become members of the Native American Church – and of interest was one of the charges made, that the members had 'bewitched' a particular individual. The Federal Government proved unenthusiastic about being asked to support charges of witchcraft, and the officious official was relieved of his government employment the same year. But even though legal sanctions no longer accept witchcraft as an offence – the last witch was hanged in Britain in 1684 – fear of the supernatural has given rise to much retaliatory aggression, and theological backing for such superstitious fear is encountered, from time to time, even in Europe today. The price of humane care of the mentally ill, and of religious freedom – both of which are involved in this matter – is vigilance.

EMOTION AND MOTIVATION

Emotions like fear and anger, and emotional habits like love, hate, and prejudice, represent two important categories of human motive. Emotional states like anxiety and guilt have some subtle and important relations to motivation, and various major theorists in psychology have explored their importance. Freud has been particularly concerned with the importance of guilt, and later thinkers such as Flugel have developed his penetrating insights into this difficult field. In particular we may note, as Freud appreciated and Dostoyevsky understood at an earlier period, that guilt may arise not merely from overt actions, but also from 'behaviour' which has occurred only in thought and fantasy. Others, for example Alfred Adler, paid attention to the motivational effects of other emotional states, notably the feeling of inferiority – and adjustments to it – which Adler regarded as a universal human phenomenon. Finally, later and contemporary psychologists have been deeply interested in relations between scientific understanding of the learning process and motivation. Learning theory, including ideas based on animal experiments, has contributed one of the ingredients in such thought, the other being derived from psycho-analysis. Of interest is the importance which contemporary theorists, interested in relations between personality and learning, such as O. H. Mowrer on the one hand, and J. Dollard and N. E. Miller on the other, have placed upon fear and anxiety. These investigators place fear and anxiety squarely in the centre of their accounts of human motivation. It is to this subject, the motivation of behaviour, that we shall next turn.

SOCIETY AND EMOTION

The social norms obviously exert a considerable influence on the expression of human emotion. There are indications that they may perform another function as well. This is hinted at by Schopenhauer and the definition he provides of human politeness as 'a tacit agreement that other people's miserable defects . . . shall on either side be ignored and not made the subject of reproach'. On this view we see politeness performing the function of protecting self-esteem, and insulating the parties concerned against emotional provocation. Schopenhauer has little doubt about the need for such norms, and sees human nature as containing 'a fund of hatred, anger, rancour and malice . . . waiting only for an opportunity of venting itself'. Elsewhere Schopenhauer views civilization as a system of restraints from which human aggression may break forth 'wherever and whenever the locks and chains of law and order fall off'. This line of thought is further explored in a more recent contribution to the subject of emotional arousal.

In 1954 Hebb and Thompson formulated a theory of human society in its relation to emotion, and emotional provocation. They take their cue from comparative psychology, which reveals man as the highest and most intelligent of the animals. But if, as they argue, emotional upset is largely the result of a break-down of thinking, then emotion is most likely to occur when thought is most complex. Thus man is seen as not only the most intelligent, but also the most emotionally vulnerable of the animals. That this is so is not obvious. A reason is found by Hebb and Thompson in the fact that this extreme susceptibility to emotion is self-concealing. Civilized society has the characteristic of providing an environment which reduces provocation to fear, anger, disgust, jealousy, and other emotions. As one piece of evidence the two psychologists point to the commonness of death. When, however, a group of 198 persons – including some nurses and some returned servicemen – were investigated, it emerged that 37 of these had never seen a dead person. Moreover 91 had seen a corpse only after it had gone through the ritualized procedure of the undertaker. A total of 66 per cent had in this way been shielded by society from the emotional upsets of death. Again Hebb and Thompson point to the educated man's confidence in his broad-mindedness and contempt for appearances. They ask us to consider people who deviate even a little from the usual, for example people who have been disfigured by injury and accident who – despite being unimpaired in speech or intellect – are unlikely to find employment readily. Merely to ask such questions of a class of students – people more than usually confident of their ability to discount externals – results, they have found, in 'a curious mixture of uneasiness and incredulity'. There are many such taboos which serve to insulate people from emotional excitement, to which people in general are so susceptible. As our lives are usually arranged, with our comfortable repertoire of taboos of this kind, we can also maintain the self-deception that as a species we are unemotional. These norms result in a certain uniformity, and as Hebb and Thompson – echoing Schopenhauer – put it, 'man is not a tame animal but inherently dangerous, to be domesticated only with great pains.' He is, for example, remarkably intolerant of others of his species who have learned different norms: the risks taken by a stranger on entering a given human society 'would not be less than that taken by a chimpanzee or a wolf encountering a group of his fellows'. Man is inhospitable to the out-grouper.

CHAPTER NINE

Motives

> There is obviously a sudden access of energy from some source within me. What is that source? Where and what are these latent reserves of energy?
>
> WILLIAM MCDOUGALL

FOREMOST among the contributions of psycho-analysis has been its uncovering of the complexity of human motivation. In this field 'common sense' has proved an uncertain guide. Everyday life may tempt us into looking for 'the motive' of a piece of behaviour in the reasons and stated intentions a person may offer for it. If today we are less inclined to accept such reasons and intentions at their face value we have learned this, partly at least, through the influence psycho-analytic thought has had. Many theories of motivation have been advanced in terms of some single principle. These one-factor theories have had their serious defenders, and still retain much influence on popular thinking. Three such theories may be mentioned. *Egoism* is the doctrine that all behaviour is motivated by self-interest. *Hedonism* holds that the pursuit of pleasure and the avoidance of displeasure (or pain) are the primary basis of motivation. The doctrine of *self-interested fear* regards fear as central to motivation, and disinterested actions as simply the result of fear of the punishments that would otherwise ensue. Such doctrines, and other one-factor theories, have been heavily criticized for over two thousand years, though we may still hear them seriously defended today.

MULTIPLE MOTIVATION

An advance to a more adequate conception of motivation is to be found in those who rejected wholeheartedly any attempt at one-factor explanations. Instead such people have argued that motivation is complex, and the actions of people result from the interaction of processes of different kinds. One such doctrine is associated with Joseph Butler, the eighteenth-century bishop of Durham who delivered perhaps the most psychologically interesting, and probably the most readable, sermons ever published. In his *Sermons on Human Nature* Butler has some interesting criticisms to make of each of the three doctrines mentioned above. His own concern is to analyse motivation in its complexity. It is from the interplay of four types of motivational processes that behaviour results. First are 'the passions'; these comprise what we would today call emotions and appetites, and fear and hunger are examples. As Butler points out, the goal of fear is not self-interest but escape from danger; the goal of hunger is not pleasure but food. Indeed, as he shows, there are many situations in which the passions conflict with the interests of the organism. Awareness of this leads Butler to note a second important motivational principle which he calls 'prudence', or 'cool self-love'. This motivates the individual in the direction of his own long-term advantages, and restrains the influence of the passions on behaviour when they conflict with this goal. Thirdly, Butler notes what he calls 'altruism' or 'benevolence'. This principle influences our conduct in the direction of the welfare of others. Its influence is akin to the influence stated by Shand – in the quotation which heads the previous chapter – of disinterested emotion evoked on behalf of others as well as on behalf of oneself. Butler makes the interesting point that the principles of prudence and benevolence do not necessarily conflict; in certain actions it is not easy to detect which is the predominant influence: what is conducive to the welfare of others is often also to one's own long-term advantage. Finally, as the dominant principle of this hierarchy of principles, we encounter 'conscience'; this exerts its influence and prompts us towards or away from certain lines of conduct in terms of the rightness and wrongness of action. Butler's conception of motivation involves viewing the personality as a hierarchy, incorporating a set of principles which exhibit interaction. His conception is of particular interest in helping us to understand long-term motivation when major decisions are involved. Much must, however, be added to his analysis to take account of some of the vicissitudes of motivation, for example the motivation of abnormal behaviour in its various forms, and of criminal and self-destructive behaviour in their wide variety. For the understanding of these we need to turn to later thinkers, particularly the psycho-analysts.

Despite widespread misconceptions to the contrary, Freud did not in any way subscribe to the one-factor kind of theory of motivation. One very important aspect of his thought concerns the realization that behaviour can be subject to over-determination. By this he means that the motivation may be more than sufficient to determine the behaviour in question: there may be a surplus of motivation. This notion is a valuable one in that it leads the investigator to continue his search rather than rest content after he has catalogued merely one or a few of the more obvious motives involved. It leads him to look carefully for some of the more complex and subtle influences which are likely to escape purely superficial examination. Freud is alert to the notion that response may occur in the presence of strongly contrary motivation, and that the anxiety and guilt-feeling which can result may themselves become important motivational influences. Those motives which are introspectively prominent to consciousness may not themselves be the really important ones; unconscious factors can operate in the sense that people are likely to deceive themselves and overlook the more irrational and more disreputable aspects of their motivation. In the case of others, however, for example others whom they dislike, the same

14. What is this?
In perception one may, in time, come to notice something not at first apparent. Similarly in motivation our initial introspections may overlook significant aspects which, as we acquire greater insight, we are alerted to notice.

irrational and disreputable motives are highly noticeable to the selective attention of the adversely biased observer. Specifically Freud's own account of motivation takes account of the interplay of conscious processes with processes of whose existence and influence the person concerned is dimly if at all aware. Deep rooted in the personality are primitive instinctive forces which the person is likely to deny or ignore at every point, but which may nevertheless be powerful determinants of what he actually does. There are aspects of the personality much modified by contact with the material and social environment, and others which operate in pursuit of immediate pleasure and reduction of tension without consideration for realism. Freud has much to say about this interaction between the ego – the aspect we identify as ourself and which has this task of making realistic adjustment – and the id, which operates more or less on the hedonism principle. In addition there is a third factor – the super-ego – which has resemblances to Butler's 'conscience', this being the motivational factor concerned with feelings of ought and obligation. We cannot wholly identify conscience and the super-ego, and are unwise to do so unless we take account of the possibilities of disorder and maladjustment in this area of the personality also. In the writings of Freud and of some of his ablest successors, much of value has emerged from their analysis of vicissitudes of the super-ego particularly when it becomes a gathering point for aggression: such aggression may result in a variety of forms of self-destruction, or may express itself – in disguised and moralized form – against other people.

THE CLASSIFICATION OF MOTIVES

Many attempts have been made to classify motives, and numerous investigators have sought to draw up lists of *human instincts*. One psychologist, after a documentary analysis of the literature, found no fewer than 400 instinctivist theories, and 6,000 postulated human instincts. The best-known of these theories is associated with William McDougall, whose revised list comprised food-seeking, disgust, sex, fear, curiosity, protectiveness, gregariousness, self-assertion, submissiveness, anger, appeal, constructiveness, acquisitiveness, laughter, comfort, rest or sleep, migration, and 'a group of very simple propensities subserving bodily needs'. McDougall's doctrine of motivation involved two concepts: instincts (or 'propensities'), which are innate, and sentiments or learned motives. The difficulty about catalogues of 'instincts' is the arbitrary nature of such listings, and although McDougall's list has proved the most influential of these there seems no reason to prefer it to other alternatives of an equally plausible kind. McDougall like Freud contributed something of value in drawing the attention of psychologists to the importance of motivation. His own motivational theory belongs to the history of the subject, rather than to contemporary thought. McDougall's original theory appeared in 1908. It did not succeed in the face of the vigorous criticism it received at the hands of his critics, but in a more general way McDougall achieved his aim. Motivation became a central topic in the subject matter of psychology. The concept of instinct has not, on the whole, played a prominent part in subsequent psychological theory, after the initial controversy. Recent years have, however, seen some re-emergence of interest in 'instinct', as a result of the work of the ethologists. These investigators – of whom Lorenz and Tinbergen are the best known – have been particularly concerned with innate processes, though their concept of instinct differs somewhat from McDougall's original notion. Recent years have seen an increasing cooperation between psychology and ethology, and it may be that instinct will again become a fashionable basis for motivational theory. In the meanwhile, however, psychological theory has favoured an alternative, to which we may next turn.

In the early 1900s, along with McDougall and Freud, Woodworth was also groping with the needs of psychology for a theory of motivation. It is on the whole Woodworth's concept of 'drive' rather than 'instinct' which has captured the attention of motivation theorists. Woodworth's theory was put forward in his book *Dynamic Psychology* of 1918, and bears evidence of the influence of both Freud and McDougall. He urged the development of a 'dynamic', motivational psychology and introduced the two concepts of *mechanism and drive*. He had in mind an analogy between human behaviour and machines. The mechanism of a machine is relatively passive, and drive is the power applied to it which makes the machine go. The notion of mechanism in psychology is taken by Woodworth to refer to the connexions between stimuli and responses that relate to how a certain action is performed. Drive is what induces the person in question to do it; and drive is conceived of, like instinct, as some kind of internal stimulation. Woodworth takes as illustration a man pitching in a baseball game. The problem of mechanism is the problem of how he aims, gauges distance, and coordinates his movements to achieve the desired end. By contrast the problem of drive includes such questions as why he engaged in this activity at all, why he performs better on one day than others, and why he pitches better against a particular opponent. The distinction, Woodworth argues, is like that we find with a machine: 'the drive here is the power applied to make the machine go; the mechanism is made to go, and is relatively passive.' Two advantages of the concept of drive over that of instinct may be noted. The first is that a hereditary basis is not assumed: we can as readily speak of secondary or learned drives, as of primary or innate ones, and as we shall see recent theorists have placed considerable emphasis on such a secondary drive as anxiety. A second advantage is that drive is an otherwise more neutral term; it did not at the time evoke the controversy which accompanied instinct with which the views of both Freud and McDougall – and their critics – had surrounded it. At any rate, for these reasons and others, drive became a highly respectable and much used concept in learning and motivation theory. Drive plays a prominent place in the complex learning theory of Hull, and in the numerous psychologists more directly or more indirectly influenced by this elaborate system. In its turn, like instinct, drive has become a much misused, controversial, and highly ambiguous concept.

A somewhat different way of classifying motives may also be noted as it draws attention to two seemingly important, mutually exclusive categories. These are *appetites, and non-appetites*. The term 'appetite' denotes motives like hunger and thirst which exert a rhythmical motivational influence on the organism.

Appetites may be learned as well as innate, and apart from the more extreme forms of drug addiction we may note among these, as important in many people's lives, the milder addictions we encounter to such substances as tea, coffee, and tobacco. And these may exert influences contrary to the welfare, or even the survival, of the organism. Elsewhere (1952) I cited two cases, both involving prisoner-of-war camps, which testify to the strength of the tobacco hunger appetite. A colleague who had been a prisoner of war told me he had once seen a man pay £115 sterling for one cigarette. His second case involved a prisoner who arrived at the camp in a state of starvation, exchanged what little food he had for tobacco, and afterwards died of hunger. As regards the coffee addiction I can cite data of my own obtained introspectively during a series of experiments involving food deprivation in which I was a subject. On the days of the experiment I was acutely aware of missing coffee – which was also denied me – more than I missed the food. The need was not for fluid as such – water would not have done and was available in any case – but for coffee as coffee. Although very hungry I would have much preferred a cup of coffee to something to eat. Many instances can be found in which learned motives, for example learned appetites, assume greater prominence, both to conscious awareness and to observation, than innate motives.

There are difficulties about classifying motives as *innate v. learned*. McDougall listed the food-seeking instinct as one of his primary motives. We need hardly quarrel with the view that food-seeking has an innate basis, but much more needs to be said. The consummatory activity of eating may be common to all food-seeking, but the process of achieving this, and indeed the goal objects which one is in fact prepared to consume, are highly varied. In this variation we notice many important aspects of the problem of motivation including both cultural influences and individual variations of personality. Thus the group has its standards, its norms, which affect its members: the Jew and the Moslem avoid pork, the Catholic meat on Friday, and the vegetarian meat altogether. And most of us confine our meat-eating to the flesh of cloven-footed animals. Interesting deviations from the more usual norms occur for example in quaint organizations like 'The Anteaters', whose members meet in Washington D.C. and consume strange dishes like hippopotamus fillets. But as we regard these variations of eating habits as strange, we should also remember that our own are defined in certain ways by conventions we implicitly accept as 'normal'. To talk about even such an obviously in-born tendency as food-seeking in terms of an instinct may be to neglect important aspects of its actual motivational influence. There is every difference in the world between the 'food-seeking instinct' of the gourmet at a well-chosen dinner, and that of the starving man whose food-seeking is broader in its range of acceptable goal objects. Yet here again we must also avoid oversimplification. Highly intense motivation may itself impose strong preferences: extreme hunger may greatly prefer bread and butter to chocolate éclairs, while extreme thirst is more happily quenched with water than with, for example, neat brandy. Moreover starvation may not be sufficient to overcome religious norms, or well-established but narrow food habits, and there are many cases on record of people starving to death because although food was available it was not acceptable to those who needed it.

The notion of a *hierarchy of motives* has been developed by A. H. Maslow in recent years. We have seen that Butler at an earlier period viewed motivation as hierarchical, certain principles being subordinated to others. Some such formulation is necessary to understand the motivation of an individual personality, in which certain motives though present are subordinated to others. Maslow conceives of man as being in a state of perpetual want, in which some motives are satisfied, and others thwarted. A man may be at the same time hungry and thirsty, and in desperate need of warmth and shelter. In the history of exploration and mountaineering many have died because they allowed their need for sleep to assume ascendancy over their warmth and shelter needs. Again, under the influence of a deliberate act of volition such a person may, though tired and hungry, proceed first to shelter, and only afterwards satisfy the sleep and food needs. Thus, in taking adequate account of the complexity of motivation, it is necessary not only to consider what motives are actually present, but also the organization of these motives into a hierarchy of precedence. It is this aspect of motivation which Maslow stresses in his notion of a hierarchy of prepotency among motives.

Without attempting any exhaustive catalogue of human motives, I would suggest three important groups within which motives be classified. These relate to the *species* of which one has membership, the *society* of the individual, and the *individual* personality as such. Among motives common to the species we may note primary appetites like hunger, thirst, and the sleep drives, together with other inborn motives previously classified as instincts. The second category reminds us of the heavy influence of social learning upon members of an area of culture. Not all individuals will exhibit uniformity in being moulded by their culture, but they will tend on the whole to conform to these cultural standards. And thirdly, we encounter the individual personality with a set of motives that distinguishes him from others, hierarchically arranged, that defines him as a person. One important investigation may be mentioned in connexion with this third category of personal motives. This was carried out at the Harvard Clinic and reported in 1938 by H. A. Murray and his colleagues. The investigators confined themselves to the study of a relatively small group of people: fifty young men of college age. Their aim was to investigate motivation in its relation to the normal personality, and in terms of differences between individuals. A large number of psychologists took part, including specialists whose skills and training extended from conditioning and learning on the one hand, to projective techniques on the other. Murray himself is co-author of the TAT (Thematic Apperception Test), one of the best known of the projective techniques for the study of fantasy and ideational behaviour. The central concept used was 'need', and a long list of needs or personal motives was drawn up from the data obtained. These needs were studied in terms of their expression both in overt behaviour and in the fantasy life of the individual. The two expressions did not always coincide, though they did with some of the needs, for example need dominance. No relation was found between public behaviour and fantasy in the case of the needs achievement and aggression. In other cases – for example the sex need – there was evidence of an inverse relation between overt expression and ideational activity.

Murray made an important contribution in providing a language in terms of which the motives which characterize one individual, and distinguish one personality from others, could be expressed. A fuller discussion of his contribution to the psychology of personality appears later (Chapter 11), but illustration may be given of some of the *needs* which emerged in the study. Some people were found to be strong on n. autonomy: a major motive for them was to initiate and organize their own activities without interference from others. Some manifested n. nurturance: a need to support, sustain, and give help to others. Nurturance may be contrasted with n. succourance, the need to be supported and helped oneself, and an inclination to 'lean on' other people. Other needs included aggression, excessive concern with self-justification, and the need for achievement. The Harvard Clinic investigation was an influential one, and has provided a basis and a terminology for much subsequent research into the personality differences we encounter in motivation. We find that people are surprisingly, even unbelievably, different from one another motivationally as in other ways. To this aspect of motivation we may now turn.

THE INDIVIDUAL PSYCHOLOGY OF MOTIVATION

Galton, as we have seen, investigated cognitive processes like thinking, remembering, and imagining. In this field he found that people exhibited considerable differences. Likewise in the motivational field is to be found evidence that personalities vary markedly. Murray has provided the basis for studies of the variations of human motivation, and in this respect his work may be compared with Galton's in the realm of variations of image life (see Chapter 11). But it is perhaps to psychoanalytic thought itself that we must turn for an understanding of some of the vicissitudes of motivation which heavily tax normal empathy. In this I shall be concerned not only with Freud himself, but with certain later investigators, notably the British psychologist J. C. Flugel, who had so much to contribute to understanding the subtler aspects of individual human motivation.

Criminality from a sense of guilt represents one style of motivation to which Freud himself drew attention. He found on investigation that in certain crimes or other anti-social actions the sense of guilt preceded the behaviour itself. In other words the individual, preoccupied with an acute sense of guilt, appeased this by committing a crime and perhaps also by being punished for it. He grasped at something to feel guilty about, and achieved a state of mind more bearable than the free-floating sense of unexplained guilt. This syndrome of motivation was examined by Dostoyevsky many years before Freud. It is in fact central to the plot of both *Crime and Punishment* and *The Brothers Karamazov*. In *Crime and Punishment* Raskolnikoff responds with guilt to his own dreams and fantasies, before any actual overt crime is committed by him. In *The Brothers Karamazov* there are four brothers. Only one of them kills their father, who is portrayed as a hateful and utterly unpleasant person; but the other three brothers – including even the saintly Alyosha – have also 'killed' their father, in fantasy though not in fact. In the end one brother is tried and convicted of the murder. Although he did not, in fact, commit it he is prepared to accept punishment for it as wholly appropriate: his imagination had loaded him with guilt for the crime. Short of these rather extreme cases we can, in more everyday life, find lesser manifestations of criminality from a sense of guilt. Guilt feeling is not infrequently detectable for purely fantasied acts. In studies of the sentiment of hatred I have found much evidence of guilt of this kind (McKellar, 1950). Using the TAT or some other projective test as an appropriate stimulus to imagining about the person they hated, I found people would often construct a fantasy of revenge. Many afterwards showed much guilt feeling because of these fantasies alone; similar fantasies may occur in daily life, and provoke similar guilt feeling. The relations between feelings of guilt on the one hand and overt actions on the other are highly complex. Criminality as such will be discussed in Chapter 13. People who have been causally guilty of crimes, and judged legally guilty, may be largely without guilt feelings. Others who have done nothing may be preoccupied with an inner sense of guilt.

Nemesism is a term coined by Flugel (1945) in connexion with a somewhat unexpected and original criticism he makes of hedonism as a theory of motivation: 'man is in certain respects not a pleasure-seeking, but a pain-seeking animal.' Thus in *Man, Morals and Society* and other writings, Flugel surveys and analyses the motivation of a large variety of nemesistic phenomena. These include a number of different types of asceticism ranging from those in which some definite gain is achieved as a result of the hardship undergone, to those in which there is a more or less direct expression of self-directed aggression. Sometimes, of course, as Flugel shows, self-aggression may assume moralistic coloration and 'chronic suicide' may occur. In some such cases it is difficult to explain them simply in terms of the motivation to kill oneself: something else is involved. Sometimes the wish to die in some highly specific way in which symbolism is fairly blatantly expressed seems to be the main thing: the wish to die, or even the wish to inflict pain on oneself, appear to be subsidiary though contributing motives. Such cases of suicide suggest something very different from the dignified 'death philosophy' of Shakespeare: the assertion on rational grounds that death is preferable to life, and, were it not for the fear of what may come after death, would be the choice of the rational man. Sometimes the means of suicide and attempted suicide is such that its very prominence defeats the act. One of the strangest cases of all was reported in 1933, and concerned a Venetian shoemaker who set out to kill himself by crucifixion. He made a cross, managed to nail his feet and his left hand to it, and wounded himself in the side with one of his shoemaking tools. Eventually, by an arrangement of pulleys he managed to get himself and the cross on to the window-sill outside his house. As there were plenty of people about at the time he was rescued within minutes, and recovered from his injuries in hospital (MacDonald, 1961). Attempted suicide by crucifixion is extremely rare: something more than a wish to die quickly, quietly, and efficiently is obviously involved. These other components, in a peculiarly idiosyncratic conception of religion, may be noted in the related case of a strange sect, the Penitentes, who are fairly strong even today in certain areas of New Mexico and Colorado. The members of the sect beat themselves with thongs made from the prickly cacti of the area, but the central part of their major ceremonies is a crucifixion of one of their number. It is considered a great honour to be chosen for this role. Nowadays the victim is merely tied to the cross until he loses consciousness, though the fact that nailing is no longer practised appears to be resented by members. The victim has been known to die under the ordeal, but is ordinarily released before death. In mentioning the Penitentes and the highly masochistic version of religion they practise I am not writing of a former age, but of what exists today as one little-studied but curious variant. This suffering, and self-aggression coloured by morality and religion, seems to meet the needs of the people concerned in a way others may find difficult to understand.

There are many syndromes of motivation of a less dramatic kind which present difficulties not only for empathy, but also for hedonism and egoism as theories of motivation. There is, for example, what Freud called the *negative therapeutic reaction*, in which the energies of the patient seem to be mobilized against getting well. Such patients manifest a need for their symptoms as something they are happier with than without, and little can be done to help them. This motivational syndrome is familiar to many physicians in general practice, as well as to psychiatrist specialists. The motivation mentioned may be compared with others we encounter elsewhere, such as the syndrome in which a man brought to trial while professing his conscious intentions to assist his own acquittal in fact does everything possible to impede the efforts of his legal advisers. And in everyday life we encounter similar paradoxes of behaviour in, for example, the inability to accept praise. An important principle of the psychology of learning, the Law of Effect, states that actions which lead to a satisfying state of affairs tend to be repeated. The psychologist originally responsible for this principle, Thorndike, began by including with it a second half: 'actions which lead to an unsatisfying state of affairs tend not to be repeated.' But he himself deleted this second half: investigations revealed that, although the effects of reward on behaviour are relatively predictable, those of punishment are relatively unpredictable. And so today we have the 'truncated' Law of Effect, this truncation recognizing the fact that for certain people apparent punishment may mask hidden rewards. Yet in certain cases the residual principle also appears to have its limitations as in the inability to accept praise. Such people react to praise as though it were blame: they are unhappy, depressed, or even angry when they receive it. For them reward is reacted to as though it masked hidden punishments.

Flugel has drawn attention to another, perhaps related, syndrome of motivation in what he calls the *Polycrates complex*. The name derives from the legend of the Greek ruler Polycrates who reacted with fear, anxiety, and inward guiltiness to a period of good fortune, and with an uneasy feeling that much unhappiness was being stored up for him. In some people, with whom others may find empathy difficult, the Polycrates motivation may assume a dominant influence on their actions, and sometimes in everyday life we encounter people who by some superstitious or ritualistic act seek to appease 'the wrath to come', particularly during times of relative good fortune. We encounter an echo of this motivation in common reactions to a spell of good weather, and the thought or spoken judgement 'we shall have to pay for this later'.

McDougall had originally hoped to deal with the individual psychology of motivation in terms of the sentiments. Sentiments, whether positive, negative, or ambivalent, are as we have seen important motives, and so with other motives their verbal expression as conscious intentions may be a dubious guide to the lines of conduct they produce. This paradoxical feature of sentiments results in part from the fact that at least some sentiments are ambivalent, that consciously felt love may for example mask hidden reserves of hostility and resentment. 'Love' is an extremely ambiguous word in any case. It is a reputable word, and this may account for its widespread use to disguise a huge variety of emotional habits of other kinds, including jealous possessiveness, and up to relatively pure hatred. As we have seen in the previous chapter, La Rochefoucauld had many witty statements to make expressing these insights, including, for example, 'If we judge love by its usual effects it resembles hatred rather than friendship.' This aspect of love is examined by Flugel in his earlier book *Men and Their Motives*, in which he examines two aspects of the love relation between man and woman: the simple direct one which he associates with Scandinavian society, and the complex one he associates with France. He uses for his purposes in contrasting these a novel which portrays the story of a young Frenchman who falls in love with a Scandinavian girl, and the intense frustrations he has to undergo because she sees no necessity for the complications he finds it necessary to inject into the relationship. This frustration and accompanying despair results from the matter-of-fact attitude of the girl, which denies the young man the pleasure of falling from ladders while attempting to reach her balcony, hiding under beds, or being chased by irate fathers with shotguns! He misses in this what Flugel calls the operation of the principle of 'greater satisfaction through inhibition'. This principle Flugel finds important in motivation generally, an avoidance of the obvious and direct, and a pursuit of the subtle which has its own attractions. Elsewhere he makes considerable use of this principle of motivation, for example in his book *The Psychology of Clothes*. To follow his own method, an example may be taken from literature. Thus Irwin Wallace in *The Prize* portrays a scene in which a young man eventually locates the lady who attracts him – who is incidentally also Scandinavian, a Swede – in a nudist colony. The author portrays the young man's surprise at the complete absence of sexual feeling on his own part towards her while in the colony – an observation many nudists confirm – but the reappearance of these feelings when she dresses and leaves with him. The relation of clothing to the sentiment of love, and to sexual emotion, is a complex one in which Flugel's writings on the subject stand pre-eminent. The principle of greater satisfaction through inhibition was implicitly recognized by earlier thinkers concerned with the limitations of hedonism as a theory of motivation: it has often been noted that direct pursuit of pleasure is often unsuccessful in achieving its goal and, as Aristotle observed at an early date, pleasure is better conceived of as a by-product of the successful functioning of other motives.

Along with Aristotle's by-product theory of pleasure may be noted the application of Flugel's principle to art. In one investigation Gombrich (1954) produced a series of photographs. The first was of some Victorian chocolate-box-style nude female figures; his observation, which the viewer is likely to share, is that these are sickly, obvious, and aesthetically unpleasing. The others are of the same paintings but photographed through distorting glass which give them a sort of cubist character; one now has to contribute effort to make sense of the figures, complication is introduced, and the effect is aesthetically very much better. Art preferences have in fact been subjected to study as a basis for understanding the personality of the beholder. From the work of Barron in this field has emerged a dimension of personality termed complexity–simplicity. The person who scores high on simplicity exhibits aesthetic preferences for the obvious and unsubtle, whereas high complexity scorers exhibit preferences which suggest the motivational influence of Flugel's 'greater satisfaction through inhibition' principle.

A number of other syndromes of motivation may be mentioned more briefly. We have already noted what Graham Wallas has called the baulked disposition: the missing of opportunities to experience an emotion like fear, and as a result making efforts or paying sums of money to achieve the experience. Wallas also refers to another syndrome which he calls 'drunkard's wit', which may apply to alcoholics or others. Here we have a man whose life is in almost every respect a total failure, and everything has gone wrong, but how does he react? He responds with laughter and humour to everything, and has found an escape in the defence of regarding nothing as serious and everything as one huge joke.

Many of the oddities of motivation uncovered by psychoanalysis, not only by Freud but also, and very important, by Anna Freud, his daughter, will be discussed in the chapter to follow on mechanisms of ego-defence. Psychologists and psycho-analysts have not been the only ones to contribute to our knowledge of these syndromes. Thus, for example, one important style of motivation has been examined by the great sociologist Veblen, and relates to the visible signs of socio-economic status. His principle relates to surplus wealth, and the fact that owners of surplus wealth tend to utilize it for the purpose of convincing others that they own it. Thus, to take examples from Veblen's own age, the fashionable lady would appear in her carriage flanked by two footmen, thus demonstrating that she could afford to keep two able-bodied men uselessly employed. Being 'fashionable' means, in effect, wearing new clothes before old ones have been worn out; niceties of polite society including good grammar and spelling indicate that one has been able to afford to waste time on these inessential things. Veblen explores numerous examples: only the well-to-do women of China had their feet bound or wore long fingernails, both of which displayed to the world that it was unnecessary for them to do productive work. The social psychology of motivation is a large field, but Veblen's ideas – although now classical – still have some application. On clothing, Flugel is impressed by the influences of what he calls 'the great masculine renunciation', the time in history when man gave up wearing attractive and colourful clothes and left the field to woman. The reasons for this he regards as complex, but of interest is the phenomenon itself which accounts for the marked differences of behaviour and motivation that still distinguish man and woman today, though not in certain former ages.

In these paragraphs I have sought to draw attention to some of the forms of motivation which occur. They exhibit great variety, and the discovery of some of these syndromes in friends and acquaintances may result in surprise comparable to that we frequently meet on discovery of variations of imagery, and of the presence of idiosyncrasies like number forms, synaesthesia, and hypnagogic imagery. Some of these aspects of motivation exhibit, I suspect, an incidence comparable to that of the falling experience, and *déjà vu*: in short they are extremely common. Others may resemble hypnagogic imagery in dividing people almost equally into two categories, while others may resemble diagram forms in being extremely rare. Their rarity is no justification for their being ignored, and indeed the rarities of motivation are valuable precisely because they challenge us to empathize with mental life markedly unlike our own. We cannot today content ourselves with merely a general theory of motivation, a theory devoted exclusively to the universal human motives. Nor should we content ourselves with crude, oversimplified theories such as hedonism and egoism, which science has long abandoned but which still retain their hold in 'common sense', though in some of its manifestations this is merely another name for superficiality or the science of yesterday in diluted form. Thus I have described a few of these variants, idiosyncrasies and apparent oddities of motivation. The list has been arbitrary but may provide some food for thought in the realm of motivation to those whose motivational life resembles the visual imager who 'cannot conceive of' how people can think without such imagery, or who is curiously shocked to discover that such oddities as number forms and colour associations are an aspect of the mental equipment of their friends, acquaintances, and spouses.

CONTEMPORARY THEORIES OF MOTIVATION

The importance of the influence of learning on motivation is fully appreciated today by some of the major contemporary theorists in this field. Of particular importance to contemporary theory are fear and anxiety. As illustration may be noted the position taken by O. H. Mowrer (1950), a leading American psychologist. Mowrer's work exhibits an unusual combination of highly original experimentation (much of it conducted on animal subjects) with profound insight into the human personality in respect of its subtleties of motivation, and an enormous breadth of knowledge which he draws on in his theorizing. Mowrer regards fear as a 'secondary' or learned drive, secondary in the sense that in his life history a person comes to fear many objects and situations which did not originally evoke the fear reaction. Fear results in a strong tendency to avoid the source of provocation, and the specific habits of avoidance which occur tell us a great deal about the individual personality and his style of motivation. Techniques used to escape, or reduce, fear and anxiety are themselves reinforced or strengthened to the extent to which they achieve this. These avoidances may themselves – viewed from outside – seem to be self-destructive yet, paradoxically enough, self-perpetuating. The reason they persist is that they are essentially devices for avoiding fear or, as it were, binding up anxiety so that it is not prominent to conscious experience. Mowrer's approach to these problems fits in well with the concept of 'ego-defences' to which the individual may resort for the purpose of keeping painful emotion such as anxiety, guilt, and inferiority feeling out of consciousness. We shall discuss some of these ego-defences, the strategies which individuals use and through which they deceive themselves, in the following chapter.

A second, and somewhat similar, standpoint is represented by J. Dollard and Neil Miller, who are like Mowrer much concerned to relate learning theory to personality and individual motivation. With Mowrer they place emphasis on fear as a secondary drive, and like Mowrer they see fear and anxiety as a major determinant of the internal avoidance processes of the individual. Some analogies can be drawn between the human personality and his problems, and the rat at a choice point in a maze – Miller is, like Mowrer, a talented animal experimentalist – and we need to know about the 'maze' each adult human being has constructed for himself. This means, in effect, a study of the structure of the individual environment he has created, and of the types of behaviour which he expects to be rewarded and punished. It means also – and Dollard is an experienced anthropologist – a study of the rewards and punishments of the social environment which constitutes the area of culture in which he lives. Of interest is Miller and Dollard's acceptance, but reformulation, of one of Freud's central concepts: the mechanism of repression, which was the first of the ego-defences with which the psycho-analysts concerned themselves. Later, as we shall see in the following chapter, they were to find and name others. Repression is a process of avoiding certain thoughts – perhaps in part originally based on punishment for using certain taboo words in speech – and it is a product of learning. The response of 'not thinking' becomes strengthened or reinforced because it avoids fear and reduces anxiety. Repression is conceived of as a continuum ranging from slight tendencies not to think about, to strongly motivated tendencies to avoid, fear-provoking items of thought. In the course of time the words which evoke ideas about the object or situation which evokes fear come to be discarded and avoided, and the process of repression is complete. Repression – not thinking about, not remembering, and ultimately being unable to think about or remember – represents the prototype of an ego-defence. It is to this, and other strategies of anxiety avoidance and self-deception, that we shall next turn.

CHAPTER TEN

Techniques of Self-Deception

'I did that', says my memory. 'I could not have done that',
says my pride, and remains inexorable. Eventually the
memory yields.   NIETZSCHE

PLATO examined certain aspects of the behaviour of the abso-
lutist ruler. Such a ruler tends to surround himself with people
who accept his ideas and, in one way or another, rid himself of
those who criticize. The result is, Plato tells us, that an ingenious
self-deception becomes available to him: he is eventually able to
seek the opinions of his associates who will reflect back to him his
own, and confirm that what he is doing is right. A similar process
has been discussed by the contemporary social psychologist
L. Doob. In his book on propaganda Doob (1949) makes the
point that one of the first victims of propaganda tends to be the
propagandist himself, the next being his close associates. Thus
the man at the top tends to build a non-conducting layer of
approving disciples between himself and those likely to criticize
or object. Divided though they are by 1,500 years, the Greek
philosopher and the American psychologist draw attention to
one unnamed technique of self-deception.

Doob goes on to suggest that the individual's repertoire of self-
deceptive techniques is extensive, and has relevance to other
people's judgements of the 'sincerity' or lack of it in his actions.
Because of man's capacity for self-deception, Doob suggests,
once we examine them the popular concepts of 'sincerity' and
'insincerity' lose much of their meaning. Two points may be
added. First, we have noted that human motivation tends to be
complex, a combination of motives of different kinds. The
ethically respectable and rational among these are likely to be
introspectively prominent to the person himself, while the disreputable and irrational ones will be apparent to those with
enmity towards him. Secondly, and because of this, there may be

a marked discrepancy between an individual's stated intentions and the obvious consequences of his actions. The techniques, which the psycho-analysts call the 'mechanisms of ego-defence' have a great deal to do with this discrepancy. Best known of these mechanisms is repression, which was noted by others before Freud. Its characteristics are well summarized in the quotation from Nietzsche at the head of this chapter.

A number of these mechanisms have been described and given names by the psycho-analysts, and Anna Freud (1936) has published probably the most important book available in this field. In this, Freud's daughter discusses repression along with projection, denial, reaction formation, isolation, and other of these mechanisms. Four general characteristics of ego-defensive mechanisms may be noted. Two of these were mentioned by E. R. Hilgard (1949), who made them the subject of his presidential address to the American Psychological Association: first, they are self-deceptive; and secondly they are defences against the conscious experience of anxiety. To this may be added the characteristic mentioned by Doob: the mechanisms are relevant to the judgements of the 'sincerity' or otherwise that we make about human actions. Finally, it may be noted that under certain circumstances the mechanisms may perform important functions of adjustment in the ordinary activity of normal human living.

EGO-DEFENCE AND ADJUSTMENT

Under some conditions we find it prudent to place distance between ourselves and a threat to our physical safety. The human personality frequently experiences threats to its self-esteem, and may similarly react with defensive activity. Anna Freud gives the name 'restriction of the ego' to one important strategy of this kind. This is admirably discussed, though not named, by William James (1890) in his discussion of self-respect. He argues that this depends upon the ratio between an individual's successes and his aspirations. Thus having devoted his life to being a psychologist he, William James, is mortified to find anybody else knowing more about it than he does; yet he is content to wallow in the grossest ignorance of Greek, about which he has no such aspirations. As Muzafer Sherif would express it, James is 'ego-involved' with psychology but not with Greek; or in Anna Freud's terms he has 'restricted his ego' in certain ways but not in others. Because of such restriction of the ego, James, like most of us, is able to accept failure in certain fields without undue humiliation. We either regard ourselves strictly as amateurs or we don't compete at all. But in other areas success and failure may mean a very great deal, and this needs to be considered if we seek to understand certain manifestations of inferiority feeling. Thus, as William James puts it, 'we have the paradox of a man shamed to death because he is the second pugilist or the second oarsman in the world. That he is able to beat the whole population of the world minus one is nothing: he has pitted himself to beat that one.'

Taking restriction of the ego as an example we can see how such mechanisms may perform useful adjustive functions. Life would be miserable and perpetually anxiety-provoking without them. Feelings of inferiority are exceedingly common. Because people are able to restrict their aspirations in certain ways, they can exert some selectivity over what they feel inferior about. Some of the other mechanisms may now be considered.

THE MECHANISM OF DENIAL

The old proverb 'there are none so blind as those who *will* not see' helps to define what the psycho-analysts call denial. 'Not seeing' may be taken to represent any of the channels of perceptual information: in general to fail to take in what is perceptually obvious, but emotionally unacceptable. Denial is well illustrated by a very common reaction to bad news: 'it isn't true', 'I don't believe it', or even 'you must be lying'. These words may be spoken by the recipient of the news even to somebody he knows well and whose word, on more emotionally neutral matters, he would accept without question.

Irving Sarnoff (1962) in discussing denial draws attention to another of its manifestations, which takes the form 'it can't happen to me'. He instances a study made of people who had been victims of the Nazi occupation. Many of these people were Jews and told of how they had been fully aware of the Nazi persecutions. Yet for a long time they managed to maintain the illusion that they themselves would be spared. They denied the personal implications of events around them and were genuinely surprised and shocked when arrested. It seems probable that this kind of denial plays an important part in the ego-defensive activity of the soldier on the battle-field, able to advance without fully realizing that he himself, and not others only, may be killed.

Denial may operate in the service of positive sentiments as in the proverbial blindness of the lover, also of negative ones as in selective imperception of the virtuous actions or motivation of people we dislike. This aspect of denial is illustrated in an experiment conducted on a group of children by Zillig in 1928. She obtained information about classroom friendships and antipathies, and set the children examination tasks. The well-liked children were instructed to make mistakes, the disliked children to perform correctly. Perception of the events by the observers was influenced by their sentiments: favourable sentiments induced them to perceive tasks as being performed correctly when they were not. Again, and fairly obviously, denial may both stem from and serve to perpetuate prejudice. Prejudice has been said to have had a brilliant past, and to look like having a promising future: very often indeed have the prejudiced asserted that members of some persecuted group 'do not feel pain in the same way as others do'. Commenting on this convenient piece of denial by persecutors, Stafford Clark draws attention to its resemblance to other assertions, such as that the fox enjoys the hunt, and the fish does not feel the hook. From his knowledge as a medical man of biology, both human and animal, Stafford Clark admits his failure to find any evidence that the pain sense is, in these various cases, absent.

Numerous examples of denial are to be found in relations between adults and children. Thus a parent may reinforce tendencies to denial by telling the child that his bruised leg, still smarting with pain, is 'all better now'. Alternatively the adult may administer some perfectly horrid – and possibly quite unnecessary – medicine saying that its taste 'isn't a bit nasty'.

There have been many instances of people wounded in battle who have not experienced pain. A well-known case of this kind of denial involved David Livingstone, who felt no pain while his arm was being partly devoured by a lion. Pain itself is a form of perception subject to increase or decrease of intensity in accord with suggestion. Kuehner (1956), writing as a dentist, refers to influences of implicit verbal suggestion. Thus dentists can unnecessarily increase the sufferings of their patients with talk about 'drilling', 'grinding', and 'chiselling'. Instead they can help by a tactful choice of words like 'cleaning out', and 'polishing', avoiding as far as possible terms implying discomfort, cutting activities, and resulting pain. Fairly obviously the physician and midwife can do much to increase pain by harping on such words as 'the pains' of childbirth. Alternatively they can help a little by habitual use of the word 'contractions' for the accompaniments of the normal process of birth.

PROJECTION AND ALLIED MECHANISMS

The word 'projection' denotes a whole family of defence mechanisms. In classical projection one person accuses another of a quality which is so obviously an attribute of the accuser that it surprises the bystander that he hasn't noticed it himself! An early observer of this form of self-deception in his patients was the eighteenth-century surgeon John Hunter. Hunter refers to one such patient, an alcoholic, who he says tended as he became intoxicated to 'refer all his own weaknesses and feelings . . . to those around him' (Hunter and MacAlpine, 1963). Thus on returning home he would insist on putting his whole family to bed, maintaining that they were too drunk to do it for themselves. This happened regularly, whenever he was intoxicated. Similarly people with considerable hostility or ambivalence towards others may preserve themselves from recognizing this fact by projecting that hostility on to others and feeling persecuted by them. An important study of the projection mechanisms was conducted in 1936 by R. R. Sears. A hundred students, members of a college fraternity, rated each other and themselves on various personal qualities, e.g. obstinacy, meanness, etc. Degree of insight was assessed by the extent to which self ratings agreed with ratings by others. When insight was low and these two diverged, Sears found a tendency for those who possessed more than an average amount of a trait to attribute it to others: a tendency to project.

One variant of projection Anna Freud calls 'identification with the aggressor'. This we may have observed in ourselves when while motoring or after treading on somebody's toe we blame *him* for putting his car or his toe in the way when we were going to put ours there! Identification with the aggressor, Anna Freud points out, is observable in certain children's games. She relates an incident concerning a six-year-old girl who on visiting the dentist ridiculed the idea that a dentist ever hurt anybody. One day she was discovered in a dreadful temper: the dentist *had hurt her*. She was cross and unfriendly, and later expressed her anger against various objects in the analyst's room: she cut up an india-rubber and a length of string into small pieces, and then turned her attention to pencils, which she proceeded to break. While not actually playing dentist, the child appeared to be trying to achieve mastery by doing actively in her play what she had suffered from the dentist.

Another mechanism is named by Anna Freud 'altruistic surrender'. This involves projection plus a rather pathological degree of identification with another person. Freud himself does not provide a name, but discusses the process whereby a parent may adopt an exaggerated vicarious satisfaction of his own thwarted needs and ambitions through his children. Anna Freud tells of a young woman who came for psycho-analysis. It emerged that she had had two great ambitions: always to be nicely dressed, and to have children of her own. When she came for analysis she was scruffy, unmarried, and childless, but betrayed an abnormal amount of interest in the dress, welfare, and children of her friends. She had emptied her own life of interests and wishes, and expended all her energies on vicarious living through others. The altruistic surrender had in this case been remarkably complete.

Related to projection is a mechanism which I have elsewhere (1952) suggested might be called *projective distortion*. In this one person attributes to another a quality which that other person does possess, but the accuser attributes it to an exaggerated extent because it is noticeably his own, and he lacks insight into this fact. Thus during persecution a member of a persecuted minority group may attribute additionally threatening qualities to his persecutors. Interesting observations, remarkable for both their insight and intellectual honesty, of this process were reported by Bettelheim. Bettelheim, a Jewish psychologist, was himself a prisoner in Nazi concentration camps. In the diary he kept he recorded evidence of a clash of stereotypes: between the Nazi's stereotype of the Jew, and the Jewish prisoner's stereotype of the Nazi. The dangers of overt expressions of hostility by the prisoners against the guards were considerable; the likelihood of overt expression of aggression varies inversely with expectation of punishment. Thus Bettelheim found evidence that under conditions which prevented overt expression of their hostility the prisoners would attribute additional hostility to the guards. This was observable to him even though genuinely persecutory behaviour by the guards was *also* obviously present. I suspect that projective distortion, along with classical projection, plays an important part in inter-personal relations of an everyday kind. In accord with the principle of economy, such sense data as are present will be used: hostility and aggression that are factually present are perceived in an exaggerated way. Moreover a person who projects his own hostility on to others is liable by this to provoke hostility in them: thus accurate perception, projective distortion, and projection may together function to reinforce the original projection.

In his famous *Maxims* La Rochefoucauld drew attention to another mechanism that resembles projection. La Rochefoucauld's mechanism involves the tendency to blame in others what we feel guilty about in ourselves. On occasion we encounter exaggerated hostility towards people who manifest, in an exaggerated way, one of the qualities of our own that we are reluctant to acknowledge. The 'righteous indignation' of the law-abiding citizen against the criminal often illustrates the mechanism. Thus the advocate of flogging who demands this punishment for a criminal accused of an aggressive crime is able to 'have his cake' in expressing his own aggression in this socially acceptable form, and 'eat it too' in so far as he can also enjoy his own self-righteousness while doing so. The La Rochefoucauld mechanism may also operate in relation to the subject's former qualities, as is wittily pointed out by Gilbert and Sullivan in *Trial by Jury*. The chorus of jurymen acknowledge that, when younger, they themselves were remarkably like the accused, but

> I'm now a respectable chap
> And shine with a virtue resplendent,
> And therefore I haven't a scrap
> Of sympathy for the defendant!

Sometimes the actions or even the presence of another person evoke guilt which manifests itself in the form of aggression. Dostoyevsky indicates his understanding of this process when in *The Brothers Karamazov* old Karamazov is asked why he has such an intense hatred for a certain person. He replies that the object of his hatred has never done him harm, but he, Karamazov, once behaved dishonourably to this other person and has ever since hated him. We tend to be emotionally involved with certain categories of other people and, as C. G. Jung remarked, 'there can be no indifference to the carrier of a projection'. Nor, we may add, to those who remind us in some way of the qualities in ourselves that we wish to repudiate. The La Rochefoucauld mechanism is by no means absent in everyday life; it operates a great deal in reactions for delinquency; and it forms a connecting link between projection proper and the mechanism of reaction formation.

REACTION FORMATION

The psychologist Flugel (1945) defines reaction formation as the development of a trait which is usually the opposite of the original trait which it cancels and keeps in check. Thus a fundamentally aggressive person may exhibit exaggerated politeness; the individual with exaggerated inferiority may manifest arrogant and dominant behaviour; and the person with an inner preoccupation with sex may manifest exaggerations of prudishness. Shakespeare was commenting on this mechanism when he made one of his characters say 'Methinks the lady doth protest too much'. One form of reaction formation has received particular attention through the work of Alfred Adler: this is what Adler calls 'over-compensation' as a reaction to feelings of inferiority. The bombastic and self-opinionated man who appears to be anything but under-confident is, on Adler's analysis, frequently a victim of acute inferiority feelings.

Reaction formations taking the form of inquisitiveness, stemming from sexual guilt, are often tiresomely obvious to others if not to the person concerned. To take an intentionally remote example, at the end of the last century a clergyman said of a certain lady of the village, 'She combines the advocacy of purity with the investigation of indecency'. It seems a little unfair that the term 'old woman' should be used to denote social nuisances of this kind of the male variety. Sometimes the apparently opposite qualities which comprise the reaction formation permit both denial and expression of the motives which underlie the reaction formation. The psycho-analyst Theodore Reik suggests the principle that it is sometimes possible to assess a person's unconscious motives from the responses his actions evoke in others. There is a kind of person of whom it has been well said 'he is out to help others, and you can tell the others by their hunted look!' It is not entirely surprising if this kind of 'helpfulness' on occasion elicits resentment from the insight of others into its underlying motivation. Similarly there are some pacifists who can express an intensity of aggression through their pacifism which may be a source of wonder to their acquaintances, as may be the hostility towards their fellow men which some anti-vivisectionists can express through their love of animals. The sentiment of love is one which, as La Rochefoucauld has observed, resembles hatred rather than friendship in certain of its manifestations. The unacknowledged motives which feed a reaction formation may be detectable to others, who may react to them rather than to consciously expressed intentions; thus a person exhibiting reaction formation may frequently complain of being misunderstood.

There are taboos other than those on aggression and sex, and there is one interesting taboo to which I. D. Suttie (1935) has drawn particular attention; it also has its bearing on reaction formation. This is the rather surprisingly strong taboo on the expression of tender emotion. In many societies people are often extremely intolerant of such expression, which may evoke responses like 'sickly sentimentality' or 'don't be silly'. This is noticeably true of the male child at certain stages of his development when 'manliness' as opposed to 'childishness' is admired; adults in love are regarded as 'silly' and 'spoony', and expressions of fondness for friends have to be disguised and covered up in some form of mock abuse. Suttie regards the taboo on tenderness and these responses as reaction formations against a craving for maternal protection and the nursery. The individual concerned is uncertain of his emancipation from childhood and reacts against it in very much the same way as the prude reacts against sex, and for the same reasons of weakness.

Another kind of reaction formation has been called by Karl Menninger the repudiation of masculinity. A person who is unsure of his masculinity may manifest this by what appear, to superficial observation, to be male qualities. He may be preoccupied with tough maleness, and anti-feminist in his general outlook. Or another manifestation that to superficial observation seems so different is Don Juanism, in which the person concerned often seems to be seeking repeated reassurances of masculinity in a series of conquests. Again, repudiated masculinity may express itself in incessant talk about actual or fantasied sexual achievements. Again the 'protest too much' characteristic of reaction formation, and the discrepancy between manifest overt qualities and their latent but unacknowledged motivation, may be apparent to others. Any of these varied forms of reaction formation may be supported by, for example, rationalization: this has sometimes been called a 'secondary mechanism' in that it supports other ego-defensive operations like repression.

THE MECHANISM OF REPRESSION

The mechanism of repression is summarized in the quotation from Nietzsche which heads this chapter. Repression was one of the first of the mechanisms to be studied, for example by Freud in close association with Breuer in their early studies of hysterical neuroses. Psycho-analysis itself stemmed in part from the treatment by Breuer of one patient, a young woman referred to as 'Anna O.'. Breuer treated her hypnotically as he found that when in her normal state 'her dread of a memory . . . inhibited its appearance' (Breuer and Freud, 1895, edition 1955). Freud similarly at first used hypnotism, but later abandoned it in favour of free association as a technique for overcoming repression and retrieving memories. Some aspects of repression, as a process of active forgetting, are well exemplified in the famous case of claustrophobia treated by Rivers (1920). The fear of enclosed spaces in the individual concerned was eventually removed when Rivers elicited recall of a wholly forgotten incident: this had involved the patient, as a child, being confined in a dark passage with a fierce and barking dog. The incident was recalled only after a long period of treatment. It was recalled with accompaniments of extreme terror: an abreaction or emotional reliving of the original experience. As a result of this repressed memory the patient had subsequently reacted to enclosed spaces alone, as though they were enclosed spaces plus a fear-producing stimulus. The origins of phobias in 'association of ideas' was suggested in 1711 by the philosopher John Jocke, who also anticipated the notion that the person concerned might actively forget – what we would now call repress – the emotionally toned memories themselves. The Rivers case of claustrophobia is a particularly interesting one in that it throws additional light upon the repression process and illustrates how repression at different levels of depth can occur. A process of analysis may not be entirely unlike that of peeling an onion, which yields layer after layer as the work progresses. Thus in the claustrophobia case mentioned Rivers elicited first one and then a second and more deeply repressed incident, before he came to the third and still more frightening incident of the dog and the dark passage. These seemed, though repressed themselves, to help to maintain the most deeply repressed memory of all. In addition to memories repressed at greater levels of depth, Freud introduced in his *Psycho-pathology of Everyday Life* the further notion of 'concealing memories'.

These, though conscious, perform the function of impeding recall of associated repressed memories for which they, as it were, offer themselves instead.

The notion of repression, as formulated by Freud, is a complex one. Repression itself is one of what were later recognized to be a repertoire of defence mechanisms which keep certain emotionally charged ideas out of consciousness. Removal of repression, like the penetration of other ego-defences, is not a task to be undertaken lightly. Accompaniments of the greater insight, improved judgement, and ultimate emotional adjustment sought may be for a time an upsurge of disturbing emotion. Thus a patient during analytic treatment may, like a patient undergoing a major surgical operation, become apparently very much worse during the treatment. It is an important part of the therapist's function to give emotional support during what may be disturbing periods in which anxiety and fear, guilt and inferiority feeling, become manifest. A competent therapist will not permit upsurges of these emotions which are in excess of what he, and the patient, can cope with. Thus in a sense timing of the process of giving insight by analysis of the ego-defences is essential. Ego-defences are after all a defence against something. In the previous chapter we have seen that other investigators like Mowrer, Miller, and Dollard have studied the self-perpetuating devices of the personality for avoiding fear and anxiety. The process of replacing these with something else in therapy may be accompanied by strong upsurges of emotion in which anxiety itself is a major component. Moreover if the therapy process proceeds too fast these defences may be replaced by others, particularly by defences of an intellectualizing kind. It would be a mistake to view the kind of 'insight' which deep analytic therapy seeks as merely something intellectual. Elsewhere I have mentioned a case of a victim of amateur analysis. He was a bad obsessional patient though 'analysed'. And he remained a bad obsessional despite his ability to talk fluently and at length about his symptoms and their causes intellectually and in technical language. Intellectual knowledge was perfectly compatible with retention of these symptoms, and in fact had constituted an ego-defensive activity of its own. This brings us to consideration of another and very interesting mechanism, which has both pathological and adjustive functions.

THE MECHANISM OF ISOLATION

In a very readable introduction to the abnormal, the psychiatrist Bernard Hart discusses certain characteristics of the normal personality. One of these is the widespread tendency people have to surround their favourite beliefs with logic-tight compartments. These are resistant to argument, and permit the entertaining of two mutually incompatible beliefs without an undue sense of inconsistency. Certain aspects of mental life exhibit compartmentalization, and isolation from others. Such compartmentalization may take many forms. One of its commoner manifestations is the remark 'I know it's silly but I can't help it', which may be said by a normal person about his action in going downstairs to turn off the gas when he is perfectly aware of having done so already. And the 'walk on the squares of the street' mechanism governs many of the activities of the compulsive-obsessional neurotic: about these activities he also is likely to make the same remark. Isolation of idea and effect is the mechanism underlying these forms of behaviour, and the compartmentalization of the two is responsible for the sense of absurdity about one's own actions.

Isolation of a related kind may play an important part in those kinds of normal thinking we call 'rational' and 'unemotional'. It is a characteristic of both scholarship and science to think in an unbiased way, that is to isolate one's pro and con sentiments from the relevant ideas. A magistrate or judge pronouncing on the law, an examiner striving to be impartial, or a psychologist trying to understand such revolting phenomena as the Nazi Party or a Negro lynching are all by the nature of their thought attempting isolation. My inclusion of the word 'revolting' – it was the way the sentence came as I wrote it – indicates that such attempts are not always successful. Other examples of adjustive activity of the isolation kind may be found in the adaptations made by the medical student to the activity of dissecting a human body. some find this very difficult indeed. Most, in the course of time, are able to isolate from disturbing emotional upset by pre-occupying themselves with the generic terms which anatomy as a subject provides, rather than the individuality of a former living human being.

A person who is too successful in the activity of isolation may be judged 'inhuman', or 'ruthless'. Thus some administrators may lose sight of the feelings and sufferings of individuals in their preoccupation with figures and other abstractions. Sometimes such isolation is achieved partly by geographical distance. Field Marshal Alexander said of his experiences as a line officer in the First World War: 'No commander above my Brigade Commander ever visited my front line.' This isolation may have been psychologically necessary to those who planned major campaigns, though whether it was always militarily desirable may well be questioned. About a million men, considering both sides, fell in the Battle of the Somme, and on the first day of the battle there were 60,000 British casualties, including 20,000 dead. Leading Generals responsible for ordering these men into action have left a record of some of the defensive activities of isolation they indulged in. After pinning a medal on a blinded soldier Joffre declared: 'I mustn't be shown any more such spectacles . . . I would no longer have the courage to give the order to attack.' Of Haig it is reported by his son that he 'felt it was his duty to refrain from visiting the casualty clearing stations because these visits made him physically sick'. Clearly this physical remoteness and wish to preserve it was a factor in maintaining an unemotional attitude to generalship, and the attitude of 'almost inhuman calm' that has been attributed to Joffre.

It is perhaps not easy to draw a line between desirable and undesirable manifestations of the mechanism of isolation. And such a distinction is not relevant to my purpose which, in attempting to be impartial, itself requires isolation. It is, however, relevant to note differences between typical cases of the normal and adjusted forms of the mechanism, for example in impartial thinking, and in some abnormal forms such as the compulsive actions and obsessional thoughts that characterize one of the main neuroses. Many interesting phenomena lie between these extremes, and they include behaviour we describe in some of the following terms: ritualistic, bureaucratic, cold and calculating, inconsistent, and excessively intellectual. The mechanism of isolation is an important one with extensions into many forms of human activity, and different types of personality.

OTHER MECHANISMS OF DEFENCE

Six of the principal mechanisms have been discussed. There are others like *displacement*, as when, for example, an angry person may choose a safer target for his aggression for whom retaliation is improbable, or impossible: the 'kicking the cat' mechanism. *Laughter and humour* may perform a variety of ego-defensive functions, as is emphasized in McDougall's theory discussed in Chapter 8. Of interest for its adjustive functions is *introjection*, by which the individual takes into his personality things external to himself. Thus, for example, introjection plays a part in building up internal standards both ethical and intellectual. Rather than continue to undergo external punishments and criticisms the mature person achieves such internal systems, and himself censors his behaviour and thought.

Some mechanisms are mainly concerned with ego-defensive strategies against threats from within. External defences include, for example, *regression*, in which the individual returns to a developmentally earlier mode of functioning. Against stress from inner threats like strong impulses, guilt, anxiety, and inferiority feeling, defences like reaction formation and isolation may be employed. Another such mechanism is *undoing*. Undoing may play an important part in compulsive behaviour, as is illustrated in fiction in the classic case of the sleep-walking Lady Macbeth rubbing her hands and thus trying to undo her sense of guilt. One specific kind of undoing has been already noted in the oddity of motivation which Freud has called 'criminality from a sense of guilt'.

There may be a variety of moralistic accompaniments of ego-defensive activity, and perhaps a mechanism of *moralization* needs to be considered as such. Freud and the psycho-analysts have paid much attention to the vicissitudes of the super-ego and the exaggerated sense of guilt. Guilt is a feeling, and like inferiority feeling may have remarkably little reference to out-side events and actions. In this connexion Freud drew attention to the fact that the super-ego of the saint may become more guilt-ridden than that of the sinner. As the sense of obligation becomes more exacting these aspirations result in more guilt feeling, and this guilt may gain impetus from self-destructive tendencies of the personality operating through moralization.

It was from the later psycho-analytic theorist J. C. Flugel (1945), rather than Freud, that there came a distinction between the 'ego-ideal' and the 'super-ego'. Freud seems to have used the two terms interchangeably. Flugel finds it desirable to regard the ego-ideal as the reality-adjusted aspect of the super-ego. It comprises the moral standards for which a person can give good reason; with this ego-ideal may be contrasted the other aspects of the super-ego which are more primitive and developmentally earlier. The primitive kind of super-ego morality may manifest itself as when, in his dreams, a civilized twentieth-century man inflicts death upon someone who has merely done him a mild disservice. The dreamer, in waking thought, would probably reject this harsh punishment, his ego-ideal morality considering merely mild reproof or a few harsh words as appropriate. Flugel judges the ego-ideal morality as desirable both socially and per-sonally, and the primitive morality of the other aspects of the super-ego as undesirable in both respects. The concept of 'the unforgivable sin' has provided much subject matter for the vicis-situdes of the super-ego in its abnormal manifestations. This we may note in psychotic depression. Yellowlees (1932) instances a patient who had committed 'the unpardonable sin'; when its content emerged it was pathetic in its triviality: eventually she confessed that this sin had been that when carving the chicken at Sunday lunch she had frequently given herself too large a helping of the breast, and too little of it to the rest of the family. Such action may be thought blameworthy by the non-psychotic, but the typically psychotic loss of perspective is illustrated in the patient's own assessment of it.

Because we are dealing with vicissitudes of the super-ego, the guilt-ridden patient's delusions should not be taken at their face value. In this instance the exaggerated sense of guilt seems to be primary, and the reason for it that the patient finds is something secondary. It is a rationalization of this feeling of guilt. These complex aspects of ego-defence and motivation are dealt with more fully by specialists in this field, for example by Flugel in his book *Man, Morals, and Society* (Penguin). In the light of his studies of phenomena of this kind Flugel himself concludes that man is, in certain important respects, not a pleasure-seeking but rather a pain-seeking animal.

CONCLUSION

There are obviously an indefinite number of strategies and variations of these to which the ego may resort. They may be directed against threats by painful and unpleasant forces from outside; alternatively they may be defences against inner threats like guilt, anxiety, and inferiority. It has seemed valuable to some investigators to provide names for certain of the main ego-defences, and several of those named have been discussed. My purpose has been to draw attention to both self-deceptive and adjustive functions which these mechanisms can perform. One may be over-alerted to looking for the operation of such mechanisms in acquaintances and friends. It is my hope that this chapter will alert the reader towards noticing first their relation to his own personality and its motivation.

CHAPTER ELEVEN

The Normal Personality

> The dynamic organization within the individual of those psychophysical systems that determine his unique adjustments to his environment.
>
> G. W. ALLPORT, defining 'personality'

IN one of the most influential books in this field Allport examined fifty definitions of personality in terms of previous usages. His own definition, which heads this chapter, stems from this study. As the modern psychologist understands the term, personality denotes the individual: his thinking and his abilities, his emotions and emotional habits, and the motives which are characteristic of him. We may if we like distinguish two aspects. First, there is the cognitive side of personality: thinking, imagery, intelligence, and abilities generally; and secondly the temperament aspect: the characteristics of the individual's emotional and motivational life. Thus we may speak of cognitive traits on the one hand, and temperament traits on the other.

A third type of trait is associated with character. Allport defines character as 'personality evaluated'. The tendency today is to follow this usage: thus honesty in money matters, dishonesty in matters of truth telling, and integrity in one's business dealings are examples of character traits. For certain practical purposes we may be interested in these or other character traits, as well as in both cognitive and temperamental personality traits.

A different approach to personality involves types rather than traits. To classify people into types is to do violence to their uniqueness, but it may prove helpful. Personality typologies have proved an impetus to thought and observation in both the pre-scientific and the scientific periods of personality study. Along with traits, types provide a vocabulary that alerts us to certain aspects of the person's characteristic behaviour. Three kinds of personality types will be noted: some that are orthodox and well established; others that have emerged from investigations but have been neglected or are less well known; and others again which may provide food for thought, and perhaps subject matter for future research.

ORTHODOX TYPOLOGIES

One of the oldest conceptions with which psychology still has dealings is the classical *doctrine of the four temperaments*. The origins of this are to be found in the Greek philosopher Empedocles (490–430 B.C.), developed by later pioneers of this early period such as Hippocrates, the 'father of medicine'. People were divided into four categories in terms of their temperament, or characteristic emotional and motivational life. These comprised the sanguine, the choleric, the melancholic, and the phlegmatic. The types may be summarized in terms of two broad temperament traits: susceptibility to emotional provocation, and intensity of emotion once aroused. Thus the sanguine and choleric types are both highly susceptible to emotional provocation; they differ in that the emotions of the sanguine person are weak, while those of the choleric are strong. The melancholic and the phlegmatic are similar in that both are resistant to provocation to emotion; they differ in that the emotional intensity of the aroused melancholic is strong, while that of the phlegmatic is weak. In connexion with this very old typology may be noted Eysenck's use of it in recent times to relate it to the results of his own researches of the last decade or so (see Figure 15).

Perhaps the best-known of modern typologies is Jung's typing of people as *introverts and extraverts*. Jung also postulated, in addition to these two attitude types, four functional types with the functions of thinking, feeling, sensation, and intuition. Thus he produced an eight-fold typology, these types including for example the thinking extravert, the thinking introvert, the feeling extravert, and the intuitive introvert. Later work has, however, largely neglected these and concentrated on the attitude types.

Two trends in the subsequent history of the typology may be noted, and both illustrate what often tends to happen to typologies in general as research becomes more sophisticated. First, the notion of introverts *v.* extraverts has given place to a measurable trait of introversion–extraversion: this trait has an important place in, for example, the personality researches of Eysenck and his colleagues (compare again the Figure 15). These investigators

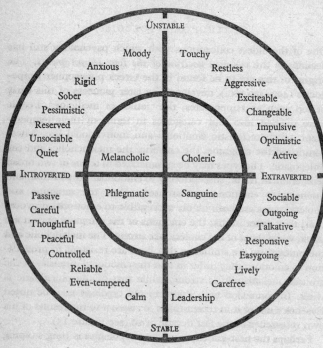

15. Eysenck's analysis of temperament tests, relating them to both dimensions of personality and the early temperament typology.

find evidence for differences between the two poles of the trait in terms of speed of learning, perceptual behaviour, and style of performance in tasks of motor skill. They differ in their motivational characteristics, their social behaviour, and the types of neurosis to which they are susceptible. Secondly, by contrast, other investigators, while accepting introversion–extraversion as a trait, have regarded the trait as composite rather than unitary. They have, for example, distinguished and developed tests for measuring separately thinking introversion-extraversion, social introversion-extraversion, and emotional introversion-extraversion. Thus a given person may be introverted in his thinking, socially extraverted, and emotionally introverted: such a person might, for example, be a professional philosopher who gets on well with other people in parties and other social situations, but prefers to be alone in times of grief rather than to seek the comfort of others. Other typologies, like Jung's, have provided subject matter for the design of tests of measurable traits, and the further analysis of the typology into component parts. (The relation of Eysenck's 'introversion–extraversion' to crime and criminality is discussed in Chapter 13.)

The development of types into testable traits is also seen in the case of a second typology, associated with Eduard Spranger and his book *Types of Men*. Spranger regarded his original types simply as reference points which, as ideal abstractions, he likened to the lines, points, and right angles of geometry. His idea was to type people in terms of their basic philosophy of life, into *six value types*. Subsequent research has indicated a sex difference, in that men tend to fall into three of Spranger's categories: the theoretical, economic, and political types. By contrast women tend more often to be of the other three: the aesthetic, religious, and social types. For some people, Spranger argued, the pursuit of knowledge is all-important: these comprised his theoretical type. Others exhibited values and long-term motivation in the direction of art or natural beauty (aesthetic type). Others pursued humanitarian goals (social), or power (political), or religion. The strongly economic type may find the theoretical type too preoccupied with 'ivory towers', while the social may regard both as cold and inhuman. The Spranger typology has given rise to a most valuable research technique in a test known as the Study of Values. Investigations with this have revealed the sex difference mentioned, and also the predicted differences between high and low scorers on the measurable value traits in terms of occupation. Thus, for example, engineers tend to score highly on the economic (applied science) value trait, while divinity students tend to record high scores on the religious value. Spranger's original typology has given rise to one valuable approach to personality differences, and it has served to remind us of the usefulness of approaching people in terms of their basic values and long-term life goals. As one of the authors of the Study of Values test, G. W. Allport, has pointed out, there are nevertheless certain omissions. Allport suggests that we should also keep in mind other kinds of people, for example the humorist: the person who guides his life, and adjusts to adversity, in terms of humour and the laughable.

William James was responsible for one typology which provides a different approach to personality in terms of *the tender minded and the toughminded*. A kind-hearted, perhaps somewhat sentimental concern for the welfare of others distinguishes the first, while 'hardness' and even 'ruthlessness' are attributes of the second. As in the case of Spranger's values, such types may be applied not only to characteristic differences between people, but also to the states of mind of one individual on different occasions. Under certain circumstances a given person may be provoked to a transient state of toughmindedness, and many situations can arouse tendermindedness in otherwise 'tough' people. Situational influences on personality should not be overlooked in our consideration of basic personality organization. In subsequent researches Eysenck found evidence that human attitudes correlate to form clusters, and he adopts the William James terms as the basis of a tendermindedness–toughmindedness general attitude trait. Thus, for example, toughmindedness may reveal itself in specific attitudes to such matters as the upbringing of children, hardness in the treatment of criminals, and considering the proper place for women as being in the home.

In his study of attitudes Eysenck found a second bipolar factor of radicalism–conservatism, and with the aid of this and the other bipolar factor proceeded to the study of the psychology of politics. Thus, in terms of their political affiliation, communists were found to be toughminded radicals, while fascists proved to be toughminded conservatives. This aspect of Eysenck's work has been criticized from a number of different standpoints. One of the most interesting of these criticisms was contributed by R. Green and B. Stacey in a paper with the provocative title 'Was Torquemada tenderminded?' They argue that, although William James would hardly have assessed this official of the Spanish Inquisition in this way, Eysenck's 'tendermindedness' proves, in fact, to be a measure of religious conservatism. Assessing Torquemada's probable responses to the questions asked, they concluded 'yes', he would have scored quite highly on the tendermindedness trait of Eysenck. Despite such criticisms the evidence on the whole supports the important point underlying Eysenck's work: attitudes form clusters. While there are individual exceptions, there are strong over-all tendencies for certain specific attitudes to go together to form larger units, whose study will greatly help in the understanding of personality. The label provided by the William James typology denotes what appears to be one important attitude variable.

Another kind of typology has had a very long history, and attempts to relate *physique and temperament*. In the fifth century B.C. Hippocrates described two opposing physical types, the one athletic and muscular, and the other slender and delicate. These showed relations to physical disease: the first proved more than averagely susceptible to apoplexy, and the second susceptible to tuberculosis. Hippocrates also found differences of temperament between these two physical types. Following these early ideas we have a tradition of attempts at typing people in terms of their physiques. Perhaps the best known of these typologies – and one which has provided a terminology for later researches into temperament – is that of Ernst Kretschmer. Kretschmer distinguished two main physique types: the pyknic, associated with plumpness and roundness, and the leptosomic (or asthenic), associated with slender and more angular body build. Kretschmer found evidence that these two types of body build were unevenly represented as between two main kinds of psychotic illness. In the pyknic the manic-depressive or cyclical psychosis occurred most commonly; the leptosome, if he developed a psychosis, tended to schizophrenia. Subsequent researches have revealed other findings of interest, for example that the prognosis of a schizophrenic – his likelihood of recovery – is poorer if he is of the leptosomic kind of body build. Kretschmer himself went on to extend his theory to embrace normal personality, and distinguished two broad temperament types which he called schizothymes and cyclothymes. We may if we choose, view schizothymia–cyclothymia as a measurable trait, as subsequent investigators such as R. B. Cattell have done. It may be noted that Kretschmer himself was interested in designing and using tests for measurement of this dimension of personality. In discussing Kretschmer's typology it is difficult to resist reference to Shakespeare's *Julius Caesar* (Act I, Scene 2), when Caesar refers to his distrust of the 'lean and hungry' Cassius who 'thinks too much'. To this Caesar adds: 'Such men are dangerous.' This passage is conveniently translated by Thouless (1935) as a diagnosis of Cassius as of the asthenic body type, therefore of schizothymic temperament. Thouless adds that Shakespeare's Caesar expresses a wish to be surrounded by pyknics. The passage reveals the strong association that has repeatedly been observed to occur between physique and temperament – an association Kretschmer and others have investigated with some profit.

Following the work of Kretschmer we encounter that of Sheldon, who, as he says, seeks to proceed to the study of personality 'from the bones and muscles upwards'. Sheldon (1944) has provided a valuable review article in this field, as well as making original contributions of his own; review articles by major investigators with originality are usually well worth reading. Like Kretschmer, Sheldon has provided his own theory of different temperament types which he associates with specific kinds of physique. I suspect, however, that the more important contribution of Sheldon has been in his studies of individual variations of the human body, rather than his contribution to temperament. To this study of physique he has brought considerable refinement of method, and of techniques of measurement. The three types of body build are: endomorphy, mesomorphy, and ectomorphy. As Sheldon points out the endomorph in his tendency to plumpness is well provided with insulation against the external world, the mesomorph's athletic body build of strong bones and well-developed muscles equips him for self-defence or flight, while the ectomorph (Kretschmer's leptosome) has sacrificed both insulation and strength of body build to greater exposure of the sense organs and accompanying sensitivity. In connexion with Sheldon's theory it is interesting to recall the very early contribution of Plato. In *The Republic* Plato portrays the ideal State, in which we find three types of people. There is the ordinary citizen with his love of comfort, and inclination to satisfy his basic needs; the soldier who is equipped by temperament and physique to defend; and the philosopher-ruler with his thoughtful approach to life and his ability to withstand emotional upset and temptation. Sheldon portrays three equivalent temperament types that he calls viscerotonic (with a tendency to endomorphic physique), somatotonic (mesomorphic physique), and cerebrotonic (ectomorphic physique). Both the components of temperament and those of physique permit quantitative expression on three seven point scales. Thus a person who was average, i.e. 4, on endomorphy, and average on ectomorphy, would score 4.4.4. the extreme endomorph would be a 7.1.1; the extreme mesomorph is a 1.7.1; and the extreme ectomorph is a 1.1.7. We find, in Sheldon, a breaking down of the notion of a typology into a quantitative expression of measurable components which may be stated with precision. This is a substantial progression from popular association of (endomorphic) plumpness with an easy-going and comfort-loving personality. Instead it is possible to investigate whether, as proves to be the case, professional soldiers tend towards mesomorphy, and to measure the amounts of the mesomorphic components usual in different types of successful athlete. Other occupational trends in relation to types of physique, and the developmental history of the various components, have been intensively studied. A useful summary of this line of investigation with particular reference to developmental study, and athletic performance, is provided by J. M. Tanner (1965), a leading British investigator in this field.

ORTHODOX BUT LESS KNOWN

In one passage of his *Discourse on the Arts and Sciences* Rousseau presented a contrast between the values of Ancient Athens and those of Sparta. He expresses his own sympathy with Sparta with its interest in military virtues rather than intellectual ones, its distrust of the Arts, and its rejection of things foreign. Thus Rousseau applauds Sparta, which, at the time Pericles in Athens was gathering around him the greatest thinkers of his day, banished from its borders 'the artists and their art, the learned and their learning'. In these two opposing areas of culture as portrayed by Rousseau we can also see the implication of differences between the ideal Spartan and the ideal Athenian, as personality types. This difference might be illustrated from the personalities of two of the more important explorers of Africa, H. M. Stanley and Emin Pasha. Emin, born Edouard Schnitzer, changed his name and adopted the Moslem religion. Alan Moorehead (1960) in his account of African exploration says of him and Stanley that there was 'hardly a single quality these two men had in common'. Emin was of the 'Athenian' personality type: he was a doctor of medicine, a botanist, and an ornithologist, and spoke about ten languages. He collected thousands of specimens of birds, plants, and animals, and made detailed studies of the languages and customs of the upper Nile. Moorehead relates how Stanley was sent at one stage to rescue Emin; we learn something of the conflicts of the two men during their subsequent journey. One biographer wrote of the 'Spartan' Stanley as *'briseur d'obstacles'*. Stanley himself wrote: 'The savage respects only force, power, boldness, and decision.' Moorehead says of Stanley that he had 'no patience for the finer shades of meaning'; he had only one way of life, 'to march unflinchingly upon his set objectives'. He had no time for collectors and scholars. Thus we can imagine numerous conflicts with Emin, 'subtle, studious and indecisive', who interrupted the march for his plant and bird collecting. One British administrator (quoted by Moorehead) described Emin Pasha as 'one of the greatest of African explorers in the sense that he tried to understand Africa and the teeming life he found there rather than treat the country merely as a blank space to be "discovered" and delineated on a map'. However different a personality, Stanley also ranks as a great explorer in another sense: his journeys in Africa resulted in the eventual completion of the difficult task of solving the geographical problems of the White Nile.

There would appear to be two rather opposing personality

types, as exemplified by Rousseau's Spartan–Athenian dimension. These have been much investigated in recent years in terms of a measurable trait that has become known as *complexity–simplicity*. The complex end of the scale is represented by the intellectual and aesthetic values, a preference for the subtle rather than the obvious, and a hospitable attitude, that is both liberal and cosmopolitan, to new ideas. The simplicity end of the scale is interested in straightforwardness; the simple personality 'does not like modern art', is intolerant of minority groups, strict in his attitudes towards crime and criminals, thinks women should be 'kept in their place', and has firm ideas about the upbringing of 'Little Willie'. This trait of complexity–simplicity has been found to correlate, as might be expected, with Eysenck's tender-mindedness–toughmindedness, but the two are far from identical. Complexity–simplicity originally emerged from the studies of two opposing tendencies which emerged in investigations of aesthetic preferences. Subsequent research revealed that these two styles of preference in art related to attitudes, specifically to attitudes about such matters as war, crime, and the treatment of women, children, and minority groups. Later studies showed occupational differences. Thus army officers tended to score at the simplicity end, and university students at the complexity end. One study of my own on tests which measure this trait supported the prediction that police officers would, on the whole, score high on simplicity. Barron (1963), a leading investigator in this field, has designed a verbal test of good reliability on which significant differences emerged between creative writers (average of 31.3) and commercial writers (average of 23.9). Barron has found that complexity is positively related to originality (as measured independently). By contrast simplicity is positively related to tendency to repression as a defence mechanism, mental rigidity, and political-economic conservatism. Extremes of the trait are of interest in relation to the abnormal. Barron's studies indicate that complexity in excess shades into psychopathy, while simplicity in excess is associated with the compulsive–obsessional personality.

In his account of *The Varieties of Religious Experience* William James (1902) distinguishes between *the once-born and the twice-*

born. This typology derives from the earlier thought of Francis W. Newman, who introduced these terms in 1852. William James, like Newman, is primarily interested in differences between people in terms of their religious life; he draws on religious writings and also on questionnaire studies, notably those of Edwin D. Starbuck on religious attitudes. William James has in mind a difference between the healthy-minded, who need to be born but once, and 'sick souls', who 'must be born twice in order to be happy'. For the once-born the world is, James says, a one-storied affair, while for the twice-born it is a double-storied mystery. There are some people who appear to be born with a personality that is harmonious and well balanced from the outset. Their impulses are consistent with one another, their passions are not excessive, and their lives are little haunted with regrets. Thus one Unitarian minister in reply to Starbuck's questions said: 'I always knew God loved me, and I was always grateful for the world He placed me in.' This for James exemplifies the once-born attitude, as did Walt Whitman, who confessed his sympathy with animals who 'do not sweat and whine about their condition' and who 'do not lie awake in the dark and weep for their sins'. To the twice-born person the once-born seems superficial and shallow. James refers to 'the disdain of the Methodist convert for the mere sky-blue healthy-minded moralist'. As illustrative of the twice-born he takes the case of Mrs Annie Besant who, as a child, would suffer the tortures of shyness, who would shrink away from strangers 'and think myself unwanted and unloved', and who would fall with eager gratitude on 'anyone who noticed me kindly'. We also see the twice-born personality with its profound inner heterogeneity in St Augustine (Bishop of Hippo) who wrote at such length of the 'struggle of two souls' within himself, who confessed to morbid scruples and dreads, and to profound shame for his own weakness of will. While he is primarily interested in the religious adjustments of these two types of personality, William James is also explicit in pointing out that religion is one way of remedying the sense of inner incompleteness of the twice-born, and replacing it with harmony and equilibrium. There are, he says, other ways also. Perhaps we may recognize well-defined cases of once-born and twice-born individuals in the history of politics and government. Perhaps we see them also in daily life.

Several typologies are implicit or explicit in the work of Freud. To one of these scant attention has been paid outside the ranks of orthodox psycho-analysts, despite its appearance in what has been assessed as a paper which ranks 'among the most important of Freud's writings' (Freud, 1914). This divides personalities into the categories of *anaclitic and narcissistic*. The typology in question serves to highlight differences between men and women, and some of the less obvious aspects of the relations between human parents and their children. By anaclitic is meant 'attached' or 'leaning on': the characteristics of the anaclitic personality, according to Freud, are his dominant need to form an attachment to a love object. By contrast the narcissistic type needs not so much to love as to be loved by somebody. Freud's explanation of the emergence of these two different trends of motivation lies in developmental psychology. He concludes that the child has originally two love objects: the woman who tends him – his mother – and himself. The mother forms the basis of the anaclitic style of motivation, or alternatively love may be directed towards the self, though in some disguised way. At this point Freud contends that there tends to be a sex difference between the anaclitic and narcissistic style of loving. Anaclitic love with its attachment to, and overvaluation of, the love object is characteristic of man; we find narcissistic love most characteristically in woman. Freud argues that women, particularly if they grow up with good looks, develop a certain self-contentment; strictly speaking it is themselves that such women love with an intensity comparable to that of man's typically anaclitic love for them. Their need lies not in loving, but in being loved.

Thus Freud seeks a clue to the understanding of human personality, and to the psychological difference between the sexes, by studying the behaviour of people in love. Two courses of loving lie open. A person may love himself narcissistically: himself as he formerly was, or as he would like to be, or someone who was once part of himself. The anaclitic type of person may love the person who feeds him (the mother or the wife) or the man who protects. Both men and women can love either anaclitically or narcissistically. On the whole, however, it is the anaclitic love of the male which complements the narcissistic love of the female. Human self-respect is intimately involved. The effect of anaclitic dependence by the man (in the typical case) upon the loved object is to diminish self-regard. This self-respect is regained if love is accepted and returned. Along with anaclitic, typically male, love goes a tendency to overestimate the loved object. Of interest is the comment by Hebb and Thompson (1954) that young men have been known to say, 'and even on credible report to feel', that they are 'not worthy' of the woman they love. But, they add, 'the converse point of view is noticeably rare.' A person in love, according to Freud, tends to exalt the loved object. Observation of people in this state of interaction – which Freud describes as 'a state suggestive of neurotic compulsion' – also helps us better to understand certain parental attitudes to children. The parents may love something that was once part of themselves. As Freud sees it, part of the charm of the child lies in his narcissism, his remoteness, and his inaccessibility. Along with this appeal on the grounds of narcissism may go the vicarious satisfaction of thwarted parental needs through the achievements of the child. The child is to have a better time than its parents. The boy may become a great hero in his father's place, and – as a tardy compensation to the mother for the man she actually married – the girl is to marry a superior male. In its extreme cases the satisfaction of thwarted parental wishes vicariously achieved through the child involves the phenomenon of altruistic surrender discussed in the previous chapter. In general, reactivated parental narcissism may achieve its satisfactions through the child.

A different aspect of personality has been studied in recent years, in the light of increased knowledge about the human tendency to agree and disagree. Analysis of responses to certain tests has yielded evidence of what have been called 'response sets', that is certain kinds of bias which enter into answers to the test questions. Couch and Keniston (1960) were thus led to make a distinction between what they call *yeasayers and naysayers*, as measured by responses to items with which people were asked to express agreement or disagreement. Earlier work, for example that of Bass (1955), had critically examined the Californian F-scale, which purports to measure authoritarianism as a personality trait. Bass arrived at the conclusion from his study that this test was primarily a measure of a tendency to acquiesce, and only secondarily a measure of authoritarianism. Couch and Keniston similarly found reason to question 'the usual assumption . . . that agreement or disagreement with a scale of items measures primarily the variable for which the test was designed'. A measure of invalidity is introduced by the tendency people have to agree, or disagree, with questions asked: this can be elicited if we ask the same question in different ways, or reverse some of the items. Interview studies by these investigators revealed striking differences in the behaviour of those who scored as yeasayers and those who scored as naysayers. The yeasayers exhibited more social extraversion, were more talkative, appeared to be less complex as personalities, and tended to wander from the point more often. The naysayers were more shy and reserved, they required more questioning and prodding, they weighed and considered each answer; the investigators concluded that for many of them 'introspection and self-analysis seemed virtually a full-time occupation'. The naysayers were more conventional in their social attitudes than the yeasayers, who seemed more ready to express their impulses 'with little concern for inter-personal consequences'. As a basic characteristic of the yeasayers the investigators find a general attitude of what they call 'stimulus acceptance', a readiness to respond affirmatively or yield willingly to both inner and outer forces. By contrast the naysayers seemed to see impulses as forces requiring control, and perhaps as threats to personal stability. They exhibited a general attitude of 'stimulus rejection': a basic unwillingness to respond to either impulses or environmental forces. More speculatively Couch and Keniston attempt to link the dichotomy to the psycho-analytic conception of the ego and its functions. The yeasayers are seen as possessing relatively passive egos, by contrast with the more actively controlling egos of the naysayers and their accompanying processes of delaying, censoring, rationalizing, sublimating, and integrating. These studies of response sets, and of individual bias towards affirmation and rejection, represent a new and promising approach to personality differences. The yeasaying–naysaying dichotomy recalls some of the traits we have examined in relation to such notions as introversion–extraversion, complexity–simplicity, and perhaps also the once-born–twice-born dichotomy. Further work with this and other response sets may be awaited with interest.

Psychologists have not been alone in endeavours to provide personality typologies. As an example from the work of other behavioural scientists we may note the work of David Riesman. In *The Lonely Crowd* (1950) and elsewhere he distinguishes between what he terms *inner-directed and other-directed personalities* and styles of motivation. A subsidiary concept is that of the tradition-directed personality. In certain parts of the world – Spain and Spanish America being clear examples – we encounter social norms which make for a basic personality structure which tends to be tradition-directed. The modal individual responds to the norms of his culture as a whole; conformity is highly valued, and deviation is relatively rare; the main sanction is that of shame. As is apparent in such cultures – and one might mention the small villages of New Mexico in the American Southwest in which the values of sixteenth-century Spain still flourish – each person is part of a closely knit community in which mass media like the printed word and radio have a minimal influence. It is exceedingly difficult for people from outside to understand the intense pressures towards absolute conformity, the dependence of members of the society upon those with whom they are in daily contact, and the rigid influences of unchallenged tradition. With the tradition-directed personality of such cultures may be contrasted the inner-directed individual in whom what H. A. Murray calls autonomy – the strong motivation to instigate and direct one's own activities – is prominent. As Riesman puts it, the inner-directed individual has early in life incorporated 'a psychic gyroscope' which results in an internal piloting of his own actions. Inner-direction is associated with the character traits we often connect with Protestantism, as opposed to Catholicism, with respect for the sanction of the written word and one's own individual interpretation of it. The capacity to 'go it alone' is characteristic of the inner-directed personality, who can remain both stable and persistent in his purposes whether or not immediate social approval from others is forthcoming. His sanction is the sense of guilt, and his authority he finds in the promptings of his own conscience. The third type of personality, or style of motivation, Riesman finds in what he calls other-direction. This he diagnoses as characteristic of dwellers in the metropolitan parts of the United States. Other-direction suggests some of the popular stereotypes of American culture of the kind we associate with supermarkets and child-dominated homes, rather than with tradition-directed Spanish Americans, or inner-directed frontiersmen and cowboys! The other-directed style of motivation, which is of course to be found in many personalities in various parts of the world, is characterized by concern with what neighbours or other people think. The individual concerned has learned to respond to a wider group, the sanctions for his conduct are to be found in anxiety about his status in their eyes, and he is in all ways different from the conformist tradition-directed person on the one hand, and the guilt-ridden but independent inner-directed personality on the other. Like others Riesman is concerned to establish some connexion between personality, with its variations, and society; his aim is to show how certain types of society may encourage the development of one kind of personality rather than others. Like Kretschmer, Riesman based his typology – or excursion into styles of motivation which may be dominant in a given society – not on speculation but on quantification and observation. One is tempted to think of extreme types in the tradition-directed peasant of southern Europe, the inner-directed Protestant martyr, and the other-directed inhabitant of suburban England or America. The sanctions of shame, guilt, and anxiety are influential among human motivational forces, and these we find in differing degrees in different personalities. Likewise, within the same classroom we may find children who reflect the values of their parents, or attempt at values of their own, in their tendency to deviate in their motivational styles towards one or other of Riesman's three types. The typology itself represents one important attempt, based on data that I have not attempted to summarize, to link personality with differences of culture, and with the process of cultural change.

LESS ORTHODOX TYPOLOGIES

The point has been well made by Allport (1938) that there are an indefinite number of different ways of typing human personalities. Our aim should be to chose those types or traits that are useful to our scientific, or other, purposes. Psychologists are not alone in using the concepts of type and trait as reference points for their work. In daily life, and in literature also, much classification of this kind goes on. Too little attention has perhaps been paid to this feature of human behaviour, the study of the concepts used and what they mean to their users. Moreover some of these classifications merit serious scientific attention for themselves as giving us new ways of looking at personalities, and as providing hypotheses for future investigation. On the one hand we have commonly-used classifications of people as 'nice' or otherwise, while on the other we have fairly specific kinds of personality which lack a well-established name, but whose detection may be important for some purpose. An example may be given. A would-be employer, selecting among a number of candidates by interview, may have in mind a wish to avoid choosing a potential source of trouble in the working unit. There is one kind of personality he may wish to choose: a man who will be able to obtain and keep the respect and perhaps affection of his subordinates as well as of those above him in the hierarchy. This interviewer may wish to avoid choosing another type of personality whose behaviour is 'different' towards his equals and superiors, on the one hand, and his subordinates on the other. The quality of being 'nice to superiors but unpleasant to subordinates' is not quite the same thing as being a 'yes-man' or a bully. It may be difficult but not impossible to detect in interview, and difficult also to discover afterwards if a mistake of selection has been made. Nevertheless it may be one which an experienced and sophisticated human being, engaged in a complex task involving categorizing his fellow men, may have firmly in mind. Psychology might well pay more attention in its researches in the future to types and traits of this general kind, which are as yet little understood.

In recent years there has been, as we have noted, some attention paid to yeasaying and naysaying as personality attributes.

These are not, however, the same qualities as those of the 'yes-man', who is known not only to the classifications of everyday life, but also to literature. An unknown eighteenth-century author contributed to literature the 'Vicar of Bray', who managed to adjust himself to the changes of religious norm and belief of the in-group over a troubled and changing period of history. Another study in literature of this personality type is to be found in Ibsen's *Emperor and Galilean*. In the first of the two plays which make up this work, under the Emperor Constantine the in-group is Christian, and the pagans are the rejected out-group. When the second play begins Constantine has been succeeded by Julian the Apostate; now it is the Christians who are the out-group, and the pagans who are the in-group. Ibsen brings out skilfully how yes-men, the vicars of Bray of their era, succeed in remaining within the approved group despite this change of religious norms. Of interest also is the process by which the Julian portrayed by Ibsen (though I suspect it is less true of the Julian of history) rids himself of 'no-men', and the honest critics of his own régime. Perhaps the 'no-man' has received less attention both in literature and in everyday classifications of other people, yet such individuals do exist, with their tendencies to reject, evaluate, and criticize even very different social systems. In connexion with the yes-man–no-man dichotomy it may be helpful to take account of the William James typology of the once-born and the twice-born. The once-born yes-man, the impulsive and sanguine disciple, or perhaps the hollow flatterer may not, in fact, survive long either in the regard of the person in authority, or in fact. More interesting is the twice-born yes-man, who as a successful courtier or diplomat is shrewd enough to avoid being totally predictable. He may learn to respond to that complex attribute which a man in authority may acquire of coming to value occasional disagreement and criticism, rather than yet another expression of the support of which he has already had a surfeit. Julian the Apostate, as portrayed by Ibsen, does not exhibit this characteristic, but there have been men in both literature and history who have shown it. The once-born no-man may also fail to survive long, or he may develop qualities of the twice-born. Initial determination to reject, to criticize, and to reform everything gives rise to greater discrimination in choosing what to oppose and what, in order to be accepted, to go along with and support. In so far as politics involves compromise and 'the art of the possible', the study of the twice-born no-man as parliamentarian would repay investigation. In a world in which committees play an increasingly important part, a fuller investigation of the life histories and influence of all four types, of yes-men and no-men in both their once-born and twice-born varieties, would provide much interesting subject matter for research. Perhaps the work that has already been done with yeasayers and naysayers may prove to be a beginning for such research.

In a later chapter we shall be concerned with human behaviour in its relation to time, and the temporal adjustments different types of personality make. A distinction between people is quite often made in daily life in terms of the temporal margins of time they allow themselves: there are those who are always on time, some who are characteristically too early, and others who are invariably too late. Again, in very practical matters like choosing a companion to share a flat or in choosing a spouse, it is wise for us to take account of another difference between people: the early risers, and the late goers to bed. The personality correlates of these well-defined temporal habits are little understood, and they are certainly not adequately covered by either existing typologies or existing personality tests. They are very important indeed to human living. Among other typologies that have relevance to inter-personal harmony and discord is one which divides what might be called the hoarders from the throwers away. Also of interest is the difference of a quite fundamental kind between what are popularly known as those with 'chips on their shoulders' and those with 'silver spoons in their mouths'. These differences presumably imply early learning, and socio-economic background, but may also overlap into such areas as child-rearing practices. The huge cultural variations that exist in relation to this have been the subject of much investigation and theory. Less attention has been paid to subcultural differences. An illustration may be found in work by Davis and Havighurst in the Chicago area, which compared and contrasted different socio-economic strata, and white and Negro groups. Differences in breast feeding, weaning, toilet training, and habits of discipline were found. Thus weaning took place earlier in the middle classes than in the lower-class groups, and children of middle-class families were expected to assume responsibilities at an earlier age. Bowel and bladder training were begun earlier with Negro children than with white children. The lower socio-economic families exhibited a more permissive attitude in relation to feeding, toilet training, and being allowed out alone. In assessing the influence of child-rearing practices upon personality we need to know more about comparable subcultural variations in Britain, and elsewhere. Much has been said about the influences of frustration and deprivation, but remarkably little is as yet known about its relation to the normal personality and its variations.

Molière, an incisive if pre-scientific typologist, explored the traits of such personality types as the hypochondriac and the hypocrite. Others like Dostoyevsky have dealt with such personalities as the fanatic, the compulsive gambler, the nihilist, the unrepentant criminal, and the saint. Somerset Maugham has described the aboulia and incapacity for sustained action of the demoralized beachcomber, and also on one occasion attempted the feat of describing in words 'a good man'. In Ibsen we have again the fanatic (in *Brand*), and also a remarkable portrait of the ineffectiveness of the sentimentalist (Hjalmer Ekdal in *The Wild Duck*). Examples in Shakespeare, as also those from recent literature, are too numerous to mention, though it may well be asked why psychology has paid so little attention to the systematic study of so many kinds of personality, their correlates, and the learning histories which have given rise to them. Both literature itself, and the implicit and explicit categories used in everyday life, provide some fascinating subject matter for future researches.

DIMENSIONS OF PERSONALITY

As we have seen, over the years there has been a tendency for personality to be approached in terms of traits rather than types. With the emergence of an interest in measurable traits came a flood of tests, good, bad, and indifferent as regards their conception and standardization. From time to time there appears a most valuable book, *The Mental Measurements Yearbook*, edited by O. K. Buros. In its successive volumes this reviews new tests which individual reviewers are asked to assess in terms of their validity, reliability, and standardization. A first essential of any test is validity: the extent to which it measures what it is supposed to measure. A second essential is reliability: the consistency with which it measures on different occasions. There are, unfortunately, many tests available of dubious reliability and uninvestigated validity, though the volumes of Buros, and the standards that have been laid down by the American Psychological Association, are some deterrent.

In 1936 G. W. Allport and H. S. Odbert produced what they called a 'psycho-lexical study' – a detailed investigation of words in English that related to personality traits. They found in all 17,953 of them. Of interest is their history. Thus some, like 'jovial' and 'lunatic', came from astrology; some emerged with the Reformation, including 'sincere', 'pious', and 'fanatic'; others came from classical times, like some we have noted in connexion with temperament, for example 'sanguine' and 'phlegmatic'. In 1946 R. B. Cattell took this list of 17,000 odd words and pruned it down to 171, which he was later able to reduce to 35 main trait clusters. He used these terms in a series of investigations with rating scales, which were subsequently treated by techniques of factor analysis to yield factors or basic personality dimensions. Cattell remains one of the most important contemporary investigators in this field, and some of his factors will be familiar to us from previous typologies, for example cyclothymia–schizothymia. Cattell's 'Sixteen Personality Factor Test' is an instance of a modern test in this field, which is designed to measure certain of his major variables. In this field it is important to keep in mind the fact that differences which divide major investigators are often highly technical ones. Moreover differences may also be more apparent than real. As Sir Godfrey Thomson – one of the founders of the method of factor analysis – has put it, 'factors depend on stated assumptions'; different assumptions may be made by different investigators, and this may affect the number and kind of factors which emerge from their researches.

A second major investigator of personality from this standpoint, already noted, is H. J. Eysenck. Eysenck himself analyses temperament into two main factors, which he calls introversion–extraversion, and neuroticism. He defends the view that it is profitable to deal with introversion–extraversion as a unitary trait. Others prefer to treat it as composite. Thus, to mention a further important figure in this field, J. P. Guilford finds five underlying components: these are summarized by the name of his test, the 'Guilford STDCR'. They comprise: social introversion (S), thinking introversion (T), depression (D), cyclothymia (C), strong mood fluctuations, and rhathymia (R), a lively, carefree, impulsive temperament. Along with Guilford we have noted Cattell, who prefers many rather than few personality dimensions. Some of the similarities and differences between Cattell and Eysenck – two main contemporary investigators – may be worth elucidating. Both draw on previous researches and ideas, whether they involve types or traits, for subject matter for refined mathematical treatment. Both are extremely productive of research data in support of their basic pursuit of the fundamental dimensions of personality, though one prefers to use two main dimensions while the other prefers to work with more factors. (Cattell, it may be noted, acknowledges the concept of 'higher order factors', which resemble closely the type of component with which Eysenck works.) One important difference lies in the preferred research techniques. We have seen that Cattell began with descriptive words and rating scales, and then went on to test design. Eysenck has been less interested in tests for numerous variables, and has chosen to relate his two main factors to other functions, notably those of perception and learning. He has sought to relate his classificatory work on personality dimensions to the learning process, to make predictions and test these by experiment. From this has emerged a theory of normal and abnormal mental life in which the extreme introvert, who tends to develop hysteria if he develops a neurosis, and the extreme extravert, who tends to what Eysenck calls the 'dysthymic' neuroses, figure prominently. Eysenck has also been interested in psychosis and finds evidence of a factor of 'psychoticism' but no support for Kretschmer's schizothymia–cyclothymia dimension. In recent years he has been interested both in criminality, and in a method of treatment of neurosis which he calls 'behaviour therapy'; this is based on the study of learning, and differs greatly in its emphasis from psycho-analytic therapy, to which Eysenck is strongly opposed. Cattell for his part has sought to apply factorial methods to the study of music, to the analysis of different areas of culture – a sort of factor analytic social psychology – and to cognitive mental life. Cognition has interested Eysenck less, his main factorial work being in the field of temperament, though as we have seen he has been intensively interested in relations between personality dimensions and the learning process.

PERSONALITY AND MOTIVATION

One of the most important investigators of the personality in the modern period is H. A. Murray (1938). A number of major contributions are associated with him. First, he was interested in normal personality and in providing a terminology for discussing it without using the reference points of abnormal psychology. Secondly, he was concerned with personalities in terms of their motivation: with the motives which distinguish one personality from another, rather than with those universal to the species. Thirdly, he sought to integrate psycho-analytic insight into the influences of unconscious mental life with orthodox psychology.

Murray makes a basic distinction between what he calls extraception and intraception. A primarily extraceptive person tends to be dominated by perception and awareness of tangible observable facts. His inclination is towards objectivity and tough-mindedness. By contrast intraceptive personalities tend to be dominated by subjective processes: personal feelings, imagination, and intangible subjective influences. They incline to tender-mindedness, indecision, and intuition. A second basic distinction is between what Murray calls conjunctivity and disjunctivity. Conjunctivity represents a high level of harmony within the personality, good integration of its component parts, and a well-ordered plan of life. Disjunctivity represents lack of integration, conflict between traits, and disorganization as regards purposes and plans. Murray is well aware of the possibilities of conflict and disharmony within personalities, ambivalences as regards personality traits; and his notion of conjunctivity–disjunctivity attempts to embrace this fact.

Murray, although a leading psychologist, also had a medical training. This, he indicates in one autobiographical passage, much affected his thinking. He tells us he learned early to take account of *both* objectively observable signs *and* subjectively reported symptoms, and to pay due attention to both. A sharp distinction between objective behaviour and introspective experience thus has little appeal for Murray, who uses as a convenient term to denote both the word 'proceeding'. A proceeding is a real or imagined interaction between the subject and some aspect of his environment. We may, if we wish, distinguish external proceedings (observable behaviour) from internal proceedings (for example dreaming and daydreaming).

Murray's central concept is that of 'need'. The word stands for a force within the personality which organizes perceptual, intellectual activity and behaviour in a certain character. On the basis of intensive studies of people, Murray set out to catalogue some of the more important human needs. This catalogue has been much used by later investigators and has the advantage we have noted of being neutral as regards any reference to the abnormal. Counteraction is one such need: people differ in this need to make up for failures by re-striving, to persist in overcoming weakness and fear and other barriers to their goals. Other needs include harm avoidance (concern with avoiding personal danger and injury), abasement (passive submission to external forces), and achievement (to excel, and to surpass others).

A second basic term is what Murray calls 'press'. Press denotes a force acting on the person from the environment. One may, for example, be submitted to a press of aggression. At this point is introduced an elegant simplification: many of the same words can be used to denote need and press. Murray uses the prefixes 'n' and 'p' to denote which is implied. Thus a given individual may exhibit 'n. counteraction' – himself be motivated to overcome obstacles – or may be subject to 'p. counteraction' – people in his environment give him this kind of encouragement. He may exhibit 'n. exhibition' – a wish to be seen and heard – or may be submitted to 'p. exhibition' – people in his vicinity thus inclined, to whom he has to adjust. Thus the need concept makes it possible to label a large number of needs, of the kinds that distinguish personalities from one another. The press concept makes it possible to label social forces which may be important in determining responses, and more general personality development.

A further feature of Murray's thought is a distinction he makes between three different layers of the normal personality. The outer layer comprises tendencies which are publicly asserted and acknowledged. The middle layer (ideational activity) is expressed in thought and fantasy, but not overtly. The inner layer consists of what the psycho-analyst would call repressed or unconscious tendencies. Relations between these three layers may be complex, as when a person's fantasy bears little relation to his overt action. It is presumably the function of psycho-analysis to produce greater conjunctivity between the inner and outer two layers. As analysis proceeds 'insight' is gained, and the person concerned becomes more aware of his latent and hitherto unacknowledged needs.

Prominent among the studies which have stemmed from Murray's work have been the investigations of McClelland (1953) and his co-workers, notably with n. achievement. McClelland sought to investigate whether it was possible to demonstrate with these personality needs the same sorts of phenomena that occur with needs like hunger and thirst. He chose need achievement, which is satisfied by success and aroused by failure, in the same way as hunger is satisfied by food and aroused by food deprivation. Numerous experiments were conducted with subjects for whom n. achievement was varied in different ways: conditions of success and failure, emphasis on achievement, and initial success followed by failure. A flood of subsequent studies has followed, some of them developmental – studying different age groups – and others cross-cultural, for example studying differences between Anglo- and Spanish-Americans. Parallel studies were conducted by McClelland on n. affiliation, the desire to be accepted by others, and n. power, gaining power over people. One interesting strand of research has taken these studies into the field of history. Content analysis of writings, available statistics, and other data have been used with a view to assessing the dominance of such needs as achievement, affiliation, and power in specific historical periods of a community. In 1965 S. A. Rudin studied statistics of death rates of seventeen countries in relation to n. achievement and n. power over the period 1925–50. On the basis of his correlations he obtained two indices: first, deaths 'due to' inhibition and repression, and secondly, deaths 'due to' acting out of impulses. It emerged that the 1925 scores on n. achievement predicted the 1930 death rate 'due to' inhibition and repression (statistics for ulcers and high blood pressure). The 1925 n. power scores predicted the 1950 death rate 'due to' aggression and acting out (murder, suicide, and alcoholism). The United States and Japan were high on all death rates. Britain, Australia, New Zealand, and Ireland were high on death rates for inhibition and low on those for acting out. Germany, South Africa, Denmark, and Switzerland had high acting-out and low inhibition death rates. Norway and the Netherlands were low on everything; for the period these countries showed the longest life expectancy. Assessment of the needs showed high n. affiliation and low achievement and power motivation. These studies show both the uses that have been made of Murray's attempt to catalogue personality motives, and represent perhaps the beginnings of an application of personality psychology to the study of history and political change.

SITUATIONAL INFLUENCES AND PERSONALITY

An aspect of behaviour which has received limited attention merits examination in connexion with the concept of personality. This is the extent to which human responses are elicited by situations, as well as emitted by the personalities of the individuals concerned. There are two kinds of information that assist us in making predictions about human activities, these being: (a) knowledge about the personality of an individual; (b) knowledge about how people in general are known to react to situations. Psychologists differ in their relative interest in these two kinds of information: some are mainly concerned with studying personality; others are mainly interested in processes like perceiving, learning, and thinking. Both forms of specialization are legitimate, but there are some areas of research in which we cannot neglect either to the exclusion of the other. One instance of this is experimentation with substances like hallucinogenic drugs. If we administer mescaline to anybody he will manifest responses of two kinds. On the one hand he will show forms of experience and behaviour that are common to all – or nearly all – subjects who take part in such an experiment. He will also manifest reactions that result from the fact that the drug has been given to *him*, John Doe, and not to Richard Roe or somebody else. The circumstances of the experiment, the situation – in this instance the drug administered – and the personality of the subject will all determine what occurs, and the predictions we make about it. Thus we may predict that our subject, like any other subject we might have chosen, will produce evidence of impressive and highly autonomous imagery reminiscent of the visual imagery of the hypnagogic state. We might be able to make the same prediction if we had given the subject LSD or psilocybin, because we know that in this respect these other two substances have similar effects to those of mescaline on people in general. But in addition we may be able to make another kind of prediction: our subject, John Doe, may exhibit mystical thinking, persecutory reactions, or other responses that derive from his personality and individual inclinations in these directions. Moreover we may be able to predict that John Doe would probably also exhibit rather similar reactions (mysticism and/or persecution feelings) in other circumstances: with alcohol, if subjected to oxygen deficiency in a decompression chamber, or as the subject in a sensory deprivation experiment. Thus our predictions express our confidence in our knowledge of relatively universal responses to known situations on the one hand, and our knowledge of specific individual personalities on the other.

The history of psychology affords many illustrations of the concern of researchers with one or other of these two kinds of prediction. Thus in the study of perception, in the early period, investigators were most concerned with the reactions of people in general. Subjects were confronted with suitably drawn lines and shapes, and the majority of them reported perceiving reversible figures: those that deviated, and did not, received scant attention. Later on psychologists became interested in the study of personality through perception. Thus they designed their investigations to elicit individual differences between John Doe and Richard Roe; to highlight this influence of personality on perceiving they used brief exposure, dim illuminations of visual material, and ambiguous subject matter like Rorschach inkblots. The more unstructured the stimulus the more the personality differences revealed themselves, and the more individuals differed from one another. The same two-fold interest of psychology has found expression in other fields, such as the study of emotion. Thus some investigators sought to find out the circumstances which lead people in general to experience an emotion like anger: circumstances denoted by words like 'thwarting', 'frustration', and 'humiliation' were found to lead predictably to anger in most people. But to achieve still higher levels of prediction in a given instance it is necessary to study the personality concerned. Thus we would need to know about John Doe's sentiments, particularly his dislikes and hatreds, and the things most likely to anger him, which might be emotionally neutral to Richard Roe.

At this point we return to the notions of types and traits. These are useful in the study of personality – the habitual characteristics of the individual – but may be helpful here also. Suitable tests may reveal him to be intelligent, introverted, toughminded, with dominant value traits of the political kind. This is a statement about his personality and its habitual responses. But we may also design situations to evoke in him manifestations of behaviour which could be called by these trait names. Thus we might design situations – those arousing emotional upset and fluster are examples – which discourage tendencies in him to behave intelligently, however habitual this is to him. It is, for example, absurd to expect to obtain – as I was once as a young psychologist asked to do – adequate performances in an intelligence test by a group of airmen who have just been marched into the testing room, and then abused for the quality of their marching by a probably unintelligent, and certainly unempathic, N.C.O. A given person may, on average, be non-superstitious, but suitable circumstances may evoke superstitious reactions from him. More information needs to be obtained about ordinarily non-superstitious personalities and their actual behaviour in relation to the ladders they encounter on their way to important interviews or examinations, and the salt they spill at their wedding breakfasts! Likewise a given personality may have a place on a scale of suggestibility, but there may be conditions under which it is mainly circumstance and not personality that wins to make him more or less suggestible than usual in the situations in which he is placed. Or, as William James puts it, each of us has as many 'selves' as we have people whose opinions we value. An understanding of the vocabulary of types and traits may help us to classify influences and the behaviours they may evoke.

Specific examples may be taken from types and traits already mentioned. First, consider tender- and tough-mindedness. A given person may be habitually high on tendermindedness, as measured on suitable tests, but following provocation of the 'I have been let down' kind may adopt a mood of toughmindedness. This may be relatively short-lived, and later he may return from this transient state to his usual personality. An interesting example is provided by Freud's concept of narcissism. Among circumstances which seem to provoke in people in general a shift towards increased narcissism is life as a patient in hospital. A person who is ordinarily much interested in the outside world, altruistic and concerned with the welfare of others, and lacking in hypochondriasis may behave very differently when visited as a patient in hospital. In common with his ward-mates he may show a much diminished mental horizon and an apathy towards events outside. He reveals enormous concern with his own body image and interest of a kind suggestive of the hypochondriacal personality. The atmosphere of his changed daily life gives rise to these responses, which may disappear soon after a return to normal outside life. These responses may be noticeable in even a short-stay patient; they may occur even with relatively minor illnesses involving little actual pain; they may become a more enduring feature of the personality of the long-stay patient who has to a larger extent absorbed the norms and expectations of the hospital situation. Similar problems merit study in relation to the influence of other institutions. Some work has been done on the effects of prisoner-of-war camps upon people in general; much more needs to be done on the temporary or more permanent effects of psychiatric hospitals on their patients.

Some personalities are more resistant to situational influences than others. This notion of inner consistency despite outside pressures is incorporated in Riesman's concept of the other-directed personality, and of various of Murray's needs, particularly n. counteraction and n. autonomy. Social psychologists are of course intimately concerned with the influences of situation upon behaviour; the notion that both personality differences and social pressures determine behaviour is incorporated in the concept of the J-curve. This may be illustrated in relation to the behaviour of motorists. In Figure 16 we have a histogram showing

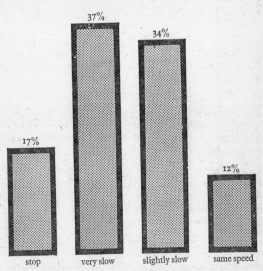

16. Behaviour of motorists at a street intersection.

the behaviour of successive motorists at a street intersection. If, however, the situation is changed by the introduction of a traffic light we have J-curve behaviour: as will be seen in Figure 17 the majority of motorists conform, but individual differences also assert themselves, and some show greater or lesser degrees of deviance. A steeper J-curve, with diminished deviation, is found to occur with the twin incentives of a traffic light and the presence of a policeman. In either case it is possible to make some

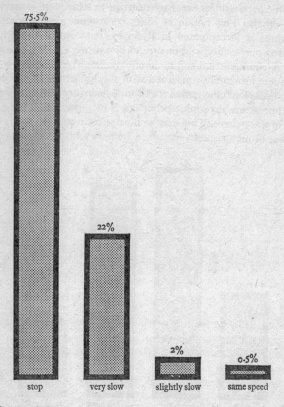

17. J-curve behaviour of motorists at street intersection with traffic lights.

prediction, perhaps even an approximate quantitative prediction, of how people in general will behave in these situations despite their individual differences of personality. Again the situation which confronts him will also influence the pedestrian in, for example, the extent to which he is influenced by outside pressure. This may be seen in one interesting study involving both controlled observation and experiment conducted by Lefkowitz *et al.* Figure 18 shows the conformity of pedestrians in obeying the

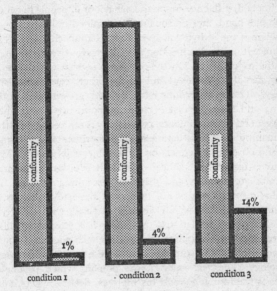

18. Conformity of pedestrians.

rule of not crossing the road when a red light is showing: under Condition 1 pedestrian behaviour at a number of red light crossings was studied, and 1 per cent deviated. Under Condition 2 an experimenter's assistant set the bad example of deviating and crossing the road, and this increased the number of nonconformists to 4 per cent; but under this condition the assistant was dressed in scruffy clothes indicative of low socio-economic status. Under Condition 3 he was dressed neatly and tidily, and the number of non-conformists who followed him in his deviation rose to 14 per cent! In these histograms we can see how the situation itself may induce regularities of behaviour, despite personality differences. And in Figure 20 we see how experimental manipulation of the situation results in altered general trends of such behaviour for certain individuals.

It has been noted that psychologists themselves exhibit differences in the relative interest they show in situational (including experimental) influences upon the behaviour of people in general, on the one hand, and personality-determined influences on the behaviour of the individual. Even today Cronbach (1957) is able to claim with some justification that there are 'two disciplines of scientific psychology'. On the one hand is what Cronbach calls 'experimental psychology' and on the other 'correlational psychology'. These two groups have, he said, grown apart in their training and their interests. The standpoint of what might be called general or experimental psychology is represented by those who manipulate the situation in an experimentally systematic way, and observe the effects on their subjects in general. Many such investigators have conceived it as their task experimentally to manipulate stimulus, and observe the resulting response. This stimulus-response analysis of behaviour has had its critics. An opposing standpoint, which we may associate with differential psychology, or 'correlational' psychology as Cronbach calls it, is represented by Thurstone, whom Cronbach quotes: 'I suggest that we dethrone the stimulus. It is only nominally the ruler of psychology. The real ruler of the domain which psychology studies is the individual and his motives, desires, wants, ambitions, cravings, aspirations' (Thurstone, 1923). The field defined by Thurstone clearly includes personality, as discussed in this chapter, and differential psychology more generally (in which Cronbach would include comparative psychology: the study of similarities and differences between different species). My own statement in relation to this issue has already been given: it is the task of the psychologist to predict, and some bases of prediction may come from the study of the effects of situations on people in general, while others come from the study of the individual as such. In the former, experimentation has proved to be the most important method, while in the latter the technique of correlation has been invaluable. Psychology should embrace both fields of study, which represent two of its important areas. It is not a question of 'either–or', but of 'both'. Cronbach himself, though like Thurstone a leading figure in correlational psychology, adopts this viewpoint. He does, however, draw attention to one interesting study conducted by E. L. Thorndike in 1954, which shows how sharply divided on this issue are psychologists in America. The subjects were psychologists, who were asked to assess the relative importance of the contributions of major psychologists. Data were factor-analysed, and revealed a factor which exhibited two poles dividing experimentally inclined psychologists of the past from correlational investigators. Moreover it emerged that the contemporary subjects showed an esteem for the experimenters which correlated negatively, to the extent of $-\cdot 80$, with their esteem for scientists who used correlational methods. This schism may diminish with time but it has certainly impeded development of the science, or, as Cronbach puts it, 'the country between has turned to desert'; there is, however, much evidence today of an increasing interaction between representatives of general psychology on the one hand and those primarily interested in individual differences on the other.

CHAPTER TWELVE

The Abnormal Personality

I've 'seen' and 'heard' people speak when they never
spoke a word. I know when I'm speaking myself, but I
don't know when other people are answering me.
PSYCHOTIC PATIENT IN INTERVIEW

SOME human beings live in a cognitively experienced environment which differs markedly from reality. Among them are
psychotic patients, like the schizophrenic quoted above, for
whom hallucination intrudes upon normal perception. In their
anxiety to assert their sanity, and to stress the differences
between themselves and the psychiatrically disturbed, the sane
have too often treated such people as this as less than human.
Throughout history difficulties for the abnormal person have
been greatly amplified by the insensitivity, stereotyped misconceptions, and lack of empathy of normal people. Only slowly
have humanity and science made their inroads, and even today
vigilance is needed to ensure that what achievements have been
made are maintained. Four aspects of scientific progress may be
summarized.

HISTORICAL ORIENTATION

A first major advance took place over 2,000 years ago when
Hippocrates (approximately 460–357 B.C.) took a firm stand
against superstition about mental illness. He and his associates
developed the full implications of the idea that such people
should be regarded as patients, and treated by the methods of
orthodox medicine. A second major advance is associated with the
discoveries of Anton Mesmer (1733–1815) about the puzzling
phenomenon of mental life later to be called 'hypnosis'. Hypnosis
is the state, and hypnotism the technique for inducing this state,
in which various phenomena, including many of the signs and
symptoms of psychiatric abnormality, can be replicated in

normal people. The work of Mesmer and later investigators brought realization of the limitations of the conclusion reached by Hippocrates. While orthodox medicine provided a starting point, there was now evidence that some characteristics of mental illness have a different kind of cause, and require a different kind of treatment. A third advance came with Emil Kraepelin (1856–1926), who is important for the descriptions, classifications, and naming that he contributed to psychiatry. His work still provides the basis of the classification of the main syndromes of mental illness. Finally we come to Sigmund Freud (1856–1939), who developed a new method of treatment for neurosis, and new techniques for investigating layers of the personality of the patient that were not readily available to introspection. Freud's work was distinguished by an intense and persistent curiosity about the individual and what was actually wrong with him. He was interested in his patients as people who were adjusting, or failing to adjust, to the stresses and difficulties of their individual lives. This interest was opportune at a time when European psychiatry – having freed itself from demonological thinking – had become somewhat preoccupied with custodial care, diagnosis, and disease entities.

PSYCHO-ANALYSIS AND THE ABNORMAL PERSONALITY

Psycho-analysis arose from the study and treatment of one of the neuroses: conversion hysteria. As we saw in Chapter 10, Freud and Joseph Breuer, with whom he was closely associated in this early period, were much interested in their thinking by one of Breuer's patients, 'Anna O.'. This young woman exhibited a large number of hysterical phenomena including paralysis, anaesthesia, amnesia, and visual disturbances. The term 'hysteria' denotes a neurosis said to be rare today, as it certainly is in Western Europe. Nevertheless it is common in Africa and the Middle East, and Abse (Arieti, 1959) during the Second World War found it often in Indian though rarely in British soldiers. It appeared to be frequent among the war neuroses of the First World War, under conditions of trench fighting (Rivers, 1920), and common also in the Vienna of Freud and Breuer. The signs and symptoms of hysteria comprise certain sensory, motor, and memory phenomena: blindness, deafness, anaesthesia, paralysis, mutism, loss of memory, and simulation of the features of other diseases of organic origin. These phenomena of hysteria appear to have no known physical cause, and indeed closely resemble the phenomena which can be produced by hypnotic suggestion. Freud appears to have been influenced not only by the case of Anna O., treated by Breuer, but also by appreciation of this resemblance between hypnotic and hysterical phenomena. Breuer and Freud's book appeared in 1895, and Breuer's treatment of Anna O. was terminated in 1892. Freud went to Paris to study under Charcot, the great French neurologist whose interest had helped to make both hysteria and hypnotism scientifically respectable. In a lecture Freud gave in 1893 he refers to Charcot's demonstration of how a hysterical symptom – a paralysis – can be produced hypnotically. A traumatic experience could be replaced, as Charcot showed, by hypnotic suggestion, the result being occurrence of the same physical symptom without any appropriate physical cause. As we have seen above, the realization that certain of the phenomena which occur in mental abnormality are of this kind stemmed from the work of Mesmer in the earlier, pre-scientific period. In the case of his patient Anna O., Breuer had used hypnotism in the treatment of symptoms of this kind. *Studies on Hysteria* is an account of four such cases, Anna O. and three cases of Freud's. From these studies emerged the notion of a 'talking cure' (the term itself was Anna's), the idea that hysterics 'suffer mainly from reminiscences', and the understanding of the process of repression. Certain of the ideas which Breuer and Freud arrived at about hysteria, its causation, and its treatment find interesting anticipation in the work of the British physician Robert Carter (see Veith, 1965). Carter is better known in medical history for his contributions to ophthalmology than to psychopathology, but in 1853 he published an account of hysteria. He noted a process of active forgetting (repression) and the influence of the norms of Victorian England in imposing restraint upon women in their recognition of emotions and particularly sexual emotions; and he advocated 'moral treatment' (psychotherapy). It is, however, to Freud himself that we must turn for the major advance of knowledge, which he developed out of the study of the hysteric, who is often an exceedingly tiresome patient. Freud introduced the term 'conversion' in connexion with hysteria, the notion being that the unacceptable and emotionally charged memories transformed (converted) themselves into a physical symptom. He wrote: 'The memory trace of the repressed idea has, after all, not been dissolved; from now on it forms the nucleus of a second psychical group' (Freud, 1894).

The cathartic or 'talking-out' cure at first involved putting the patient into the hypnotic state. Both Freud and Breuer initially used this method, though in 1892 when treating his patient 'Elizabeth' – apparently a strong-minded young woman – Freud abandoned hypnotism for what he at first called a 'concentration' technique. On one occasion Elizabeth objected to Freud's interruptions when she was answering his questions. Thus, Freud's biographer tells us, 'he took the hint', and there followed 'another step towards free association' (Jones, 1953). Since the new method of free association assumed central importance in the subsequent development of psycho-analysis, one of Freud's later papers merits special mention. In this paper, 'On Beginning the Treatment' (1913), he explains what he meant by 'free association' and makes explicit his recommendations for its use. This paper discusses the basic pact made between therapist and patient, upon which the whole analysis depends: what Freud called the 'fundamental rule of analysis'. This was the instruction to free-associate. The subject was told that his thoughts must in no way be censored by him because they seemed irrelevant; he must be absolutely honest and 'never leave anything out because, for some reason or other, it is unpleasant to tell it'. Freud likens the requirement of free association, in accord with the fundamental rule of analysis, to the situation of a traveller at the window of a railway carriage describing to somebody else the changing view outside; only in the case of free association it is a matter of reporting – without omission of any kind – what is going on inside rather than outside. Elsewhere (1952) I have discussed in some detail the strong temptations that exist to censor and omit, and the ways in which both conscious and unconscious resistances impede free-associative activity. To obey the rule required by the analyst of the patient, however seemingly simple, is in fact exceedingly difficult. One analyst has defined psycho-analysis itself as a process of making the patient aware of the difficulty, if not the impossibility, of obeying the single rule which it imposes. In learning about these difficulties the patient acquires insight into his personality and his own preferred mechanisms of ego-defence (see Chapter 10).

Psycho-analysis began with hysteria, but did not long confine itself to its study. Before the turn of the century Freud had published papers about other neuroses: obsessions, phobias, and the anxiety states. He had become interested also in psychotic phenomena, notably those of paranoia and psychotic depression. Larger contributions were to follow at a later date in the study of psychoses: for example a detailed analysis of the paranoid schizophrenia of Schreber in 1911, and, with *Mourning and Melancholia* of 1917, a detailed excursion into the psychopathology of depression. Central to all this work was the method of free association, whose relation to subsidiary techniques may be mentioned. Thus Freud's approach to dream interpretation has often been misunderstood. His book *The Interpretation of Dreams* was regarded by Freud himself as his most important work. As we shall see below, many earlier thinkers had found, in the study of dreams, a basis for understanding psychosis. To Freud the dream also provides a means of insight into many of the phenomena of neuroses, the self-deceptive operations of the normal personality, and unconscious motivation generally. He did not argue for the 'interpretation' of dreams in terms of some kind of standard 'dream book' code which provided the answers by a process of translation. Freud did not in fact advocate interpretation of dream symbols as such, but rather interpretation of symbols and other dream content through free association. To understand a dream the first requirement is the presence of the dreamer, and the second, eliciting the free associations he himself provides to his own dream. Of interest was Freud's reply when the Surrealist André Breton wrote asking for a contribution to an anthology on dreams. Freud refused, and the reasons for his refusal are fundamental to an understanding of his whole approach. He replied that 'without the dreamer's associations, without knowledge of the circumstances . . . dreams tell me nothing' (quoted in Gombrich, 1954). Thus, in many respects, in his attempts to study the human personality Freud's method was not unlike Galton's. Referring to the association of ideas Galton wrote: 'The furniture of a man's mind chiefly consists in his recollections and the bonds that unite them . . . it must differ greatly in different minds according to individual experiences' (Galton, 1883). What Freud actually advocated was something more acceptable than merely the blind interpretation of symbols, or symptoms: it was a linking-up of items of thought, including dreams, with other associations and emotional preoccupations. It must be admitted that Freud himself was not always consistent in following his own rule. Particularly in studies of art and literature – thought products other than dreams – he quite often proceeded in the absence of the author of the thought product and his free associations. This applies for example to Freud's study of the delusions and hallucinations of Schreber, a man whom he never met but whose autobiographical notes he used in his study of psychosis.

As psycho-analysis developed, and with it a widening interest in many kinds of abnormal – and normal – personality, certain formal arrangements came to be made. It became the requirement that the analyst should himself be analysed as part of his training. In the light of this the question has sometimes been asked, 'Who analysed Freud?' A three-fold answer can be given: (a) Freud himself; (b) the record of the analysis appears in *The Interpretation of Dreams*; (c) Wilhelm Fliess helped Freud in carrying the burden of analyst. To amplify (c): in the period when Freud was carrying out probably the most persistently sustained introspective study ever conducted – his book on dreams – he was in regular correspondence with Fliess. Fliess, another physician, was a close intellectual friend, a man receptive to many of Freud's early ideas, and an obvious source of moral support. Unfortunately the letters of Fliess to Freud have not survived, but Freud's letters to Fliess have been preserved and published (Bonaparte, Freud A., and Kris (eds.), 1954). They comprise a valuable supplement to Freud's published writings, and a source of additional information on his own analysis.

The study of the state of hypnosis contributed a new way of thinking about the abnormal personality, particularly the neuroses. Freud and the psycho-analysts were themselves heirs to this reorientation in the revolution of thought which they provided. After ceasing to use hypnotism Freud studied the personality in its 'normal' state, and moreover did much to blur the sharp distinction between 'normal' and 'abnormal'. As A. A. Brill, the analyst, wrote after his translation of one of Freud's books, Freud found that 'mechanisms so glaringly observed in the psycho-neuroses and psychoses could usually be demonstrated in a lesser degree in normal persons'. In widening the concept of self-knowledge Freud also widened the possibilities of empathy, though empathy with the forms of mental life we call 'psychotic' remains a matter of considerable difficulty.

EMPATHY WITH THE PSYCHOTIC

A traditional distinction differentiates the neuroses from the psychoses. Among the neuroses we encounter syndromes like hysteria, anxiety states, the compulsive-obsessional neuroses, and the phobias. The psychoses subdivide into those of an organic kind with known physical causes, and the functional psychoses – like schizophrenia, paranoia, and psychotic depression – which lack any known physical cause. As we have seen it is today widely believed that biochemical explanations for at least some of the functional psychoses may eventually be found (see Chapter 3). On the whole it is the psychoses rather than the neuroses which present the greater problems of empathy and understanding for the normal person. Freud contributed the beginnings of such an understanding in the case of one important category of mental illness: neurotic and psychotic depression. He found this in an examination of human mourning and bereavement. The bereaved person is not merely miserable and unhappy, but may also be overwhelmed with guilt feelings about his actions and omissions in relation to the deceased. Such guilt, in normal people, can often be peculiarly excessive; this is also an outstanding characteristic of psychiatric cases of depression. Again, in normal personalities, such guilt may arise from ideational activity and fantasy, as well as from overt actions. Normal people may resemble patients closely in that they exhibit guilt feeling about the wrong things, and in their pursuit of rather pathetic rationalizations they seek to explain this guiltiness to themselves. A reading of Freud's *Mourning and Melancholia* (1917), and the thought it provokes about bereavement, are an excellent beginning to the understanding of one important family of mental illnesses. In this family we encounter psychotic depression, which in Western Europe is the commonest of the psychoses.

Other psychotic illnesses, like paranoia and schizophrenia, provide greater problems of empathy. Most difficult of all to understand are schizophrenics: in connexion with such patients seven possible bases for empathy will be suggested. First, in accord with one old and frequently restated idea on this subject, it is helpful to keep in mind one's own dreams and nightmares. The fantasy-dominated world of the schizophrenic may be likened to that of dream life: an intrusion into wakefulness of A-thinking processes of the kind that the normal personality is able to confine to his periods of sleep. In some schizophrenic patients there has been a manifest failure to achieve satisfactory inter-personal relations with others: in their psychosis they have evolved a more satisfactory fantasy world. In other patients the resemblance lies less with the wish-fulfilment kind of dream than with nightmare in its most anxiety-ridden and terror-producing aspects. Many thinkers have stressed this resemblance. Thus Jung describes the schizophrenic as 'a sleeping person in a waking world', while McDougall writes, 'Schizophrenia is a dream state, a prolonged half-waking dream or fantasy . . . as in sleep he has lost contact with the world about him'. In psychosis we encounter an invasion of waking consciousness by thoughts, images, and impulses that seem strange and foreign to the personality. Among such patients are many who are perfectly capable of such introspection, and explanation to us about what it is like. Thus, as the highly intelligent schizophrenic quoted at the head of this chapter was able to explain, it is exceedingly difficult to adjust to real events when one 'sees' and 'hears' things that do not in fact occur. Also important in many forms of psychosis are delusions which replace the beliefs that provide frames of reference to the normal person, as hallucination replaces normal perception. Delusions may be of persecution which has no basis in fact, or of grandeur or personal unworthiness; other delusions affect the body image, and delusions of bodily change are a common accompaniment of schizophrenia. A marked autonomy of mental life, and the occurrence of thoughts, images, and impulses which seem foreign to oneself, may give rise to another kind of delusion. In delusions of influence the patient feels himself to be under the control of somebody else, or perhaps he interprets this in a persecutory way: some 'enemy' is putting thoughts into his head, or manipulating his actions. It is easy to understand how these phenomena could be interpreted in terms of 'possession' by evil spirits in a former age, or in a superstitious community today.

A second basis for empathy may be found in the study of how normal people respond to severe strains and hardships, such as life in concentration camps. In fact many of the institutions of former ages in which psychotics were confined must have very closely resembled concentration camps. The records of the ignorantly brutal or intentionally sadistic acts perpetrated on the mentally ill are revolting in a way that is comparable only to those perpetrated on political prisoners and persecuted minorities in more recent times. It is important not to deceive ourselves into assigning all this to the past: in many countries today are to be found backward institutions where overcrowding, ignorance, and much else prevail. But consider the position even of a patient in a modern, humane, and scientifically enlightened psychiatric hospital. We noted, when discussing perception, that people respond emotionally and in other ways not to the actual situations of their environment, but to that environment as they perceive it to be. For many psychotics the discrepancy between the two can be considerable, because of hallucination, delusion, and other disturbances. Thus the perceived environment, the hospital, may be to the patient himself something very different from the humane institution it is. His sufferings, though fantasied, are none the less very real to the person who lives with them. Daily life retains a nightmare-like quality, and the people around may seem to express human malevolence at its worst. The unpredictability of a psychotic's changeable emotions and impulsive actions may be difficult to explain in terms of his actual environment; it becomes very understandable indeed in terms of that environment as he perceives it.

A third basis for empathy comes from the study of development: in practical matters the psychotic patient may exhibit many resemblances to the child. Although this resemblance is not complete, and psychotic 'regression' is not necessarily regress over normal development, this notion may help us. The child may need help, not merely in such matters as dressing, feeding, and toilet, but also in having explained to him things he finds puzzling. Many psychiatric nurses adopt something of the role of 'mother' or 'father' to their charges. Allowances have constantly to be made for a patient who, like a child, is not wholly responsible, and who may also need considerable protection. With reference to the later stages of psychiatric nursing, when the patient is moving towards recovery and discharge from the hospital, the analogy may be taken further. As the child progresses into adolescence and towards adulthood, the protectiveness of adults may be a source of irritation and discouragement. During the period before discharge a patient may have to undergo the strains of 'acting normal', and his problems in this period resemble those of the young adult who is trying to behave like a 'grown-up'. Again there are many intelligent patients who are fully capable of appreciating and communicating these difficulties.

A fourth basis of empathy is to be found in some of the variations of normal mental life discussed earlier. The raw materials for much of the content of a psychosis can be drawn by a patient from subjective experiences which he shares with non-psychotics. He may, for example, be too preoccupied with his own body image, and bodily sensations like aches and strains may be reacted to with a peculiarly psychotic kind of hypochondria. Again spots and rashes may become for him 'wounds' inflicted by his enemies, minor discomforts 'tortures' administered by the hospital staff, or evidence of 'wireless waves' passed through his body by people trying to influence or injure him. As we have noted, one frequent schizophrenic reaction is delusions of bodily change; we have seen that there are many circumstances, including the hypnagogic period before sleep, which provide raw materials for delusion of this kind. Moreover if normal people can experience phenomena like hypnagogic and hypnopompic imagery, body-image changes, *déjà vu*, and the like, psychotics are not exempt. It is of considerable interest to hear intelligent psychotic patients describe some such odd variant of normal experience, and interpret it in the same way as would a non-psychotic, because it doesn't happen to fit in with his delusions. But in addition there are other patients for whom such experiences do fit in, and for whose psychosis they provide subject matter.

A fifth basis for empathy will be mentioned briefly. It has already been discussed, and some other aspects will be discussed later. This is the experimental production, in normal people, of phenomena closely resembling those of abnormal mental life. Thus as we have seen, sensory deprivation and hallucinogen experiments, and experiments with stroboscopic flashes, can produce hallucination and other phenomena. The hallucinogenic drugs in particular provide a powerful technique with great potential as a training device to allow psychiatrists, psychologists, and others professionally concerned to have first-hand experience of psychotic-like phenomena in themselves. As we noted earlier, a new orientation towards mental abnormality arose from investigations of the hypnotic state, in which many phenomena of neurosis and psychosis may be produced. There are many good reasons for continued serious scientific research with hypnosis, not the least important of them being the opportunity such work provides for widened powers of empathy.

A sixth basis for empathy comes from an understanding of social psychology, anthropology, and related sciences. In particular, any patient is like other people in being subject to the perceptual surroundings and social norms of his own area of culture. We realize this more easily if we alert ourselves to our own culture by returning to it after examining others. Thus a Navajo Indian living as he is even today in a witchcraft-conscious culture may well accept the A-thinking processes which invade his consciousness as the results of bewitchment and malevolent logic. In some of the more puritanical and guilt-ridden areas of northern Scotland we encounter a rather specific kind of depression in a category of patients in which the idea of having 'committed the unpardonable sin' is very prominent. In our own hospital wards patients may be members of the same radio and television audience as the community generally. These mass media have proved of enormous benefit to psychiatric hospitals in giving patients a way of spending their time, and in lightening the problems of control for the nurses. The same programmes can, however, also provide subject matter for the content of a psychosis, as when a patient interprets them as 'messages' sent to himself. Whether it is through mass media like radio or the printed word, or from some other source, the information available to a patient is likely to be reflected in his illness. Like other people, psychotic patients are liable to be affected by the fashions and social norms of their day and age. Thus in twentieth-century Europe delusions and hallucinations often take on the garb of popular science: electronics, space travel, and nuclear warfare. In less developed societies, as we have seen, as in medieval Europe, possession by evil spirits and witchcraft were notions that affected the content.

A seventh and final basis of empathy is the most important of all. It is the realization that a patient, even if he is a severely disturbed psychotic, remains a human person. He is remarkably like other people in many, perhaps most, respects. Several specific illustrations will be taken: all relate to severe cases of psychosis. One such patient was a good chess player, another a dependable fourth at bridge, a third a poet, and the fourth an accountant by profession. It is obviously wise to take account of such facts. The chess player, though severely deluded, enjoyed playing and invariably won. The bridge player was, as is rarely the case with psychotics, an aggressive and extremely dangerous man when his delusions were activated; yet he frequently played bridge with the superintendent of the hospital and came to be welcomed for his skill. Similarly the poet appreciated the opportunity and materials with which to indulge his interest. And a highly intelligent man, the trained accountant, understandably objected to being given no opportunity to work with figures, but being given instead the kind of occupational therapy more likely to have appealed to an amateur carpenter. In their range of interests and basic human needs, patients strongly resemble non-psychotics. They may, for example, be smokers who appreciate a cigarette, or may like being visited at the hospital by their relatives and friends. The residual normality of a patient should never be forgotten, if only in the interests of his immediate happiness: as a foundation on which an eventual cure may be built it should always be recognized and wherever possible reinforced.

Normal people, with their own memories of admission to general hospitals, may be able to understand the additional problems of the psychotic patient. Savage (1956) argues that we do many things to the psychotic which do not help. When, for example, a schizophrenic is desperately trying to retain his hold on reality we take him to a series of new environments: the admission ward of a hospital, perhaps a police station, or a psychiatric institution. In hospital, every few hours new faces appear as new nurses take over. In this connexion may be mentioned the importance of the insight, and patience, of psychiatric nurses and others who work for long hours with psychiatric patients. Even granted valuable modern aids, like television sets in the wards, such work is exacting. The overcrowded conditions, obsolete buildings, and staff shortages that mostly tend to prevail do not help. Moreover psychiatric patients, like other patients, can be exceedingly difficult and provocative.

EXPERIMENTAL PSYCHOPATHOLOGY

Many of the phenomena of neurosis and psychosis can be simulated in normal people by appropriate experimental procedures. Moreover when appropriate safeguards are adopted these effects are reversible: it is possible to use not only the introspections of the subject at the time, but also the retrospections of the normal subject afterwards, as a source of further information. Induction of the state of hypnosis by the technique of hypnotism is one such method. An illustration of its use in the study of negative hallucination and dissociated perceptual activity has been considered in Chapter 2. Despite its long history the full possibilities of hypnotism as a technique of scientific research have certainly not been exhausted. With it can be produced a large number of sensory, motor, and memory phenomena, many of which closely resemble those that occur spontaneously in the neurosis of hysteria. In considering ways in which normal people can extend their capacity for empathy with the psychotic patient, I have referred to the use of hallucinogenic drugs. Other aspects of hallucinogen research were discussed in an earlier section (Chapter 3). Their use in studying pathological forms of thinking, which have some resemblance to the thinking of the psychotic, will now be considered. As was noted in Chapter 3, leading investigators in the hallucinogen field, such as Smythies and Woolley, have argued for more attention to be paid to the relation of these drugs to the phenomena of thinking. My comments relate mainly to experiments with mescaline.

Some time after the administration of the drug the thought of the subject exhibits evidence of deterioration: it has a more crude, slipshod, and all-or-nothing quality about it. We encounter the phenomenon of 'overinclusion', often regarded as a characteristic of schizophrenic thought. In the case of the subject this involves a readiness to assert similarities of a kind that are by no means always apparent to the experimenters. To introspection the experience resembles closely the subjective effects of nitrous oxide, as reported by William James on himself as a subject (1897). James refers to an awareness of seeing logical relations 'with an apparent subtlety and instantaneity to which normal consciousness offers no parallel'. If, however, these thoughts are written down, as James puts it 'one is left staring at a few disjointed words and phrases'. Sometimes, as we have seen, with the hallucinogens as with nitrous oxide, these reactions are accompanied by mystical overtones. At any rate mescaline provides admirable opportunities for study of a loosening and alteration of normal standards of R-thinking. On occasion associative thinking, of a kind strongly reminiscent of the sub-vocal thought of certain schizophrenic patients, may be observed. Of particular interest was the reaction of one of our subjects in a mescaline experiment, when asked to explain in other words the proverb 'people who live in glass houses . . .' She found herself thinking about the parable of the 'mote and the beam' and was about to offer this as an alternative statement of the proverb, but further thoughts intervened. She decided to go over again, in her mind, the connexions between the proverb and the parable. Those she found caused her dismay: they were purely associative, and not logical. These comprised: glass houses – glass – crystal – crystal palace – palace – castle – moat – mote – mote-and-beam parable. The linkage depended very much on the crucial clang association 'moat–mote'. So, without saying anything to the experimenters she returned to the problem. And now she found the linkages: throwing stones – retaliation – unless unassailable don't throw stones – one rarely is unassailable – therefore don't throw stones – mote and beam parable. Of interest is the way in which this subject could connect the proverb to the parable in two ways: one by A-thinking and association, and the other by R-thinking and logical connexion. Our subjects frequently explained their long hesitations before replying to questions put by the experimenters in this way. Often the associations to the words spoken to them led them into subsidiary lines of association: sometimes indeed they would forget, as a result of this, the question asked. In interview schizophrenic patients will explain that something very similar is going on in their own mental life.

A peculiar feature of much psychotic thought is its lack of connexions. In this respect we encounter the concept of 'the knight's move of the schizophrenic'. The patient resembles the knight which, in a game of chess, jumps over an intervening square. Something very similar can happen in a model psychosis experiment. From the introspections and retrospective reports of subjects we can see how this can come about. Because of the flood of associations that are passing through his consciousness the subject may respond not to a question he is asked, but to what is suggested by one of these associations. He grasps at one of the many associations that are occurring, and puts it into words, relevant or not. On other occasions he responds not to the question asked, but to some question associatively linked with it in his own consciousness. Both phenomena have frequently been observed, or rather reported to researchers, by intelligent schizophrenics with some capacity for introspection. We can study these and other forms of blockage of thought – failure to respond to questions – in model psychosis experiments. Other sources of blockage noted by our own subjects included loss of vocabulary (particularly loss of abstract words), and suspiciousness involving the thought 'how much of myself am I revealing if I answer'. In this last case we encounter experimentally produced phenomena that help us to understand the problems of paranoid reactions, and paranoid schizophrenics. Such information can be used in a practical way by a psychiatrist or clinical psychologist who, having formerly been subject in an experiment, understands the variety of reasons which may cause a blockage in a patient's responses. The same observable phenomenon – the patient not replying – may result from a variety of differing subjective conditions, as we have seen. Hallucinogen experiments can enlarge the powers of empathy in the former subject who, in his role of interviewer, can say with understanding to a patient 'is it X, Y, or Z that is preventing you from answering?'

Another phenomenon of schizophrenic thinking is the 'neologism'. Neologisms are of two kinds: invented words, or idiosyncratic usages of established words. Neither are of much value in communication, though on occasion a conscientious therapist will set out to learn and thus be able to use a given patient's neologisms. Neologisms also occur in model psychosis experiments, through which we can examine in more detail reasons for their occurrence. They may result from hallucination or imagery, in that a patient or subject finds ordinary vocabulary insufficient to refer to the strange things he alone 'sees'. Again because of an over-active flood of associations a patient or subject may be tempted to coin neologisms, or through some strange connexion that occurs to him to refer to a familiar object with an unrelated word. Along with neologisms as an impediment to communication may be mentioned perseveration: this is the tendency for thinking to block, and result in endless repetition of some stereotyped word or phrase. Perseverations of this kind can occur under experimental conditions. An amusing example is provided by Steinberg when during a nitrous oxide experiment one subject started to draw an analogy with a gramophone record, and perseverated. This resulted in 'can't help laughing, laughing, laughing; feel like a gramophone record, record, record . . .'

Some attention may be paid to the use of analogy in psychotic, and model psychotic, thinking. A distinctive feature of the kind of thinking we call sane is retention of the ability to be aware of a difference between figurative and literal meanings. A sane person may use a simile or metaphor to express his meaning as when, for example, he says the human brain behaves, in certain respects, as if it were a machine. This sense of 'as if' is retained. But 'loss of the as if' as it might be called is one interesting phenomenon of both model psychotic and natural psychotic thinking. This loss may itself be a matter of degree. An illustration may be taken from two of our mescaline experiments. In the first of these, during lunch, the subject was put off by the fact that she saw the surface of the piece of bread she was trying to eat as 'alive with small yellow ants'. These were in fact crumbs, but reassurance by the experimenters to this effect perhaps understandably did not help. Another subject, in an almost identical situation during lunch, had the same subjective experience. He was, however, able to bring himself to eat the bread 'ants and all', and do so quite cheerfully. In the first instance the subject, despite intellectual awareness and much reassurance, found it impossible to adjust to the visual appearance. The second subject was able, though with some reluctance as he admitted, to make this adjustment. These difficulties help us to understand the problems of a hallucinated psychotic, and the fact that mere intellectual insight may not be enough. In a hallucinogen experiment a normal subject may or may not be able to retain his awareness of 'as if' of the kind 'the bread I am eating looks as if its crumbs are living, moving organisms'. Only rarely is the psychotic patient, for whom perception may have been largely replaced by hallucination, able to retain this sense of 'as if'. The retention or loss of this is particularly important during an upsurge of autonomous mental processes that the person concerned feels unable to control. A normal person may say, 'It feels as if somebody else is putting thoughts into my head'. For his part the psychotic may say, 'Somebody *is* putting thoughts into my head': here we see a basis on which delusions can begin to develop.

SOCIAL INFLUENCES ON ABNORMALITY

The abnormal personality is, like the normal personality, a product of his culture. This involves us in the context of geography and history, both of which are only too often forgotten. Thus it might be said that today certain syndromes like the kind of conversion hysterias studied by Breuer and Freud, about the beginning of this century in Vienna, are rare. We may also be tempted into saying that mental illnesses of the kind that result from malnutrition, dietary deficiency, and infection are rare. And we may add that the notion of possession by evil spirits, and a demonological way of thinking about psychiatric matters, is something from which the mentally abnormal patient has now escaped. This is all very well but only if we are content to be so parochial as to view these problems from the relatively comfortable perspective of twentieth-century Europe. The poverty, lack of education, and widespread superstition that Europe, and North America, lack today are characteristic of many parts of the twentieth-century world.

In 1966 a conference of psychiatrists working in Africa and the Middle East was held in Khartoum, the first of its kind to be held in Africa. Those present discussed their problems in dealing with illiteracy, malnutrition, and deep-rooted superstition. It emerged that in such countries as Zambia, the Sudan, and Sierra Leone both patients and their relatives regularly attribute psychiatric illness to witchcraft and spirit possession. In Sierra Leone, for instance, we find evidence of something reminiscent of medieval European witchcraft in resort to natural means when supernatural means failed: the use of poisons and hallucinogens to produce psychotic reactions. One psychiatrist, working in Nigeria with depressed patients, explained the kind of problems he had, and the solution he had arrived at in handling them. In using electro-convulsive treatment he had abandoned his previous tendency to explain to and argue with patients and relatives who persisted in their supernatural interpretation. He now defended his treatment to a patient convinced he was the victim of malevolent magic, by asserting that he as a psychiatrist with his apparatus had and would use still more powerful magic. In Europe the condition G.P.I. (general paralysis of the insane) is no longer a major source of admission to hospitals. By contrast a study of one East African hospital revealed that 20 per cent of the patients were suffering from neurosyphilitic infection of the central nervous system of this kind.

The rarity of classic conversion hysteria seems to be associated with education and general sophistication. On the African continent, as in India, it is very common, and it has been classified as the commonest of all the neuroses in Egypt. Robert Carter writing in 1853 found hysteria to be very common indeed in the England of his day and age. As we have seen, Carter anticipated Freud in several interesting respects. He placed emphasis on the low status of woman, and on the pressures for her to conceal her emotions in general, and her sexual emotions in particular. In these circumstances she could 'produce an apparently serious illness and thus make herself an object of great attention to all around her' (quoted by Veith, 1965). Of the women of Vienna of his day Adler remarked that many of their qualities had nothing to do with femininity as such, but were rather those of the underdog. This remark is no longer appropriate in Western Europe today, but may still have application in certain parts of the world. Of interest for example is a psychiatric illness that affects women called 'lata', which was first described in Malaya. It has also been reported in Java, Japan, Thailand, and China. The patient enters into a peculiar state in which she passively imitates what is said and done around her. She may say or shout obscene words that she would not ordinarily utter. Lata has been associated with the inferior and restricted role of women in the parts of the world where it occurs. It is but one of many syndromes to be found in some areas of culture but not others. Arieti and Meth (in Arieti, 1959) report in detail on a most interesting collection of syndromes of this kind, from various parts of the modern world.

The norms of our own society do not favour a supernatural

interpretation of either mental illness itself or the activities of those who treat it. It is otherwise in some parts of the world. On these issues Galton (1883) reminds us of how custom and tradition can set the stamp of its approval and disapproval, and thus affect subjective experience itself. He wrote: 'When popular opinion is of a matter-of-fact kind the seers of visions keep quiet . . . but let the tide of opinion change and grow favourable to supernaturalism, then the seers of visions come to the front.' There are many societies in which the major deviations, and more minor harmless ones, which we ourselves discourage are fostered. Under such conditions, as Galton says, 'the faintly perceived fantasies of ordinary persons become invested by the authority of reverend men with a claim to serious regard; they are consequently attended to and encouraged, and they increase in definition through being habitually dwelt upon.' As an illustration of how cultural norms can affect psychiatric illness, and public reactions to it, I shall consider the American Indians of the South-west.

A distinction may be made between the pueblo- or village-dwelling Indians and the nomadic Navajo. In both cases, witchcraft is still widely feared and is regarded as a major cause of both physical and mental illnesses. The notion of possession by spirits is also accepted, and this of course applies not only to the relatives but also to the patient himself. Two schizophrenic patients I have interviewed may be contrasted. The one, a European, was acutely aware of the autonomous processes going on inside him and his own inability to control them: he said that it seemed like 'another self playing the fool inside me'. The other patient, a Navajo Indian, described similar autonomous processes in terms of spirit possession: his illness itself had been caused by malevolent witchcraft. Kaplan and Johnson (1964) have examined in detail the main syndromes of Navajo psychopathology. What we ourselves might call 'fits', whether of epileptic or hysterical origin, are relatively common. The Navajo themselves speak of 'moth craziness', and the causes are to be found in violation of certain Navajo taboos by the person afflicted. The specific agent is 'a moth' which grows up inside the head of the patient just behind the eyes, and as it flies about the patient throws himself about. Just as the moth is attracted to the fire so also is the patient, who may during his fit throw himself into a fire. Another Navajo syndrome described by Kaplan and Johnson is 'ghost sickness'; its phenomena include anxiety and generalized fear, together with hallucination. This condition is caused by malevolent witchcraft, and subsequent possession by evil spirits. The Indian methods of treatment for these and other ailments involve one or other of a large number of ceremonies called 'sings'. These ceremonies are specific to groups of illnesses: thus for some the ceremony of the 'Holy Way' is used, and for others the ceremony of the 'Evil Way'. At such ceremonies, which may go on for several days, ingredients like wild tobacco may be used. The Navajo schizophrenic whose interview I mentioned above had been treated at such a ceremony, and during it a small arrow head had been inserted in the back of his head for curative purposes. This he had removed, and he was now – at a psychiatric hospital – undergoing more orthodox treatment. Specific men skilled in this work take part in the 'sing', and also in the preliminary work of a diagnostic kind. Chanting and singing form part of these ceremonies, together with the specific Navajo practice of making sand-paintings, which are and must be destroyed at the end of the ceremony. There is apparently widespread confidence in these ceremonies. Any beneficial effects we may ourselves interpret differently in terms of our own concepts like suggestion, social acceptance, and reassurance. The Navajo comprise today the largest single group of American Indians. Their reservation occupies 24,000 square miles extending into the States of Arizona, New Mexico, Utah and Colorado. The remoteness of the 84,000 Indians who live in this area is considerable – many speak only their own Navajo language – and the remoteness of their thought, not least about problems of mental illness, from our own is still today considerable.

MENTAL ILLNESS AND THE LAW

The 1959 Mental Health Act was an important advance of English law which did much to reduce confusions over the translation between psychiatric and legal categories. The law now distinguished: (1) mental illness; (2) arrested or incomplete development of mind; (3) psychopathic disorder; (4) any other disorder or disability of mind. Apart from the fact that psychiatrists and psychologists do not, today, talk about 'mind' in this way, this was a substantial improvement in many ways. The law recognized by implication the occurrence of a number of serious abnormalities of personality which did not possess any known physical cause. The psychiatric categories of intellectual subnormality, neurosis, psychosis, and psychopathic personality were allowed for. Brief mention may be made of category (2), recognizable as intellectual subnormality. The 1959 Act subdivided this into the categories of 'subnormal' and 'severely subnormal', and, as the Act recognizes, either type may be present from birth or develop later from brain injury, infection, premature onset of senility, or other causes. Apart from such matters as the need for care and protection, and insulation from exploitation by other people, the intellectually subnormal individual is not ordinarily a problem for the law.

It is otherwise with the psychopath, who has often in the past been confused with the intellectually subnormal. His deficiencies are not those of simple-mindedness, but in the area of conscience and sense of responsibility. Psychopaths thus represent one category of mental abnormality of considerable interest to criminal law: such people may well clash with the rules of their society by either drifting into or actively engaging in some form of anti-social activity. In the next chapter this type of personality will be discussed in more detail. The remaining two legal categories of the 1959 Act presumably overlap with the remaining psychiatric categories, including those of neurosis and psychosis. One kind of neurotic whose behaviour may result in criminal activities is the compulsive-obsessional. In this connexion the word 'mania' is sometimes used in a semi-popular way, as in kleptomania for compulsive larceny, and pyromania for compulsive arson. Certain sexual offenders are also of this type, and in fact it is to the compulsive-obsessional neuroses rather than, as is often supposed, to psychopathy that we must turn for the more typical kinds of abnormal sexual offences. Most neurotics of the compulsive-obsessional kind, like most psychotics, create, however, no kind of legal problem. In schizophrenia, or perhaps more properly 'the schizophrenias', we may on occasion encounter anti-social and criminal behaviour stemming from hallucination, delusion, or other typical schizophrenic phenomena.

One form of psychosis may provide on occasion considerable problems for the law: this is paranoia. True paranoia, a relatively uncommon type but a particularly interesting one, may be distinguished from paranoid reactions. Paranoid reactions may occur for a variety of reasons, including physical causes like brain injuries; they are not themselves uncommon and range from minor eccentricities to more major ones, in all of which exaggerated suspiciousness and undue sensitivity in dealing with other people are prominent characteristics. True paranoia may be illustrated from one case history and associated events which have had a great deal of historical significance and importance legally. One afternoon on Friday, 20 January 1843, a London official called Drummond was walking down Whitehall. Somewhere between the Admiralty and the Horse Guards a man approached him, put the muzzle of a pistol to his back, and fired. The would-be assassin was apprehended almost immediately, and it emerged that his name was Daniel McNaghten. Some days later – rather unexpectedly – Drummond died from his wounds, and McNaghten was charged with murder. In the early days of the trial the motive of the crime seemed obscure, and questions were asked about the possible mental abnormality of the accused.

As a personality NcNaghten proved to be a dignified, solitary, and reserved man who had made few contacts with other people. His landlady was called as a witness, and she told the court that he had repeatedly told her that certain persons, 'Catholics and Jesuits', were plotting against him, and seeking his life. Evidence was also given that, some time before, McNaghten had sought police protection. Recently he had bought a brace of pistols for self-defence. He was a man of good character, and had hitherto been a law-abiding citizen. There was nothing at all against him except that, according to *The Times* of the day, 'he was a Radical in his politics, and inclined to infidelity in religion'.

330

This judgement is itself interesting as representing a sane misinterpretation of a system of delusions, or insane beliefs. McNaghten's delusions bore little resemblance to either 'radicalism' or 'infidelity' as ordinarily understood, then or since. Only as these delusions began to be penetrated did McNaghten's motive for the crime begin to emerge. He had developed the idea that his original persecutors, the Catholics, had been joined in their conspiracy against him by the Tory Party. (The Tories at the time were carrying out a policy of sympathy towards Irish Catholics.) And so he had set out to shoot the Tory leader, Sir Robert Peel. He had succeeded in fact in killing Drummond instead: the evidence suggested a genuine mistake by McNaghten. At the trial the word 'monomania' was used, but today a diagnosis of paranoia would almost certainly have been reached. McNaghten was, in fact, a rather rare kind of psychotic. His personality was distinguished by well-systematized delusions of persecution, absence of hallucination, and a loss of perspective from brooding over his fancied dangers and grievances. He was otherwise a respectable citizen who behaved normally in other ways, and on subjects other than his imagined persecutions. Because of his mental state he was found not guilty, and escaped the death penalty. From 1843 he was held at Bethlem Hospital, and in 1864 transferred to the newly established Broadmoor Institution where in 1865 he died. As a result of the case of McNaghten, and the subsequent actions of the Judges and the House of Lords, there emerged the McNaghten Rules. These became the basis of court decisions in subsequent cases of murder if questions of the mental abnormality of the accused were raised. Many legally important, and psychologically interesting, cases of allegedly abnormal murderers were tried under the McNaghten Rules, though these have become a matter of less concern in England since the introduction of the plea of 'diminished responsibility'. The Rules, it may be added, have often been evoked when abnormality of a very different kind from that of McNaghten has been alleged or sustained. The McNaghten Rules remain the basis of such law in several Commonwealth countries, and in many American States. We shall not, however, concern ourselves further with the application of the Rules, at this stage. McNaghten himself represents a historically important case of true paranoia.

From true paranoia may be distinguished the much commoner forms of paranoid reactions. There are many people we encounter whom we tend to regard as unduly sensitive, or excessively touchy, and who are prone to see insult or provocation where none is intended. Such personalities range from the relatively normal to the more severe instances of paranoid reaction, and there are many such people outside psychiatric hospitals. Some of them are a considerable nuisance to Local Authorities, the police, and others as a source of sincere but spurious complaints against their fellow men. The paranoid personality is prone to project. On the whole, he does not like other people very much, and he may project his hostilities on to them: thus he achieves the transformation from 'I am against them' to 'they are against me'. Complaints against neighbours may be real, but others may have their authorship in a paranoid personality. Some such people even seek police protection because of the belief that they are being pursued with sexual intent by somebody who may, in fact, be quite unaware of their existence. Emphasis must be placed on the existence in the outside world of such personalities, who may make their presence, and their considerable nuisance value, more known to the police than to psychiatrists. In relation to such delusions, plausibility is all-important. A person who has delusions about being persecuted by a six-foot-high white rabbit is unlikely to achieve much in the way of either sympathy or belief from others. But a person who is deluded about the tendency of his neighbours to leave on their wireless late at night at full volume, or otherwise to provoke him, may be a considerable nuisance to housing authorities and others. Such delusions may, of course, create their own subject matter. The deluded individual who feels he is being provoked by neighbours or colleagues and who retaliates may provoke actual hostile acts, and thus fresh subject matter for further delusion.

CHAPTER THIRTEEN

Crime and Criminality

> Crime is assignable to no single universal cause . . . it
> springs from a wide variety, and usually from a multipli-
> city, of alternative and converging influences.
>
> SIR CYRIL BURT

IN the first pages of one of the classics of the psychological study
of crime Sir Cyril Burt argues for a rational and fact-finding
approach to these complex problems. Burt (1925) presents us
with a singularly heartless case of murder. The criminal in
question had tripped his victim into a canal in London, had
kicked away his fingers each time he tried to clutch the bank,
and watched him 'with jibes and taunts while his body went
under'. In the end the murderer confessed to his crime. And it
is when we turn from the crime to the criminal that feelings of
indignation change to include elements of something else: intellectual concern and perhaps even compassion. Burt describes the
individual causally responsible as he first met him: 'a sobbing
little urchin . . . a scared and tattered bundle of grubbiness and
grief'. His age was seven and a half years. The child, to whom
Burt refers as 'Jerry Jones', with his name still on the roll of an
infant school, had added to his history of truancy and theft the
crime of murder, and had taken another boy's life. Murder committed by a child forces upon us the necessity for clear thinking
about two issues: the inappropriateness of a purely emotional
reaction to crime, and the problem of what to do with the
offender. It suggests the unreality of any rigid formula from the
Old Testament or elsewhere, and the necessity for scientific
inquiry into some exceedingly complex problems.

This alternative, the collection of factual information, has
prevailed. Its pioneers included William Healy (1915), working
in Chicago, and Cyril Burt, working in London. Thus Burt's
book *The Young Delinquent* deals with individuals and is rich in
case histories, but also provides detailed statistical information

about the family circumstances, social background, and economic environment of the offenders. In some forms of crime, group membership is important, and in 1927 Frederick Thrasher presented a study in this field, a factual inquiry into 13,313 gangs in Chicago. By the 1930s the studies of Sheldon and Eleanor Glueck were under way: like many other scientific investigators of criminology the Gluecks sought to develop 'prediction tables' that would enable them, given background information about the personalities concerned, to predict the influences of this upon crime and delinquency. In a few decades criminology – as a branch of behavioural science to which psychologists, sociologists, anthropologists, and others have contributed – has advanced a great deal. Since 1957 in Britain the Home Office has had its own research unit concerned with these issues. The inevitable result of increasing knowledge has been the formulation of more precise questions. It is no longer appropriate to ask crude questions like 'Should criminals be punished or treated?' The relation of the numerous different kinds of criminal behaviour to the wide variety of 'treatments' and 'punishments' is a matter for detailed research. There seems to be no alternative to patient and painstaking fact collection in the face of some exceedingly complex problems, though here the modern computer is a powerful ally. The Home Secretary expressed this awareness in 1966 when he said, 'It is important that we act not on our emotions but on the basis of the facts.' Relevant 'facts' can, as is now realized, come from detailed statistical and biographical studies of the kind pioneered in Britain by Cyril Burt when he began his work as psychologist to the London County Council. Moreover the 'facts' about crime are not only complex; they also vary between different societies, and are liable to change through time.

SOCIAL NORMS AND CRIME

'Crime' represents one kind of deviation from the norms, or standards, of a society. These norms themselves exhibit both historical and geographical variations. A historically remote example may be taken from a trial which took place in England in 1602. The trial itself is of interest in that it provides one of the first records we have of medical witnesses appearing in court. Hunter and MacAlpine (1963) refer to the case of Elizabeth Jackson who, it was claimed in that year, had bewitched a fourteen-year-old child. The girl's symptoms had included loss of speech, fits, anaesthesias, and paralysis. Medical witnesses, Drs Jordan and Argent, interpreted these as evidence of psychiatric illness. But the judge, and jury, responded in terms of the norms of their day and age. Since the girl had had harsh words with the accused, Elizabeth Jackson, the cause of her troubles lay in bewitchment. The jury found the old woman guilty of witchcraft. The judge, Lord Anderson, declared that the land was full of witches; he himself had hanged twenty-six of them. Of the medical testimony given he said, 'I know they are learned and wise . . . I care not for your judgement'. For the crime of witchcraft, of which she was found guilty, the old woman was sentenced to stand in the pillory four times, together with a year of imprisonment. Any judge and jury who today made such a decision would be assessed as at least superstitious, and possibly psychotic. But Judge Anderson and the jury concerned responded to the social norms of their age, as did many others. Thus for long periods of history European rulers were able to execute their political enemies for the crime of 'high treason'. This crime was elastically defined. It is today, in Europe, defined more narrowly, though in parts of the world both imprisonment and execution are still used for 'crimes' of a political kind.

The formalized social norms we call 'the law' have changed even in recent years. Thus in Britain today suicide is not regarded as a crime, and moreover the survivor of a suicide pact is not, as was formerly the case, charged with murder. What is and what is not a crime depends very much on the norms of the society in which the behaviour in question occurs. The law itself may change in a brief period of time so that what was previously legal now becomes criminal behaviour. Thus, on 16 January 1920, in the United States, national prohibition became the law of the country. As Toch (1961) puts it, 'Drinking became a crime the next day, and remained so for thirteen years.' Again, to take another American example, the Harrison Act of 1914 created a new category of crime, and from then onwards the behaviour of all narcotics users, other than those under medical supervision, became criminal. A third, more recent, example may be taken. Again in the United States, on 5 January 1967 the act of trading with Rhodesia became a crime, and punishable by up to ten years' imprisonment. As in the previous examples the actions in question had not up till this date been criminal. Many such examples could be taken to show how temporal factors can affect the legal and formalized norms of a society, and thus the definition of what is and is not criminal behaviour.

The law comprises one of several kinds of social norm. As we have seen it exhibits temporal variations, and there are also variations of a geographical kind. Thus, to consider again the United States, there is considerable variation between different States as to what is and what is not a violation of the law in the matter of drinking alcohol. In some 'minors', who are not permitted to drink, are defined as people under 21, whereas in others under 18 is – as in Britain – taken as the norm. By contrast, in Louisiana, perhaps as the result of the historical influences of immigrants from France, wine may be drunk by people at a younger age than even 18. In this we can see how habits of thought and traditions can themselves influence the formalized norms we call the law. The law itself is only one kind of social norm. Important also are the mores. The term 'mores' was introduced into the behavioural sciences by Graham Sumner (1906), and it refers to those rules of society whose violation is liable to provoke strong social disapproval. It is 'immoral' to violate the mores, and 'illegal' to violate the law. What is immoral may also be illegal, as is the case with many forms of behaviour of the cruelty and unprovoked-aggression kind. Nevertheless what is illegal is not necessarily a violation of the mores. Thus, for example, in Britain minor customs offences, while undoubtedly illegal, do not carry with them the same kind of social disapproval as occurs with violations of the mores. It is when the mores and the law become too much out of gear with one another that the social reformer can perform a useful function.

In Chapter 11 we encountered J-curve behaviour as an indication of how the law, or some rule, can operate as a norm. With a

J-curve distribution we have behaviour involving conformity by the majority, and both lesser and greater deviations from it by smaller minorities. Since motoring offences occupy the major part of the time of modern courts of law, it is of interest to consider motoring behaviour from this standpoint. Figure 19

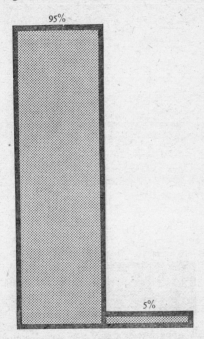

19. The rule operates as a norm: the majority of motorists stopped at the red light.

presents observations made some years ago of more than 4,000 private cars proceeding along the Great West Road near London (*The Observer*, 31 July 1960). This figure shows how the red light of the traffic signals was effective in producing a J-shaped distribution: a substantial majority conformed with the law. The same did not apply in the case of the 40 m.p.h. speed limit, as will be seen in Figure 20. In this case an overwhelmingly

large number of cars violated the rule. The third figures related
to observations of my own made during one evening in Sheffield,
relating to the rule that parked cars should display parking lights.
Again there is no indication of J-type behaviour, and a considerable majority of owners of cars made no attempt to conform. The

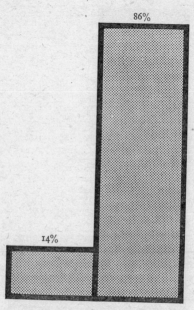

20. The rule fails to operate as a norm: an overwhelming majority of
motorists failed to adhere to the 40 m.p.h. speed limit.

deviation shown in this case, Figure 21, may seem less important
than that of Figure 20: the report in the *Observer* showed that in
fact the majority of vehicles failed to conform to the rule in a
large number of other respects. For example, no less than 94 per
cent of motor cycles disregarded the 40 m.p.h. speed limit, 66
per cent of taxis disregarded the red light, and certain makes of
car were conspicuously badly driven by many of the criteria.

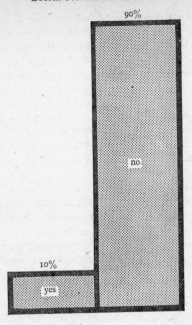

21. Failure of behaviour to conform to a legal norm: the histogram indicates that 90 of 100 parked vehicles were not displaying parking lights, in a city requiring this by law. They were observed between 5.30 and 5.40 p.m. after dark on a winter's evening. (Lighting-up time was 4.30 p.m.) A J-curve of conformity does not occur: the majority failed to conform.

Some of these deviations seem to be important ones for road safety reasons. Others, for example not lighting up in a well-lit street when parked, may be less important. It might be argued that the practice of certain cities (for example London) of not requiring this is desirable. On the other hand rules which are too openly and frequently violated need to be reviewed, with a view to a definite decision as to whether the rule in question should be changed or enforced. In any case the extent of conformity, and the effectiveness of enforcement, can be studied by methods of observation: the presence or absence of J-curves or J-type histograms, and their steepness. As new rules are introduced – for example the rule of giving way to vehicles that are actually on a roundabout – the extent to which these rules are observed, and enforced, can be investigated by this simple observational method. If official bodies do not undertake such investigations, citizens themselves may decide to do so and publish their results. Thus the investigation reported in the *Observer*, from which illustrations have been taken, was of this kind. It was conducted for four months, during which period the road behaviour of 8,063 vehicles was recorded by four private citizens who were concerned about these problems.

On occasion research findings can help us to reorientate our thinking as when, for example, the mores of a given culture lag somewhat behind its law. The researches of T. C. Willett (1964) into serious motoring offences provide such a reorientation. On the whole, with such offences, the evidence shows that juries are considerably more likely than magistrates to acquit the offender. A plausible explanation of this is that the juryman is unduly likely to identify himself with the accused, and perhaps to adopt the ego-defensive reaction 'there but for the grace of God go I'. Willett's findings are instructive on this point. He studied 653 convictions for serious motoring offences over the period 1957–9 in the London area. And he found that 23 per cent of the individuals concerned had previous convictions for non-motoring offences. In all 32 per cent of the offenders had either had such convictions, or were strongly suspected by the police of having committed other violations of the law. Thus one third of the dangerous motorists were revealed as by no means the kind of person a law-abiding citizen would be happy to identify himself with.

If the respectable citizen has his social norms, so may also be the case with the criminal community. One of the important early studies in this field was the work of Sutherland (1937), who dealt with one relatively specialized kind of criminal, 'the professional thief'. With this group, and at the time at which he worked, Sutherland found clear evidence of a criminal subculture with its own norms. Professional thieves exhibited considerable group loyalty. Moreover they were highly group-conscious: they were aware of their membership of their group, jealous of its norms, and resistant to invasions by others who did not follow the correct rules of stealing. Entry to the profession occurred through a system of apprenticeship, and recruitment frequently took place within the prisons. Sutherland also unearthed much information about how changes through time could affect specialization. He quotes one confidence man who admitted to him that times were hard and he had thus had to resort to other kinds of theft. He told Sutherland that a few years ago he would not have been prepared to be seen in the street with another man, a man with whom he now regularly consorted. This, he explained, was not because of snobbery, but purely for business reasons: as a relatively high-ranking member of the underworld it was necessary for him to keep up his reputation as such. In a more recent study Warburton (1965) studied a group of long-term prisoners in an American jail; the prison authorities chose the forty men with the worst records for prison discipline. Most of them had committed armed robbery. Warburton reports that their attitudes, their casual conversation, their humour even, all carried the implication that 'they wanted this way of life and were determined to go on with it'. Of interest was their reaction to the investigators, whom the long-term prisoners 'considered small fry compared with themselves'. Warburton reports amazement on the part of the prisoners after inquiring about the researchers' salaries, and discovering that they were low. While cooperative, their general attitude to the research 'was of an obliging nobility'. There are, as many studies have shown, sub-groupings of a hierarchical kind within crime: in prisons, for example, prisoners who have committed crimes against children tend to be looked down upon and harshly treated by the others. In the Warburton study the investigators report that the recalcitrant group of mainly armed robbers, 'many of whom ranked front page news in the national newspapers', were considerably put out when they discovered that a burglar had, in fact, got into the sample.

Prisoners of the type studied by Warburton represent one extreme type. Human behaviour exhibits a remarkably complete continuum. Just as the eccentric shades into the abnormal, so also is there a continuum between the normal, the ethically dubious, and the criminal. This is apparent for example in relation to larceny offences. We may be tempted to condemn landlords who charge excessive rents or 'key money'; their actions may or may not be illegal. An unpleasant feature of the criminal subculture is the marginal person, such as one prepared to let rooms to the London prostitute at a very high rent, being fully aware of her calling. Again the charging of excessive prices for goods in a shop may not itself be an offence against the law, nor may the ethically dubious practices of certain moneylenders and their recovery agents. More definitely criminal are the actions of the 'fence' who receives stolen goods, whose behaviour may in fact be remarkably similar. Thus Winick (1961) reports that the average cash paid by the fence for goods brought to him in the New York area is 12 per cent of the value of the goods. This form of exploitation of the criminal by the fence greatly affects one kind of potential criminal, the drug addict. Because of his small return from the fence, and the high price he has to pay for his drugs – another instance of exploitation – the addict's incentive to repeated theft is considerable. To maintain his addiction each addict thus becomes what Winick calls 'a kind of continuing one-man crime wave'. And moreover the Federal Bureau of Narcotics gave as their 1960 estimate the number of no less than 45,000 drug addicts in the United States. Thus both the norms of society – for example those of the United States Federal Government which define drug addiction as a crime – and those of the subculture itself – the exploitation of the addict by the 'fence' and the drug peddler – influence and help to increase criminal behaviour.

Of interest is a related kind of problem, that of the alcoholic offender, who is in certain respects better placed. Thus an organization like Alcoholics Anonymous can operate helpfully, while its equivalent Narcotics Anonymous has difficulties precisely because the people who need help are cautious: their addiction is a crime, while addiction to alcohol is not in itself criminal. In discussing alcoholic offenders Rubington (1961) draws attention to the importance of developmental factors which make drunkenness a 'crime of middle age'. As age increases, alcohol tolerance becomes lessened, so that relatively small doses induce intoxication. Thus, as Rubington points out, there is evidence that arrests for serious offences to which alcohol has contributed tend to occur earlier in life. There is a shift to arrests exclusively for drunkenness in later life. American statistics show that, apart from motoring offences, more people are charged with drunkenness than any other offence. The contribution of alcohol to other offences is probably considerable. In one respect Winick (1961) suggests the influences of narcotics and alcohol on offences tend to differ. Alcohol is, on the whole, associated with crimes of violence but – contrary to popular presuppositions to the contrary – the drug offender is more inclined to take part in crimes against property than against persons. Heroin – which presents the main problem of American drug addiction – is more likely to lead to larceny offences than those involving violence.

American Federal law is stricter than English law about narcotics. Similarly, within a given area of culture non-criminal individuals and institutions exhibit variations in respect to offences. For an offence to come before the courts it is necessary for some injured party either to report it to the police or otherwise to seek redress. This is likely not to occur, for example, in connexion with certain types of sexual offence. Of interest also, in this connexion, is larceny, and a study done by Martin (1962) in relation to employees. One aspect of Martin's research concerned the distinction that employers make between 'stealing' and 'pilfering' by employees. Examples of acts classified by employers as 'pilfering' included taking small items in small quantity, such as screws and nails and stationery. Money taken in any amount, items over a given value, and goods taken in large quantities were given as examples of 'stealing'. In general taking on impulse, occasionally taking, and taking for oneself alone tended to define the category of pilfering. But premeditated taking, repeated taking (even of small amounts), and taking for resale tended to be regarded by employers as instances of stealing. There were, as might be anticipated, differences between smaller and larger firms in their strictness of definition of the category of stealing. Nevertheless differentiations of the kind indicated tended to be made, and they not only serve to remind us of the continuum between crime and anti-social behaviour not formally classified as such; they also draw attention to the 'dark figure', the submerged part of the iceberg of crime: this includes both undetected crime, and crime which does not come before the courts. As Wilkins (1962) points out crimes known to the police 'do not include a large proportion of crimes committed'. Wilkins adds that any changes which occur in conventions affecting 'crimes worth notifying' would materially influence the statistics of crimes known.

PERSONALITY AND CRIME

Eysenck (1964), in discussing crime from the standpoint of the criminal's personality, finds it helpful to take account of related but non-criminal forms of deviant behaviour. Thus, as we have seen, Willett's study of motoring offences may give us something of a clue to understanding the type of personality more than ordinarily likely to indulge in crime. Eysenck thus takes account of a research by B. J. Fine of traffic violations and minor accidents. Fine worked with a group of first-year students of the University of Minnesota, and obtained data on minor road offences in which some of these had been involved. Those with unsatisfactory driving records were found to score more highly than did the other students on Eysenck's personality dimensions of neuroticism and extraversion. In an earlier section we have noted how Eysenck was led in his previous studies of personality to view it in terms of two major dimensions: emotional stability or otherwise (neuroticism), and introversion-extraversion. Figure 15 on page 276 illustrates this analysis of personality. Thus the traffic violators of Fine's study fall into the top right segment of the figure. Also of interest is a study by Sybil Eysenck of unmarried mothers at a London hospital, who scored more highly on neuroticism and on extraversion than otherwise comparable married mothers. In other words they fall into the same segment. This also proves to be the case with various researches into criminals themselves, cited by Eysenck. He refers for example to Warburton's study of difficult and recalcitrant prisoners in one American jail (subsequently published, Warburton, 1965).

Warburton describes his subjects as 'chiefly anxious extraverts': they were measurably high on Cattell's test of anxiety (which resembles Eysenck's neuroticism variable), and also on Cattell tests of extraversion. Eysenck also refers to personality testing of psychopathic personalities (see below), which again places them in this top right segment. He cites data on Australian prisoners, both male and female, whose test results again put them into this top right segment. We have seen that formalized social norms define what is and what is not a crime. Nevertheless such norms, whatever they happen to be for the area of culture concerned, provide something from which individuals may deviate. Eysenck has attempted to provide a scheme for prediction of the kinds of personalities more than averagely liable to deviate. In this respect he is pin-pointing a type of personality structure which merits more detailed study; it includes both criminals and other types of deviation.

In twentieth-century Britain some forms of criminal behaviour, for example those classified under the heading of 'larceny', are extremely common. Others are exceedingly rare. Since novelty tends to provoke interests, and with it news value, we might expect that it is unrepresentative crimes that tend to receive maximum press attention. This proves to be the case. However tragic the exceptional cases which may arouse strong emotion as well as wide publicity, it is realistic to begin by recognizing them as unrepresentative. On average crime is sordidly uninteresting. Murder, for example, is usually a domestic affair, particularly when the victims are women: women are mainly murdered by husbands, fathers, and other close relatives, or at least people known to them. Men have a statistically greater chance of being murdered by strangers, though for both men and women it is predominantly spouses, friends and relatives, and acquaintances who are responsible. The murder of a child is particularly likely to provoke strong emotion in the law-abiding citizen. Yet again, as Home Office figures for the period 1955–60 show, approximately three quarters of child victims are killed by a parent or other older relative. Newspaper reports tend to give an exceedingly unbalanced picture in these and other respects.

Nevertheless the press performs – though often with smaller

headlines – its function of reporting the more usual forms of crime. Some illustration of their variety may be taken from one newspaper's coverage during a week of August 1966. Two brothers were jailed for breaking in and stealing cash and cigarettes, valued at £15. A woman was fined £45, and £65 costs, for malicious damage to property she had been responsible for during a vendetta against a neighbour. There were several cases of arson, from different parts of the country. A confidence man, pretending to be a salesman, had robbed two elderly ladies of £50. Numerous other impostors, frequently representing themselves as tradesmen or officials, had gained entry into houses through the front door: then, when left alone by the house-holder, they had committed thefts. The newspaper carried a warning to readers about a minor epidemic of this form of crime. Very many assaults, and numerous drunken and other brawls which resulted in police-court proceedings, were reported. Of some news interest, in this monotonous series of cases, was one irate pedestrian who had squirted a soda-water fountain in a driver's face, and resisted arrest when a policeman had inter-vened! Among other offences reported were numerous burglaries, a few instances of anonymous phone calls, night prowling, church desecration, and malicious damage. 'Crime' in Britain in the 1960s obviously involves a wide variety of different acts which – to use an analogy from the study of perception – provide inconspicuous 'ground' to the 'figure' to which the press and other mass media give major attention. Perhaps the acts themselves provide something of a clue to the kinds of people who engage in them? This may be considered in relation to one important category of crime, larceny.

The law makes distinctions between the huge variety of larceny offences. Different charges are made, and different penalties are prescribed if the guilt of the accused is sustained. One offender may operate as a relatively specialized career-criminal as a burglar with considerable skill in his 'trade'; an-other finds a door unlocked and enters a house where he steals; a third shoplifts; a fourth commits robbery with violence; and a fifth operates as a confidence trickster at a tourist resort. The facts that criminals may exercise choice in the type of crime they commit, commit them in a particular way, and repeat such actions are of interest. Police officers have told me that on occasion, when they investigate a given instance of larceny, the matter may be so clear-cut that they find themselves saying to themselves, 'Obviously old Johnny Doe did this.' If two people as habitual offenders commit crimes that are distinguishable, may it not prove to be the case that they have measurably different personalities? Moreover with categories of offence, and offenders classified by their offence, are we not even more likely to find measurable personality differences? This very reasonable idea, that the categories of the law itself are useful as a guide to psychological research into criminal personalities, as formulated for example by Tong (1958), has, on the whole, proved fruitful. Working with a population of intellectually subnormal offenders Tong found measurable differences between, for example, sexual and larceny offenders. Moreover he found that the nature of the offence assisted him to demonstrate other differences within these two categories of larceny and sexual offence. Let us take an extreme example: we would not expect to find confidence men with their attributes of social skill, smooth talk, and 'front' at the lower levels of intelligence, as measured by standard tests. As Burt found in his early researches there are some habitual offenders of superior rather than inferior intelligence: a look at the crimes themselves may help us to place these on an intellectual scale. Moreover in connexion with property offences, there is evidence of two rather distinct types of offender. One such individual will never under any circumstances carry a weapon and will not, if interrupted, exhibit violence in resisting arrest. We might reasonably expect him, as a personality, to differ from leading members of some of the adult Chicago gangs that Frederick Thrasher studied, and different also from the strong-arm assistants of a contemporary London protection racket. Arson for example is a rather peculiarly specific kind of offence. Obviously there are different sub-types, and MacDonald (1961) gives a long list of motives from arsonists themselves. These range from jealousy and revenge, through wishes to defraud insurance companies, to attention-attracting and the wish to hide the evidence of some other crime. Nevertheless with one group of offenders McKerracher and Dacre (1966) have found certain features which distinguished the group as a whole from others. Although self-mutilation and self wounding was a frequent feature of the arsonist they conclude that arson in the group studied, as measured by test results and biographical information, involves aggression but an aggression channelled against property, not persons. In this respect the arsonists resembled the drug offenders studied by Winick (1961) in American society: on average offences against persons, as opposed to property, had rarely occurred.

THE PSYCHOPATH

Psychiatry uses the diagnosis 'psychopathic personality' for one type of severely abnormal personality that is, by definition, neither neurotic nor psychotic. The 1959 Mental Health Act recognized psychopathy as a legal category and defined it as 'a persistent disorder or disability of mind, whether or not including subnormality of intelligence, which results in abnormally aggressive or seriously irresponsible conduct on the part of the patient, and requires or is susceptible to medical treatment'. The notion of psychopathy derives historically from the concept of 'moral insanity' formulated in 1835 by J. C. Prichard: Prichard's concept was undoubtedly broader than that of 'psychopathy' as understood today. He included in it, however, phenomena like 'expressions of intense malevolence, without ground or provocation actual or supposed' (Prichard, 1835, in Hunter and Mac-Alpine, 1963). Prichard also adds that 'a propensity to theft' is often a feature of moral insanity. Personalities today diagnosed as psychopathic vary greatly; among their number we encounter some liable to acts of aggression of a seemingly unprovoked kind, and others to varied sorts of irresponsible behaviour including larceny. The psychopath is particularly liable to clash with the law. Where psychopathy ends and criminality on the one hand, and other types of abnormality on the other, begin is by no means a clear-cut issue. Moreover for many psychiatrists the diagnosis of psychopathic personality has become a kind of rubbish heap for cases not readily classifiable in other ways. There are, however, signs of a tendency towards a more narrow use of the term by psychiatrists. In the meantime British law has now accepted a category of severely abnormal people who are neither neurotic nor psychotic.

Following a study of psychopaths in one security hospital Murphy (1961) listed seven distinguishing characteristics: egocentricity and lack of relations with other people, disregard for accepted social standards, absence of guilt feeling, failure to learn from punishment, emotional immaturity, impulsiveness, and apparently motiveless behaviour. Classificatory psychiatry sometimes distinguishes the 'inadequate psychopath', the shiftless individual who may drift into criminal activity, from the 'aggressive psychopath', who may commit seemingly meaningless crimes of violence including murder. In absolute terms homicidal psychopaths, like for example the murderer Neville Heath, represent only a small minority of psychopaths, and a tiny minority of criminals. Most psychopaths, it should be stressed, tend to be a nuisance – often a considerable nuisance – but are not, in this way, a danger to society. There is, I believe with others who would seek to define and limit more strictly the use of the term 'psychopathy', justification for distinguishing this type of personality from others. Neither the actions nor the motives of such people are easy to explain in terms of normal behaviour. Nor are we helped, in seeking empathy and explanation, by studying neurotic and psychotic patients. The personality of the psychotic kind may himself be quite unable either to explain his motivation, or to predict his likelihood or otherwise of repeating the offence. In his very comprehensive study of psychopathy Cleckley (1955) turns to literature in attempts to give some understanding of this kind of personality. He instances Iago, whose malevolence is 'without motivation in the ordinary sense', and Edmund in *King Lear*, whose extremes of cruelty illustrate one kind of psychopathy. To Cleckley's list from Shakespeare might be added the determined trouble-maker Tybalt of *Romeo and Juliet*, who, despite knowledge of the law which prescribes exile for the next offender, is determined – with or without provocation – to pick a fight, which ultimately ends in the murder of Mercutio. Other instances found by Cleckley in literature include old Karamazov, whom Dostoyevsky portrays with the psychopath's active pursuit of folly and buffoonery and who 'immerses himself in indignity for its own sake'. The typical emotional shallowness of the psychopath Cleckley sees skilfully portrayed by Somerset Maugham in Mildred, one of the central characters in *Of Human Bondage*, with her characteristic insensitivity and ingratitude for the sincere efforts of others to help her. These last examples serve to remind us that not all psychopaths are aggressive and dangerous; some are merely coldly insensitive to the feelings of others about them, and blind towards their own welfare. (See also Cleckley in Arieti, 1959.)

The most obvious defect of the psychopath is his lack of restraint on his own impulses. He is characteristically unreliable in such matters as telling the truth, keeping promises, or repaying the money he is very likely to borrow. The psychopath has been likened to an otherwise intact motor car with very defective brakes. If for 'brakes' we read 'conscience' or 'super-ego', then we come some way towards understanding the type of personality involved. But it is only the beginning of an understanding. The car itself – the outward personality – may be well polished and seemingly sound: in other words the psychopath quite often has a good front, and a capacity for glib talk which misleads his victims for a time. What Cleckley calls 'the mask of sanity' obscures the underlying personality, as he exhibits charm and the outward appearance of sincerity. Thus he readily finds victims, and former victims acquire a hunted look. It is indeed often difficult to reconcile the outrageous conduct recorded in the case history notes on a psychopath with the patient one actually meets. Thus psychopaths quite often withdraw from the scene leaving their earlier, now thoroughly informed victims and their current protectors, who are as yet unaware of the psychopath's true character, fighting among themselves. The current victims often feel that their predecessors have unfairly misjudged this charming person. They learn, in time, that others have been, like themselves, unwisely tolerant.

A case history contributed by the psycho-analyst Karl Abraham (1925) gives an indication of the burdens the psychopath inflicts on others. It also reminds us that not all psychopaths who clash with the law are physically aggressive or in this way dangerous. Abraham refers to the man in question as 'N', and takes him as an illustration of the kind of psychopath known to his victims and the law as 'swindlers' and 'confidence men'. His observations relate to N's period of war service. When N began his life in the army his superiors knew about his past, which included several periods of imprisonment. Nevertheless the same thing happened in the army as had happened before. First N gained sympathy and confidence, and then he abused this trust: given money to spend on behalf of his company, he used it for his own purposes. On being caught out he did not return to his regiment, but moved to another town, and promoted himself to corporal. Later N, having by now assumed the stripes of a sergeant, went to Budapest but was eventually caught, and returned for military imprisonment in his original garrison town. There he soon got on to such excellent terms with his captors that he escaped without any difficulty. Next, armed with papers he had forged, he travelled all over Germany, masquerading as a gentleman of leisure, and subsequently as an art critic. He readily obtained money by false pretences, and by the time he again reached Budapest had put on the uniform of an officer. As Abraham says, by now 'the charges against him had assumed vast proportions'. These included desertion, pretending to hold a commission, and numerous frauds, forgeries and embezzlements. Despite this N seemed to have no difficulty at all in winning everybody over by exerting his charm. When Abraham, himself a medical officer, first went to see N, who was supposed to be imprisoned under guard, he was surprised to find no guard on the door. Instead, on entering the room he found N sitting at the table drawing. One of the guards was posing as a model for this portrait, and the other guard was looking on admiringly. Abraham made detailed inquiries from N about his previous life history, inquiries which he wisely verified from other sources. He found a long list of delinquencies from early years. Thus, on one occasion, as a child N went to a stationer's shop, represented himself as the son of a general, and arranged to receive goods on credit. He was aged six at the time. The history of a personality of this kind with 'an inner necessity to be amiable' is fascinating in terms of his long criminal record, which contained, incidentally, no crimes of violence. In such instances we can see that the psychopath, despite his peculiar deficiencies in the area of conscience, may be highly intelligent and possessed of considerable social skill. A striking feature of Abraham's case is the evidence it affords of the psychopath's ability to 'manipulate' people. The story has been told of one psychiatrist who was in doubt about his diagnosis of a patient: was he, or was he not, a psychopath? His problem was solved when he found himself driving his patient home after therapy and he *knew* he was dealing with a psychopath. As the 1959 Mental Health Act recognizes, psychopathy is unrelated to intelligence, and some highly intelligent patients are diagnosable as psychopathic. To cite quantitative evidence on this point, Warburton (1965) in his study of 'a sample of psychopathic American criminals' found a wide range of intelligence scores. With a modified form of the Army Classification Test he found, in this sample, an average intelligence quotient of 103. Moreover half of his sample of 38 prisoners scored over 100, and 6 of them scored over 140. Despite prolonged misunderstandings to the contrary, psychopathy has no direct relation to intelligence.

If we seek to define psychopathy in a positive way, rather than negatively as a residue of otherwise undiagnosable personalities, more can be said. It would be a mistake to regard such personalities merely in terms of their deficiencies of conscience. In Freudian terms, more than the super-ego is involved: there are also abnormalities of the ego, and of the id. The ego of the normal personality performs the function of permitting him to adjust to the demands of reality, and to exercise restraint on his actions on the grounds of prudence and long-term self-interest. Ego strength reveals itself in concern with the future as well as the immediate present, and in capacity for carrying through long-term purposes. Normal people may on occasion forget themselves, lose their tempers, or perform impulsive acts. If so they tend to experience guilt feelings because of these lapses, as a result of the activity of the super-ego. Again, in the normal personality the id is the seat of the impulses and the reservoir of emotional energy; this reservoir is adequate to permit him to form attachments, and perhaps also sentiments of dislike, towards other people. In all these aspects involving the functions of ego, super-ego, and id, the psychopath is different. His ego is notoriously weak, and his ability to face the realities of the present, to pursue long-term goals in the future, and to learn from the past is extremely limited. He exhibits his incompetence in facing what Alfred Adler has called the 'three great problems of life': adjustment to other people, to employment, and to a satisfactory love relationship. In these respects the abnormalities of the psychopath's id, as a source of emotional energy and thus of ability to form sufficiently strong sentiments, become apparent. His emotional life is shallow, motivational energy is lacking, and he is without the resources needed to establish real and lasting relationships with other people. If his impulses overcome the restraints of the ego and of the super-ego it is less because these impulses are unduly strong than because these restraints are so weak as barely to exist at all. The weakness of the psychopath's super-ego has been noted, and with it go both a lack of interest in right and wrong and a peculiar absence of perspective in such matters. Thus one psychopathic murderer who had killed three people was indignant that the press had not been fair to him: they had omitted to mention his various acts of kindness, such as putting a pillow under the head of one of his victims (MacDonald, 1961). Other psychopathic acts of aggression are typically unprovoked and seemingly motiveless; they are not continuous with normal acts of aggression except possibly those of the alcoholically intoxicated person.

The purposeless nature of the motivation, and accompanying shallowness of emotion, may be emphasized. It is not always easy to draw a sharp distinction between the psychopath's anti-social behaviour and that of the 'normal' criminal, but one basis of distinction may be found just in this. As Cleckley points out, it is possible to empathize with the ordinary criminal in that we can see that he is trying to get something, like money, that we all want, but is using means that we ourselves shun. The purposes of the psychopath are more obscure. Moreover his incompetence in adjusting to reality shows up here as elsewhere in his inability to take realistic precautions against getting caught, and his lack of skill in this as in other occupations. Tony Parker's book *The Unknown Citizen*, published by Penguin Books, provides a detailed history of 'Charlie Smith' and his repeated larcenies. Charlie Smith was found to be of average intelligence (Terman-Merrill I.Q. of 106), but is described as 'an inadequate and unstable person'. His sentences, always for some form of theft and always without any component of violence, totalled in the end 26 years; his average period of freedom between sentences was 11 weeks. The problems for society provided by the inadequate psychopath of this kind are discussed in Parker's book.

Aggressive psychopaths may differ markedly from inoffensive nuisances like Parker's 'Charlie Smith'. The attitudes of the psychopathic murderer towards 'right and wrong' differs from that of the psychotic murderer. A deluded psychotic like McNaghten may believe his acts to be merely those of justifiable self-defence against his enemies and persecutors; a hallucinated schizophrenic may have received 'divine commands' through his 'voices' to perform the act in question. Psychopaths exhibit other reactions. Examples may be taken from two psychopathic murderers in interview. One of them when asked why it is more wrong to kill than to steal answered that the law's penalty for murder is greater than for theft. Detailed questioning failed to elicit any idea whatsoever of 'rightness or wrongness' apart from the amount of punishment legally prescribed for being caught after the act. The second psychopathic murderer was different in that he confessed to having no memory of having killed his victim at all, nor any awareness of the very large number of stab wounds he had in fact inflicted. His response to the question 'If you were released from institutional care do you think you might do it again?' was chilling: he replied, with at least superficial signs of sincerity, 'I don't know, but I really do hope I wouldn't'. The murder was motiveless by ordinary standards, and the murderer seemed wholly unable to throw any light on this motiveless act. In our courts of law we are very much in need of finding some way of communicating clearly about such personalities as these, and the kinds of questions usually asked of psychiatric witnesses ordinarily fail to elicit the essentials. If we exclude the severely intellectually subnormal, there are few people who are unable to talk about 'right and wrong' when interviewed. But in psychotic delusion and hallucination on the one hand, and psychopathy on the other, we encounter quite different variations from the normal in this matter. The aggressive psychopath can be a very serious danger to society. The assumption by the general public, and sometimes the law also, that prison rather than a security psychiatric institution is the proper place for offenders of this kind is misguided. It is both unfortunate and dangerous for very practical reasons. In various countries there have been cases in which such individuals, after release from prison for some minor offence, have gone on to commit a major one, sometimes murder. Such people are much more appropriately kept in special security institutions rather than allowed into the prison system, from which they may be prematurely released at the end of their sentences, or earlier for good behaviour. The possibility that on release an aggressive psychopath will go out and commit a more serious offence is not something to be taken lightly. There is one way in which aggressive psychopaths, who include some of the most vicious personalities we are likely to encounter anywhere, can perform a positive function. Safely locked up in special institutions with one hundred per cent security from which escape has been made impossible, they can provide highly valuable information. Research into the personality of such people may permit others of their kind to be discovered before, and not after, they have committed major crimes. The need for such research cannot be overestimated.

MURDER

The first difficulty of murder is differentiating the act itself from acts of a very similar kind. An example may be taken. On 9 September 1966 two police officers stopped a motorist in a north of England town: his car's number plates appeared to them to be false. The motorist, when questioned, suddenly produced a revolver, threatened them with it, and then pulled the trigger four times. The gun did not go off, but when recovered was found to be loaded in all chambers. Subsequently the motorist was charged with 'having a firearm with intention to resist arrest'. Only chance, a lucky accident, prevented the offence from being in law one of murder. During the same year the murder in London of three police officers, under rather similar circumstances when they stopped a motor car, provoked widespread national concern. The incident in the northern town passed unnoticed, as did other incidents elsewhere. For example, in December the same year another police officer, this time in Canterbury, went out to investigate a car. He was attacked by four men and knocked to the ground. Later he found that a stab cut in his left tunic pocket had penetrated deeply into his notebook: again only a fortunate accident appears to have saved his life. On other occasions other fortuitous factors like the good health of the victim, or the availability of prompt and skilled medical attention, may prevent murder occurring. Thus in studying murder, whether for the purpose of crime prevention or for research, we are immediately confronted with the problem of differentiating what is in law 'murder' from psychologically very similar acts which did not result in a death.

As we have seen there are many inaccurate and stereotyped ideas about the offence of murder. Despite beliefs to the contrary, the majority of murders involve the family, close relations, or friends. The commonest murderer is somebody who is emotionally close, or at least acquainted with, the victim: it is rare for strangers to be chosen. Moreover many murderers who are undoubtedly guilty of the crime are not available for trial because approximately one fifth of them commit suicide after the act. There are occasions too, as when a murder follows a struggle between two people, when the victim might well have happened to be the offender. In a comprehensive study of this area of crime MacDonald (1961) draws attention to the fact that certain types of people tend to get themselves murdered: thus it is well for us to make some attempt to understand the personality of victims as well as of offenders. Among such victims MacDonald includes 'the tormenter', of whom he says: 'The autocratic mother or wife who is constantly criticizing her son or husband may find that even a worm will turn.' Thus such a person may well die, within the family, at the hands of his or her own former victim. More generally MacDonald produces statistics and case

356

histories to show how, in a variety of different ways, the crime may be the result of provocation by the deceased. Again statistics reveal that murder is an occupational hazard not only of prostitutes, but also of blackmailers. Perhaps, however, it is in the case of brawls that we can see most clearly how in crimes like murder and attempted murder the moral blamelessness of the victim cannot always be presumed. The victim's own acts may have been potentially homicidal.

Studies of the weapon used may be of considerable value in connexion with prevention. In the United States shooting proves itself to be the most frequent method, being responsible for approximately 50 per cent of cases. Gibson and Klein (1961) in a British Home Office study show that murder by shooting is rare in Britain: it accounts for only 16 per cent of cases when the offender is a man, and 11·6 per cent of cases when she is a woman. (The figures given by MacDonald for the United States are respectively 52 and 40 per cent.) Since in the United States murder is a State, not a Federal, offence, subcultural differences are important, as are differences of State law. There is for example a well-established relationship between a low expenditure of State money on education and a high incidence of the form of murder known as 'lynching'. Custom and tradition may also be important in other ways. As we have seen in Texas, where the tradition of defence of one's property with one's gun is firmly established, three things are found: firearms are readily available, the concept of justifiable homicide in law is a very broad one, and the murder rate is extremely high. In Britain murder is most commonly committed either with no weapon at all, or with some blunt instrument: these account for approximately 50 per cent of cases. Home Office figures before the Homicide Act give the figure of 49·3 per cent; after the Act the figure was 61·8 per cent. The much lower figures for murder by shooting of Britain by contrast with certain American States like Arizona and Texas give no reason for complacency. Murder by shooting, and attempted murder, we have seen illustrated already in the cases of the five police officer victims or potential victims mentioned. Since a proportion of these cases involve murder by a criminal who is apprehended, or interrupted, in the course of some other crime, a practical lesson might be learned from British history. In earlier times smugglers who carried firearms were subject to much more severe penalties than were smugglers who did not or who merely resisted arrest in some other way. What happened was that smugglers developed the practice of not arming themselves with a gun: they usually carried a stick with which they were, if necessary, prepared to resist arrest. In some respects they resembled one category of larceny offenders who differ from the other category in that they do not carry weapons. A differential scale of penalty for the criminals who do, and who do not, when apprehended prove to be possessed of guns merits examination. In the meantime the possession of weapons of any kind by known criminals might well be made the matter for increasingly severe penalties. Subsequent statistical follow-ups will reveal whether this suggested change of the law, and of habits of sentencing, is justified by its effects: meanwhile the implicit hypothesis involved would seem to be a not improbable one.

In crimes which involve murder by shooting, as in crimes which are associated with drug addiction, there are obviously very important cultural differences between the United States and Britain. American researches cannot be safely used, without considerable caution, in assessing general trends: on the other hand they may still prove of value in indicating the variety of the people, and forms of behaviour, that are involved. Of interest, for example, are some of the cases dealt with by Thrasher in his early studies of the Chicago underworld. For instance, he provides data which support the frequently heard contention that mass media like the press and the film affect this and other crimes. A whole series of burglaries is reported in which the offenders, when apprehended, admitted that they had had a model of the 'I'd seen it in the movies' kind. Thrasher discusses the Loeb and Leopold case: the murder by these two young men of a fellow student, Richard Franks, with the apparent motive of committing the 'perfect crime'. The influence of Dostoyevsky's novel *Crime and Punishment* on this murder is perhaps a remote one, though Richard Loeb admitted being influenced by the substantial library of books about crime which he possessed. Anyway the Loeb–Leopold crime itself had many imitators. Thrasher refers to an epidemic of 'perfect crimes' which followed in Chicago, California, and Minnesota. Moreover, press publicity resulted in national barriers being crossed, and Thrasher points out that two university students in Sicily committed a detailed imitation of the crime. In this case the lawyers based their defence on the fascination the Loeb–Leopold crime had had for the accused. Burt, in his London study reported in *The Young Delinquent*, also found evidence for imitative crime; he regards it, however, as more typically the act of an intellectually subnormal offender. Fashions change, as does available reading matter. Thrasher's own subjects, in the juvenile Chicago gangs, had reading preferences for the Tarzan novels. In the 1960s when children have, on occasion, injured themselves by trying to imitate the flying activities of their heroes – in a period of enthusiasm for Batman and Robin – it is apparent that the influences of mass media upon unwise, antisocial, or criminal behaviour merit continuing study. One such inquiry into the mass media from this standpoint is being conducted by the Council of Europe. An American Senate subcommittee is conducting another specifically into the possible effects of television on juvenile delinquency.

For the most part murder in literature, aside from instances in which the written word may produce imitative crime, is extremely unlike the typical murders that concern the police. Thus Boyd (1961), writing as a psychologist, has analysed some of these differences. Worthy of investigation is the process by which a skilled writer can provide interest, entertainment, and pleasure out of a subject matter of murder. From its origins in Dostoyevsky, Wilkie Collins, and Edgar Allan Poe has developed a substantial literature of this kind, some of it of high quality. Contemporary authors of lighter fiction of this kind often achieve their effect by treating the crime itself as an event, without dwelling on the details, and then concentrating on the process of detection which has an appeal to many comparable to that of a chess problem. An element of fantasy, for example eccentricity on the part of the detective, whether he be Holmes himself, Poirot, or Dr Fell, is an important ingredient for some authors. What is achieved has considerable remoteness from the facts of real murder of the kind which Rackham (1966) has called 'psychological distance'. Such distance, as Rackham shows, in a highly original investigation, may be of a variety of kinds: it may be geographical or historical, or can be achieved by making the characters concerned in some way unreal. Thus, for example, we are less disturbed by a case of cruelty occurring in the remote past, or in some distant part of the world, than one in our immediate vicinity.

The understanding of how people are able to make effective use of the mechanism of isolation (see Chapter 10), and achieve psychological distance, is one of the more important tasks for scientific psychology to achieve. In this respect an analysis of thought products such as books, plays, and films is by no means irrelevant. Shakespeare, for instance, not once but many times made great literature from a subject matter of crime including murder itself in some of its more horrible forms. The citizen, whether as juryman, police officer, pathologist, or in some other capacity such as scientific criminologist, may have to perform the difficult task of thinking unemotionally, and judging impartially in accord with the evidence. At times, to do this, it is necessary for the thinker to resort to the abstract categories of psychological distance; at others it is equally necessary for him to examine the facts themselves in their detail, however emotionally repugnant they may be. This achievement is as difficult as it is socially important.

*

In this chapter it has been possible to touch only lightly upon a huge subject, and to mention only a few of the many kinds of crime. As we have seen, human behaviour exhibits a continuum ranging from the virtuous, through the usual, to the ethically objectionable, and finally to the criminal. Different cultures have defined, and still do define, differently their category of the criminal. Here also, as in the case of the study of minor deviations from the psychiatrically normal, minor deviations from the norms may assist us to understand actual criminality. Prediction of criminal behaviour, the ultimate practical goal, is not unlike the goal of the scientific criminologist seeking understanding.

Four bases for such prediction might be suggested. First, a knowledge of the behaviour of people in general – behaviour which is universal, or nearly universal, within the species – may help. Thus for example statistics show that men are more liable than women to be victims of murder at the hands of strangers. This danger seems to be particularly evident in the case of police officers who, like men in general and unlike women, are more likely to interrupt some other crime. Study of the behaviour of human and other living organisms, and of relations between flight and aggression, may assist us. In Chapter 8 we discussed how fear and the flight reaction can, when escape is prevented, lead to aggressive attack: this may have some application to the understanding of violence, assault, and homicide in certain types of offence. Secondly, another basis for prediction is to be found in a given area of culture, and the social norms to which its members show conformity. Thus in some communities toughness and aggression are a way of life, while criminal subcultures themselves may have definite norms of their own. Study of such norms may assist prediction, understanding, and control. Thirdly, predictability also comes from the study of individual personalities. The assault by Daniel McNaghten on Drummond cannot be explained in terms of either general psychology or social norms: it resulted from McNaghten's personality, and his paranoid delusions. Study of such personalities in borstals, prisons, and elsewhere at an earlier date might well have prevented the subsequent tragedy of later major crimes. This is particularly so in the case of the abnormal offender: thus the murderer Neville Heath was executed without being even properly interviewed, much less scientifically studied, by anybody. The loss of such data, if we are seriously interested in preventing future crimes of a similar kind, and if we are concerned in the early detection of the kinds of people likely to commit them, is little short of tragic. Fourthly, prediction may come from analysis of situational influences upon behaviour, and from study of the effects specific situations are likely to produce. Thus, for example, while situations likely to produce road accidents have been much studied, we have been neglectful of the study of situations which provoke anger. The effects of impatience, irritation, and anger upon road users and upon road accidents, and the circumstances which provoke these emotions, merit detailed investigation. Again MacDonald, in his studies of homicide, has drawn attention to numerous occasions on which the situation itself was such that a murder was likely to occur. He reports evidence that on many such occasions the potential victims, and the appropriate authorities, were singularly resistant to recognition of the obvious.

Crime and criminality are subjects of enormous difficulty and complexity: they embrace many different kinds of behaviour and personality. Some predictions can nevertheless be made; as knowledge grows about general, social, individual, and situational influences on behaviour, these predictions will increase in number. From crime itself we may turn to courts of law, and the influences which these have on the accused, and other people present. Some attention will also be paid to civil, as well as to criminal, proceedings in courts.

CHAPTER FOURTEEN

Forensic Psychology

The court room and the human foundations which support
it are full of points at which scientific inquiry and reform
are needed.   HANS TOCH

FORENSIC psychology will be taken to mean application of the
methods and findings of psychology to problems of law, including
human behaviour in court, study of types of personalities likely
to be of interest to the courts, police procedures of investigation,
and related matters such as, for instance, the study of human
lying. This branch of the subject already exists and is taught in
several American universities. Its content is defined in a book
edited by Hans Toch (1961) of Michigan State University, where
about a thousand students a year take such a course. Forensic
psychology may be distinguished from criminology, forensic
psychiatry, and prison psychology, though it has important
points of contact with these and other subjects. Two aspects may
be distinguished. First is its practical side, as when a psychologist
appears as an expert witness in court, advises a court, assists a
police investigation, or conducts experiments in connexion with
a specific case. Second is its more background function, as when
researches are conducted into such matters as jury decision
making, reliability or otherwise of human testimony, and the
influence of sentiments and prejudices on perception and
opinion.

Civil as well as criminal law may be kept in mind. There are,
in this area, many disputes which do not find their way as far as
the courts, where expert scientific assistance on psychological
problems may help. Of interest are several disputes of the textile
industry to which Michel Chevreul (1835) makes reference in his
important early work on colour perception. In France at this
time, conflicts arose between drapers and manufacturers of cloth,
several of which Chevreul tells us he was able 'to settle amicably

by demonstrating to the parties that they had no possible case for litigation'. In one such instance cloths had been supplied in colour on which were printed black shapes; the drapers complained that the blacks were not true, but themselves varied considerably. Those on the red backgrounds had a greenish shade, on violet they were greyish-yellow, and on blue they were orange-brown. They were not the uniform blacks that the drapers had ordered. By experiments Chevreul demonstrated that the dispute arose not from the dyes, but from ignorance of the perceptual qualities of colour: in each case the blacks had taken on the complementary hue of the coloured background. The difficulties were settled without litigation, following these demonstrations.

THE PSYCHOLOGIST AS EXPERT WITNESS

One of the earliest cases in which a psychologist appeared as an expert witness in court concerns civil rather than criminal law. This involved Karl Marbe, the Würzburg psychologist, who was called in a civil case involving a railway accident. Marbe drew on his knowledge of reaction time. He was able to convince the court, with appropriate laboratory findings in support, that the driver of the train concerned could not have reacted more rapidly than he did. On the evidence presented the driver was absolved from responsibility for the accident. This early case shows how the psychologist as experimentalist, and not only the clinical psychologist, can provide relevant expert testimony.

In 1910 the Belgian psychologist Varendonck was called as an expert witness in a different kind of case. For the preliminary hearing Varendonck was given the task of evaluating the evidence of two little girls who had alleged a criminal assault on them. He decided to conduct an investigation with other children of similar age and social background, and to these he submitted questions similar to those the two girls had been asked. His subjects were 22 children aged 8 years. When asked the leading question, 'Didn't a man approach you?' and invited to name him, 7 of the children wrote down a name. The experimenter continued with similar questions including, 'Wasn't it Mr A?'

and 17 of the 22 children said that it was. The Belgian psychologist's evidence did more than merely prevent a miscarriage of justice. It communicated to the court something of the psychologist's sophisticated knowledge of the influence of suggestion upon human testimony.

An important influence on modern forensic psychology was the work of G. M. Gilbert at the Nuremberg trial. Following his studies of the principal Nazi accused, Gilbert was later to establish the courses mentioned above at Michigan State University. Later Gilbert appeared as a witness for the prosecution in the trial of Adolf Eichmann. His evidence included a documentary confession that he had obtained from one of the Nuremberg witnesses, Colonel Hoess, who had been executed many years before the trial of Eichmann. Gilbert had asked Hoess to write an account of how mass extermination of human life, 10,000 people a day at Auschwitz concentration camp, had been organized. This document fully implicated Eichmann in these murders, at which both Hoess and Eichmann had assisted. The evidence proved highly damaging to the denials of the accused, and greatly strengthened the case of the prosecution. In this instance we are reminded that the prosecution, as well as the defence, may well make use of the psychologist as an expert witness.

A different kind of use of the testimony of psychologists has been discussed more fully elsewhere (McKellar, 1952). This involved a civil case in which a Negro took proceedings against an American railway company for refusing to serve him in one of its dining cars. The decision of the court went in favour of the Negro. The company concerned subsequently made special provision, set up a table separated by a partition from the rest of the car, and argued that such segregation did not constitute discrimination 'provided facilities are equal'. When the issue came before the Supreme Court two psychologists, Deutscher and Chein, assisted in preparing the evidence. A questionnaire and covering letter were sent to some 800 behavioural scientists, including psychologists and anthropologists. Of the 517 who replied 90 per cent indicated their opinion that segregation had detrimental effects even if equal facilities were provided. A further 83 per cent gave the opinion that such segregation had harmful effects on those enforcing it as well as on those who were discriminated against.

In recent years in America, though to a lesser extent in Britain, psychologists – particularly clinical psychologists – have appeared as expert witnesses in court. A fuller understanding by judges, magistrates, and lawyers of what they can and cannot contribute may encourage courts to make wider use of such testimony. To make explicit any personal bias in this matter perhaps I should add that on the one occasion – which I have no particular urge to repeat – on which I appeared in this capacity myself it was before an American court as an expert witness in a murder trial. The testimony I was asked to give was on hallucination on the one hand and normal aggression on the other, these being two subjects into which I have researched. Scrupulous fairness was observable on the part of the District Attorney who prosecuted, on the one hand, and on the part of the judge on the other. On the whole I felt myself to have been very fairly treated by the court.

Other witnesses have been much less happy about their experiences. Courts of law, on the whole, tend to mistrust expert witnesses, particularly those who represent any profession whose name begins with 'psych—'. Moreover, since psychiatrists have been much more often called than psychologists two unfortunate results have followed. First, courts in Britain are largely unaware of the many and differing contributions that psychologists could make in areas remote from psychiatry; some examples have been given above. Secondly, psychologists when they do appear often receive inappropriate mistrust resulting from confusion with members of another profession. Certainly in this chapter I hope to show that the bad reputation that psychiatrists have with the courts – a reputation which through confusion the psychologist is liable to have to share – results from something more complex than merely deserved reputation. There have, however, been psychiatrists, as there have been psychologists, who have performed far from adequately in the witness box, particularly under cross-examination. Jeffery (1964) reports on several such cases, in which for example psychologist witnesses were subjected to the technique of 'selective demolition', being cross-examined on individual questions asked, and answers given in, intelligence tests. Some witnesses were also tempted into making highly fanciful and speculative interpretations of Rorschach and other projective tests. These interpretations were then treated devastatingly in the subsequent part of the cross-examination. This paper suggests the wisdom of both prior training and caution once in the box. Courts deal harshly with pretence, with unsupported opinions, and with lapses into pomposity. The inability to say 'I don't know' has much to do with the failures of the psychologists quoted in the article. By contrast, from the murder trial in which I myself appeared as an expert witness in the United States, I quote a more satisfactory performance. The witness concerned was Dr John Clarke, a clinical psychologist, who had submitted the accused to a considerable number of tests. The cross-examination may be quoted at one point when the attorney sought to elicit an opinion on the behaviour of the accused, in court.

ATTORNEY: You said, Doctor, that the accused became emotionally excited while you were testing and interviewing him?

WITNESS: Yes.

ATTORNEY: When the same matters came up in the court, didn't you see him become emotionally excited?

WITNESS: No.

ATTORNEY: Why not?

WITNESS: Because from where I was sitting I could only see the back of his head.

This extract from the cross-examination is the more interesting in the context of the cross-examination as a whole, which was an extended one. During this the attorney tempted the witness in every possible way to engage in rash speculation about the emotional life of the accused. The witness, for his part, stuck firmly to what he had seen and heard of the actual behaviour of the accused, during the many hours he had tested him. He refused, politely but firmly, to go beyond the information available to him.

There have been too many expert witnesses who have gone to testify unprepared, whether as expert witnesses or as witnesses on ordinary points of fact. Any citizen may find himself in this position, and it is desirable that he should be forewarned. As a teacher I have been concerned to instruct my own students, who, as psychologists, may themselves one day be called as expert witnesses. Valuable help has been obtained at Sheffield University from our Forensic Medicine Department, and from colleagues who are experienced in appearing in court as expert witnesses. In this respect it seems desirable that psychologists should learn not only from forensic psychiatrists. There are other professional men who are at present considerably more acceptable to courts of law than either psychiatrists or psychologists. Thus on occasion courts are interested in such questions as whether medical opinion supports the view that an accused was drunk at the time of an offence. On other occasions they seek information on such matters as the cause and time of death. Medical specialists, prominent among them pathologists, who can tell them these things are acceptable to the court, and are often well experienced in the hazardous business of appearing in the witness stand. They often have useful information to impart from which people about to testify for the first time, or witnesses representing relatively inexperienced professions like psychology, have much to learn.

THE COURTROOM SITUATION

The behaviour and subjective experiences of people, in courts of law as elsewhere, are a legitimate part of the subject matter of psychology. First may be noted the territorial character of the situation. For some people, such as magistrates and judges, lawyers and barristers, the courtroom is familiar territory. For others it may provide a situation in which emotion seriously interferes with thinking, among such people being plaintiff and defendant, juryman and witness, and an accused himself. Under the influence of anxiety, awe, or plain fear, ordinarily intelligent people may behave stupidly. Those who are honestly attempting to tell the truth may give a convincing impression of deceit. And under cross-examination, with accompanying fluster, even experienced expert witnesses may appear both incompetent and unintelligent. Moreover in the elementary matter of audibility many courtrooms leave much to be desired. A combination of bad acoustics and the lowered voice of a frightened witness results in much of the evidence not being heard from the public gallery; one hopes that the juryman on such occasions fares better.

An excellent precedent is written into the legal code of the State of California: 'It is the right of a witness to be protected from irrelevant, improper, or insulting questions, and from harsh and insulting demeanour.' It is the task of any chairman to exercise control over what is going on under his chairmanship. The presiding magistrate or judge is a kind of chairman, and if he is a good one he accepts his responsibility to protect interested parties, including witnesses, where this is necessary. Much depends on the judge or magistrate, and what he is, or is not, prepared to permit in his court. This is the more important in that many laymen – witnesses, jurymen, or accused – enter court unaware of the debate character of court proceedings. A court case is not a kind of scientific investigation designed to elicit the truth, but resembles more closely a debate between prosecution and defence, with the judge acting as a kind of referee or chairman. It is his task to impose and insist on certain rules. Fairly obviously debating is an uncertain way of arriving at the truth, or a sensible course of action, particularly when the issues are complex. In discussions with police officers I have often found them indignant about the way in which a weak judge or magistrate permits excess in the matter of cross-examination by barristers appearing for the defence.

Another category of people who may undergo stress resulting from the debate character of a court of law are expert witnesses. An extreme case concerned one pathologist who went into the witness box expecting a routine cross-examination. He was there for three days. Moreover, in this instance, there are good grounds for believing that his inability to stand up to this prolonged ordeal did not help the course of justice. Sometimes a witness may perform badly under cross-examination because of some unwise oversimplification he is not permitted to correct. An instance of this took place during the Straffen murder trial, when a psychiatrist witness was questioned about Straffen's intelligence quotient. In the previous examination-in-chief he had said that the I.Q. was 63. He had then added, most unwisely, that this meant '63 per cent' of normal intelligence. Subsequently in a harassing cross-examination by the prosecution, which seized upon this mistake, he was asked awkward questions like 'how could a person have an I.Q. of more than 100?' We are used to thinking of 100 as the top point of a percentage scale, but it is the *average* I.Q. which is 100. The I.Q. is not, of course, a percentage but a ratio of mental age to chronological age, the resulting figure being multiplied by 100; thus when M.A. = C.A. in the average case $\frac{\text{M.A.}}{\text{C.A.}} \times 100 = 100$. The equation of intelligence quotient with a percentage was thus a bad error, and one which the prosecuting barrister did not hesitate to exploit. Harassed by repeated questions, given little time to answer them, and frequently interrupted while answering, the witness had no opportunity to correct his error and explain what he meant. The result was disastrous, not least from the point of view of the communication of relevant information to the jury.

To continue with this question of the debating atmosphere of the court: a somewhat different problem faced another expert witness in another murder trial. There were some vigorous exchanges between a formidable prosecutor, Sir Hartley Shawcross, and an experienced forensic psychiatrist, Dr Henry Yellowlees. The word 'paranoia' had been used, and Shawcross had asked whether the term 'paranoia' (a medical term) was included in the legal category 'disease of mind'. Yellowlees had assented. Shawcross had then produced a text-book of psychiatry which stated that paranoia was not a 'disease' but rather an 'intellectual anomaly'. He then asked the witness: 'Do you not agree?' Dr Yellowlees, as the witness concerned, exhibited his determination to communicate clearly to the court, despite this skilful debating question. He said: 'I do *not* agree with any *sentence* taken out of its context applying to anyone thirty years after the writer has died, but I agree entirely with *the views* expressed in that chapter.' In other words the witness insisted on the importance of the meaning the words were meant to convey, but refused to be trapped by an experienced cross-examiner's use of the words the text-book writer had happened to use in conveying his meaning. He was lucid in his communication of these relevant facts to the court, and rightly so: accidental similarities and differences between medical and legal words should not be the basis on which a jury can be expected to come to its decision.

Particularly in cases in which the mental abnormality of an accused is claimed, expert witnesses may appear to disagree when they do not. Psychiatrists and others may differ only in how they equate the technical terms of their own speciality to the legal categories. Thus the legal category of 'disease of mind' may be important to the court: it occurs in the McNaghten Rules, which still prevail in many countries and many American States. Some psychiatrists have interpreted 'disease of mind' to mean 'psychosis', while others have interpreted it more broadly to include psychopathy as well. Thus two expert witnesses may appear and may be asked, 'Is this man suffering from a disease of mind?' One may say 'yes' and the other 'no'. Both if given the chance, which in many famous British murder trials they were not, would have been prepared to agree if asked, 'Is this man a psychopath?' The confusion of the jury, who are laymen both as regards medicine and as regards law, faced with these subtle problems of translation as between medical and legal terms, must be considerable. This confusion may be added to if, under the stress of cross-examination, a psychiatrist witness resorts to peculiar uses of language of his own. Thus during one trial I heard one psychiatrist witness, during almost his whole testimony, use the word 'normal' to mean 'not psychotic'. The cross-examining barrister did not fail to exploit this error, spent much time listing the obviously extremely abnormal conduct of the accused, and kept the witness saying 'yes' that the man in question was 'normal'. The word had for the witness his own private meaning 'yes abnormal, but not psychotic'.

Some university teachers find it more difficult to lecture on subjects about which they are well informed than those of which they have limited knowledge. The same problem may confront a witness, particularly an expert witness, who is asked seemingly innocent – though actually complex – questions in court. If he is well informed on the matter the witness possesses a network of associations, and an awareness of complexities which it may be exceedingly difficult to begin to explain. It is most difficult of all to explain to those who believe, or pretend to believe, that the issues are simple. Scientists and teachers on the whole tend to discourage dogmatism in their colleagues and students, and to have considerable doubts about the intellectual value of the opinions of those who exhibit it. In this respect courts of law, and teachers in universities, possess somewhat different conceptions of 'an expert'. Police officers with whom I have discussed this issue incline, on the whole, to the view that it is the testimony of witnesses who exhibit confident dogmatism that tends to be accepted. Experiments on testimony conducted with classes of police officers have been on the whole successful in convincing them that it is possible to be absolutely certain and absolutely wrong. Yet obviously many problems can arise in the courts from these facts. The systems of knowledge of the lawyer who asks the questions, and of the expert witness who is required to answer, are different. Each is disposed by his training to make distinctions which may have little meaning to the other. Thus for example a cross-examining barrister was successful in getting an expert witness to agree that the accused was suffering from 'disease of character' and not 'disease of mind'. This distinction was legally very important indeed, but is not meaningful to medical science. A psychiatrist, by contrast, may wish to make distinctions between 'true paranoia', 'paranoid schizophrenia', 'paranoid personality', and 'paranoid reactions'. An illustration of this may be taken from a case which occurred in Jamaica in which the woman psychiatrist called said in the examination-in-chief that the accused had 'a paranoid reaction resulting from brain damage: the "punch drunk" reaction'. In subsequent cross-examination she was asked, 'You say this man has paranoia?' Fortunately in this case the witness was permitted to explain what she meant and make the distinction. Paranoia, discussed in a previous chapter, is a psychosis which has no ascertainable accompaniments of brain injury. By 'paranoid reaction' she had meant that the man accused had persecutory delusions for which brain injury seemed to have been responsible. This distinction could be made, was permitted to be made, and was relevant to the evidence. Unfortunately this does not always happen either because of the debate character of a court's proceedings, or because the systems of knowledge of the expert witness and the lawyer are so different. An expert witness may be asked a question which seems a simple question to everyone else present, but to which no man who is truly an expert can answer 'yes' or 'no'. Under these circumstances an experienced pathologist expert witness advises the witness to resort to the procedure of saying, 'I cannot answer the question as asked without misleading the court'. The witness cannot otherwise be sure about how either his 'yes' or his 'no' will be understood. Very probably it will be interpreted differently by the different people present.

As we have seen, much depends in a major criminal case upon the judge. Sometimes he does not help. Up till the time of the 1959 Mental Health Act the law made little provision for distinguishing between the categories of 'intellectually subnormal' and 'psychopath'. There was in fact much confusion between the two. On one occasion when a lawyer, in the Court of Appeal, attempted to make the distinction he was sharply rebuked by a former Lord Chief Justice. Mr Justice Goddard added: 'Jurymen are not college professors . . . it would only confuse them to go into metaphysical and philosophical distinctions.' This distinction between low intelligence and the absence of conscience and usual moral standards of psychopathy is not one which it is difficult to make. The 1959 Act now makes explicit in law the fact that a psychopath may be of normal, average, or superior intelligence. Psychopathy has, as such, no particular relation to intelligence. Unfortunately up till the time of the Act many cases came before the courts in which the accused were both intellectually subnormal and psychopathic. The result was considerable confusion, and, as we have seen, judges did not always help those who sought to make these necessary distinctions.

THE PERSONALITY OF THE ABNORMAL OFFENDER

In a trial for murder the law is interested in the possible abnormality of the accused in three main respects. First, the state of the accused at the time of trial is relevant to his 'fitness to plead': this means that he should be able to understand the evidence and instruct his counsel. Secondly, the trial is concerned with the state of mind of the accused when the offence was committed: thus the McNaghten Rules, and their alternatives, relate to the time of the act. Thirdly, if he is found 'legally insane' the law is interested in the normality or otherwise in relation to disposal. This is obviously especially important under systems of law which involve a death penalty which effectively ensures that mistakes cannot afterwards be undone. Such mistakes do occur. As early as 1932 E. M. Borchard was able to produce a book called *Convicting the Innocent* which dealt with no fewer than sixty-five people who, in Britain or America, had been convicted and subsequently found to be innocent.

The presence of mental abnormality in an accused is not necessarily relevant to the offence committed. An obvious example would be a man with a compulsion to steal motor cars who had run over somebody with the car he has stolen. His kleptomania may be genuine and still irrelevant to a charge of manslaughter brought against him. Thus in the trial of Daniel McNaghten, following his examination by nine physicians the opinion was advanced that 'the deed of murder followed immediately from the delusions'. The defence of insanity in cases involving murder has been part of English law since the time of Edward I. But McNaghten's case, and the subsequent Rules which emerged from it, set an important precedent for later trials. This applied not only to England itself, but elsewhere as well. The McNaghten Rules are still important in many American States (murder being a State and not a Federal offence), and also in many Commonwealth countries, for example Australia and New Zealand. In England the 1957 Homicide Act (see below) brought in the further possibility of a plea of 'diminished responsibility', which produced considerable changes in legal practice. Nevertheless some of the legally and psychologically most interesting cases of murder tried in Britain were tried under the McNaghten Rules, and admirably illustrate certain of the difficulties that impede clear and unambiguous communication in court. This may now be considered.

In a previous chapter we saw that Daniel McNaghten would probably have been diagnosed today as a case of 'true paranoia', that is as a somewhat rare kind of psychotic. The fact that many people tried in England under the McNaghten Rules, for which McNaghten's case provided a basis, have been quite different personalities, has not helped clear communication in court about them. In McNaghten's own case the trial was stopped, and he was found 'not guilty on the grounds of insanity'. The decision at the trial gave rise to much public concern. One Member of Parliament went so far as to move for permission to bring a bill to abolish altogether the plea of insanity in cases of murder, but fortunately the proposal found no seconder. Instead the House of Lords submitted certain questions to the judges of England, and the answers given to these form the McNaghten Rules. Five main questions were asked. It is part of the answer to the second and third questions that is usually quoted as 'The McNaghten Rules', though we must not forget that the judges had many other things to say. Among these was their decision 'that every man is to be presumed sane . . . until the contrary is proved'. Thus although in respect of guilt the burden of proof rests with the prosecution, in the matter of insanity the burden of proof rests with the defence. The central part of the Rules may be quoted.

It must be clearly proved that, at the time of committing of the act, the party accused was labouring under such a defect of reason from disease of the mind, as not to know the nature and quality of the act he was doing, or if he did know it that he did not know he was doing what was wrong.

The above text is important as virtually every one of its words has been debated and interpreted in court. Our concern is with the difficulties which this statement introduces as a basis of communication between people whose concepts and ways of thinking are markedly different. There have, in fact, been occasions on which the common sense of the court has prevailed and reasonable decisions have been reached despite the difficulties of the words of the formula. But unfortunately there have also been other occasions, when these words have proved a fertile source of ambiguity and confusion.

An example may be taken in the term 'wrong', which appears in the statement quoted above. 'Wrong' was interpreted by the judges who drew up the rules – as is clear from their answer to the first of the five questions put to them – to mean 'contrary to the law'. The same interpretation has prevailed in British and those American State courts which use the Rule. It may not, however, be obvious to an expert witness that he should not take at its apparent meaning the question 'Did he know he was doing wrong?' The witness must realize, and many witnesses obviously haven't realized this, that the question really means 'Did he know he was acting contrary to the law?' To be asked one question in words which form another question is confusing. It has proved to be confusing enough in England; but even greater confusions can occur in different American States where the Mc-Naghten Rules prevail. The law between States differs. Thus for example the question 'Did the accused know he was doing wrong?' (i.e. acting contrary to the law) might be answered 'yes' in New Mexico, but 'no' in Texas. There are certain acts which are contrary to New Mexican law which would be condoned under the somewhat excessively broad interpretation of 'justifiable homicide' that prevails in Texas. In this matter I am referring to an actual case which I observed, that was tried in New Mexico close to the Texas border. Under the McNaghten Rules (which prevail in both States) the psychiatrist witnesses were being asked a seemingly simple question about 'wrong', but they were in fact being asked a very complex question indeed: they were being asked to assess the knowledge that the man on trial for murder possessed about comparative law. It is very probable in this case that the accused was faulty in his knowledge – though a subsequent interview with him to ascertain this was not practicable. Evidence at the trial indicated that he believed himself fully justified in the murder he had committed, and for which he was convicted. But if he had been tried twenty miles further east, in Texas, he would probably have been acquitted. There, his feeling of justification would have coincided with Texan State law.

The phrase about knowing 'the nature and quality of the act' may be noted. There have been occasions when judges themselves have sought, quite unhelpfully, to explain to the jury what this phrase meant. At one British trial, the judge's illustration was that if a man strangled somebody, and all the time thought he was merely squeezing the juice out of an orange, 'that would be a case of not knowing the nature and quality of the act'. One standard legal text-book takes the illustration of 'sawing somebody in two while thinking one is merely sawing up a log of wood'. If these figments of legal imagining are taken by a gullible juryman to be the kind of thing to look for in an accused, it is not surprising that they fail to find them. Other presuppositions may be brought into the courtroom by the jury themselves, for example if 'schizophrenia' is mentioned they may be looking for a 'split mind' of the Jekyll–Hyde type. With this presupposition, reinforced so often by the press, a juryman may well decide – despite the medical evidence – that the accused can't be a schizophrenic and isn't legally insane.

'Disease of mind' is a phrase which has resulted in many confusions. As we have seen different expert witnesses interpret this legal category differently, and may appear to disagree when in fact they do not. It will be noted that for a McNaghten plea to be sustained 'disease of mind' must be established. Some subtle problems arise from a tradition of English law which distinguishes between 'disease of mind' and 'mental defect', as two mutually exclusive categories. Unfortunately it is a habit of speech of psychologists, which they have taught to psychiatrists, to use the term 'mental deficiency' when they mean to indicate intellectual subnormality. Unfortunately the lawyer's concept of 'mental defect' and the psychologist's concept of 'mental deficiency' are liable to be confused. Thus a psychiatrist or psychologist who is innocently attempting to communicate the fact that a man is intellectually subnormal may be understood to be saying 'he is not suffering from disease of mind'. He is, in short, conceding that the McNaghten Rules do not apply. Since he is in fact trying to communicate something quite different he is liable to be unaware of the concession he is making to the prosecution.

Another subtle problem arising from the McNaghten Rules concerns its phrase 'defect of reason', which like 'disease of mind' must also be established. We have seen that many people have been tried under the McNaghten Rules who have in no way at all resembled McNaghten himself, as personalities. Is 'defect of reason' to be taken to mean acting under the influence of delusions, as McNaghten undoubtedly was? Or is it to be taken to include intellectual subnormality, an obvious attribute of many of the people subsequently tried under the Rules? The cross-examining barrister may himself be unaware of the ambiguity of his question to the witness about presence or absence of 'defect of reason'. Alternatively he may skilfully exploit this ambiguity for the purpose of confusing the witness with an apparently simple question. In either case the witness is in a difficult position, as he either does not realize the problem that confronts him, or if he is aware of it he has no idea how his 'yes' or his 'no' will be interpreted by the court. Here as often the McNaghten Rules tend to provoke rather random answers to ambiguous questions. The underlying issues are two: (1) is the accused intellectually subnormal? (2) is he influenced by delusions in his thinking? If asked this way both questions can be answered briefly, and the answers are unlikely to be misunderstood.

IMPROVEMENT OF COURT COMMUNICATION

The Homicide Act of 1957 introduced a new rule which, as Connolly (1963) has pointed out, had the purpose of saving 'the judge having to pass a formal sentence of death in a case of insanity outside the McNaghten Rules'. If under this rule 'diminished responsibility' can be established then the offence becomes manslaughter and not murder. This defence is allowed when the accused

was suffering from such abnormality of mind (whether arising from a condition of arrested or retarded development of mind or any inherent causes or induced by disease or injury) as substantially impaired his mental responsibility for his acts or omissions or being a party to the killing.

As with the McNaghten Rules the burden of proof of diminished responsibility lies with the defence. The introduction of this newer measure has been an advantage from the point of increased clarity of communication in court. In particular the McNaghten formula did not easily apply to intellectually subnormal offenders on the one hand, and psychopaths on the other. A law formulated round the case of a dignified, reserved, but severely deluded paranoiac does not readily permit stretching to cover unambiguous communication about a homicidal psychopath. Thus for example McNaghten himself and a man like Neville Heath were quite different kinds of personalities. The diminished responsibility plea favours less confused discussion in court about these other types of abnormal offender.

American States differ markedly in the systems of law they use. Some still use the McNaghten Rules. Others take as their basis 'The Durham Decision'; it operates in for example the District of Columbia. Of importance to legal reform and clear communication in court is the present activity of the Washington School of Psychiatry. Under the direction of Judge David Bazelon this is conducting a comprehensive investigation into 'Psychiatry and the Law'. Judge Bazelon, of the American Supreme Court, was himself responsible in 1954 for probably the most far-reaching attempt to replace the McNaghten Rules by something more up to date. This was the Durham Decision. Under the Durham Rule

an accused is not criminally responsible if his unlawful act was the product of mental disease or mental defect.

In this rule it will be noted that the category of 'mental defect' as well as that of 'mental disease' is explicitly included. The Durham Rule has, on the whole, been well received by many responsible legal and psychiatric experts. But any legal test is likely to give rise to problems of communication. These problems can be reduced in several ways. Better education will minimize barriers that stem from presuppositions and stereotypes. Responsible chairmanship from the Bench can help to remove barriers arising from the atmosphere of debate of courtroom proceedings. Newer formulations like those of diminished responsibility and the Durham Rule may assist in the problems of translation as between the categories of the law and those of the expert witness. One leading American forensic psychiatrist has commented on the Durham Rule in these terms: 'Nearly all the articles which have appeared in both legal and psychiatric journals have praised the Durham Rule as "sound psychiatrically and legally"' (Overholser, 1959; edition 1965). We can, however, be confident that neither the Durham Rule nor its alternatives will wholly remove the difficulties of communication in court about mental abnormality. The rule leaves it for jurymen to decide, as a matter of fact not of law, whether the accused is insane or not. Jurymen, as laymen, are often tenacious in their adherence to presuppositions and stereotypes about mental illness. Of great importance I suspect are detailed exchanges, outside the courtroom, between lawyers and expert witnesses, so that each may learn about the concepts of the other. For some years now the Institute of Advanced Legal Studies, of London University, has held regular inter-disciplinary meetings at which such exchanges, in depth, have taken place. Much can also be achieved, more informally, to help remove what Roger Bacon, many centuries ago, listed as four main obstacles to the attainment of truth. These were submission to unworthy authority, submission to custom, submission to popular prejudice, and concealment of ignorance by pretended wisdom.

CHAPTER FIFTEEN

The Present and the Future

I don't care who owns the problem, I just want to understand it.   GEORGE MILLER

THE growing points of scientific disciplines have often been found on their frontiers with others. Traditional divisions between the main branches of human inquiry are not wholly appropriate today. Many of them stem from Aristotle, whose dates were, after all, 384–322 B.C. These divisions are breaking down, new disciplines are being established, and in the meantime human curiosity continues. As far as psychology itself is concerned it will be wise to welcome hospitably invasions from other specialists, though on the strict understanding that return visits will be allowed. Professor George Miller, Chairman of the Psychology Department at Harvard, has himself made significant contributions on the frontier between psychology and linguistics. His statement, as a guiding principle for the future, holds much wisdom.

FRONTIERS OF PSYCHOLOGY

In Chapter 1, when trying to put human psychology within its broader framework, I argued that the scientific study of the behaviour of living organisms had hardly begun. Future developments in the understanding of behaviour within the evolutionary system as a whole inevitably depend on close collaboration with zoology. Perhaps for too long, in its adolescent years, psychology has regarded physics as its scientific model. At any rate interaction with the biological sciences, not less than the physical sciences, is very much with us today. One such interaction is with a group of men, trained as zoologists, who are called 'ethologists'. Best known of these are Lorenz and Tinburgen. Another of the ethologists has gone so far as to suggest that the term 'comparative psychology' should be abandoned altogether in favour of 'ethology'. This point of view is understandable, as are defensive operations by psychologists against it: there seems to be no good reason to abandon or rename a well-established area of psychology because of a new movement in zoology, however important. Yet under whichever label ultimately prevails we can certainly look forward to detailed study of similarities and differences of the behaviour of different species, and much profitable interaction between researchers trained in the two disciplines.

Genetics has made enormous progress in the last decade. The biochemical basis of inheritance is beginning to be understood in terms of the 'genetic code' contained in the DNA (deoxyribonucleic acid) of the nucleus of the cell itself. Another protein, RNA (ribonucleic acid), transmits this coded information from the DNA within the nucleus to the growing cells. Here again we can see the development of scientific knowledge at the frontiers of different scientific disciplines. Moreover, while geneticists have traditionally been preoccupied with the inheritance of structure, there is now a growing and lively interest also in the genetics of behaviour. Like many other things, what is today called 'psychogenetics' had its origins in the intense intellectual curiosity and broad perspective of Galton. From Galton's interest in intelligence, and the genetics of families in which high ability occurred, emerged techniques for intelligence testing. Galton was interested in the inheritance of other aspects of cognitive mental life, such as diagram forms. He was also the father of the method of twin study. As is now known, approximately one quarter of all twins are of the identical twin type. In them heredity is, as it were, held constant, and the differences which emerge between such identical twins can be investigated as studies of the effects of social influences, and the learning process. Twin studies have repeatedly shown that the measurable intelligence of identical twins reared apart is remarkably similar. Other twin studies have contributed evidence of the extent of hereditary predisposition to personality abnormalities such as psychosis, neurosis, and homosexuality. Twin studies have even been applied with success to the study of criminality (compare Eysenck, 1964). For many years the psychologist, with his interest in behaviour, has followed the geneticist, with his concern mainly with structure, into the field of animal experimentation. In rats cognitive traits have been studied, for example the maze-learning behaviour of successive generations of strains of 'maze bright' and 'maze dull' rats. Temperamental traits have been similarly investigated, for example in Britain by Broadhurst with his 'emotionally stable' and 'emotionally unstable' strains of rats. More recently psychologists have employed the geneticists' own favourite subject, the Drosophila fruit fly. Numerous generations of these fast-breeding organisms have been studied in terms of such behavioural qualities as general activity and food preferences. Thus Connolly (1966) used a wild type of Pacific strain of these organisms, *Drosophila melanogaster*, and bred selectively for activity. Activity was measured by distance covered in three different types of apparatus: two types of straight runway, and one circular runway marked off in units of distance covered. After twenty-five generations, statistical differences between the two selectively bred groups emerged; the experiments have continued through subsequent generations. But if Drosophila can breed faster than either rats or men, computers can 'breed' faster still. In stimulating the breeding of 'statistical drosophila' the computer has proved its value to the geneticist himself. It is likely to be of similar use to investigators of the genetics of behaviour.

One of the most vigorous areas of psychological research in Britain, the United States, Canada, and Soviet Russia has only been lightly touched on in this book. This is physiological psychology. The huge contributions of British investigators to neurology have naturally promoted work in this country. The proximity in the University of McGill of two distinguished scientists, Penfield in neurology, and Hebb in psychology, has assisted Canadian advances in this field. Soviet Russia is also mentioned explicitly in that a strongly physiological tradition prevails in much Russian psychology for historical reasons. Thus, certainly until very recent years at least, students of psychology in Russia have been required – as part of their course – to dissect the whole human body. Some younger Russian psychologists have expressed to me the opinion that they personally had at least as intensive a course in anatomy and physiology as had contemporaries who were medical students. At any rate they get a great deal, and this helps to account for the strongly physiologizing tendency in much theory, and the character of much research. Investigation of the relations between molar events (behaviour of the organism in its environment) and molecular events (processes within the organism) remains an important trend in contemporary psychology in many parts of the world.

The future importance of another frontier area is perhaps less obvious. It concerns two of the most central topics of psychology: perception and remembering. The psychologist shares with representatives of several other disciplines an interest in the problem of establishing with accuracy the facts about a past event. Two of these other disciplines are history and law. Moreover there are instances in which what was initially of importance to courts of law proved later to be of concern to the historian. Emphasis has been placed on one such instance: the trial of the principal Nazi leaders at Nuremberg. Another was the assassination of President Kennedy. Whether we are dealing with events that interest law or history or events in which the two shade into one another, there is much that psychology has to contribute. While new and appropriate experiments involving perceiving and remembering can be designed, much can be learned from repetitions, with slight modifications, of well-tried experiments. Thus Ward (1949) showed how the familiar serial reproduction experiment can be modified so as to replicate in the laboratory the processes of historical change. As we have seen, in the United States, and to a lesser extent in Britain also, psychologists are making valuable contributions to problems of law, either as expert witnesses in court, or as background researchers. Research into the closely related problems of history have hardly begun, and may well prove to be exceedingly important. Much could be contributed, through serial reproduction and other experiments, to the understanding of the myths of history, the propaganda of the past, and the stereotypes that have survived about people and events of former ages.

In his *Introduction to Social Psychology* of 1908 William McDougall pointed to the 'remarkable fact' that psychology had neither established itself, nor been commonly recognized as 'the essential common foundation on which all the social sciences . . . must be built'. He sought to remedy this by giving central importance to motivation as a problem, and by formulating a theory of his own in this field. Murray, as we have seen in earlier sections (Chapters 9 and 11), sought to study motives not as universal human phenomena, but in terms of personality differences. Subsequent investigators have made considerable use of Murray's index of 'needs' or individual motivational variables. One group of investigators has used both Murray's concepts and his technique the Thematic Apperception Test in the field of the social sciences. Murray showed that we can study an individual personality in terms of the stories and narratives he constructs in response to TAT pictures. McClelland and his associates proceeded on the assumption that we can do the same thing with social groups, for example nations at particular stages of their history. Analysis, similar in principle to the analysis of TAT records, can be used on the products of a culture: its plays and other literary productions, children's readers used in the classroom, and even popular songs can be similarly analysed. Particular attention has been paid to four of Murray's motives: n. achievement, n. affiliation, n. aggression, and n. power. Thus for example 400 years of English history were examined by content analysis of popular dramas as index of n. achievement. The study revealed, from this content analysis, a peak of n. achievement in the reign of Henry VIII extending to Elizabeth, a trough in the seventeenth and eighteenth centuries, and a second peak with the Industrial Revolution. A study of street ballads over the same period yielded a similar graph. Different nations at the same period of time have been compared by similar methods. As at the time McDougall wrote (1908), the psychologist has not yet provided an adequate scientific basis for many of the interests of disciplines like politics, economics, and history. Yet the researches mentioned represent one line of attack on these problems. They are, incidentally, taking place along the pathway originally suggested by McDougall: motivation theory, and its

o

development. Among other attempts of a related kind may be noted work such as that of R. B. Cattell, in using the technique of factor analysis in the statistical study of nations. On the basis of available statistics Cattell has found it possible to classify national differences into certain dimensions, somewhat resembling personality dimensions. We might for example expect information of a statistical kind on such matters as annual death rate from tuberculosis or cancer; number of men eminent in art, science, and literature; number of telephones per head of population, to yield inter-correlations. This proves to be the case and has yielded, in subsequent factor analysis, variables like matriarchal–patriarchal, affluence *v.* narrow poverty, and the like. These Cattell regards as at least the beginnings of a study of some of the basic dimensions of nations. Whichever of these two methods – McClelland's or Cattell's – is used, or whether some alternative emerges, progress towards the goal which McDougall envisaged is likely to be made in the next decades.

SCIENTIFIC NAMING

We gain greater ability to deal with a complex subject matter by having words, particularly precisely defined words, with which to discuss it. The point was made at an early date by J. B. Watson, who equated what the psycho-analysts called 'the unconscious' with what he called 'the unverbalized'. More recently Skinner – in defending a more sophisticated version of behaviourism – has said: 'To know is very largely to be able to talk about.' Throughout the history of human thought different thinkers have repeatedly stressed the importance and usefulness of being able to name objects, events, and processes. Thus as Crowther (1966) has pointed out, the invention of the word 'physicist' and even the word 'scientist' stems from William Whewell's introduction to the language of science of 1840. In this period physics faced problems similar to those which confront psychology today. Michael Faraday found himself in difficulties over describing the numerous electrical phenomena he had discovered, and lacked words with which to name them. We are, for example, indebted to Faraday's own personal physician, Dr Nicholl, for suggesting the term 'electrode'. Fortunately perhaps the good doctor's further suggestions, 'eisode' and 'exode', were replaced, on the suggestion Whewell made to Faraday, by the terms 'anode' and 'cathode'.

Karl Linnaeus provided the biological sciences with one of their most powerful tools in his linguistical and logically sophisticated system of naming that permitted the classification of all living things, both plant and animal. The subject matter of psychology – experience and behaviour – awaits such a contribution. Of special interest is the fact that Linnaeus, whose biology differed from the subsequent biology of Darwin in fundamental ways, nevertheless provided a way of naming of enormous use to post-Darwinian biology. We may contrast the nomenclature provided by too many of the psychologists who have contributed to this field. The names provided have often proved of limited value precisely because they were so theoretically loaded. An example can be found in the work of one major theorist of considerable stature and importance in the history of psychology. Clarke L. Hull's nomenclature was a complex system of words and symbols, but this was too closely related to his theory of learning, a theory which today has a more than uncertain future. Had this nomenclature been of a theoretically more neutral kind it might well have survived in a way it probably will not. Thus, to return to physics, we have noted the contribution of William Whewell, who was heavily involved with its nomenclature. As part of his contribution when the physical sciences were similarly concerned with naming, Whewell drew up seventeen criteria to govern the invention of new scientific names. One of these criteria stated that terms which imply theoretical views should be advisable only in so far as the theory in question has been proved (Crowther, 1966).

Criteria of this lack of theoretical neutrality can also be made of many of the terms which stem from Freud. When Freud looked to the available psychology of his day he found it irrelevant to his purposes: irrelevant to the understanding of the human personality, its motives, and problems of adjustment. Thus he himself contributed something to fill this gap and, together with much theory, provided names for the complex processes he uncovered.

In accord with the dictum Skinner was later to state – 'to know is largely to be able to talk about' – Freud sought to spell out the processes of mental conflict as interactions between 'ego', 'id', and 'super-ego'. Unfortunately acceptance of this terminology carries with it strong tendencies to reification. As Bruner has put it, we are too readily tempted to personify these names of complex processes as 'little men', and are tempted to think of Freud's theory as 'peopled by actors'. Thus Bruner refers to 'the blind, energetic, pleasure-seeking id', the ego 'battling for its being by diverting the energy of the others to its own use', while 'the priggish and punitive super-ego' surveys the fight. Unfortunately elsewhere are other constructs of Freudian theory which also lend themselves to concrete forms of thinking. In 1957 I discussed this tendency in Freud's terminology in more detail, for example his concept of the libido, which one is tempted to think of with an irrelevant surplus of meaning belonging more properly to electricity and plumbing. Some of these overtones have dated rather badly, and may lose by seeming 'unfashionable' to the modern thinker. It is unfortunate that Freud – who contributed so much – should have provided a terminology with both theoretical and irrelevantly concrete overtones. Here as often the close relation between a terminology and its related theory has tended to impede the pursuit of observation. The point is well made by R. H. Thouless (1935), who argues that, if in the ordinary course of development there is, before the age of five years, a strong attachment by the child to the parent of the opposite sex, this *in itself* is well worth knowing. It is important in and for itself whether we are convinced or otherwise of the Freudian theory of the Oedipus complex. Too rarely have psychologists since Freud approached this aspect of child development in accord with this admirable suggestion. They have been preoccupied – in too many books, and too many symposia – with 'proving' or 'disproving' the Oedipus theory.

In its progress towards the maturity of a science there is much evidence that psychology has misspent much of its adolescence in attempting prematurely to develop 'grown-up ways', alias a body of 'grown-up' scientific theory. The division of the psychologists of the past into quasi-militant camps of adherents of rival theories has not helped matters. Group-conscious groups in science, as elsewhere, tend to be loyal to their party: the end result is much wasted effort. Ultimately it does not matter much whether Freud, or Hull, or some other great thinker was 'right' or 'wrong'. Science is a collective enterprise, and its methods are eclectic. Thus the correctness or otherwise of a given thinker is in the end only a matter of historical interest. What does matter is that a tested system of knowledge be built up with as little time and effort as possible spent on irrelevancies.

THEORY IN PSYCHOLOGY

This book has, on the whole, attempted to avoid theory. This is not because I am opposed to, or uninterested in it. On the contrary, elsewhere (1957, Chapter 11) I have been concerned with both theory itself, and the understanding of the psychology of the kinds of thinking we call 'theorizing'. In many fields of psychology of the kind we have examined, theory is premature: basic information is lacking. Theory in psychology might be likened to the curves we draw through points on a sheet of graph paper. If there are two few points – or observations – then there are many different lines – or theories – that can be drawn through them. When observations are limited in number, then the alternative theories possible may be very numerous. To reduce their number we need more points, more observations, that will restrict and more closely define the graph lines that can be drawn. Here we are concerned with the relation between fact-collecting, or accumulation of observations as I would prefer to call it, and theory. Not all observations are of equal value: some are mere observations of little interest, while others are theoretically important, or have hypothesis-forming attributes. In terms of our analogy some observations provide us with more than one point on the graph paper through which we seek to draw our curve. Moreover, on occasion, a single observation may be crucial in establishing a theory: since we cannot define a graph by a single point it is apparent that here the analogy used breaks down.

Illustrations of observations of this kind may be found for

example in the process of testing certain negative assertions of the sort that are sometimes made in psychology. Several instances occur, for example, in the study of the state of hypnosis. It has been held that: (1) you cannot hypnotize a person against his own volition; (2) you cannot hypnotize a psychotic; (3) you cannot induce a person when hypnotized to perform a self-destructive act (e.g., in one experiment, grasp a live rattlesnake); (4) you cannot induce a person to perform a criminal act of a kind that is contrary to the acts that he would perform when not hypnotized. Contrary instances have been provided in the case of all four assertions. It is apparent that a single positive instance, in each case, is sufficient to refute the negative assertion provided the observation is itself valid. The relation between theory (or the hypotheses generated by a theory) and observation may be complex in positive statements of the 'if . . . then' kind. Thus it may be argued 'if my hypothesis is valid then so and so will occur'. Even when so and so is observed we cannot conclude that this upholds the hypothesis in question unless we have ensured that uncontrolled variables have been wholly eliminated. The *post hoc, ergo propter hoc* kind of reasoning can be misleading in scientific investigations, as in everyday life situations. A friend of mine was scratched by a black cat on Hallowe'en Eve: the following day he passed his driving test. On occasion superstitious thinking is tempted to infer a relation between two such events, though this temptation is best resisted. The same caution is best kept in mind in, for example, studying the effects of a given treatment in the cure of a mental illness. There is much food for thought in the principle of medicine: 'it is less important to cure a patient than to happen to be treating him when he gets better.' Recovery may occur for a variety of reasons which are quite unrelated to the treatment being used. Dr Shaw, a seventeenth-century physician, made this point at an early date and wrote about 'cures' effected not by the treatment used but by 'nature, accident, or imagination' (Hunter and MacAlpine, 1963). Medical practitioners themselves tend to be twice-born in these matters today, though a pathologist colleague tells me that jurymen and others are often extremely gullible about such assertions. They learn that the deceased 'died after his last meal';

there is not necessarily any connexion between the meal itself (e.g. poisoning) and the death, and, moreover, one may overlook the fact that in any case everybody dies after his last meal. Many of the conventions upon which logical inference, and scientific investigation, depend in thinking are quite often violated in the forms of thinking that occur in everyday life.

As we have seen technical terminology may play an important part in scientific thinking. As the ideas of a science and its accompanying technical terms become widely known serial reproduction may occur: this, as we have seen, tends to be accompanied by omission and distortion, dramatization and simplification, and general misunderstanding. Sumner (1906), who himself was an important contributer to the terminology of the social sciences, has likened the process of popularization to the wear and tear and debasement of a coinage: the 'coins', alias initial ideas and terms, are, he says, 'smoothed down by wear until they are only discs of metal'. It remains, Sumner argues, a continuing problem for responsible thinkers to be working all the time 'trying to re-coin them' and thus give the ideas and concepts of science 'at least partial reality'. Psycho-analysis has suffered much from this debasement process. Earlier I tried to show that Freud and his successors had very substantial contributions to make to the understanding of human motivation: they were concerned to deal with this problem in its full complexity, and were equipped with detailed knowledge of human ego-defences and self-deception. The idea that, as regards motivation, psycho-analysis 'reduced everything to sex' has as much relation to original Freudian theory as the popularization by T. H. Huxley had to Darwin. Freud and his associates became understandably sensitive about having to explain exceedingly complex, and emotionally disturbing ideas to highly prejudiced people who basically did not understand. A distinction can perhaps be maintained between 'mere ignorance', which expresses itself with a simple 'I don't know', and a different kind of ignorance with overtones of arrogance, rigidly impenetrable defences of deafness, and strong emotion. Today a different kind of criticism of psycho-analysis must nevertheless be maintained. The 'truth' about complex matters has never been revealed to any individual thinker, or observer. Science is, of necessity, eclectic, and the insights of any scientist, however great his stature, must inevitably be only partial. The most important interactions between psychologists and psycho-analysts must be on the basis of this recognition.

THE CONVENTIONS OF A SCIENCE

Like other sciences psychology involves observation, including measurement when possible, a subsequent highly systematic kind of thinking, and the products of such thoughts. These products include rules for the classification of the phenomena studied, and rules for making predictions about them. In other words formal conventions define, and restrict, thinking of the kind we call scientific psychologizing. This definition and restriction merit emphasis. Few specialists have failed to find themselves, on occasion, in the embarrassing position of being asked questions which they are not able to answer. Their questioner, himself not a specialist, quite honestly expects an answer to what seems to him a simple question. In this respect the psychologist, whose subject matter, experience, and behaviour are likely to interest other people, resembles the expert witness in court. Often, like the expert witness, he may have to answer, 'I don't know', but perhaps even more often he is forced to reply, 'I cannot answer your question, as asked, without being misleading.' Reasons for these difficulties merit examination. They vary. Some questions about subjective experience or observable behaviour have not, as yet, provoked the curiosity of psychologists, who have not always in the past been broad enough in their conception of their subject matter. Others are confused and meaningless. Others again involve reformulation in technical terms, unknown to the questioner, before what really interests him about what he is asking can be clarified. Many questions are the product of verbal ambiguity: a good illustration comes from the discussion by Koffka (1935) of the question 'Do human beings have instincts?' Koffka quickly makes the point 'It depends on what you mean by "instincts".' He goes on to explain that if we mean stereotyped forms of patterned response of the kind common in the insect world, then human beings have few if any instincts. But if by 'instincts' we mean basic needs which are directed towards specific goal objects, then in this sense we may speak about human instincts. My brief summary of how one historically important psychologist brought out the complexities of a seemingly simple question does not do justice either to his answer, or to the complex problems involved. But it helps to illustrate one common kind of question-and-answer situation in which the psychologist, or psychology student, frequently finds himself.

There are other questions that are not meaningful in the sense that there is no conceivable way in which they could be answered. Thouless (1935) takes as an example a question like 'Does the mind occupy space?' Apart from the verbal problems about what the questioner means by 'the mind' – a psychologist could, for example, give a kind of answer to a question about where people locate their 'self' – some insuperable difficulties are presented by a question which is not scientifically answerable. A different kind of question might well be confused with questions of this non-meaningful kind. I shall take as illustration the question 'Do animals dream?' This may look, at first, like a question which is not scientifically answerable. But as we have seen, as a result of an important scientific breakthrough in the discovery of the rapid eye movements which appear to accompany dreams, a kind of answer can now be given. In the last essence we can't answer the question. The evidence that somebody, presumably a man and never an animal, has had a dream is his introspective (or more strictly retrospective) report. But if we are prepared to accept the occurrence of recordable eye movements of a particular kind as evidence of dreams, there are research data which show that animals can and do dream. Many other issues about dreams are of this kind. Questions which once seemed wholly unanswerable now permit a kind of answer. Here we can see how a new procedure can provide a valuable enlargement of the subject matter of a science.

In their early years university students of psychology – like those studying other subjects – are not unlike laymen. They ask the kind of questions which teachers with intellectual integrity often can't answer. In their later years they themselves build up a schema, or system of knowledge, and learn to understand this problem of their teachers. In this respect they come to resemble expert witnesses in court. Very understandably their questioners, parents or relatives, become impatient and dubious about the value of their studies. Some data on this point may be of interest. I am indebted to my colleague Bernard Dodd, who recently conducted a small inquiry with our own students, and their questions. Each was asked to think up 100 questions representing both (a) questions non-psychologists would be likely to ask, and (b) questions they themselves felt they ought to be able to answer on completion of their degree studies. Thus, for example, in Chapter 2 we saw that the study of perception has been called 'the psychologist's psychology'. It embraces issues and problems that are not likely to be in the mind of the student when he begins his studies of psychology, but which are likely to interest him as his knowledge of it grows and deepens. Thus 'perception' was one of the categories into which Mr Dodd was able to classify many of the questions received from his subjects. Other categories comprised motivation, intelligence, instinct, animal behaviour, teaching and learning, persuasion and social control, physiological mechanisms underlying behaviour, child development, and mental illness. He found it necessary to add a category into which many of the non-psychologist questions fell, and called it 'concept of mind'. This included questions about telepathy, faith healing, and ghosts, and others such as 'Can you read my mind?' and 'Is there an unconscious?' The data obtained from the students as a whole varied from the highly sophisticated and theoretical (questions about shape discrimination, theories of psychology, vigilance and attention, and research procedures), to the more naïve (child upbringing, and 'Is heredity more important than environment?'). Others dealt with professional matters, like 'What knowledge does the clinical psychologist (or industrial psychologist) need to possess?' This small investigation illuminated the point: as one builds up a system of knowledge the seemingly obvious reveals hidden complexities, and hitherto unthought-of questions arise.

Technical terms may be a source of irritation to the nonspecialist, and a nuisance in communication between disciplines, but some such terms are necessary. The work of a teacher is, in part, one of communication of new words which help the learner to think with greater precision. As we have seen, Linnaeus provided the biological sciences with a system of naming vast inter-disciplinary value. It permitted the systematic labelling of all known plants and animals, and provided a way of fitting into the system new ones as they were discovered. Psychology awaits its Linnaeus, but in the meantime a good dictionary or glossary of terms is a valuable acquisition by any potential learner. As knowledge is extended other problems arise, and established technical terms may not be adequate. Thus, as we have seen, Robert Holt argues with justification that the term 'hallucination' has been unduly extended in psychology. A more detailed terminology is needed to cover the wide range of phenomena we encounter in sensory deprivation, hallucinogen, and other such experiments. As we have seen, Faraday, Whewell, and others had similar problems of naming for newly observed phenomena in the early period of physical science. Such problems as these may affect investigators working within some area of a subject. In psychology a good example we have considered is the study of time estimation. In my experience it is simply not possible for two people, even two psychologists familiar with the terminology of their science, to discuss time estimation without preliminaries. These preliminaries include a period in which the terms they will use in their speech are discussed, explained, defined, and agreed. On a subsequent occasion they can talk about the complex phenomena involved with reduced likelihood of ambiguity and confusion. The concept of a family joke is not irrelevant: within the family group certain words and allusions become meaningful, and have use as relatively precise vehicles of communication. Scientific terminology has something of the character of an agreed family language, or repertoire of family jokes. But a group of investigators interested in a particular set of problems may develop concepts of their own, and words they can use to one another in communication. In time these may be accepted by their discipline as a whole, or – perhaps more often – they are abandoned after they have served their immediate, but very useful, purpose. Terminology itself provides us with one of the reasons why an outgrouper's questions cannot always be answered as asked. It is also, as we have seen, one of the barriers to communication in court between representatives of such different disciplines as medicine and the law.

In considering the future development of any discipline it is desirable to alert ourselves to differences between necessary conventions and purely habitual traditions. Although in a sense the founder of the subject in its modern period, Wundt did much to impose a crippling orthodoxy upon it, which others had to break through before progress could be made. Robert Watson (1963) – not to be confused with J. B. Watson – writing as a historian of psychology, assesses Wundt as 'inalterably opposed to the application of psychology'. Thus others in time had to overcome this tradition in laying the foundations of the educational, industrial, clinical, and other applications of the science. Wundt was also wholly unsympathic to the study of individual differences and showed this lack of sympathy in quite practical ways to those like J. M. Cattell who were interested. For him psychology was concerned with the general character of mental life as exhibited by adult, normal, educated human beings. Those who came later, like the behaviourist J. B. Watson, had much to overcome in establishing the legitimacy of the study of, for example, child development and animal experimentation.

Yet in his turn Watson imposed an orthodoxy. Like many people he was more interesting in what he affirmed – the need to study animals and children – than in what he denied – the legitimacy of the method of introspective report – and from this psychology has suffered a great deal. Even today the legacy of Watson's attempt to make psychology 'a purely objective experimental branch of natural science' is with us in its negative aspects. Thus Harlow in 1957 criticized with vigour 'the deification of extremely rigid experimental method [which] once threatened to lead to the exclusion of many problems of importance from the domain of the experimental analysis of behaviour'. Others, for example Sanford (1965), have put this point even more vigorously and have complained of the widespread lack of 'psychological insight and sensitivity' in too many psychologists, 'who have never had occasion to look at any one person, let alone themselves'. Sanford adds: 'The plain fact is that our young psychological researchers do not know what goes on in human beings, and their work shows it.' While I should not go all the way with Sanford, perhaps he has a point of substance when he stresses for example the weakness of much work precisely because experimenters have not submitted themselves to – and introspected in – their own experimental set-up. Watsonian phobias about introspection have resulted in an undesirable legacy of negative attitude towards such reports. It would seem more appropriate today for this to be replaced with something positive: an attitude which alerts the investigator to subjective phenomena, and preferably a training in the family of techniques subsumed under the term 'introspection'. . . .

*

And what of the future? This must build upon the kind of tested knowledge about natural phenomena we know as 'science', including the science of experience and behaviour. As we have seen, since the foundations of Wundt's laboratory nearly a century ago, psychology has changed much. Moreover the environment in which human behaviour occurs has also changed, as have problems of adjustment in it. Thus as Baroness Wootton has pointed out the invention of the internal combustion engine, and with it the motor car, has revolutionized the problems of courts of law. The motor car presents the law with its largest single category of offences. In relation to these, and to accident prevention, psychology has some important contributions to make. The aeroplane has produced other problems for psychological research. As recently as 1896 Lord Kelvin, a distinguished physical scientist, declared that he had 'not the smallest molecule of faith in aerial navigation other than the balloon'. But aviation has nevertheless advanced, and with it the application of psychology to the work of the armed forces.* Emergence of jet flight has stretched the conventions that traditionally defined man's environment. It is possible, because of commercial jet travel,

* Very important indeed was the early work of Craik (posthumous 1966) in this field. A valuable summary of later researches has been provided by Broadbent (1961).

for a passenger to leave Sydney at 4 p.m. on a Friday afternoon and reach San Francisco on Friday morning. The internationally determined Date Line was more appropriate to steamships than to modern aviation. Thus new problems of behavioural adjustment emerge, and new issues for psychological research: among these have been noted the intrusions of subjective experiences of the hallucination kind during cloud or high-altitude flight. Development of rocket travel has added a new field of research. In the same year as the Russians launched their first Sputnik, 1957, the Astronomer Royal told the press 'space travel is utter bilge'. This recorded opinion was later reported by *The Times* (6 January 1967). It now seems a strange one when, within a decade, the Moon has been landed on and the surface of Mars has been photographed by aerial photography. The photographs of Mars were taken in 1965 by Mariner IV at a distance of approximately 325,000,000 miles from where this book is being read now. In the 1960s many psychologists are engaged in the problems of training and research that surround space travel. In this connexion we encounter the notion of 'spin off', the term used for other applications of findings that have emerged from space research. Thus for example useful knowledge about skills, in relation to remote control and remote handling of equipment, has emerged from these investigations: this knowledge has some important applications to more orthodox industrial psychology. Of special interest to psychologists, in connexion with the question of manned expeditions to the Moon, or robot or manned expeditions to Mars, are the new environments involved. Additional stresses, and their effects on human thought, perception, and performance, are being given intensive study.

In a survey of possible environments of the future Clarke (1962) has pointed to the advances of speed of travel. The 1950s saw entry into the speed range of 1,000–10,000 m.p.h. And the 1960s saw entry into the next bracket of 10,000–100,000 m.p.h. Of interest in connexion with plans for landing a manned space craft on the Moon are speeds which are now taken for granted: it is envisaged that such a craft will travel initially at 25,000 m.p.h. but will slow down to 1,000 m.p.h. for the final stages of the journey. These enormous speeds, and the distances of travel that they may make possible, create problems in which close interaction between engineering and physics on the one hand, and psychology on the other, becomes additionally necessary. Psychology has made some very important advances in this field of design of equipment, increasingly complex equipment, in accord with the known characteristics of its human user. In addition to equipment like motor cars, aeroplanes, and space craft, there is also the equipment used on earth for human living: houses and other buildings. In 1936 Graham Wallas in his book *The Great Society* envisaged 'a future science of architectural psychology'. This science is now firmly under way, and Departments of Architecture, and Building Science, are now actively cooperating with psychology. New disciplines are emerging, frontiers between disciplines are breaking down, and many valuable applications are still to be made between psychology and established subjects. Examples that have been discussed include the biological sciences generally, history, linguistics, and the professional areas of medicine and law.

At one university where I have worked there is a hall of residence for students with a board which lists past and present student presidents from 1952 onwards. It allows for the future, with a second column beginning with 1968, and a similarly blank third column that makes provision for the Session 2001–2. If psychology, as the scientific study of experience and behaviour, is taught at this university when Mr X, president for the year 2001–2, holds office it will have changed in ways I cannot hope to predict. It will, I suspect, have developed greatly on its frontiers with other sciences, including some that are emerging now and some that will emerge later. Mr X and his contemporaries will, I hope, enrol for the course: it should prove an interesting study.

References

ABERCROMBIE, M. L. J. (1960) *The Anatomy of Judgment*. London: Hutchinson.

ABRAHAM, K. (1925) 'The History of an Impostor in the Light of Psycho-analytic Knowledge'. In Fliess, R. (ed.), *The Psycho-analytic Reader*, London: Hogarth (1950).

AGNEW, M. (1922) 'A Comparison of the Auditory Images of Musicians, Psychologists, and Children'. *Psychological Monographs*, 51.

ALLPORT, G. W. (1937) *Pattern and Growth in Personality*. Edition 1961. New York: Holt, Rinehart, and Winston.

ALLPORT, G. W. (1938) *Personality*. London: Constable.

ALLPORT, G. W., and POSTMAN, L. (1947) *The Psychology of Rumour*. New York: Holt.

ANDREWS, T. G. (1943) 'A Factorial Analysis of Responses to the Comic'. *Journal of General Psychology*, 28.

ANTROBUS, JUDITH S. (1962) 'Patterns of Dreaming and Dream Recall'. Unpublished doctoral thesis, Teachers' College, Columbia University.

ARDIS, J. A., and MCKELLAR, P. (1956) 'Hypnagogic Imagery and Mescaline'. *Journal of Mental Science*, 102:426.

ARIETI, S. (1959) *American Handbook of Psychiatry*, Vols. I, II (1959), and III (1966). 1965 edition. New York: Basic Books.

ASERINSKY, E., and KLEITMAN, N. (1953) 'Regularly Occurring Periods of Eye Motility and Concomitant Phenomena During Sleep'. *Science*, 118.

BAERG, W. J. (1958) *The Tarantula*. Lawrence: University of Kansas Press.

BARNETT, B. (1965) 'Witchcraft, Psychopathology, and Hallucinations'. *British Journal of Psychiatry*, 111:474.

BARRATT, P. E. (1953) 'Imagery and Thinking'. *Australian Journal of Psychology*, 5:2.

BARRON, F. (1963) 'Discovering the Creative Personality'. *College Admissions 10: The Behavioural Sciences and Education*. New York: College Entrance Examination Board.

BARTLETT, F. C. (1932) *Remembering*. Cambridge: University Press.

BASS, B. M. (1955) 'Authoritarianism or Acquiescence'. *Journal of Abnormal and Social Psychology*, 51.

References

BELBIN, E. (1956) 'The Effects of Propaganda on Recall, Recognition and Behaviour'. *British Journal of Psychology*, 47:3.

BERTALANFFY, L. VON (1956) 'A Biologist Looks at Human Nature'. *Scientific Monthly*, 82.

BIRCH, L. B. (1963) 'The Teacher as Learner'. In symposium, 'The Teacher and the Learner', *Bulletin of the British Psychological Society*, 16:50.

BONAPARTE, M., FREUD, A., and KRIS, E. (eds., 1954) *The Origins of Psycho-Analysis: Letters to Wilhelm Fliess*. London: Imago.

BOYD, S. (1961) 'Homicide in Fiction'. In MacDonald, J. M. (ed., 1961), q.v.

BOYD, S., and ROBERTS, A. (1963) 'Psychomycology'. *American Psychologist*, 18.

BREUER, J., and FREUD, S. (1895) *Studies in Hysteria*. Standard Edition of Freud, Vol. 2. London: Hogarth.

BRUNER, J. S. (1964) 'Some Theorems on Instruction Illustrated with Reference to Mathematics'. Chapter 13 in Hilgard, E. R. (ed.), *Theories of Learning and Instruction*. Chicago: University Press.

BURT, C. (1921) *Mental and Scholastic Tests*. Edition 1949. London: Staples.

BURT, C. (1925) *The Young Delinquent*. Edition 1957. London: University Press.

BURT, C. (1949) 'The Structure of the Mind: a Review of the Results of Factor Analysis': *British Journal of Educational Psychology*, 19.

CANTRIL, H., *et al* (1940) *The Invasion from Mars*. Princeton: University Press.

CERLOTTI, A., in (ed.) Crocket, R., *et al* (eds., 1963), q.v.

CHEVREUL, M. E. (1835) *The Principles of the Harmony and Contrast of Colours*. Edition 1870. Trs. C. Martel. London: Bell and Daldy.

CLARKE, A. C. (1962) *Profiles of the Future*. London: Gollancz.

CLECKLEY, H. (1955) *The Mask of Sanity*. St Louis: Mosby.

COHEN, J. (1958) *Humanistic Psychology*. London: Allen and Unwin.

CONNOLLY, K. J. (1963) Chapter in Tidmarsh, M., Halloran, J. D., and Connolly, K. J., *Capital Punishment*. London: Sheed and Ward.

CONNOLLY, K. J. (1966) 'Locomotor Activity in Drosophila'. *Animal Behaviour*, 14.

CONNOLLY, K., and MCKELLAR, P. (1963) 'Forensic Psychology'. *Bulletin of the British Psychological Society*, 16:51.

COUCH, A., and KENISTON, K. (1960) 'Yeasayers and Naysayers: Agreeing Response Set as a Personality Variable'. *Journal of Abnormal and Social Psychology*, 60.

CRAIK, K. (1966) *The Nature of Psychology: a Selection of Papers*,

References

Essays and Other Writings by the late Kenneth J. W. Craik (ed. Sherwood, S. L.). Cambridge University Press.

CROCKET, R., et al. (eds., 1963) *Hallucinogenic Drugs and their Psychotherapeutic Use*. London: Lewis.

CRONBACH, L. J. (1957) 'The Two Disciplines of Scientific Psychology'. *American Psychologist*, 12.

CROWTHER, J. G. (1966) 'When "Scientist" was New'. *New Scientist*, 29:485.

CURRAN, F. J., and SCHILDER, P. (1937) 'Experiments in Repetition and Recall'. *Journal of Genetic Psychology*, 5.

DEMENT, W., and KLEITMAN, N. (1957) 'The Relation of Eye Movement During Sleep to Dream Activity: an Objective Method for the Study of Dreaming'. *Journal of Experimental Psychology*, 53:5.

DESAI, M. M. (1939) 'Surprise: a Historical and Experimental Study'. *British Journal of Psychology*, Monograph Supplement, 22.

DEUTSCHER, M., and CHEIN, I. (1948) 'The Psychological Effects of Enforced Segregation: a Survey of Social Science Opinion'. *Journal of Psychology*, 26.

DOLLARD, J., and MILLER, N. E. (1950) *Personality and Psycho-therapy*. New York: McGraw-Hill.

DOOB, L. (1949) *Public Opinion and Propaganda*. New York: Cresset Press.

DORCUS, R. M. (1956) *Hypnosis and its Therapeutic Applications*. New York: McGraw-Hill.

EBIN, D. (ed., 1961) *The Drug Experience*. New York: Grove Press.

ERICKSON, M. H. (1938) 'A Study of Clinical and Experimental Findings on Hypnotic Deafness'. *Journal of General Psychology*, 19.

EYSENCK, H. J. (1964) *Crime and Personality*. London: Routledge.

EYSENCK, S. B. G., and EYSENCK, H. J. (1963) 'The Validity of Questionnaire and Rating Assessments of Extraversion and Neuroticism and their Factorial Stability'. *British Journal of Psychology*, 54:1.

FLUGEL, J. C. (1934) *Men and Their Motives*. London: Kegan Paul.

FLUGEL, J. C. (1945) *Man, Morals and Society*. London: Duckworth.

FLUGEL, J. C. (1954) 'Humour and Laughter'. In Lindzey, G. (ed.), *Handbook of Social Psychology*. Cambridge, Mass.: Addison-Wesley.

FRAISSE, P. (1964) *The Psychology of Time*. London: Eyre and Spottiswoode.

FRANKENHEUSER, M. (1959) *Estimation of Time: an Experimental Study*. Stockholm: Almqvist and Wiksell.

FRASER, J. (1900) 'A New Visual Illusion of Direction'. *British Journal of Psychology*, 2.

FREEDMAN, S., and MARKS, P. A. (1956) 'Visual Imagery Produced by

References

Rhythmic Photic Stimulation: Personality Correlates and Phenomenology'. *British Journal of Psychology*, 56:1

FREUD, A. (1936) *The Ego and the Mechanisms of Defence*. London: Hogarth.

FREUD, S. (1894) 'The Neuro-psychoses of Defence'. In *Early Psycho-Analytic Publications*, Standard Edition of Freud, Vol. 3, ed. J. Strachey. Edition 1962. London: Hogarth.

FREUD, S. (1900) *The Interpretation of Dreams*. Standard Edition of Freud, Vols. 4–5. Edition 1953. London: Hogarth.

FREUD, S. (1913) *On Beginning the Treatment*. Standard Edition of Freud, Vol. 12. Edition 1958. London: Hogarth.

FREUD, S. (1914) *On Narcissism*. Standard Edition of Freud, Vol. 14. London: Hogarth.

GALTON, F. (1883) *Inquiries into Human Faculty*. London: Macmillan.

GARWOOD, K. W. S. (1961) 'A Psychological Study of Human Fear'. Unpublished Ph.D. thesis, University of Sheffield.

GETZELS, J. W., and JACKSON, P. W. (1962) *Creativity and Intelligence*. London: Wiley.

GIBSON, E., and KLEIN, S. (1961) *Murder : Home Office Research Report*. London: H.M.S.O.

GILBERT, G. M. (1948) *Nuremberg Diary*. London: Eyre and Spottiswoode.

GOMBRICH, E. H. (1954) 'Psycho-analysis and the History of Art'. *International Journal of Psycho-Analysis*, 35.

GORDON, R. (1962) *Stereotypy of Imaging and Belief. British Journal of Psychology, Monograph Supplement*. Cambridge: University Press.

GUILFORD, J. P. (1950) 'Creativity'. *American Psychologist*, 5:9.

GUILFORD, J. P. (1959) 'Three Faces of Intellect'. *American Psychologist*, 14.

HARPER, R. J. C., ANDERSON, C. C., CHRISTENSEN, C. M., and HUNKA, S. M. (1964) *The Cognitive Processes : Readings*. New Jersey: Prentice Hall.

HART, B. (1912) *The Psychology of Insanity*. Cambridge University Press.

HEALY, W. (1915) *The Individual Delinquent*. Boston: Little, Brown.

HEARNSHAW, L. S. (1956) 'Temporal Integration and Behaviour'. *Bulletin of the British Psychological Society*, 30:1.

HEBB, D. O. (1949) *The Organization of Behaviour*. New York: Wiley.

HEBB, D. O. (1953) 'On Human Thought'. *Canadian Journal of Psychology*, 7. 3.

HEBB, D. O. (1960) 'The American Revolution'. *American Psychologist*, 15.

References

HEBB, D. O., and THOMPSON, W. R. (1954) 'The Social Significance of Animal Studies'. Chapter 15 in Lindzey, G. (ed.), *Handbook of Social Psychology*. Cambridge, Mass.: Addison Wesley.

HEDIGER, H. (1955) *Studies of the Psychology and Behaviour of Captive Animals in Zoos and Circuses*. London: Butterworths.

HEIDER, F. (1958) *The Psychology of Interpersonal Relations*. New York: Wiley.

HILGARD, E. R. (1948) *Theories of Learning*. New York: Appleton Century.

HILGARD, E. R. (1949) 'Human Motives and the Concept of the Self'. *American Psychologist*, 4.

HILGARD, E. R. (ed., 1964) *Theories of Learning and Instruction*. Chicago: University Press.

HOLT, R. R. (1964) 'Imagery: the Return of the Ostracized'. *American Psychologist*, 19:4.

HORNE, A. (1962) *The Price of Glory: Verdun 1916*. London: Macmillan. Harmondsworth: Penguin Books.

HUNTER, I. M. L. (1957) *Memory*. Edition 1964. Harmondsworth: Penguin Books.

HUNTER, I. M. L. (1962) 'An Exceptional Talent for Calculative Thinking'. *British Journal of Psychology*, 53.

HUNTER, R., and MACALPINE, I. (1963) *Three Hundred Years of Psychiatry, 1535–1860*. London: Oxford University Press.

JAENSCH, E. R. (1930) *Eidetic Imagery*. London: Kegan Paul.

JAMES, W. (1890) *The Principles of Psychology*. London: Macmillan.

JAMES, W. (1897) *The Will to Believe and other Essays*. New York: Longmans.

JAMES, W. (1902) *The Varieties of Religious Experience*. Edition 1928. London: Longmans.

JEFFERY, R. (1964) 'The Psychologist as an Expert Witness on the Issue of Insanity'. *American Psychologist*, 19.

JENKINS, J. G. and DALLENBACH, K. M. (1924) 'Oblivescence during Sleep and Waking'. *American Journal of Psychology*, 25.

JENKINS, J. J., and PATERSON, D. G. (1961) *Studies in Individual Differences*. New York: Appleton Century.

JONES, E. (1953) *The Life and Work of Sigmund Freud, 1856–1900*, Vol. 1. New York: Basic Books.

KAPLAN, B., and JOHNSON, D. (1964). 'The Social Meaning of Navajo Psychopathology and Psychotherapy'. In Kiev, A. (ed.), *Magic, Faith and Healing*. Glencoe: Free Press.

KAY, H. (1955) 'Learning and Retaining Verbal Material'. *British Journal of Psychology*, 46.

References

KIMBLE, D. P. (ed.) *The Anatomy of Memory*. Palo Alto: Science and Behaviour Books.

KIMMINS, C. W. (1937) *Children's Dreams*. London: Allen and Unwin.

KLEITMAN, N. (1939) *Sleep and Wakefulness*. Enlarged edition 1963. Chicago University Press.

KLÜVER, H. (1928) *Mescal: the Divine Plant and its Psychological Effects*. London: Paul.

KLÜVER, H. (1942) 'Mechanisms of Hallucinations'. In McNemer, Q., and Merrill, M. (eds.), *Studies in Personality*. New York: McGraw-Hill.

KOFFKA, K. (1935) *Principles of Gestalt Psychology*. London: Kegan Paul.

KUEHNER, G. F. (1956) 'Hypnosis in Dentistry'. In Dorcus, R.M. (ed.), *Hypnosis and its Therapeutic Applications*. New York: McGraw Hill.

LEANING, F. E. (1925), 'An Introductory Study of Hypnagogic Phenomena'. *Proceedings of the Society for Psychical Research*, 35.

LE SHAN, L. L. (1952) 'Time Orientation and Social Class'. *Journal of Abnormal and Social Psychology*, 47.

LOEHLIN, J. C. (1959) 'The Influence of Different Activities on the Apparent Length of Time'. *Psychological Monograph*, 73:4.

LOXLEY, F. D. (1962) 'Subjective Experiences During a Brief Period of Controlled Sensory Isolation'. Unpublished dissertation, University of Sheffield.

MCCLELLAND, D. C. (1955) 'The Psychology of Mental Content Reconsidered'. *Psychological Review*, 62.

MCCLELLAND, D. C., *et al.* (1953) *The Achievement Motive*. New York: Appleton Century.

MACDONALD, J. M. (1961) *The Murderer and his Victim*. Springfield, Illinois: Thomas.

MCDOUGALL, W. (1926) *An Outline of Abnormal Psychology*. London: Methuen.

MCKELLAR, P. (1949) 'The Emotion of Anger in the Expression of Human Aggressiveness'. *British Journal of Psychology*, 39:3.

MCKELLAR, P. (1950) 'Provocation to Anger in the Development of Attitudes of Hostility'. *British Journal of Psychology*, 40:3.

MCKELLAR, P. (1952) *A Text-book of Human Psychology*. London: Cohen and West.

MCKELLAR, P. (1957) *Imagination and Thinking*. London: Cohen and West. New York: Basic Books.

MCKELLAR, P. (1962) 'The Method of Introspection'. In Scher, J. M. (ed.), *Theories of the Mind*. New York: Free Press of Glencoe.

References

MCKELLAR, P. (1963) 'Thinking, Remembering, and Imagining'. Chapter 7 in Howells, J. C. (ed.); *Modern Perspectives in Child Psychiatry*. Edinburgh: Oliver and Boyd.

MCKELLAR, P. (1963) 'Three Aspects of the Psychology of Originality in Human Thinking'. *British Journal of Aesthetics*, 3: 2.

MCKELLAR, P. (1965) 'The Investigation of Mental Images'. In Barnett, S. A., and McLaren, A. (eds.), *Penguin Science Survey, 1965: B*. Harmondsworth: Penguin Books.

MCKELLAR, P., and SIMPSON, L. (1954) 'Between Wakefulness and Sleep: Hypnagogic Imagery'. *British Journal of Psychology*, 45.

MCKELLAR, P., and TONN, H. (1967) 'Negative Hallucination, Dissociation, and the "Five Stamps" Experiment'. *British Journal of Social Psychiatry*, 1: 4.

MCKERRACHER, D. W., and DACRE, A. J. I. (1966) 'A Study of Arsonists in a Special Security Hospital'. *British Journal of Psychiatry*, 112: 492.

MACE, C. A. (1950) 'Introspection and Analysis'. In Black, M. (ed.), *Philosophical Analysis*. Cornell University Press.

MACKWORTH, N. H. (1965) 'Originality'. *American Psychologist*, 20.

MARTIN, J. P. (1962) *Offenders as Employees*. London: Macmillan.

MAYHEW, C. (1963) Contribution to Crocket, R., Sandison, R. A., and Walk, A. (eds.), *Hallucinogenic Drugs and Their Psychotherapeutic Use*. London: Lewis.

MEDNICK, S. A. (1963) 'The Associative Basis of the Creative Process'. In Mednick, M. T., and Mednick, S. A. (eds.), *Research in Personality*. New York: Holt.

MILLER, G. A. (1962) *Psychology: the Science of Mental Life*. New York: Harper.

MINTZ, A. (1948) 'Schizophrenic Speech and Sleepy Speech'. *Journal of Abnormal and Social Psychology*, 43.

MOOREHEAD, A. (1960) *The White Nile*. London: Hamish Hamilton.

MOWRER, O. H. (1950) *Learning Theory and Personality Dynamics*. New York: Ronald.

MURPHY, I. C. (1961) 'Stress Reactivity and Anti-social Aggression'. Unpublished Ph.D. thesis, University of Sheffield.

MURRAY, H. A., *et al.* (1938) *Explorations in Personality*. Edition 1962. New York: Science Editions Inc.

NATADZE, R. (1960) 'Emergence of Set on the Basis of Imaginal Situations'. *British Journal of Psychology*, 51: 3.

O'NEILL, W. (1957) *An Introduction to Method in Psychology*. New York and London: Cambridge University Press.

References

ORME, J. E. (1969) *Time, Experience, and Behaviour*. London: Iliffe.

ORNE, M. T. (1962) 'Hypnotically Induced Hallucinations'. In West, L. J. (ed.), q.v.

OSMOND, H., and SMYTHIES, J. (1952) 'Schizophrenia: a New Approach'. *Journal of Mental Science*, 98.

OSWALD, I. (1966) *Sleep*. Harmondsworth: Penguin Books.

OSWALD, I. (1962) *Sleeping and Waking*. Amsterdam: Elsevier.

OVERHOLSER, W. (1965) 'Major Principles of Forensic Psychiatry'. In Arieti, S. (ed.), q.v.

OWENS, A. C. (1963) 'A Study of Mental Imagery'. Unpublished Ph.D. thesis, University of Liverpool.

PEAR, T. H. (1922) 'Number Forms'. *Manchester Memoirs*, 66: 2.

PECK, L. and HODGES, R. (1937) 'A Study of Racial Differences in Eidetic Imagery of Pre-school Children'. *Journal of Genetic Psychology*, 51.

PRENTISS, D. W. and MORGAN, F. P. (1895) 'Anhalonium lewinii (Mescal Buttons)'. *Therapeutic Gazette*, 3rd series.

PRINCE, M. (1922) 'An Experimental Study of the Mechanism of Hallucinations'. *British Journal of Medical Psychology*, 2: 3.

RABIN, A. I. (1961) 'Psychopathic Personalities'. In Toch, H. (ed.), q.v.

RACKHAM, N. (1966) 'An Investigation of Psychological Distance as a Factor Influencing Children's Judgments'. Unpublished dissertation, University of Sheffield.

RAWCLIFFE, D. H. (1952) *The Psychology of the Occult*. London: Ridgway.

RICHARDSON, L. F. (1948) 'War Moods'. *Psychometrika*, 13.

RICHARDSON, A. (1965) 'The Place of Subjective Experience in Contemporary Psychology'. *British Journal of Psychology*, 56: 2.

RIESMAN, D. (1950) *The Lonely Crowd*. Edition 1962. New Haven and London: Yale University Press.

RIVERS, W. H. R. (1920) *Instinct and the Unconscious*. Cambridge: University Press.

RIVERS, W. H. R. (1923) *Conflict and Dream*. London: Kegan Paul.

RUBINGTON, E. (1961) 'The Alcoholic Offender and His Treatment'. Chapter in Toch, H. (ed.), q.v.

SANFORD, N. (1965) 'Will Psychologists Study Human Problems?' *American Psychologist*, 20.

SARNOFF, I. (1962) *Personality Dynamics and Development*. New York: Wiley.

SAVAGE, C. (1956) 'The LSD Psychosis as a Transaction Between

References

Psychiatrist and Patient'. In Cholden, L. (ed.), *Lysergic Acid Diethylamide and Mescaline in Experimental Psychiatry*. New York: Grune and Stratton.

SCHMIDEBERG, M. (1959) 'Tolerance in Upbringing and Its Abuses'. *International Journal of Social Psychiatry*, 5:2.

SCHRAMM, W. (1960) *Mass Communications*. University of Illinois Press.

SEMEONOFF, B. (ed., 1966) *Personality Assessment*. Harmondsworth: Penguin Books.

SHAND, A. F. (1896) 'Character and the Emotions'. *Mind*, 5.

SHAND, A. F. (1914) *The Foundations of Character*. London: Macmillan.

SHAND, A. F. (1922) Contribution to symposium 'The Relations of Complex and Sentiment'. *British Journal of Psychology*, 1922.

SHELDON, W. H. (1944) 'Constitutional Factors in Personality'. Chapter 17 in Hunt, J. McV. (ed.), *Personality and the Behaviour Disorders*. New York: Ronald.

SIDGWICK, H.A. (1894) 'Report of the Census of Hallucinations'. *Proceedings of the Society for Psychical Research*, 26:10.

SILBERER, H. (1909) 'Reports on a Method of Eliciting and Observing Certain Symbolic Hallucination Phenomena'. In Rapaport, D. (ed., 1951), *Organization and Pathology of Thought*. New York: Columbia University Press.

SIM, M. (1963) *Guide to Psychiatry*. Edinburgh: Livingstone.

SIMON, B. (1957) *Psychology in the Soviet Union*. London: Routledge.

SIMPSON, L., MCKELLAR, P. (1955) 'Types of Synaesthesia'. *Journal of Mental Science*, 100:422.

SINGER, J. (1966) *Daydreaming: an Introduction to the Experimental Study of Inner Experience*. New York: Random House.

SINGER, J. L., and ANTROBUS, J. S. (1963) 'A Factor-analytic Study of Daydreaming'. *Perceptual and Motor Skills, Monograph Supplement*, 3-v.17.

SINGER, J. L. and ANTROBUS, J. S. (1965) 'Eye Movements during Fantasies'. *Archives of General Psychiatry*, 12.

SMYTHIES, J. R. (1959) 'The Stroboscopic Patterns. Part I: The Dark Phase'. *British Journal of Psychology*, 50:2.

SMYTHIES, J. R. (1959) 'The Stroboscopic Patterns. Part II: The Phenomenology of the Bright Phase and After Images'. *British Journal of Psychology*, 50.

SMYTHIES, J. R. (1960) 'The Stroboscopic Patterns. Part III: Further Experiments and Discussion'. *British Journal of Psychology*, 51.

References

START, K. B., and RICHARDSON, A. (1965) 'Imagery and Mental Practice'. *British Journal of Educational Psychology*, 34.

STEINBERG, H. (1955) 'Changes in Time Perception Induced by an Anaesthetic Drug'. *British Journal of Psychology*, 46.

STEINBERG, H. (1956) 'Abnormal Behaviour Induced by Nitrous Oxide'. *British Journal of Psychology*, 47:3.

STERN, W. (1939) 'The Psychology of Testimony'. *Journal of Abnormal and Social Psychology*, 34.

STURT, M. (1925) *The Psychology of Time*. London: Kegan Paul.

SUMMERFIEL D. A. and STEINBERG, H. (1957) 'Reducing Interference in Forgetting'. *Quarterly Journal of Experimental Psychology*, 9.

SUMNER, W. G. (1906) *Folkways*. Boston: Ginn.

SUTHERLAND, E. H. (1937) *The Professional Thief*. Chicago: Crowell.

SUTTIE, I. D. (1935) *The Origins of Love and Hate*. London: Kegan Paul. Harmondsworth: Penguin Books (1960).

TANNER, J. M. (1965) 'Physique and Athletic Performance'. In Barnett, S. A., and McLaren, A. (eds.), *Penguin Science Survey, 1965: B*. Harmondsworth: Penguin Books.

THOULESS, R. H. (1935) *General and Social Psychology*. Edition 1951. London: University Tutorial Press.

THURSTONE, L. L. (1923) 'The Stimulus Response Fallacy in Psychology'. *Psychological Review*, 30.

THURSTONE, L. L. (ed., 1952) *Applications of Psychology*. New York: Harper.

TOCH, H. (1961) *Legal and Criminal Psychology*. New York: Holt.

TONG, J. E. (1958) 'Stress Reactivity and its Relation to Disordered Behaviour in Mental Defective Subjects'. Unpublished Ph.D. thesis, University of Sheffield.

VANDELL, R. A., DAVIS, R. A., and CLUGSTON, H. (1943) 'The Function of Mental Practice in the Acquisition of Motor Skills'. *Journal of General Psychology*, 29.

VEITH, I. (1965) *Hysteria: the History of a Disease*. Chicago University Press.

VERNON, J. A. (1963) *Inside the Black Room*. London: Souvenir Press, Penguin Books, 1966.

WALKER, N. (1965) *Crime and Punishment in Britain*. Edinburgh University Press.

WARBURTON, F. W. (1965) 'Observations on a Sample of Psychopathic American Criminals'. *Behavioural Research Therapy*, 3.

WATSON, R. (1963) *The Great Psychologists: Aristotle to Freud*. Philadelphia: Lippincott.

References

WARD, T. H. G. (1949) 'An Experiment on Serial Reproduction with Special Reference to the Changes in the Design of Early Coin Types'. *British Journal of Psychology*, 39:3.

WEIR MITCHELL, S. (1896) 'Remarks on the Effects of Anhalonium Lewinii (the Mescal Button)'. *British Medical Journal* II: 1625.

WEST, L. J. (ed., 1962) *Hallucinations*. New York: Grune and Stratton.

WILKINS, L. T. (1962) 'Criminality: an Operational Research Approach'. In Welford, A. T., *et al.* (eds.), *Society: Problems and Methods of Study*. London: Routledge.

WILLETT, T. C. (1964) *The Criminal on the Road*. London: Tavistock Press.

WINICK, C. (1961) 'The Drug Addict and His Treatment'. In Toch, H. (ed.), q.v.

WOODWORTH, R. S. (1931) *Contemporary Schools of Psychology*. Edition 1938. London: Methuen.

WOODWORTH, R. S. (1938) *Experimental Psychology*. Revised edition with Schlosberg, H., 1955. London: Methuen.

WOOLLEY, D. W. (1962) *The Biochemical Basis of Psychoses*. New York: Wiley.

YELLOWLEES, H. (1932) *Clinical Lectures on Psychological Medicine*. London: Churchill.

YELLOWLEES, H. (1953) *To Define True Madness*. Harmondsworth: Penguin Books.

ZILBOORG, G. (1941) *A History of Medical Psychology*. New York: Norton.

Index

415

Some other books published by Penguins are
described on the following pages.

THE PSYCHOLOGY OF
INTERPERSONAL BEHAVIOUR

Michael Argyle

Looks, gestures, and tones of voice may be powerful factors when people meet. Moreover these rapid and subtle messages are highly co-ordinated.

Experimental techniques have recently been developed for studying the *minutiae* of social behaviour scientifically: these are described here by a social psychologist. The study of social interaction demands a 'language' of its own, to which Michael Argyle supplies a clear key. But the reader will not be slow to grasp that 'the motivation of social interaction', 'the synchronization of styles of behaviour' between two or more people, and 'the presentation of a self-image' refer to things we encounter every day.

Certain specific skills, such as interviewing, group leadership, public speaking, and even child-rearing, are discussed in the light of the latest research, and the author devotes a good deal of space to mental health and to training in social skill. His outline of what amounts to a break-through in psychological analysis makes this a book which the student of psychology may well find indispensable; and the relevance of his material to everyday life offers irresistible reading to the plain man.

SELF AND OTHERS

R. D. Laing

To withstand the pressures of conforming we must understand how insidiously they attack. To develop genuine, creative relationships we must be aware of a person's capacity to inhibit, control, or liberate another.

In this study of the patterns of interaction between people Dr Laing, author of *The Divided Self*, attempts to unravel some of the knots in which we unfailingly tie ourselves. Taking his examples both from literature and case material, he shows that 'every relationship implies definition of self by other and other by self' and that if the self does not receive confirmation by its contacts with others or if the attributions that others ascribe to it are contradictory its position becomes untenable and it may break down.

'Peculiarly fascinating in that it enables the reader to share what may be termed the poetic insight of a scientifically educated mind' – *Lancet*

Also available

The Divided Self

The Politics of Experience and the Bird of Paradise

Sanity, Madness and the Family
(with A. Esterson)

WHAT FREUD REALLY SAID

David Stafford-Clark

The name of Freud is used (often by those who have never read a word he wrote) to excuse any and every licence, from anarchy to sex-worship. Yet, as a writer, the founder of psychoanalysis deployed over three million words in order to state, very clearly and simply, what he had concluded from his clinical experience with patients.

This first brief summary of Freud's theories has been made by Dr Stafford-Clark, the director of the York Clinic and author of *Psychiatry Today*. Here the general reader will find the core of Freud's own pronouncements about hysteria and anxiety, the interpretation of dreams, the unconscious mind, sexuality, the nature of the neuroses and the technique of psychoanalysis, as well as his speculations on art, literature, and life.

Dr Stafford-Clark's exact recital of Freud's revolutionary concepts is an essential corrective to almost half a century of misrepresentation.

THE INTEGRITY OF THE PERSONALITY

Anthony Storr

'Self-realization is not an anti-social principle; it is firmly based on the fact that men need each other in order to be themselves.'

With this axiom of psychology Anthony Storr, at the outset of an excellent and simple study of human personality, counters the fear expressed by Bertrand Russell and others that analytical psycho-therapy may tend to produce an anarchical race of Byrons or Hitlers.

Tolerant and impartial in tone, his book stands securely on the ground that is common to Freudian, Jungian, and other schools of psychology. Maintaining that many roads lead to self-realization, he discusses in successive chapters the mental mazes of identification, introjection, projection, and dissociation, through which the individual, sooner or later, must find his way on the path to maturity.

'The book is well written, concise and clear, and is cordially recommended' – *Mental Health*

'He deals frankly, in comprehensible terms, with the hypotheses the therapist uses in treatment' – *British Medical Journal*

'His emphasis on the beliefs shared rather than the areas of controversy is right for a book intended for the lay public' – *Lancet*

THE PSYCHOTIC

Andrew Crowcroft

'Am I mad?'

Consciously or unconsciously, this agonizing question has been asked by millions of those who, for any reason, have felt themselves to be set apart from others in their childhood. Madness provides one of the commonest unfounded fears of neurotics.

A consultant psychiatrist explains in this new study, as exactly as the conditions permits, what madness is. Drawing a clear line between psychosis and neurosis, he takes us into the world of madness by two paths: first through a survey of what specialists now know about psychotic breakdown, and secondly through a brilliant comparison between broken patterns of thought and feeling in childhood and the shattered world of the psychotic. The author interprets much experience and behaviour on the lines of Melanie Klein's theory of early emotional development and admits, through her, a debt to Freud. But Freud specialized in the psychoneuroses.

And Dr Crowcroft's book, with its clear outline of social and physical treatments available today, is concerned with psychosis – true madness – in a way which has not previously been attempted in a popular edition.

PSYCHOLOGY OF CHILDHOOD AND ADOLESCENCE

C. I. Sandström

In this concise study of the processes of growing up Professor Sandström has produced a book which, although it is perfectly suited to the initial needs of university students and teachers in training, will appeal almost as much to parents and ordinary readers. His text covers the whole story of human physical and mental growth from conception to puberty.

Outlining the scope and history of developmental psychology Professor Sandström goes on to detail the stages of growth in the womb, during the months after birth, and (year by year) up to the age of ten. There follow chapters on physical development, learning and perception, motivation, language and thought, intelligence, the emotions, social adjustment, and personality. The special conditions of puberty and of schooling are handled in the final chapters.

Throughout this masterly study the author necessarily refers to 'norms of development': these neatly represent the average stages of growing up, but (as Professor Mace comments in his introduction) they must only be applied to individual children with caution.